D0791465

AN AUTHOR'S GUIDE TO SOCIAL WORK JOURNALS

5TH EDITION

NASW PRESS

National Association of Social Workers
Washington, DC

James J. Kelly, PhD, ACSW, LCSW, *President*
Elizabeth J. Clark, PhD, ACSW, MPH, *Executive Director*

Cheryl Y. Bradley, *Publisher*
Lisa M. O'Hearn, *Managing Editor*
Wayson Jones, *Proofreader*

Cover by Eye to Eye Design
Interior design by Circle Graphics
Printed and bound by Victor Graphics

Library of Congress Cataloging-in-Publication Data

An author's guide to social work journals / [edited by] Terry Cluse-Tolar, Stephanie Souza, Michel Coconis.
   p. cm.
  Includes bibliographical references and index.
  Rev. ed. of: An author's guide to social work journals / National Association of Social Workers. 4th ed. c1997.
  ISBN 0-87101-392-4 (alk. paper)
  1. Social service—United States—Periodicals—Directories. 2. Social service—Periodicals—Directories. 3. Social service literature—Publishing—United States. 4. Social service literature—Publishing. I. Cluse-Tolar, Terry. II. Souza, Stephanie. III. Coconis, Michel. IV. National Association of Social Workers
  HV85.A93 2009
  016.361305—dc22

                                                                                    2009034544

Printed in the United States of America

Contents

Foreword

I have always depended on *An Author's Guide to Social Work Journals,* especially in my early days as an academic and a researcher, and later as a mentor. It has been a valuable tool in deciding the best fit for my manuscripts and helping me learn about the breadth of journals available. The fourth edition of the book was published in 1997, and a lot has changed since then. Many journals have moved from requiring authors to send in five hard copies of their manuscripts to requiring electronic submission either online or through email. Some journals have ceased publication since the last volume was published, and there have many new journals, both in print and online, that have begun publication.

This volume covers over 200 journals and includes new title such as *Advances in Social Work, Critical Social Work,* the *Journal of Evidence-Based Social Work,* and *Qualitative Social Work.* Authors using this tool should find increased coverage of internationally oriented journals and a new international subject category making them easier to find.

My thanks go to Jeanne C. Marsh, who served as the editor of the last edition and to Henry Mendelsohn, who served as editor for the three volumes before that. My thanks also go to Lisa O'Hearn from NASW Press, who has been patient with me while overseeing this venture. Also my thanks go to Stephanie Souza, Michel Coconis, and Deb Gossert who put countless hours into this project.

> **Terry Cluse-Tolar**
> *Chair*
> Social Work Department
> University of Toledo

Categories of Information for Each Journal

Title	Name of journal
Previous Title	Previous name of journal, if applicable.
Editorial Focus	The types of articles (research, review, theoretical, and so forth) that the editor or editorial board seek, in addition to such features as letters, notices, research in brief, book reviews, and so forth.
Audience	Discipline and types of subscribers, such as practitioners, faculty, libraries, etc.
Special Themes	Content or subject areas of particular interest to the journal.
Where Indexed/ Abstracted	Sources where the journal is indexed or abstracted.
Year Established	Year of first volume; if there have been interruptions or if the journal has been retitled at any point, please note.
Circulation	Size of subscriber list.
Frequency	How often the journal is published each year.
Months Issued	The months or seasons the journal is published.
No. of Articles	Number of articles per issue.

SUBMISSION

Address	Full address for submission of manuscripts.
Number of Copies	Number of copies the author should submit.
Disk Submission	Are disks required for submission? Are they required for accepted manuscripts? What word processing formats are accepted?
Online Submission	Is online submission required? What word processing formats are accepted? What is the website used for submissions?

FORMAT OF MANUSCRIPT

Cover Sheet	Information to be included on cover sheet, if required.
Abstract	Number of words needed, if an abstract is required.
Key Words	Are key words required? How many?
Length	Desired or maximum number of pages.
Margins	Correct margin settings.
Spacing	Spacing – single, double, or triple – required.

STYLE

Name of Guide	Suggested style guide or statement of availability of style requirements from editor or publisher
Subheadings	How much to include, if required.
References	Proper style.
Footnotes	How to include, if required or accepted.
Tables or Figures	Format. Is camera-ready copy required for all art? Or does the journal provide graphic services for a fee?

REVIEW PROCESS

Type	Information on review process, whether it is anonymous or not. Peer review?
Queries	Does the editor welcome or accept query letters?
Acknowledgment	Method by which manuscripts are acknowledged; also, instructions for including a self-addressed, stamped envelope or postcard, if required.
Review Time	Estimated length of time from receipt of manuscript to the time the author is notified of a decision.
Revisions	How revisions are handled; requirements for resubmission.
Acceptance Rate	Estimate of the approximate percentage of manuscripts accepted.
Return of Manuscript	Are manuscripts returned? Should authors include a self-addressed, stamped envelope for return of manuscript?
Lag Time to Print	Estimate of the usual length of time between acceptance and publication.

CHARGES TO AUTHOR

Author Alterations   Does the journal charge authors for alterations in proofs? If so, what are the charges?

Page Charges   Does the journal issue page charges? If so, are they for expedited publication? What are the charges?

Processing   Does the journal charge for processing manuscripts?

REPRINT, SUBSCRIPTION, AND CONTACT INFORMATION

Reprint Policy   Policy on purchase of reprints or free provision of reprints; address for reprints?

Book Reviews   Does the journal publish book reviews? Does it accept unsolicited book reviews? How should books for review or reviews be submitted? To whom and where?

Subscriptions   Directions for obtaining subscription orders and cost of one-year subscription.

Affiliation   Name of professional association or institution, if any, with which the journal is affiliated.

E-Mail Address   Editor's or publisher's address and purposes for use.

Website   Home page of publisher or journal.

ADMINISTRATION

Administration in Social Work
Advances in Social Work
The Clinical Supervisor
Evaluation and Program Planning; an International Journal
International Journal of Volunteer Administration
Journal of Nonprofit & Public Sector Marketing
Journal of Policy Analysis and Management
Journal of Social Service Research
Journal of Technology in Human Services
Nonprofit and Voluntary Sector Quarterly
Social Work in Public Health

AGING AND THE AGED

Activities, Adaptation & Aging
Aging and Mental Health
American Journal of Alzheimer's Disease and Other
    Dementias
Clinical Gerontologist
Dementia: International Journal of Social Research &
    Practice
The Gerontologist
International Journal of Aging and Human Development
Journal of Aging & Social Policy
Journal of Aging Studies
Journal of Elder Abuse & Neglect
Journal of Geriatric Drug Therapy
Journal of Gerontological Social Work
Journal of Nutrition for the Elderly
Journal of Women and Aging
Omega: Journal of Death and Dying
Physical & Occupational Therapy in Geriatrics
Psychology and Aging

CHILDREN AND FAMILIES/
CHILD AND FAMILY WELFARE

American Journal of Family Therapy
American Journal of Sexuality Education
Attachment & Human Development
Child Abuse & Neglect, The International Journal
Child & Adolescent Social Work Journal
Child & Family Behavior Therapy
Child and Youth Care Forum: Journal of Research and
    Practice in Children's Services
Child & Youth Services
Child Maltreatment – Journal of the American
    Professional Society on the Abuse of Children
Child Psychiatry and Human Development
Children and Youth Services Review

Child Welfare
Contemporary Family Therapy
Families in Society: The Journal of Contemporary Human
    Services
Family Preservation Journal
Family Process
Family Relations: Interdisciplinary Journal of Applied
    Family Studies
Journal of Child and Adolescent Group Therapy
Journal of Child & Adolescent Substance Abuse
Journal of Child and Adolescent Trauma
Journal of Child Psychology and Psychiatry
Journal of Child Sexual Abuse
Journal of Children and Poverty
Journal of Divorce & Remarriage
Journal of Family Issues
Journal of Family Psychology
Journal of Family Psychotherapy
Journal of Family Social Work
Journal of Family Violence
Journal of Feminist Family Therapy
Journal of Marriage & the Family
Journal of Pediatric Psychology
Journal of Public Child Welfare
Journal of Sex and Marital Therapy
Journal of Sexual Aggression
Journal of Youth and Adolescence
Journal of Youth Studies
Marriage & Family Review
Merrill-Palmer Quarterly: Journal of Developmental
    Psychology
Physical & Occupational Therapy in Pediatrics
Residential Treatment for Children and Youth
Social Work Forum

EDUCATION/SCHOOLS

American Journal of Sexuality Education
Arête
British Journal of Social Work
Children & Schools: A Journal of Social Work Practice
Journal of Applied School Psychology
Journal of Baccalaureate Social Work
Journal of Lesbian Studies
Journal of Practice Teaching and Learning
Journal of Social Work Education
Journal of Teaching in Social Work
The New Social Worker: The Magazine for Social Work
    Professional Development Students and
    Recent Graduates
School Social Work Journal
Social Work Education: The International Journal

GENERAL SOCIAL WORK

Advances in Social Work
American Sociological Review
Arête
Australian Social Work
Behavioral & Social Sciences Librarian
British Journal of Psychotherapy
British Journal of Social Work
Groupwork Ethics & Social Welfare
The Indian Journal of Social Work
International Journal of Social Welfare
Journal of Evidence-Based Social Work
Journal of Human Behavior in the Social Environment
Journal of Social Work Values and Ethics
Qualitative Social Work: Research and Practice
Research & Practice in Social Sciences
Research on Social Work Practice
Smith College Studies in Social Work
Social Work
Social Work and Social Sciences Review
Social Work Research
Society

HEALTH AND HEALTH CARE

The American Journal of Hospice & Palliative Care
Death Studies
Healing Ministry
Health Affairs
Health & Social Work
Health Care Financing Review
Health Psychology
Home Health Care Services Quarterly
International Journal of Sexual Health
Journal of LGBT Health Research
Journal of Pain & Palliative Care Pharmacotherapy
Journal of Psychosocial Oncology
Journal of Social Work in Disability and Rehabilitation
Occupational Therapy in Health Care
Omega: Journal of Death and Dying
Physical & Occupational Therapy in Geriatrics
SCI Psychosocial Process
Social Work in Health Care
Social Work in Public Health
Women and Health

INTERNATIONAL SOCIAL WORK/ISSUES

Australian Journal of Social Work
British Journal of Psychotherapy
British Journal of Social Work
Canadian Journal of Human Sexuality
China Journal of Social Work
Critical Social Policy
Global Social Policy
The Indian Journal of Social Work
International Journal of Aging and Human Development
International Journal of Culture and Mental Health

International Journal of Mental Health
International Journal of Psychiatry in Medicine
International Journal of Sexual Health
International Journal of Social Welfare
International Journal of Volunteer Administration
International Social Work
Journal of Comparative Social Welfare
Journal of Global Social Work Practice
Journal of Immigrant and Refugee Studies
Journal of Peace Research
Practice: Social Work in Action
Social Development Issues
Social Work & Society
Studies in Social Justice
Traumatology

MENTAL HEALTH/MENTAL ILLNESS

Aging and Mental Health
American Journal of Community Psychology
American Journal of Orthopsychiatry
American Journal of Sexuality Education
American Psychologist
British Journal of Psychotherapy
Bulletin of the Menninger Clinic
The Canadian Journal of Human Sexuality
Clinical Gerontologist
Clinical Social Work Journal
The Clinical Supervisor
Community Mental Health Journal
Contemporary Family Therapy
Death Studies
Developmental Psychology
Groupwork
Healing Ministry
Health Affairs
Health & Social Work
Health Psychology
The Indian Journal of Social Work
International Journal of Mental Health
International Journal of Culture and Mental Health
The International Journal of Psychiatry in Medicine
Journal of Abnormal Psychology
Journal of Aggression, Maltreatment, and
    Trauma (JAMT)
Journal of Applied Research in Intellectual Disabilities
Journal of Autism and Developmental Disorders
Journal of Child and Adolescent Trauma
Journal of Child Psychology and Psychiatry & Allied
    Disciplines
Journal of Child Sexual Abuse
Journal of Consulting and Clinical Psychology
Journal of Counseling Psychology
Journal of Gay and Lesbian Mental Health
Journal of General Psychology
Journal of Genetic Psychology
Journal of Homosexuality
Journal of Interpersonal Violence

Journal of Offender Rehabilitation
Journal of Pediatric Psychology
Journal of Personality and Social Psychology
Journal of Poetry Therapy
Journal of Police Crisis Negotiations
Journal of Sex and Marital Therapy
Journal of Sexual Aggression
Journal of Social Psychology
Journal of Spirituality in Mental Health
Journal of Traumatic Stress
Merrill-Palmer Quarterly: Journal of Developmental
    Psychology
Occupational Therapy in Mental Health
Psychiatric Services
Psychoanalytic Social Work
Psychological Assessment
Psychology and Aging
Psychotherapy Theory, Research, Practice, and Training
Qualitative Social Work
Small Group Research
Smith College Studies in Social Work
Social Work
Social Work in Mental Health
Suicide and Life-Threatening Behavior
Traumatology
Women and Therapy

OCCUPATIONAL AND INDUSTRIAL SERVICES

Journal of Workplace Behavioral Health
Occupational Therapy in Health Care
Occupational Therapy in Mental Health

SOCIAL ISSUES AND SOCIAL PROBLEMS

Affilia: Journal of Women and Social Work
American Psychologist
American Sociological Review
Community Development
Critical Social Work
Federal Probation
Hastings Center Report
International Social Work
Journal of Children and Poverty
Journal of Community Practice
Journal of Family and Economic Issues
Journal of Interpersonal Violence
Journal of Offender Rehabilitation
Journal of Peace Research
Journal of Police Crisis Negotiations
Journal of Policy Practice
Journal of Poverty
Journal of Prevention & Intervention in the Community
Journal of Progressive Human Services
Journal of Religion and Spirituality in Social Work
Journal of Social Issues
Journal of Social Service Research
Journal of Sociology and Social Welfare

Policy & Practice
Social Development Issues
Social Service Review
Social Work
Social Work and Christianity: An International Journal
Social Work and Social Sciences Review
Society
Suicide and Life-Threatening Behavior
Violence Against Women
Journal of Women, Politics, & Policy

SOCIAL POLICY/SOCIAL ACTION

Critical Social Policy
Critical Social Work
Hastings Center Report
Journal of Nonprofit & Public Sector Marketing
Journal of Policy Analysis and Management
Journal of Policy Practice
Journal of Progressive Human Services
Journal of Religion and Spirituality in Social Work
Journal of Social Service Research
Journal of Sociology and Social Welfare
Nonprofit and Voluntary Sector Quarterly
Policy & Practice
Reflections: Narratives of Professional Helping
Social Service Review
Social Work
Social Work and Social Sciences Review
Social Work in Public Health
Social Work with Groups
Studies in Social Justice

SPECIAL POPULATIONS

Affilia: Journal of Women and Social Work
Australian Social Work
Child Welfare
Gender & Society
The Indian Journal of Social Work
Jewish Social Work Forum
Journal of Bisexuality
Journal of Black Studies
Journal of Ethnic and Cultural Diversity in Social Work
Journal of Forensic Social Work
Journal of Gay & Lesbian Mental Health
Journal of Gay and Lesbian Social Services
Journal of HIV/AIDS & Social Services
Journal of Homosexuality
Journal of LGBT Health Research
Journal of LGBT Youth
Journal of Offender Rehabilitation
Journal of Social Work in Disability & Rehabilitation
Journal of Visual Impairment & Blindness
Journal of Women, Politics, & Policy
Omega: Journal of Death and Dying
Women and Health
Women and Therapy

SUBSTANCE USE AND ABUSE/ALCOHOLISM

Alcoholism Treatment Quarterly
American Journal of Drug and Alcohol Abuse
Journal of Addictive Diseases
Journal of Child & Adolescent Substance Abuse
Journal of Drug Issues

Journal of Dual Diagnosis
Journal of Social Work Practice in the Addictions
Journal of Studies on Alcohol and Drugs
Journal of Workplace Behavioral Health
Substance Abuse

ACTIVITIES, ADAPTATION & AGING

Current Title	*Activities, Adaptation, & Aging*
Previous Title	N/A.
Editorial Focus	Established as the primary journal for activity professionals, *Activities, Adaptation & Aging* provides a professional outlet for formal and informal research regarding the therapeutic implications of activities on quality-of-life issues and overall life satisfaction — in either institutional or community settings — for the elderly. This journal also continues to provide timely and useful case studies and program evaluations. *Activities, Adaptation & Aging* addresses such topics as evidence-based practice, evaluation, assessment of psychosocial history, culture and its influence on meaningful activity, activities and caregivers, volunteerism, and successful aging. The journal promotes a strong interdisciplinary thrust, drawing upon knowledge from the disciplines of physical, art, music, recreational, and occupational therapy; and social work, nursing, psychiatry, and medicine.
Audience	Activity directors, health care professionals, social workers in health care settings.
Special Themes	None noted.
Where Indexed/ Abstracted	Abstracts in Social Geronotology; AgeLine; CINAHL; EBSCOhost; Leisure, Recreation, and Tourism Abstracts; PsycINFO; Social Work Abstracts; Sociological Abstracts.
Year Established	1980
Circulation	Not specified.
Frequency	Quarterly.
Months Issued	Seasonally, months not specified.
No. of Articles per Issue	4–7.

SUBMISSIONS

Postal Mailing Address	Linnea Couture, Editor, Activities, Adaptation & Aging, 3555 S. Carr St., Lakewood, CO 80235.
Method for Submission	Surface mail, disk, e-mail.
Number of Copies	1
Disk Submission	If submitting a disk, it should be prepared using MS Word or WordPerfect and should be clearly labeled with the authors' names, file name, and software program.
Online or E-mail Submission Allowed or Required	Authors are encouraged to submit electronically, either by sending a disk to the editor or sending the manuscript by e-mail.

FORMAT OF MANUSCRIPT

Cover Sheet	Separate sheet that does not go out for review: Full title, authors' names, degrees, professional titles, designation of corresponding author with full address, phone numbers, fax number, and date of submission.
Abstract	Each article should be summarized in an abstract of not more than 100 words. Avoid abbreviations, diagrams, and reference to the text in the abstract.
Key Words	3–10 key words typed beneath the abstract.
Length	12–25 pages, including abstract and references.
Margins	Minimum of 1 inch on all sides.
Spacing	Double spaced.

STYLE

Name of Guide	*Publication Manual of the American Psychological Association.*
Subheadings	See style guide.
References	See style guide.
Footnotes	See style guide.
Tables or Figures	Tables and figures (illustrations) should not be embedded in the text, but should be included as separate sheets or files. A short descriptive title should appear above each table with a clear legend and any footnotes suitably identified below. All units must be included. Figures should be completely labeled, taking into account necessary size reduction. Captions should be typed, double-spaced, on a separate sheet.
	Illustrations submitted (line drawings, halftones, photos, photomicrographs, etc.) should be clean originals or digital files. Digital files are recommended for highest quality reproduction and should follow these guidelines:

- 300 dpi or higher, sized to fit on journal page, EPS, TIFF, or PSD format only.
- Submitted as separate files, not embedded in text files
- Color illustrations will be considered for publication; however, the author will be required to bear the full cost involved in color art reproduction. Color art can be purchased for online-only reproduction or for print and online reproduction. Color reprints can only be ordered if print and online reproduction costs are paid. Rates for color art reproduction are: Online-only reproduction: $225 for the first page of color; $100 per page for the next three pages of color. A maximum charge of $525 applies. Print and online reproduction: $900 for the first page of color; $450 for the next three pages of color. A custom quote will be provided for articles with more than four pages of color.

REVIEW PROCESS

Type of Review	Blind peer review.
Queries	Not specified.
Acknowledgment	Enclose a regular, self-addressed, stamped envelope with submission.
Review Time	Approximately 3–4 months.
Revisions	Not specified.
Acceptance Rate	Approximately 63%.
Return of Manuscript	Enclose a large, self-addressed, stamped envelope with submission.
Lag Time to Print	Approximately 6–12 months.

CHARGES TO AUTHOR

Author Alterations	Page proofs are sent to the designated author using Taylor & Francis' Central Article Tracking System (CATS). They must be carefully checked and returned within 48 hours of receipt.
Page Charges	Not specified.
Processing	Not specified.

REPRINT, SUBSCRIPTION, AND CONTACT INFORMATION

Reprint Policy	Reprints of individual articles are available for order at the time authors review page proofs. A discount on reprints is available to authors who order before print publication. Each corresponding author will receive 3 complete issues in which the article publishes and a complimentary PDF. This file is for personal use only and may not be copied and disseminated in any form without prior written permission from Taylor and Francis Group, LLC.
Book Reviews	Yes, contact editor.
Subscriptions	Print and online subscriptions available from the website.
Affiliation	Not specified.
E-Mail Address	lcouture@totallongtermcare.org
Website	http://www.informaworld.com/smpp/title~db=all~content=t792303956~tab=summary

ADMINISTRATION IN SOCIAL WORK

Current Title	*Administration in Social Work*
Previous Title	N/A.
Editorial Focus	*Administration in Social Work* is a highly respected, peer-reviewed journal that has provided timely, relevant information to human services administrators, managers, and educators for more than a quarter century. The journal keeps readers up to date on theory, practice, and research, with special attention given to the relationship between social administration and social policy planning.
Audience	Managers of social welfare agencies, academics interested in nonprofit organizations and management.
Special Themes	Performance of nonprofit social welfare agencies, organizational dynamics, management practice.
Where Indexed/ Abstracted	Academic Search; ASSIA: Applied Social Sciences Index & Abstracts; CINAHL; Current Abstracts; Current Contents/Social and Behavioral Sciences; Human Resources Abstracts; Journal Citation Report/Social Sciences Edition; MasterFile Premier; PsycINFO; Public Administration Abstracts; Sociological Abstracts; Social Sciences Citation Index; Social Scisearch; Social Services Abstracts; SocIndex Databases; TOC Premier.
Year Established	1977
Circulation	782
Frequency	4 issues per year.
Months Issued	January, April, July, October.
No. of Articles per Issue	4–5.

SUBMISSIONS

Postal Mailing Address	To editor: Leon Ginsberg, PhD, ACSW, Program Director and Research Professor, Social Work Program, Appalachian State University, PO Box 32115, Boone, NC 28608-2115. Best mailing address is 318 Leaning Tree Rd., Columbia, SC 29223.
Method for Submission	E-mail or surface mail.
Number of Copies	4.
Disk Submission	Electronic submission either as an e-mail attachment or via disk/diskette.
Online or E-mail Submission Allowed or Required	Yes: ginsberglh@appstate.edu

FORMAT OF MANUSCRIPT

Cover Sheet	Cover page must be submitted with manuscript indicating only the title for anonymity. Each manuscript must be accompanied by a statement that it has not been published elsewhere and that it has not been submitted simultaneously for publication elsewhere. Authors are responsible for obtaining permission to reproduce copyrighted material from other sources and are required to sign an agreement for the transfer of copyright to the publisher. All accepted manuscripts, artwork, and photographs become the property of the publisher.
Abstract	Yes: Each article should be summarized in an abstract of not more than 100 words. Avoid abbreviations, diagrams, and reference to the text in the abstract.
Key Words	5–6 key words.
Length	15–18 pages, including abstract and references.
Margins	1 inch on all sides.
Spacing	Double spaced; number pages consecutively throughout manuscript.

STYLE

Name of Guide	*Publication Manual of the American Psychological Association.*
Subheadings	See style guide.
References	See style guide.
Footnotes	See style guide.
Tables or Figures	Tables and figures (illustrations) should not be embedded in the text, but should be included as separate sheets or files. A short descriptive title should appear above each table with a clear legend and any footnotes suitably identified below. All units must be included. Figures should be completely labeled, taking into account necessary size reduction. Captions should be typed, double-spaced, on a separate sheet.

Illustrations submitted (line drawings, halftones, photos, photomicrographs) should be clean originals or digital files. Digital files are recommended for highest quality reproduction and should follow these guidelines: 300 dpi or higher, sized to fit journal page, EPS, TIFF, or PSD format only, submitted as separate files, not embedded in text files.

REVIEW PROCESS

Type of Review	Anonymous.
Queries	Queries accepted.
Acknowledgment	Enclose a regular, self-addressed stamped, envelope with submission.
Review Time	Approximately 3–4 months.
Revisions	Author receives reviewers' critiques and a letter summarizing needed changes from the editor. Page proofs are sent to the designated author using Taylor & Francis' Central Article Tracking System (CATS). They must be carefully checked and returned within 48 hours of receipt.
Acceptance Rate	Approximately 25%.
Return of Manuscript	Manuscript returned if author encloses a self-addressed, stamped 9" × 12" envelope.
Lag Time to Print	Approximately 12 months.

CHARGES TO AUTHOR

Author Alterations	Not specified.
Page Charges	Color illustrations will be considered for publication; however, the author will be required to bear the full cost involved in color art reproduction. Color art can be purchased for online only reproduction or for print and online reproduction. Color reprints can only be ordered if print and online reproduction costs are paid. Rates for color art reproduction are: Online-only reproduction: $225 for the first page of color; $100 per page for the next three pages of color. A maximum charge of $525 applies. Print and online reproduction: $900 for the first page of color; $450 per page for the next three pages of color. A custom quote will be provided for articles with more than four pages of color.
Processing	Not specified.

REPRINT, SUBSCRIPTION, AND CONTACT INFORMATION

Reprint Policy	Reprints of individual articles are available for order at the time authors review page proofs. A discount on reprints is available to authors who order before print publication. Each corresponding author will receive 3 complete issues in which the article publishes and a complimentary PDF. This file is for personal use only and may not be copied and disseminated in any form without prior written permission from Taylor and Francis Group, LLC.
Book Reviews	Book reviews published. Send books for review to Professor Madeleine Stoner, Book Review Editor, Administration in Social Work, University of Southern California, School of Social Work, Los Angeles, CA 90089-0411.
Subscriptions	Subscriptions are on a per-volume basis only. The following prices are for the current document only for addresses in the United States. Subscriptions must be prepaid. Individuals $65 (paid by personal check), Institutions $140 (examples: corporations, departments, institutes, social and health service agencies/hospitals), Libraries and subscription agencies $235 (whenever purchased either directly or through a subscription, and agency). All subscriptions, reprints and advertising should be directed to The Haworth Press, Inc., 10 Alice Street, Binghamton, NY 13904-1580; Phone (607) 722-5857.
Affiliation	The National Network of Social Work Managers Inc.
E-Mail Address	rino@sowk.usc.edu
Website	www.informaworld.com

ADVANCES IN SOCIAL WORK

Current Title	*Advances in Social Work*
Previous Title	N/A.
Editorial Focus	*Advances in Social Work* is committed to enhancing the linkage among social work practice, research, and education. Accordingly, the journal addresses current issues, challenges, and responses facing social work practice and education. The journal invites discussion and development of innovations in social work practice and their implications for social work research and education. *Advances in Social Work* seeks to publish empirical, conceptual, and theoretical articles that make substantial contributions to the field in all areas of social work, including clinical practice, community organization, social administration, social policy, planning, and program evaluation.
Audience	Social work researchers, educators and practitioners.
Special Themes	Not specified.
Where Indexed/ Abstracted	Directory of Open Access Journals; Google; Google Scholar. Working on further indexing by Ovid (Social Work Abstracts), Social Service Abstracts, and ProQuest.
Year Established	2000
Circulation	Open access online—free, unlimited.
Frequency	Twice a year.
Months Issued	June and December.
No. of Articles per Issue	7–10.

SUBMISSIONS

Postal Mailing Address	Not specified. The journal is now an open-access, online journal.
Method for Submission	Online submission required.
Number of Copies	Not specified.
Disk Submission	N/A.
Online or E-mail Submission Allowed or Required	Online submission required.

FORMAT OF MANUSCRIPT

Cover Sheet	Author information to be uploaded as a separate, supplementary file.
Abstract	150 words or less.
Key Words	3–5 words.
Length	15–20 pages, including references, tables, figures.
Margins	1.5 inches.
Spacing	Single spaced. Times New Roman 11-pt font. Please use Microsoft Word.

STYLE

Name of Guide	*Publication Manual of the American Psychological Association.*
Subheadings	See style guide.
References	See style guide.
Footnotes	Endnotes if necessary.
Tables or Figures	Embedded in text.

REVIEW PROCESS

Type of Review	Blind peer review.
Queries	Not specified.
Acknowledgment	Not specified.
Review Time	Approximately 1–2 months.
Revisions	Approximately 2–4 months.
Acceptance Rate	Approximately 40%–60%.
Return of Manuscript	N/A.
Lag Time to Print	Usually less than 6 months from final acceptance.

REPRINT, SUBSCRIPTION, AND CONTACT INFORMATION

Reprint Policy	None—freely available online for unlimited downloads.
Book Reviews	No.
Subscriptions	N/A, open access.
Affiliation	Indiana University School of Social Work.
E-Mail Address	wbarton@iupui.edu
Website	http://journals.iupui.edu/index.php/advancesinsocialwork/index

AFFILIA—JOURNAL OF WOMEN AND SOCIAL WORK

Current Title	*Affilia: Journal of Women and Social Work*
Previous Title	N/A.
Editorial Focus	*Affilia: Journal of Women and Social Work* is dedicated to the discussion and development of feminist values, theories, and knowledge as they relate to social work and social welfare research, education, and practice. All forms of writing and analysis will be considered, and a range of feminist perspectives will be encouraged. The intent of *Affilia* is to bring insight and knowledge to the task of eliminating discrimination and oppression, especially with respect to gender, race, ethnicity, class, age, disability, and sexual and affectional preference.
Audience	Social work and women's studies researchers, practitioners, educators, and administrators.
Special Themes	Psychosocial empowerment of women. Ongoing topics of interest include: The nature of female–male alliances for dealing with gender oppression in social work contexts, Psychosocial development and gender: Are women more peace-loving than men? What will/should "feminism" look like in the 21st century? The application of formal theory to feminist perspectives in social work practice: How to make a stronger case for generalizing feminist analyses to varieties of context.
Where Indexed/ Abstracted	CINAHL; Criminal justice Abstracts; EBSCOhost; PsycINFO; Social Work Abstracts; SocINFO; Women Studies Abstracts.
Year Established	1986.
Circulation	60.
Frequency	Quarterly.
Months Issued	February, May, August, November.
No. of Articles per Issue	Not specified.

SUBMISSIONS

Postal Mailing Address	Fariyal Ross-Sheriff, Co-Editor for Manuscripts, Affilia, Howard University School of Social Work, 601 Howard Place NW, Washington, DC 20059.
Method for Submission	Surface mail, disk.
Number of Copies	4
Disk Submission	After editing, a corrected copy of the manuscript saved on a disk must be returned with the final hard copy.
Online or E-mail Submission Allowed or Required	No.

FORMAT OF MANUSCRIPT

Cover Sheet	Authors should supply a separate cover sheet with name of the author(s) and other identifying information.
Abstract	Abstract of fewer than 100 words should accompany the manuscript.
Key Words	Not specified.
Length	20 pages, or 25 pages for manuscripts reporting on qualitative or historic research.
Margins	Not specified.
Spacing	Double spaced.

STYLE

Name of Guide	*Publication Manual of the American Psychological Association.*
Subheadings	See style guide.
References	See style guide.
Footnotes	There is no place for notes or comments in the References section or footnotes in the text. Such notes should be incorporated into the text if they are pertinent. Simple asides will not be included.
Tables or Figures	Not specified.

REVIEW PROCESS

Type of Review	Anonymous peer review.
Queries	Not specified.
Acknowledgment	Not specified.

Review Time	Not specified.
Revisions	Not specified.
Acceptance Rate	Not specified.
Return of Manuscript	Not specified.
Lag Time to Print	Not specified.

CHARGES TO AUTHOR

Author Alterations	Not specified.
Page Charges	Not specified.
Processing	Not specified.

REPRINT, SUBSCRIPTION, AND CONTACT INFORMATION

Reprint Policy	If you are seeking one copy of an article that was published in a SAGE journal, please purchase the article through the pay-per-view function (PPV) on the journal's online platform. Your PPV purchase will allow you to access, download, and print a copy of the article. To locate the journal article you are interested in, start here: http://online.sagepub.com. SAGE provides reprints for orders with a minimum quantity of 50. Orders for 49 or fewer copies will be fulfilled with permission.
Book Reviews	Yes, contact book review editor.
Subscriptions	Print and online subscriptions available from the website.
Affiliation	Not specified.
E-Mail Address	info@sagepub.com
Website	http://aff.sagepub.com/

AGING AND MENTAL HEALTH

Current Title	*Aging and Mental Health*
Previous Title	N/A.
Editorial Focus	*Aging and Mental Health* provides a forum for the rapidly expanding field, which investigates the relationship between the aging process and mental health. It addresses the mental changes associated with normal and abnormal or pathological aging, as well as the psychological and psychiatric problems of the aging population. The journal covers the biological, psychological, and social aspects of aging as they relate to mental health. In particular, it encourages an integrated approach between the various biopsychosocial processes and etiological factors associated with psychological changes in the elderly. It also emphasizes the various strategies, therapies, and services that may be directed at improving the mental health of the elderly. In this way, the journal has a strong alliance between the theoretical, experimental, and applied sciences across a range of issues affecting mental health and aging. The journal provides an original and dynamic focus to help integrate the normal and abnormal aspects of mental health in aging. In addition, theoretical issues can be set in the context of the important new practical developments in this field.
Audience	Clinical and academic disciplines in the field of mental health and aging, including psychiatry, psychology, nursing, gerontology.
Special Themes	Special sections published on a regular basis.
Where Indexed/ Abstracted	AgeInfo; AgeLine; Cumulative Index to Nursing & Allied Health Literature; Current Contents/Social and Behavioral Sciences; EMBASE/Excerpta Medica; International Bibliography of Social Sciences (IBSS); Linguistics & Language Behaviour Abstracts; Index Medicus/MEDLINE; PsycINFO/PsychLIT; Research Alert; SCI (Science Citation Index); SCOPUS; Social Care Online; Social Sciences Citation Index; Social Scisearch; Social Services Abstracts; Sociological Abstracts.
Year Established	1997
Circulation	Internationally in over 40 countries.
Frequency	6 issues per year, to increase to 8 in 2010.
Months Issued	January, March, May, July, September, November.
No. of Articles per Issue	Approximately 17 original articles, plus 1 editorial.

SUBMISSIONS

Postal Mailing Address	Not necessary, online submission required. Submissions: http://mc.manuscriptcentral.com/camh. It is a condition of publication that authors assign copyright or license the publication rights to their articles, including abstracts, to Taylor & Francis. This enables us to ensure full copyright protection and to disseminate the article, and the journal, to the widest possible readership in print and electronic formats as appropriate. Authors retain many rights under the Taylor & Francis rights policies, which can be found at www.informaworld.com/authors_journals_copyright_position. Authors are themselves responsible for obtaining permission to reproduce copyrighted material from other sources.
Method for Submission	Electronic form via website.
Number of Copies	2
Disk Submission	N/A.
Online or E-mail Submission Allowed or Required	Online only as a single file. Accepted word processing formats: Word XP 2003, Word XP 2007, Word Mac 2004, and Word Mac 2008. Templates available on website.

FORMATION OF MANUSCRIPT

Cover Sheet	The cover sheet should include the title of the paper, first name, middle initial(s) and last name of the author(s), a short institutional address for each author, and an abbreviated title (for running headlines within the article). At the bottom of the page, give the full name and address (including telephone and fax numbers and e-mail address if possible) of the author to whom all correspondence (including proofs) should be sent. Pages should be numbered.
Abstract	The main text should be preceded by a short structured abstract, accompanied by a list of keywords. The abstract should not contain more than 250 words. The abstract should be arranged as follows: Title of manuscript; name of journal; abstract text containing the following headings: Objectives, Method, Results, and Conclusion.

Key Words A list of 3–5 keywords should be provided. Words already used in the title should be avoided if possible.

Length Manuscripts may be in the form of: (i) regular articles not usually exceeding 5,000 words (under special circumstances, the Editors will consider articles up to 10,000 words); or (ii) short reports not exceeding 2,000 words.

Margins At least 2.5 cm (1 inch).

Spacing Double spaced.

STYLE

Name of Guide *The Publication Manual of the American Psychological Association* (Taylor & Francis Style No. 4 can be accessed via website link to article style). The text should normally be divided into sections with the headings Introduction, Methods, Results, and Discussion.

Subheadings Subheadings should be used within some sections to clarify their content. Within the text section, headings and subheadings should be typed on a separate line without numbering, indentation, or bold or italic typeface.

References Taylor & Francis Style A, (APA) can be accessed via website link to references. References are cited in the text in alphabetical order (the same way they appear in the reference list), separated by a semicolon. (Green, 2002; Harlow, 1983). If you have two authors with the same last name, use first initials with the last names. (E. Johnson, 2001; L. Johnson, 1998).

Footnotes No.

Tables or Figures Tables should be submitted on separate pages, numbered in Arabic numerals, and their position indicated in the text (e.g. Table 1). Each table should have a short, self-explanatory title. Vertical rules should not be used to separate columns. Units should appear in parentheses in the column heading, but not in the body of the table. Any explanatory notes should be given as a footnote at the bottom of the table. All measurements must be cited in SI units. All illustrations (including photographs, graphs and diagrams) should be referred to as Figures and their position indicated in the text (e.g. Fig. 3). Each should be submitted numbered on the back with the figure number (Arabic numerals) and the title of the paper. The captions of all figures should be submitted on a separate page, should include keys to symbols, and should make interpretation possible without reference to the text. Figures should ideally be professionally drawn and designed with the format of the journal (A4 portrait, 297 × 210 mm) in mind and should be capable of reduction.

REVIEW PROCESS

Type of Review Editor screening followed by anonymous peer reviews, normally 2.

Queries Queries are welcomed.

Acknowledgment Manuscripts acknowledged automatically via standard e-mail letter from website.

Review Time Approximately 2 months.

Revisions Approximately 1 month.

Acceptance Rate Approximately 50%.

Return of Manuscript N/A.

Lag Time to Print Approximately 6 months.

CHARGES TO AUTHOR

Author Alterations No charge, but only typographical corrections are allowed.

Page Charges No charges for pages.

Processing No charge; free sample copy provided.

REPRINT, SUBSCRIPTION, AND CONTACT INFORMATION

Reprint Policy Purchased via website reprints@tandf.co.uk

Book Reviews Book reviews are submitted by e-mail to Professor Murna Downs, m.downs@bradford.ac.uk.

Subscriptions Subscribe online at www.tandf.co.uk/journals/titles/13607863.asp.

Affiliation N/A.

E-Mail Address Queries on submissions to the editor: amh@ucl.ac.uk. For queries on publications or manuscripts: authorqueries@tandf.co.uk.

Website www.tandf.co.uk/journal

ALCOHOLISM TREATMENT QUARTERLY

Current Title	*Alcoholism Treatment Quarterly*
Previous Title	N/A.
Editorial Focus	The journal explores the 'how-to' approaches of intervention and therapy by presenting case studies and commentaries by counselors and therapists.
Audience	Social workers, addiction counselors, psychologists, and nurses.
Special Themes	*Alcoholism Treatment Quarterly* particularly welcomes material giving the personal and humanistic aspects of professional alcoholism counseling and therapy from both the counselor/therapist's view as well as that of the client.
Where Indexed/ Abstracted	Abstracts in Anthropology; Academic Search Complete (EBSCO); CINAHL Full Text; Criminal Justice Abstracts; E-Psyche; Family Index Database; National Criminal Justice Reference Services; ProQuest CSA; PsycINFO; Scopus; SocINDEX.
Year Established	1984.
Circulation	375.
Frequency	Quarterly.
Months Issued	January, April, July, October.
No. of Articles per Issue	7–10.

SUBMISSIONS

Postal Mailing Address	Thomas F. McGovern, EdD; Department of Neuropsychiatry, Texas Tech University, Health Sciences Center, 3601 4th Street, Lubbock, TX 79430-0001; e-mail preferred.
Method for Submission	Surface mail and e-mail.
Number of Copies	3.
Disk Submission	Yes.
Online or E-mail Submission Allowed or Required	Yes: Thomas.McGovern@ttuhsc.edu.

FORMAT OF MANUSCRIPT

Cover Sheet	Yes, please include author name and contact information on cover sheet only.
Abstract	Yes, 100 words or less.
Key Words	Yes, 5–10 words.
Length	Not specified.
Margins	1 inch.
Spacing	Double spaced.

STYLE

Name of Guide	*Publication Manual of the American Psychological Association.*
Subheadings	Not specified.
References	See style guide.
Footnotes	Not specified.
Tables or Figures	Yes, camera ready. See Page charges below.

REVIEW PROCESS

Type of Review	Blind peer review.
Queries	Thomas.McGovern@ttuhsc.edu.
Acknowledgment	Yes, via e-mail.
Review Time	We aim for 2 months.
Revisions	Yes, revise and resubmit.
Acceptance Rate	Approximately 70%.
Return of Manuscript	Yes, if rejected only.
Lag Time to Print	We aim for a maximum of 6 months.

CHARGES TO AUTHOR

Author Alterations	No charges; authors have 48 hours to check and return proofs.
Page Charges	For color figures; Online-only color figure fees: $225 for first page of color, $100 per page for next three pages. Maximum charge of $525. Print and online color figure fees: $900 for first page of color, $450 per page for next three pages of color.
Processing	No.

REPRINT, SUBSCRIPTION, AND CONTACT INFORMATION

Reprint Policy	Corresponding author receives 3 print issues and complimentary PDF file of article.
Book Reviews	Yes, to Thomas.McGovern@ttuhsc.edu.
Subscriptions	$770 Institutional, $120 Personal.
Affiliation	Routledge Journals, an imprint of Taylor and Francis Group.
E-Mail Address	CustomerService@TaylorandFrancis.com
Website	www.Informaworld.com/WATQ

AMERICAN JOURNAL OF ALZHEIMER'S DISEASE AND OTHER DEMENTIA

Current Title	*American Journal of Alzheimer's Disease and Other Dementia*
Previous Title	*American Journal of Alzheimer's Disease*
Editorial Focus	This journal provides down-to-earth clinical information on practical medical, psychiatric, and nursing issues, new and forthcoming diagnostic tools, psychosocial issues, practice-oriented clinical research, and administrative and legal issues.
Audience	The journal is for and by professionals on the front lines of Alzheimer's care, dementia, and clinical depression, especially physicians, nurses, psychiatrists, healthcare administrators, and other related healthcare specialists who deal with patients having dementias and families every day.
Special Themes	Not specified.
Where Indexed/ Abstracted	Abstracts in Social Gerontology; AgeLine; Current Abstracts; EBSCOhost; Family Index; MEDLINE; PsycINFO; SCOPUS; Social Work Abstracts.
Year Established	1986
Circulation	Not specified.
Frequency	Bimonthly.
Months Issued	February, April, June, August, October, December.
No. of Articles per Issue	7–10.

SUBMISSIONS

Postal Mailing Address	Mail submissions not accepted.
Method for Submission	Manuscripts should be submitted to http://mc.manuscriptcentral.com/ajad.
Number of Copies	1 copy through the online system.
Disk Submission	Not necessary.
Online or E-mail Submission Allowed or Required	Online submission required.

FORMAT OF MANUSCRIPT

Cover Sheet	The title should not be longer than 96 characters in length including spaces, punctuation, and subtitle. The full names or initials, highest academic degrees, and institutional affiliations (including the city and state) for each author should be included.
Abstract	Abstracts should be fewer than 150 words and should summarize key points and conclusions. For research articles, the background/rationale, methods, and results and conclusions should be summarized.
Key Words	4–6 keywords should be listed at the end of the abstract.
Length	There is no formal word limitation; however, manuscripts over 4,500 words are discouraged.
Margins	Not specified.
Spacing	Not specified.

STYLE

Name of Guide	*American Medical Association Manual of Style.*
Subheadings	See style guide.
References	See style guide.
Footnotes	See style guide.
Tables or Figures	See style guide.

REVIEW PROCESS

Type of Review	Peer review.
Queries	Contact the editor.
Acknowledgment	Acknowledgment generated automatically by online submission system.
Review Time	Several weeks.
Revisions	Per editor instruction.
Acceptance Rate	Approximately 50%.
Return of Manuscript	Not specified.
Lag Time to Print	Not specified.

CHARGES TO AUTHOR

Author Alterations	Not specified.
Page Charges	Not specified.
Processing	Not specified.

REPRINT, SUBSCRIPTION, AND CONTACT INFORMATION

Reprint Policy	Reprints may be ordered by using the special reprint order form that will accompany author proofs.
Book Reviews	Not specified.
Subscriptions	Information available through the website at: www.sagepub.com.
Affiliation	Not specified.
E-Mail Address	ajadod@verizon.net
Website	http://alzheimers.sagepub.com

AMERICAN JOURNAL OF COMMUNITY PSYCHOLOGY

Current Title	*American Journal of Community Psychology*
Previous Title	N/A.
Editorial Focus	Community Research.
Audience	Researchers and Practitioners.
Special Themes	Not specified.
Where Indexed/ Abstracted	PsycINFO; PsychLIT.
Year Established	1975
Circulation	3,500
Frequency	Quarterly.
Months Issued	March, June, September, December.
No. of Articles per Issue	12–15.

SUBMISSIONS

Postal Mailing Address	William Davidson, PhD, Editor in Chief, 132 Psychology; MSU; E. Lansing, MI 48824-1116.
Method for Submission	Surface mail.
Number of Copies	4
Disk Submission	
Online or E-mail Submission Allowed or Required	Yes, after January 1, 2010.

FORMAT OF MANUSCRIPT

Cover Sheet	Yes.
Abstract	Yes.
Key Words	Yes.
Length	25–60 pages.
Margins	1 inch.
Spacing	Double-spaced.

STYLE

Name of Guide	*Publication Manual of the American Psychological Association.*
Subheadings	Yes.
References	Yes.
Footnotes	Yes.
Tables or Figures	Yes.

REVIEW PROCESS

Type of Review	Blind.
Queries	Not specified.
Acknowledgment	Yes.
Review Time	Approximately 65 days.
Revisions	Yes.
Acceptance Rate	Approximately 11%.
Return of Manuscript	Yes, by request.
Lag Time to Print	Approximately 3–6 months.

CHARGES TO AUTHOR

Author Alterations	Yes.
Page Charges	No.
Processing	No.

REPRINT, SUBSCRIPTION, AND CONTACT INFORMATION

Reprint Policy	Yes.
Book Reviews	No.

Subscriptions	Yes.
Affiliation	Division 27 of APA, The Society for Community Research and Action.
E-Mail Address	davidso7@msu.edu
Website	No.

AMERICAN JOURNAL OF DRUG AND ALCOHOL ABUSE

Current Title	*American Journal of Drug and Alcohol Abuse*
Previous Title	N/A.
Editorial Focus	Substance use research, clinical and applied, with a particular interest in innovative methodologies, technologies, and research translation into practice.
Audience	Not specified.
Special Themes	N/A.
Where Indexed/ Abstracted	Academic Search Complete; Biological Abstracts; Biomedical Reference Collection: Comprehensive; BIOSIS Previews; Consumer Health Complete; Current Contents/Social and Behavioral Sciences; EMBASE; EMCARE; ETOH; Health and Safety Abstracts; Journal Citation Reports/ Social Sciences Edition; PASCAL; Popline; PsycINFO; PubMed/MEDLINE; Risk Abstracts; SCOPUS, Social Sciences Citation Index; Social SciSearch; Social Services Abstracts; Sociological Abstracts.
Year Established	1984.
Circulation	300.
Frequency	Bimonthly; 6 issues per year.
Months Issued	January, March, May, July September, November.
No. of Articles per Issue	15–18.

SUBMISSIONS

Postal Mailing Address	Electronic submission only: Manuscript Central/Scholar One.
Method for Submission	Electronic submission only: Manuscript Central/Scholar One.
Number of Copies	1 blinded, 1 complete including cover page with author name and affiliations.
Disk Submission	Electronic submission only: Manuscript Central/Scholar One.
Online or E-mail Submission Allowed or Required	Online submission required.

FORMAT OF MANUSCRIPT

Cover Sheet	Manuscript title; Authors names, credentials, and affiliation; manuscript details including # of words, pages, figures, and tables.
Abstract	250 words.
Key Words	5–6 key words required.
Length	Approximately 2,400 words per manuscript not including abstract or references but some variation depending on article type.
Margins	1 inch all around.
Spacing	Double-spaced.

STYLE

Name of Guide	*Publication Manual of the American Publication Manual;* see "Instructions to Authors" on *AJDAA* site for additional details.
Subheadings	As appropriate.
References	Numeric format in order of appearance in manuscript.
Footnotes	Not accepted.
Tables or Figures	As appropriate to further clarify study results. Must include a tables/figures legend.

REVIEW PROCESS

Type of Review	Anonymous; 2–3 reviewers.
Queries	1–10.
Acknowledgment	Auto generated e-mail upon online manuscript submission.
Review Time	Approximately 8–12 weeks.
Revisions	Approximately 8–12 weeks.
Acceptance Rate	Approximately 50–60%.
Return of Manuscript	N/A: online submission only.
Lag Time to Print	Approximately 4–6 months.

CHARGES TO AUTHOR

Author Alterations   N/A.

Page Charges   N/A.

Processing   All manuscript print info that author requests to be in color is at author's expense; charges do not apply to online manuscript info.

REPRINT, SUBSCRIPTION, AND CONTACT INFORMATION

Reprint Policy   Reprints of any article published in the journal are available to order on the InformaWorld website.

Book Reviews   Book reviews can be sent through Manuscript Central as regular article submissions.

Subscriptions   Subscriptions can be ordered and processed through the InformaWorld website.

Affiliation   Informa Healthcare.

E-Mail Address   Not specified.

Website   www.informaworld.com/ajdaa

AMERICAN JOURNAL OF FAMILY THERAPY

Current Title	*American Journal of Family Therapy*
Previous Title	*International Journal of Family Counseling*
Editorial Focus	You will find the latest techniques for treating families, theory on normal and dysfunctional family relationships, research on sexuality and intimacy, the effects of traditional and alternative family styles, community approaches to family intervention, and more.
Audience	Marriage and family therapists, psychiatrists, psychologists, allied health and mental health practitioners, counselors, clinical social workers, physicians, nurses, clergy practitioners.
Special Themes	Not specified.
Where Indexed/ Abstracted	AgeLine; Criminal Justice Abstracts; EBSCOhost; PsycINFO; Social Services Abstracts; Sociological Abstracts; Violence and Abuse Abstracts.
Year Established	1970
Circulation	Not specified.
Frequency	5 times per year.
Months Issued	Not specified.
No. of Articles per Issue	5–7.

SUBMISSIONS

Postal Mailing Address	Dr. S. Richard Sauber, Editor, AFT, Suite 300, 20283 State Road 7, Boca Raton, FL 33498.
Method for Submission	Three copies of each manuscript and return postage should be sent to the journal editor.
Number of Copies	3
Disk Submission	Authors are strongly encouraged to submit manuscripts on disk. The disk should be prepared using MS Word or WordPerfect and should be clearly labeled with the authors' names, file name, and software program. A hardcopy printout that exactly matches the disk must be supplied.
Online or E-mail Submission Allowed or Required	Not specified.

FORMAT OF MANUSCRIPT

Cover Sheet	Not specified.
Abstract	Each article should be summarized in an abstract of not more that 100 words.
Key Words	Yes.
Length	16–20 pages.
Margins	1 inch on all sides.
Spacing	Double-spaced.

STYLE

Name of Guide	*Publication Manual of the American Psychological Association.*
Subheadings	See style guide.
References	See style guide.
Footnotes	See style guide.
Tables or Figures	Tables and figures should not be embedded in the text, but should be included as separate sheets or files. A short descriptive title should appear above each table with a clear legend and any footnotes suitably identified below. All units must be included. Figures should be completely labeled, taking into account necessary size reduction. Captions should be typed, double-spaced, on a separate sheet. All original figures should be clearly marked in pencil on the reverse side with the number, author's name, and top edge indicated.

REVIEW PROCESS

Type of Review	Anonymous peer review.
Queries	Not specified.
Acknowledgment	Include self-addressed, stamped envelope when submitting manuscript.
Review Time	Not specified.
Revisions	Not specified.
Acceptance Rate	Not specified.
Return of Manuscript	Include a 9" × 12" self-addressed, stamped envelope when submitting manuscript.
Lag Time to Print	Not specified.

REPRINT, SUBSCRIPTION, AND CONTACT INFORMATION

Reprint Policy   Each corresponding author will receive one copy of the issue in which the article appears. Reprints of individual articles are available for order at the time authors review page proofs. A discount on reprints is available to authors who order before print publication.

Book Reviews   Contact book review editor.

Subscriptions   Taylor & Francis, Inc., 325 Chestnut Street, Suite 800, Philadelphia, PA 19106.

Affiliation   Not specified.

E-Mail Address   journals@routledge.com

Website   http://www.informaworld.com/smpp/title~db=all~content=t713722633~tab=summary

AMERICAN JOURNAL OF HOSPICE & PALLIATIVE CARE

Current Title	*American Journal of Hospice & Palliative Medicine*
Previous Title	*American Journal of Hospice & Palliative Care (pre 1994).*
Editorial Focus	Editorials, original research articles, reviews, case reports, literature and humanities, commentaries, sounding boards, book reviews, end-of-life vignettes, letters to the editor, ongoing series like the Ethics Roundtable, etc.
Audience	The multidisciplinary team: physicians, nurses, social workers, chaplains, psychologists, volunteer coordinators, and others involved in the total care of the patient.
Special Themes	None.
Where Indexed/ Abstracted	AgeLine; CINAHL, Current Contents: Clinical Medicine; Index Medicus; MEDLINE; NISC; Science Citation Index Expanded (Web of Science).
Year Established	1984
Circulation	6,000
Frequency	Bimonthly.
Months Issued	February, March; April, May; June, July; August, September, October, November, December, January.
No. of Articles per Issue	14

SUBMISSIONS

Postal Mailing Address	128 Ridgetop Drive, Gray, TN 37615.
Method for Submission	E-mail, electronic via website.
Number of Copies	1
Disk Submission	No.
Online or E-mail Submission Allowed or Required	Yes. mc.manuscriptcentral.com/ajhpm; robertenck@comcast.net.

FORMAT OF MANUSCRIPTS

Cover Sheet	Authors' names and affiliations, and corresponding author's address, e-mail, phone and fax Number.
Abstract	125 words.
Key Words	6–8.
Length	No limit.
Margins	N/A.
Spacing	N/A.

STYLE

Name of Guide	No specific style.
Subheadings	Abstract, Introduction, Methods, Results, Discussion, Conclusions for research manuscripts.
References	AMA style.
Footnotes	N/A.
Tables or Figures	Word format or pdf.

REVIEW PROCESS

Type of Review	2 peer reviewers with authors blinded to reviewers.
Queries	Yes. mc.manuscriptcentral.com/ajhpm; robertenck@comcast.net.
Acknowledgment	E-mail.
Review Time	Approximately 6–8 weeks.
Revisions	Reviewed by editorial staff.
Acceptance Rate	Approximately 80%.
Return of Manuscript	No.
Lag Time to Print	Approximately 9 months.

REPRINT, SUBSCRIPTION, AND CONTACT INFORMATION

Reprint Policy	Contact Sage Publications.
Book Reviews	Yes, send to editorial office.

Subscriptions	$219 for individual.
Affiliation	None.
E-Mail Address	robertenck@comcast.net
Website	Sagepub.com

AMERICAN JOURNAL OF ORTHOPSYCHIATRY

Current Title	*American Journal of Orthopsychiatry*
Previous Title	N/A.
Editorial Focus	The journal is dedicated to informing public policy and professional practice and to the expansion of knowledge relating to mental health and human development from a multidisciplinary and interprofessional perspective.
Audience	Social workers, psychologists, psychiatrists, psychiatric nurses, educators, and professionals in a broad range of allied disciplines.
Special Themes	Not specified.
Where Indexed/ Abstracted	Addiction Abstracts; Applied Social Science Index & Abstracts; Biological Abstracts; Criminal Justice Abstracts; Index Medicus; MEDLINE; NARIC Guide to Disability and Rehabilitation Periodicals; PsycINFO; Research in Higher Education; Social Sciences Index; Social Welfare and Social Services Abstracts; Social Work Abstracts; Sociological Abstracts; Studies on Women Abstracts; Westlaw.
Year Established	1930
Circulation	1,536 paid.
Frequency	Quarterly.
Months Issued	January, April, July, October.
No. of Articles per Issue	Not specified.

SUBMISSIONS

Postal Mailing Address	General correspondence may be sent to the editor, Nancy Felipe Russo at AJOrthopsychiatry@gmail.com.
Method for Submission	Manuscripts should be submitted electronically through the Manuscript Submission Portal at http://www.jbo.com/jbo3/submissions/dsp_jbo.cfm?journal_code=ort.
Number of Copies	N/A.
Disk Submission	No.
Online or E-mail Submission Allowed or Required	Online submission as noted above.

FORMAT OF MANUSCRIPT

Cover Sheet	Cover letter with mailing address, daytime telephone number, and fax number (if available).
Abstract	The abstract should be a maximum of 180 words typed on a separate page.
Key Words	Supply up to five keywords or brief phrases.
Length	Manuscripts are limited to 30 pages, inclusive of references, tables, and figures.
Margins	Wide.
Spacing	Double-spaced.

STYLE

Name of Guide	*Publication Manual of the American Psychological Association.*
Subheadings	See style guide.
References	List references in alphabetical order. Each listed reference should be cited in text, and each text citation should be listed in the References section. Follow style guide.
Footnotes	Footnotes should be worked back into the text or deleted, if possible. Where essential, they should appear on a page by themselves following the references and be indicated by superscript Arabic numerals.
Tables or Figures	Only photocopies or computer-generated duplicates should be submitted, as rejected manuscripts are disposed of following review.

REVIEW PROCESS

Type of Review	Masked peer review.
Queries	Letters of inquiry unaccompanied by manuscript are discouraged.
Acknowledgment	All submissions are acknowledged on receipt.
Review Time	Approximately 3–5 months.
Revisions	May be requested by the editor subsequent to review; resubmissions are subject to further review.
Acceptance Rate	Approximately 15%.

Return of Manuscript Not returned.

Lag Time to Print Approximately 12–18 months.

REPRINT, SUBSCRIPTION, AND CONTACT INFORMATION

Reprint Policy Authors are invited to order reprints at their own expense.

Book Reviews None. Companion quarterly, *Readings: A Journal of Reviews and Commentary in Mental Health,* publishes book reviews, all invited by the editors.

Subscriptions American Psychological Association, Subscriptions, 750 First Street, NE, Washington, DC 20002-4242.

Affiliation American Orthopsychiatric Association

E-Mail Address AJOrthopsychiatry@gmail.com

Website http://www.apa.org/journals/ort/description.html

AMERICAN JOURNAL OF SEXUALITY EDUCATION

Current Title	*American Journal of Sexuality Education*
Previous Title	*Journal of Sex Education & Therapy.*
Editorial Focus	This peer-reviewed journal provides sexuality educators and trainers with current research about sexuality education programming, best practices, sample lesson plans, reports on curriculum development and assessment, literature reviews, scholarly commentary, educational program reports, media reviews (books, videos, internet resources, and curricula), and letters to the editor.
Audience	Sexuality educators and trainers, public health workers, social workers.
Special Themes	Content for the journal will always be diverse, including but certainly not limited to teaching about pregnancy prevention, sexually transmitted infections, sexual coercion, healthy versus unhealthy relationships, sexual orientation and identity, sexual response, sexual decision-making, gender identity, and more.
Where Indexed/ Abstracted	Academic Search Complete; Criminal Justice Abstracts; Current Abstracts; Education Research Complete; Family Index Database; Index Copernicus; Social Service Abstracts; Social Work Abstracts; TOC Premier.
Year Established	2005.
Circulation	169.
Frequency	4 times per year.
Months Issued	January, April, July, October.
No. of Articles per Issue	5.

SUBMISSIONS

Postal Mailing Address	sexedjournal@hotmail.com
Method for Submission	E-mail.
Number of Copies	N/A.
Disk Submission	N/A.
Online or E-mail Submission Allowed or Required	Required.

FORMAT OF MANUSCRIPT

Cover Sheet	Full title; author names; professional titles; designation of one author as corresponding author with address, phone, fax, and e-mail address.
Abstract	100–150 words.
Key Words	None required.
Length	25 pages maximum for full-length paper.
Margins	1 inch on all sides.
Spacing	Double-spaced throughout paper, including references.

STYLE

Name of Guide	*Publication Manual of the American Psychological Association.*
Subheadings	As needed, see style guide.
References	See style guide.
Footnotes	With rare exceptions limited to author acknowledgements, including funding and permissions. Separate page entitled "Footnotes".
Tables or Figures	Tables and figures (illustrations) should not be embedded in the text, but should be included as separate sheets or files. A short descriptive title should appear above each table with a clear legend and any footnotes suitably identified below. All units must be included. Figures should be completely labeled, taking into account necessary size reduction. Captions should be typed, double-spaced, on a separate sheet.

REVIEW PROCESS

Type of Review	All articles in this journal have undergone rigorous peer review, based on initial editor screening and anonymous refereeing by between four and eight referees.
Queries	Queries to editor by letter, phone, or e-mail are welcomed.
Acknowledgment	By letter.

Review Time	Authors are notified after 1–3 months. Reviewers are asked to submit reviews within 3 weeks of receipt.
Revisions	Manuscripts may be sent to the same or different reviewers after revision. Three copies of revised manuscript are required, along with cover letter explaining all modifications and/or reasons for not making recommended changes.
Acceptance Rate	Unknown at present due to change in editor and format.
Return of Manuscript	Not returned.
Lag Time to Print	Approximately 6–12 months.

CHARGES TO AUTHOR

Author Alterations	N/A.
Page Charges	Color illustrations will be considered for publication; however, the author will be required to bear the full cost involved in color art reproduction. Color art can be purchased for online-only reproduction or for print and online reproduction. Color reprints can only be ordered if print and online reproduction costs are paid. Rates for color art reproduction are: Online-only reproduction: $225 for the first page of color; $100 per page for the next three pages of color. A maximum charge of $525 applies. Print and online reproduction: $900 for the first page of color; $450 per page for the next three pages of color. A custom quote will be provided for articles with more than four pages of color.
Processing	N/A.

REPRINT, SUBSCRIPTION, AND CONTACT INFORMATION

Reprint Policy	Reprints of individual articles are available for order at the time authors review page proofs. A discount on reprints is available to authors who order before print publication. Each corresponding author will receive 3 complete issues in which the article publishes and a complimentary PDF. This file is for personal use only and may not be copied and disseminated in any form without prior written permission from Taylor and Francis Group, LLC.
Book Reviews	Yes; send books for review to Taylor & Francis, 325 Chestnut Street, Suite 800, Philadelphia, PA 19106; electronic media can be forward to the editor at: sexedjournal@hotmail.com.
Subscriptions	www.tandf.co.uk/journals/wajs or 1.800.354.1420, press "4" or customer.service@taylorandfrancis.com.
Affiliation	N/A.
E-Mail Address	sexedjournal@hotmail.com
Website	www.tandf.co.uk/journals/wajs

AMERICAN PSYCHOLOGIST

Current Title	*American Psychologist*
Previous Title	N/A.
Editorial Focus	*American Psychologist* contains archival documents and articles covering current issues in psychology, the science and practice of psychology, and psychology's contribution to public policy.
Audience	Researchers in the discipline, faculty, libraries.
Special Themes	Not specified.
Where Indexed/ Abstracted	Academic Index; Applied Social Science Index & Abstracts; Chemical Abstracts; Child Development Abstracts; Communication Abstracts; Criminal Justice Abstracts; Current Index to Journals in Education; Index Medicus; Management Contents; PsycINFO; Research in Higher Education; Risk Abstracts; Sage Family Studies Abstracts; Social Sciences Index; Social Work Abstracts; Studies on Women & Gender Abstracts.
Year Established	1946.
Circulation	Not specified.
Frequency	9 times per year.
Months Issued	January, February, April, May, July, September, October, November, December.
No. of Articles per Issue	Not specified.

SUBMISSIONS

Postal Mailing Address	American Psychological Association, 750 First Street, NE, Washington, DC 20002-4242.
Method for Submission	Manuscripts should be submitted electronically through the Manuscript Submission Portal at http://www.jbo.com/jbo3/submissions/dsp_jbo.cfm?journal_code=amp.
Number of Copies	N/A.
Disk Submission	No.
Online or E-mail Submission Allowed or Required	Online submission as noted above.

FORMAT OF MANUSCRIPT

Cover Sheet	Refer to Instructions to Authors in each issue.
Abstract	All manuscripts must include an abstract containing a maximum of 250 words typed on a separate page.
Key Words	Supply up to five keywords or brief phrases.
Length	May not exceed 35 double-spaced pages in length, including the cover page, abstract, references, tables, and figures.
Margins	Not specified.
Spacing	Double-spaced.

STYLE

Name of Guide	*Publication Manual of the American Psychological Association.*
Subheadings	See style guide.
References	See style guide.
Footnotes	See style guide.
Tables or Figures	See style guide.

REVIEW PROCESS

Type of Review	Masked peer review.
Queries	General queries can be sent to the editor at: APeditor@apa.org.
Acknowledgment	Not specified.
Review Time	Not specified.
Revisions	Not specified.
Acceptance Rate	Not specified; however, approximately 70% of author-submitted manuscripts are returned without review within 30 days for a host of reasons: Empirical manuscripts are more appropriate for one of the APA primary journals; the topic of the manuscript or style of the writing is too specialized for the broad AP readership; the same topic was recently covered in the journal; inappropriate content or style; or other, more typical reasons such as the paper does not offer a major contribution to the field or is simply not written well enough.

Return of Manuscript	Manuscripts are not returned. Authors encouraged to save an electronic copy upon submission.
Lag Time to Print	Not specified.

CHARGES TO AUTHOR

Author Alterations	Authors are billed for alterations in proofs.
Page Charges	Not specified.
Processing	Not specified.

REPRINT, SUBSCRIPTION, AND CONTACT INFORMATION

Reprint Policy	Not specified.
Book Reviews	Not specified.
Subscriptions	American Psychological Association, Subscriptions, 750 First Street, NE, Washington, DC 20002-4242; can also be ordered online.
Affiliation	American Psychological Association.
E-Mail Address	APeditor@apa.org
Website	http://www.apa.org/journals/amp/

AMERICAN SOCIOLOGICAL REVIEW

Current Title	*American Sociological Review*
Previous Title	N/A.
Editorial Focus	The journal publishes original works of interest to the sociology discipline in general, new theoretical developments, results of research that advance our understanding of fundamental social processes, and important methodological innovations. All areas of sociology are welcome in the *American Sociological Review*. Emphasis is on exceptional quality and general interest.
Audience	Sociologists and other social scientists, in academic and applied settings; libraries.
Special Themes	No thematic issues are published.
Where Indexed/ Abstracted	Abstracts in Anthropology; Abstracts in Social Gerontology; AgeLine, Criminal Justice Abstracts; EBSCOhost; Educational Research Abstracts Online; Family Studies Abstracts; Historical Abstracts; PsycINFO; Social Work Abstracts; Sociological Abstracts; Urban Studies Abstracts.
Year Established	1936.
Circulation	Not specified.
Frequency	Bimonthly.
Months Issued	February, April, June, August, October, December.
No. of Articles per Issue	6–8.

SUBMISSIONS

Postal Mailing Address	AMERICAN SOCIOLOGICAL REVIEW, Vanderbilt University, PMB 351803, 2301 Vanderbilt Place, Nashville, TN 37235.
Method for Submission	Hard copy required by mail. You must also submit an electronic file of the manuscript saved onto floppy disk or CD. Acceptable program files include MS Word, WordPerfect, and Excel. Do not send PDF files.
Number of Copies	2.
Disk Submission	Required.
Online or E-mail Submission Allowed or Required	No.

FORMAT OF MANUSCRIPT

Cover Sheet	Title page should include full article title, author(s) name(s) and affiliation(s), a "running head," and word count of the manuscript.
Abstract	One paragraph of 150–200 words.
Key Words	Not specified.
Length	ASR Articles may be any length, from short reports (e.g., 10 to 20 pages) to full-length articles (e.g., 30–40 pages) as well as qualitative and historical papers, which may need more space (e.g. 50–60 pages).
Margins	1 inch.
Spacing	Double-spaced.

STYLE

Name of Guide	*American Sociological Association Style Guide,* available through the ASA website.
Subheadings	A maximum of three levels of subheadings are sufficient.
References	See style guide.
Footnotes	See style guide.
Tables or Figures	Preferred table programs are MS Word (Table function) or Excel.

REVIEW PROCESS

Type of Review	Electronic, blinded peer review.
Queries	Editor's discretion.
Acknowledgment	ASR will acknowledge the receipt of your manuscript if you provide your e-mail address.
Review Time	Not specified.
Revisions	See ASA style guide.
Acceptance Rate	Not specified.
Return of Manuscript	Manuscripts are not returned after review.
Lag Time to Print	Not specified.

CHARGES TO AUTHOR

Author Alterations	None.
Page Charges	Voluntary contributions requested if author has research funds for that purpose.
Processing	$15; waived for student members.

REPRINT, SUBSCRIPTION, AND CONTACT INFORMATION

Reprint Policy	Not specified.
Book Reviews	Not specified.
Subscriptions	American Sociological Review, 1430 K Street, NW, Suite 600, Washington, DC 20005, or e-mail subscriptions@asanet.org.
Affiliation	American Sociological Association.
E-Mail Address	ASR@osu.edu
Website	http://www.asanet.org

ARETE

Current Title	*Arête*
Previous Title	*N/A.*
Editorial Focus	We seek manuscripts written in a scholarly manner with clear and precise development of ideas. Each manuscript should include implications for social work practice, social work education, or both.
Audience	Professionals, educators, practitioners.
Special Themes	Social work education, new teaching models, social welfare issues in the South.
Where Indexed/ Abstracted	Social Work Abstracts; Sociological Abstracts.
Year Established	1970.
Circulation	3,000+.
Frequency	Semiannually.
Months Issued	May and December.
No. of Articles per Issue	5–7.

SUBMISSIONS

Postal Mailing Address	Terry A. Wolfer, PhD, Editor, Arête College of Social Work, University of South Carolina, Columbia, SC 29208.
Method for Submission	Electronic submission via website. We prefer that authors submit manuscripts electronically. Save your manuscript in Microsoft Word format. Attach the manuscript to an e-mail message addressed to arete@gwm.sc.edu. Write "manuscript submission" in the subject line of the e-mail message. If necessary, authors may send four paper copies of a manuscript addressed to: Terry A. Wolfer, PhD, Editor, Arête College of Social Work, University of South Carolina, Columbia, SC 29208.
Number of Copies	If necessary, authors may send four paper copies of a manuscript addressed to: Terry A. Wolfer, PhD, Editor, Arête College of Social Work, University of South Carolina, Columbia, SC 29208.
Disk Submission	If necessary: see above.
Online or E-mail Submission Allowed or Required	E-mail submission strongly preferred.

FORMAT OF MANUSCRIPT

Cover Sheet	As a separate attachment, include a cover sheet with the manuscript title; running head; and author's name, affiliation, and complete contact information (e-mail, postal address, telephone, and fax).
Abstract	As the first page of the manuscript, include an abstract of no more than 100 words. Insert a hard return at the end of the abstract, to begin the manuscript text on the next page. Remove author's name from the abstract or body of the manuscript (replace it with "author citation").
Key Words	Yes.
Length	We prefer manuscripts with no more than 5,000 words of text (approximately 16 typewritten pages), not including references.
Margins	1 inch.
Spacing	Double spaced.

STYLE

Name of Guide	*Publication Manual of the American Psychological Association.*
Subheadings	See style guide.
References	See style guide.
Footnotes	See style guide.
Tables or Figures	See style guide.

REVIEW PROCESS

Type of Review	Anonymous review by three reviewers: usually members of Arête's editorial review board but occasionally guest reviewers with special expertise or members of the College of Social Work faculty.

Queries	Yes.
Acknowledgment	Yes.
Review Time	Approximately 3 months.
Revisions	Editor specifies required revisions.
Acceptance Rate	The journal editor makes a disposition based on the comments and recommendations made by reviewers and on his own reading of a manuscript. The usual dispositions include the following: 1) reject, 2) reject but invite the author(s) to revise and resubmit, 3) conditional acceptance, and 4) acceptance. With the disposition letter, we send copies of the reviewer comments. The initial manuscript review process generally takes up to 3 months.
Return of Manuscript	Not returned.
Lag Time to Print	Approximately 6 months.

CHARGES TO AUTHOR

Author Alterations	Not specified.
Page Charges	Not specified.
Processing	Not specified.

REPRINT, SUBSCRIPTION, AND CONTACT INFORMATION

Reprint Policy	Upon publication of a manuscript, we send each author two complimentary copies of the issue in which it appears.
Book Reviews	None.
Subscriptions	See website.
Affiliation	University of South Carolina College of Social Work.
E-Mail Address	arete@gwm.sc.edu
Website	http://cosw.sc.edu/arete/

ATTACHMENT & HUMAN DEVELOPMENT

Current Title	*Attachment & Human Development*
Previous Title	
Editorial Focus	*Attachment & Human Development* addresses the growing demand for a clear presentation of ideas, methods and research based on attachment theory. The journal provides a forum for the presentation and discussion of scientific theories about emotional and cognitive development, internal representations and social processes. The following types of articles are accepted: (a) Empirical reports - The paper should conform to APA standards, with a legible abstract (100–150 words), followed by sections that include an introduction, method, results, and discussion; (b) Theory/review papers - the paper should make an original, testable and/or useful extension/revision to theory and previous literature concerning attachment processes and human development; (c) Clinical case studies – authors should provide an account of previous clinical theory in an organized and up-to-date manner distinct from the clinical case material.
Audience	The journal is relevant to practitioners and institutions within the domains of psychology, psychiatry, psychotherapy and related disciplines including nursing and social work.
Special Themes	Attachment theory, developmental psychology, emotional and cognitive development, internal representations and social processes.
Where Indexed/ Abstracted	CareData; Combined Health Information Database (CHID); Community Care; Cumulative Index to Nursing and Allied Health Literature (CINAHL); Current Contents EMBASE/Excerpta Medica; Family and Society Studies Worldwide; Family Index Database; Social and Behavioral Sciences; MEDLINE/Index Medicus; Pascal; Psychological Abstracts/PsycINFO; SCOPUS; Social Sciences Citation Index; ISI Alerting Services; Social Scisearch Studies on Women and Gender Abstracts.
Year Established	1999
Circulation	Unspecified.
Frequency	6 times a year
Months Issued	January, March, May, July, September, November
No. of Articles per Issue	Average 4–6 articles

SUBMISSIONS

Postal Mailing Address	Professor Howard Steele, Psychology Department, Graduate Faculty, New School University, 80 Fifth Avenue, New York, NY 10003, USA
Method for Submission	Manuscripts accepted through postal mail or by e-mail.
Number of Copies	Three: one original and two copies.
Disk Submission	N/A
Online or E-mail Submission Allowed or Required	E-mail submissions to the Editor are preferred. Please send an electronic copy of the manuscript to steeleh@newschool.edu.

FORMAT OF MANUSCRIPT

Cover Sheet	Yes - all the authors of a paper should include their full names, affiliations, postal addresses, telephone and fax numbers and e-mail addresses on the cover page only of the manuscript. One author should be identified as the corresponding author.
Abstract	100–150 words.
Key Words	Up to 7 keywords.
Length	All submissions should include an abstract and ordinarily be about 6,000 words in length, not exceeding 7,500 words in total, though occasionally longer papers are considered.
Margins	4 cm minimum margins.
Spacing	Double spacing required throughout.

STYLE

Name of Guide	Please refer to the following website for the journal style guide: http://www.tandf.co.uk/journals/titles14616734.asp.
Subheadings	A. Bold initial cap only, B. *Bold italic initial cap only,* C. *Italic initial cap only,* D. *Italic initial cap only,* text runs on
References	Please use the *Publication Manual of the American Psychological Association* for points of detail.

Footnotes	Footnotes are not normally permitted, but endnotes may be used if necessary.
Tables or Figures	Tables should be laid out clearly and supplied on separate pages, with an indication within the text of their approximate location. Vertical lines should be omitted and horizontal lines limited to those indicating the top and bottom of the table, below column headings and above summed totals. Totals and percentages should be labeled clearly.

REVIEW PROCESS

Type of Review	Double anonymous peer review.
Queries	Please direct queries to steeleh@newschool.edu.
Acknowledgment	Not specified.
Review Time	Not specified.
Revisions	Material may be accepted subject to minor or major revisions, rejected, or rejected with the option to resubmit.
Acceptance Rate	Not specified.
Return of Manuscript	N/A
Lag Time to Print	Not specified.

REPRINT, SUBSCRIPTION, AND CONTACT INFORMATION

Reprint Policy	Corresponding authors can receive free online access to their article through our website (www.informaworld.com) and a complimentary copy of the issue containing their article. Additional reprints can be ordered through Rightslink® when proofs are received or alternatively on our journals website. If you have any queries, please contact our reprints department at reprints@tandf.co.uk.
Book Reviews	Not specified.
Subscriptions	T&F Customer Services, Sheepen Place, Colchester, Essex, CO3 3LP, UK; Tel: +44 (0) 20 7017 5544; Fax: +44 (0) 20 7017 5198 Email: subscriptions@tandf.co.uk
Affiliation	The International Attachment Network (IAN)
E-Mail Address	Editor, Howard Steele: steeleh@newschool.edu
Website	www.tandf.co.uk/journals

AUSTRALIAN SOCIAL WORK

Current Title	*Australian Social Work*
Previous Title	*Forum, Australian Journal of Social Work.*
Editorial Focus	Original research, theoretical papers, and critical reviews that reflect current thinking and trends in social work and build on existing knowledge. The journal also publishes reviews of relevant professional literature, and commentary and analysis of social policies and encourages debate in the form of reader commentary on articles.
Audience	Social workers and social welfare professionals—practitioners and academics, libraries.
Special Themes	Calls for papers and special theme issues are a regular feature.
Where Indexed/ Abstracted	APAIS: Australian Public Affairs Information Service; ASSIA: Applied Social Sciences Index and Abstracts; Cinahl; Australian Education Index (Online); Cumulative Index to Nursing & Allied Health Literature; Ecology Abstracts (Bethesda); Environmental Sciences and Pollution Management; Family Index; OCLC; Ovid; PsychINFO; Research into Higher Education Abstracts; Risk Abstracts (Online Edition); SCOPUS; Social Services Abstracts; Social Work Abstracts; Sociological Abstracts; Swets Information Services; Thomson Gale (Gale Group).
Year Established	1948.
Circulation	Approximately 6,500.
Frequency	Quarterly.
Months Issued	March, June, September, December.
No. of Articles per Issue	7–8.

SUBMISSIONS

Postal Mailing Address	E-mail only: asw-vic@bigpond.net.au.
Method for Submission	Electronic form via website.
Number of Copies	Two versions of each manuscript are required: one de-identified with author details removed; one full copy with author details included.
Disk Submission	N/A.
Online or E-mail Submission Allowed or Required	Manuscript Central: http://mc.manuscriptcentral.com/rasw.

FORMAT OF MANUSCRIPT

Cover Sheet	Title page to include name of author(s), qualifications, institutional affiliation, postal address, e-mail address, telephone and fax numbers.
Abstract	Abstract required. Maximum 150 words. Should outline: questions investigated, design; essential findings, main conclusions.
Key Words	Required (3–6 key words).
Length	Maximum 6,000 words (shorter contributions accepted).
Margins	Not specified.
Spacing	Double-spaced.

STYLE

Name of Guide	*Publication Manual of the American Psychological Association.*
Subheadings	Required; see style guide.
References	Required; see style guide.
Footnotes	No footnotes. Endnotes only if necessary.
Tables or Figures	See APA style guide.

REVIEW PROCESS

Type of Review	Anonymous peer review by at least two referees.
Queries	Manuscripts submitted for review only.
Acknowledgment	By e-mail.
Review Time	Approximately 3 months.
Revisions	Within 6 months.
Acceptance Rate	Approximately 48%.
Return of Manuscript	N/A.
Lag Time to Print	Approximately 9 months.

CHARGES TO AUTHOR

Author Alterations   N/A.
Page Charges   N/A.
Processing   N/A.

REPRINT, SUBSCRIPTION, AND CONTACT INFORMATION

Reprint Policy   Corresponding authors receive 50 free reprints, free online access to their article (www.informaworld.com), and a complimentary copy of the issue containing their article.

Book Reviews   Published in each issue. Sought by book review editor.

Subscriptions   Institutional: A$241 (print + online), A$229 (online only). Personal: A$131.

Affiliation   Australian Association of Social Workers Ltd (AASW).

E-Mail Address   customerservice@taylorandfrancis.com; tf.enquiries@tfinforma.com

Website   http://www.tandf.co.uk/journals/asw

BEHAVIORAL & SOCIAL SCIENCES LIBRARIAN

Current Title	*Behavioral and Social Sciences Librarian*
Previous Title	N/A.
Editorial Focus	Production, collection, organization, retrieval, and use of social science information.
Audience	Scholars, researchers, publishers, database producers, librarians, and information specialists working in public libraries, colleges and universities, government, applied research centers, data archives, foundations, professional organizations, and the commercial sector.
Special Themes	Descriptive and critical analyses of information resources with particular subdiscipline; publishing trends; use and user studies; reference service and bibliographic instruction; indexing, abstracting, thesaurus building, and database construction; bibliographic and numeric databases, and social science data files and data archives.
Where Indexed/ Abstracted	Abstracts in Social Gerontology: Applied Social Sciences Index & Abstracts (Online: ASSI via Data-Star) (CD-ROM: ASSIA Plus); CINAHL (Cumulative Index to Nursing & Allied Health Literature); CNPIEC Reference Guide: Chinese National Directory of Foreign Periodicals; Current Awareness Bulletin; Current Contents; Clinical Education; Current Literature on Aging; Educational Administration Abstracts (EAA); Index to Periodical Articles Related to Law: Information Reports & Bibliographies; Information Science Abstracts; Informed Librarian; INSPEC Information Services; International Bulletin of Bibliography on Education; INTERNET ACCESS (and additional networks) Bulletin Board for Libraries (BUBL), coverage of information resources on INTERNET, JANET and other network; Library & Information Science Abstracts (LISA); Library Literature; Newsletter of Library and Information Services; Public Affairs Information Bulletin (PAIS); Referativnyi Zhurnal (Abstracts Journal of the Institute of Scientific Information of the Republic of Russia); Sage Public Administration Abstracts (SPAA); Social Work Abstracts.
Year Established	1979.
Circulation	282.
Frequency	Quarterly.
Months Issued	Not specified.
No. of Articles per Issue	6–10 per issue.

SUBMISSIONS

Postal Mailing Address	Lisa Romero Head, Communications Library, University of Illinois, 122 Gregory Hall, 810 South Wright Street, Urbana, IL 61801 L-ROMERO@illinois.edu.
Method for Submission	E-mail.
Number of Copies	1.
Disk Submission	Authors of accepted manuscripts are asked to submit a disk, preferably in Microsoft Word.
Online or E-mail Submission Allowed or Required	Allowed.

FORMAT OF MANUSCRIPT

Cover Sheet	Separate sheet, which does not go out for review. Full title; author names; degrees; professional titles; designation of one author with full address, phone numbers, e-mail address, and fax number; date of submission.
Abstract	Approximately 100 words.
Key Words	5–6 words that identify article content.
Length	5–50 pages, including references and abstract. Lengthier manuscripts may be considered, but only at the discretion of the editor. Sometimes, lengthier manuscripts may be considered if they can be divided up into sections for publication in successive issues.
Margins	1 inch on all sides.
Spacing	Double-spaced for all copy except title page.

STYLE

Name of Guide	*Chicago Manual of Style.*
Subheadings	Use as needed to guide reader through the article. No more than 4 levels.
References	Author-date citation style; see style guide.
Footnotes	No footnotes preferred; incorporate into text.

Tables or Figures	Type tables double-spaced. Submit camera-ready art (300-dpi resolution or better) for all figures. Place each table or figure on a separate, numbered page at the end of the manuscript.

REVIEW PROCESS

Type of Review	"Double blind" anonymous peer review. 3 reviewers plus editor-in-chief read the manuscript in an anonymous review.
Queries	Authors are encouraged to read the journal to determine if their subject matter would be appropriate.
Acknowledgment	Enclose a regular, self-addressed, stamped envelope with submission.
Review Time	Approximately 3–4 months.
Revisions	See journal.
Acceptance Rate	Not specified.
Return of Manuscript	Only if 9" × 12" self-addressed, stamped envelope is enclosed.
Lag Time to Print	Approximately 6–12 months.

CHARGES TO AUTHOR

Author Alterations	Not specified.
Page Charges	Not specified.
Processing	Not specified.

REPRINT, SUBSCRIPTION, AND CONTACT INFORMATION

Reprint Policy	All authors receive 2 complimentary copies of the issue in which the article appears. Authors receive reprint order forms to purchase additional reprinted copies.
Book Reviews	Does not include.
Subscriptions	Taylor & Francis subscriptions@tandf.co.uk.
Affiliation	Not specified.
E-Mail Address	Not specified.
Website	Not specified.

BRITISH JOURNAL OF PSYCHOTHERAPY

Current Title	*British Journal of Psychotherapy*
Previous Title	N/A.
Editorial Focus	Although psychoanalytic psychotherapy is its primary focus, the journal has traditionally sought to make links and comparisons with other therapeutic methods. Its aim, therefore, although not necessarily integrative, is inclusive. It is a journal for working clinicians, addressing their professional concerns: developments in research, considerations of theory and technique, applications of psychoanalytic thinking, and the politics of the profession.
Audience	Psychologists, medical or nursing professionals, social workers, or other related professionals.
Special Themes	Comparison between forms of schools of psychotherapy, and between therapies.
Where Indexed/ Abstracted	Current Abstracts; EBSCOhost; Family Index; PsycINFO; Social Work Abstracts.
Year Established	1984.
Circulation	Not specified.
Frequency	Quarterly.
Months Issued	February, May, August, and November.
No. of Articles per Issue	5–7.

SUBMISSIONS

Postal Mailing Address	No submissions are accepted by mail.
Method for Submission	The preferred method of submission for manuscripts is via e-mail to janinesternberg@hotmail.com with the manuscript as an attachment in Word format. If electronic submission is not possible, four copies of the printed ms should be sent to the Editor at the address given above.
Number of Copies	4 copies if sent by mail.
Disk Submission	Not required.
Online or E-mail Submission Allowed or Required	E-mail submission preferred.

FORMAT OF MANUSCRIPT

Cover Sheet	Please include, separately, the author's name; the manuscript title; and the author's contact address, e-mail address, telephone number and fax.
Abstract	An abstract of no more than 150 words should be submitted.
Key Words	Five key words are also required.
Length	Average length of manuscripts should be around 5,000 to 8,000 words, not including references or abstract.
Margins	1 inch all around.
Spacing	Double-spaced.

STYLE

Name of Guide	*Harvard Style.*
Subheadings	Follow style guide.
References	Follow style guide.
Footnotes	Follow style guide.
Tables or Figures	Follow style guide.

REVIEW PROCESS

Type of Review	Anonymous peer review.
Queries	Contact editor.
Acknowledgment	Not specified.
Review Time	Not specified.
Revisions	After the manuscript has been peer reviewed the author/s will be asked to make any necessary corrections to the manuscript.
Acceptance Rate	Not specified.
Return of Manuscript	Not specified.
Lag Time to Print	Not specified.

CHARGES TO AUTHOR

Author Alterations   For major alterations at proof.

REPRINT, SUBSCRIPTION, AND CONTACT INFORMATION

Reprint Policy   If you are interested in small quantities of your article, you may purchase individual copies of the back issue that contains the article through our Customer Services: subscriptions@sagepub.co.uk or call +44 (0) 20 7324 8701 for availability.

Book Reviews   If you wish to submit a book for review, please first contact Liane Aukin, Book Reviews Editor, at laukin@btinternet.com.

Subscriptions   Please do not send books without contacting the Book Reviews Editor for an address.

Affiliation   British Association of Psychotherapists.

E-Mail Address   janinesternberg@hotmail.com

Website   http://www.bap-psychotherapy.org/content.jsp

BRITISH JOURNAL OF SOCIAL WORK

Current Title	*British Journal of Social Work*
Previous Title	N/A.
Editorial Focus	Any aspect of social work practice, research, theory, and education; research notes; critical commentaries; book reviews.
Audience	Social work educators, researchers, practitioners, and managers.
Special Themes	1 special issue per year
Where Indexed/ Abstracted	ASSIA, British Humanities Index; Caredata Abstracts (NISW); CINAHL (Cumulative Index to Nursing and Allied Health Literature); Criminology, Penology, & Police Science; e-psyche; Family Scholar Publications; Family Studies Human Resources Abstracts; ISI: Social Sciences Citation Index; Research Alert, Scisearch, and Current Contents/Social & Behavioral Sciences; NISC; Periodicals Contents Index, PsycINFO, Public Affairs Information Services, Research on Social Work Practice, Social Planning/Policy and Development Abstracts, Social Service Abstracts, Social Work Abstracts, Social Work Research and Abstracts, Sociological Abstracts, Studies on Women & Gender Abstracts.
Year Established	1970.
Circulation	4,893 worldwide at end of 2008.
Frequency	8 issues per year
Months Issued	January, February, April, June, July, September, October, December.
No. of Articles per Issue	10.

SUBMISSIONS

Postal Mailing Address	Sue Hanson, Centre for Applied Childhood Studies, University of Huddersfield, Queensgate, Huddersfield HD1 3DH, England.
Method for Submission	Electronic form via Website.
Number of Copies	1 electronic copy only.
Disk Submission	No.
Online or E-mail Submission Allowed or Required	Online via Website only.

FORMAT OF MANUSCRIPT

Cover Sheet	Yes; see style guide on journal website.
Abstract	150–200 words.
Key Words	Maximum 5 words.
Length	Maximum 7,000.
Margins	Wide.
Spacing	Double-spaced, font 12.

STYLE

Name of Guide	See style guide on journal website.
Subheadings	See style guide on journal website.
References	See style guide on journal website.
Footnotes	See style guide on journal website.
Tables or Figures	See style guide on journal website.

REVIEW PROCESS

Type of Review	Anonymous peer review, normally 2 reviewers.
Queries	Accepted and welcomed.
Acknowledgment	Computer-generated via website.
Review Time	Approximately 6–8 weeks.
Revisions	Feedback from reviewers and editorial decision provided by via e-mail via website.
Acceptance Rate	Approximately 55%.
Return of Manuscript	N/A.
Lag Time to Print	Approximately 15–18 months; manuscript available on Advance Access on website approximately 6 weeks from acceptance.

REPRINT, SUBSCRIPTION, AND CONTACT INFORMATION

Reprint Policy	special.sales@oxfordjournals.org.
Book Reviews	Dr. Carolyn Taylor, Department of Applied Social Science, University of Lancaster, Bowland North, Lancaster LA1 4YT. c.p.taylor@lancaster.ac.uk.
Subscriptions	jnls.cust.serv@oxfordjournals.org.
Affiliation	British Association of Social Workers.
E-Mail Address	s.m.hanson@hud.ac.uk
Website	http://bjsw.oxfordjournals.org/

BULLETIN OF THE MENNINGER CLINIC

Current Title	*Bulletin of the Menninger Clinic*
Previous Title	N/A.
Editorial Focus	Offers a psychodynamic perspective on the application of theory and research in outpatient psycho-therapy, attachment theory, and developments in cognitive neuroscience and psychopathologies, as well as the integration of different modes of therapy.
Audience	Psychiatrists, psychologists, psychoanalysts, psychiatric social workers, psychiatric nurses.
Special Themes	Current treatment approaches, specific psychiatric disorders, clinical and theoretical articles and literature reviews, clinical case series reports, brief communications, and book reviews.
Where Indexed/ Abstracted	Academic Abstracts; Bell & Howell Information and Learning; Biological Abstracts; Current Contents/Social & Behavioral Sciences; Digest of Neurology & Psychology; Excerpta Medica/EMBASE; Hospital and Health Administration Index; Index Medicus/MEDLINE; PsycINFO; Research Alert; Social Sciences Citation Index; Social SciSearch.
Year Established	1936.
Circulation	800.
Frequency	Quarterly.
Months Issued	January, April, July, October.
No. of Articles per Issue	4.

SUBMISSIONS

Postal Mailing Address	The Managing Editor, Bulletin of the Menninger Clinic, P.O. Box 4406, Topeka, KS 66604-0406.
Method for Submission	Surface mail.
Number of Copies	4.
Disk Submission	Authors of accepted manuscripts are asked to submit a disk, preferably in Microsoft Word or Word Perfect.
Online or E-mail Submission Allowed or Required	Yes, it is allowed. E-mail can be sent to Mary Donohue at mdonohue@menninger.edu.

FORMAT OF MANUSCRIPT

Cover Sheet	Required.
Abstract	Required.
Key Words	N/A.
Length	Manuscripts should not exceed 20 pages (including references, tables, etc.); longer papers may be accepted at the discretion of the Editorial Board.
Margins	1 inch all sides.
Spacing	Double-spaced for all copy except title page.

STYLE

Name of Guide	*Publication Manual of the American Psychological Association.*
Subheadings	Use as needed to guide reader; preferably only 3 levels.
References	Author-date citation style; reference list includes only sources cited in text.
Footnotes	Keep footnotes to a minimum; incorporate such information into text.
Tables or Figures	Tables should be submitted in Excel or, alternatively, in a tabular format in Microsoft Word or WordPerfect for the PC. Graphs and Figures should be submitted in Excel, Illustrator, Photoshop, or equivalent art programs. Alternatively, they may be submitted in an importable file format, such as JPEG, EPS, or TIFF. Graphs and figures submitted in hard copy only will be scanned to an exportable file for placement, with possible compromise in image quality.

REVIEW PROCESS

Type of Review	All manuscripts, including invited papers, are subject to anonymous peer review.
Queries	Query letters acceptable, and authors should read journal to determine whether their manuscripts are appropriate.
Acknowledgment	Acknowledgement letter sent to on receipt of manuscript.
Review Time	3–4 months.
Revisions	Submit 2 copies with cover letter describing revisions and/or explaining why revisions were not made.
Acceptance Rate	Approximately 40%–50% (annual rate varies).

Return of Manuscript	Manuscripts are not returned.
Lag Time to Print	Approximately 6–8 months.

CHARGES TO AUTHOR

Author Alterations	N/A.
Page Charges	N/A.
Processing	N/A.

REPRINT, SUBSCRIPTION, AND CONTACT INFORMATION

Reprint Policy	All authors receive 1 complimentary copy of issue in which their article appears. Authors receive reprint order forms to purchase additional copies of article.
Book Reviews	By invitation only; send books for review to Book Review Editor, Bulletin of the Menninger Clinic, P.O. Box 4406, Topeka, KS 66604-0406.
Subscriptions	Bulletin of the Menninger Clinic, Guilford Publications, Inc., 72 Spring Street, New York, NY 10012; phone: 800-365-7006, ext. 3 or 212-431-9800; fax: 212-966-6708; e-mail: news@guilford.com.
Affiliation	The Menninger Clinic.
E-Mail Address	mdonohue@menninger.edu
Website	http://www.menningerclinic.com/

THE CANADIAN JOURNAL OF HUMAN SEXUALITY

Current Title	*The Canadian Journal of Human Sexuality*
Previous Title	N/A
Editorial Focus	Quantitative and qualitative research, literature reviews, and critical analyses.
Audience	Researchers, health and social service professionals, libraries, students.
Special Themes	Not specified.
Where Indexed/ Abstracted	Applied Social Sciences Index and Abstracts (ASSIA); Cumulative Index to Nursing and Allied Health Literature (CINAHL); EMBASE/Exerpta Medica; Expanded Academic Index; Psychological Abstracts/PsycINFO; Social Work Abstracts; Sociological Abstracts; plus others.
Year Established	1997.
Circulation	500.
Frequency	Quarterly.
Months Issued	Spring, summer, fall, winter.
No. of Articles per Issue	6–10.

SUBMISSIONS

Postal Mailing Address	Michael Barrett, Editor, *The Canadian Journal of Human Sexuality,* SIECCAN, 850 Coxwell Avenue, Toronto, ON, M4C 5R1, Canada. Submissions should be e-mailed to alex@sieccan.org with "Submission to CJHS" in the subject line.
Method for Submission	E-mail.
Number of Copies	1 by e-mail.
Disk Submission	No.
Online or E-mail Submission Allowed or Required	Yes.

FORMAT OF MANUSCRIPT

Cover Sheet	Title, name, affiliation, contact information (cover sheet will be removed prior to review).
Abstract	100–200 words.
Key Words	No.
Length	15–30 double-spaced pages not including tables or references.
Margins	1 inch.
Spacing	Double-spaced.

STYLE

Name of Guide	*Publication Manual of the American Psychological Association.*
Subheadings	As needed.
References	See style guide.
Footnotes	See style guide.
Tables or Figures	Tables and figures should be numbered and referred to by number in the text. Tables/figures should be provided after the references.

REVIEW PROCESS

Type of Review	Anonymous peer review.
Queries	Yes.
Acknowledgment	Editor e-mails acknowledgement of receipt.
Review Time	3–4 months.
Revisions	Revised manuscript submitted with description of revisions.
Acceptance Rate	Approximately 30%.
Return of Manuscript	No.
Lag Time to Print	Approximately 3 months after acceptance.

CHARGES TO AUTHOR

Author Alterations	None.
Page Charges	None.
Processing	None.

REPRINT, SUBSCRIPTION, AND CONTACT INFORMATION

Reprint Policy	Authors sent 4 copies of journal. Reprints can be made available at cost.
Book Reviews	Yes.
Subscriptions	$40 for individuals, $60 for institutions. For subscription information, call 416-466-5304.
Affiliation	*The Canadian Journal of Human Sexuality* is a publication of SIECCAN, the Sex Information and Education Council of Canada.
E-Mail Address	sieccan@web.ca
Website	www.sieccan.org

CHILD ABUSE & NEGLECT: THE INTERNATIONAL JOURNAL

Current Title	*Child Abuse & Neglect: The International journal*
Previous Title	N/A.
Editorial Focus	This journal provides an international, multidisciplinary forum on all aspects of child abuse and neglect, with special emphasis on prevention and treatment; the scope extends further to all those aspects of life which either favor or hinder child development.
Audience	Includes but is not limited to: psychologists, lawyers, psychiatrists, nurses, social workers, sociologists, public health workers, law enforcement, educators, pediatricians, and anthropologists.
Special Themes	Not specified.
Where Indexed/ Abstracted	Adolescent Mental Health Abstracts; Child Development Abstracts and Bibliography; Criminal Justice Abstracts; Current Contents/Social & Behavioral Sciences; Current Index to Journals in Education; ERA (Educational Research Abstracts Online); ERIC; MEDLINE; Psychological Abstracts; PsycINFO; Social Work Abstracts; Sociological Abstracts.
Year Established	1977.
Circulation	Not specified.
Frequency	12 times per year.
Months Issued	Monthly.
No. of Articles per Issue	5–8.

SUBMISSIONS

Postal Mailing Address	Contact editorial office.
Method for Submission	Authors should use the Elsevier Editorial System (EES) online submission site: http://ees.elsevier.com/chiabuneg/; instructions are provided at each step of the submission process. Please note that even though manuscript source files are converted to PDF at submission for the review process, these source files are needed for further processing when papers are accepted. Manuscripts submitted as PDF files will not be accepted.
Number of Copies	Not specified.
Disk Submission	Not specified.
Online or E-mail Submission Allowed or Required	For those authors unable to utilize the EES system, the journal will accept submissions sent directly to the editorial office; please contact the office (mary.roth@yale.edu; telephone 1.203.271.9950) for instructions.

FORMAT OF MANUSCRIPT

Cover Sheet	To facilitate blind reviews, all indication of authorship, including acknowledgements, must be limited to this page. Title page should include (1) full article title; (2) name, affiliation including city and state/country for each author at the time of the work; (3) name, mailing address, telephone, fax, and e-mail of corresponding author; (4) name and complete address for reprint requests; (5) all acknowledgements and support notes.
Abstract	A structured abstract not to exceed 350 words in length covering the main factual points is required.
Key Words	Not specified.
Length	Not specified.
Margins	Not specified.
Spacing	Double-spaced.

STYLE

Name of Guide	*Publication Manual of the American Psychological Association.*
Subheadings	See style guide.
References	See style guide.
Footnotes	Use of footnotes is not permitted. If the footnoted material is needed, it should be incorporated into the text itself.
Tables or Figures	Cite each table/figure clearly in text. Tables should be arranged one to a page, with a self-contained title that is understandable without reference to the text. Figures should be computer generated, one per page, with legends. Tables and figures cannot be submitted as part of the text file, but should be submitted as separate files under "Tables" or "Figures" from the drop-down menu on the file submission page.

REVIEW PROCESS

Type of Review	Blind peer review.
Queries	E-mail mary.roth@yale.edu
Acknowledgment	All initial submissions are acknowledged on receipt.
Review Time	Not specified.
Revisions	No rewriting of the original manuscript as accepted is allowed in the proof stage.
Acceptance Rate	Not specified.
Return of Manuscript	Authors should save an electronic copy of the manuscript that has been submitted.
Lag Time to Print	Scheduling and production processes currently take 6 months once manuscripts are accepted and all required information is in house.

CHARGES TO AUTHOR

Author Alterations	Only if major alterations to page proofs.

REPRINT, SUBSCRIPTION, AND CONTACT INFORMATION

Reprint Policy	The corresponding author, at no cost, will be provided with a PDF file of the article via e-mail or, alternatively, 25 free paper offprints. The PDF file is a watermarked version of the published article and includes a coversheet with the journal cover image and a disclaimer outlining terms and conditions of use. Orders for additional reprints must be received before printing in order to qualify for lower prepublication rates (coauthor requirements must be included on this form).
Book Reviews	Not specified.
Subscriptions	Available through the website at: http://www.elsevier.com/wps/find/journaldescription.cws_home/586/bibliographic.
Affiliation	International Society for the Prevention of Child Abuse and Neglect.
E-Mail Address	mary.roth@yale.edu
Website	http://ispcan.org/

CHILD & ADOLESCENT SOCIAL WORK JOURNAL

Current Title	*Child and Adolescent Social Work Journal*
Previous Title	N/A.
Editorial Focus	*Child and Adolescent Social Work Journal* features original peer-reviewed articles that focus on clinical social work practice with children, adolescents, and their families. This international journal addresses current issues in the field of social work drawn from theory, direct practice, research, and social policy, as well as focuses on problems affecting specific populations in special settings.
Audience	Practitioners, educators, researchers, policymakers, university libraries and their faculty and student patrons.
Special Themes	*Child and Adolescent Social Work Journal* publishes papers on a wide range of topics in a variety of populations, such as refugee children, pregnant and parenting adolescents, homeless runaway youth, and families with transgender/gender-dissonant children. Papers on clinical social work practice in special settings, such as emotionally disturbed youth in foster care, juvenile offenders with mental health problems in prison, and antisocial behavior of urban youth in public housing, are published. Descriptions of models and programs designed to relate to specific populations and specialized issues, as well as practice evaluation reports, are encouraged. The journal also publishes book reviews.
Where Indexed/ Abstracted	CSA Social Services Abstracts; CSA Sociological Abstracts; Family & Society Studies Worldwide; PsycINFO; Risk Abstracts; SCOPUS; Social Science Index; Studies on Women and Gender Abstracts.
Year Established	1984.
Circulation	Available to millions of desktops worldwide via Springer's platform, SpringerLink.
Frequency	Bimonthly.
Months Issued	February, April, June, August, October, December.
No. of Articles per Issue	Approximately 7.

SUBMISSIONS

Postal Mailing Address	N/A.
Method for Submission	Electronic form via website.
Number of Copies	N/A.
Disk Submission	None.
Online or E-mail Submission Allowed or Required	Online submission at: http://casw.edmgr.com Acceptable submission file formats include Word, WordPerfect, RTF, TXT, and LaTeX for manuscripts and TIFF, GIF, JPEG, EPS, PPT, and Postscript for figures (artwork). PDF is not an acceptable file format.

FORMAT OF MANUSCRIPT

Cover Sheet	In order to facilitate masked (previously termed "double-blind") review, leave all identifying information off the manuscript, including the title page and the electronic file name. Appropriate identifying information is attached automatically to the electronic file. Upon initial submission, the title page should include only the title of the article.
	An additional title page should be uploaded as a separate submission item and should include the title of the article, author's name (with degree), and author's affiliation. Academic affiliations of all authors should be included. The affiliation should comprise the department, institution (usually university or company), city, and state (or nation) and should be typed as a footnote to the author's name. This title page should also include the complete mailing address, telephone number, fax number, and e-mail address of the one author designated to review proofs.
Abstract	An abstract is to be provided, preferably approximately 100 words.
Key Words	A list of 3–5 key words is to be provided directly below the abstract. Key words should express the precise content of the manuscript, as they are used for indexing purposes.
Length	No specific minimum or maximum.
Margins	Type double-spaced using generous margins on all sides.
Spacing	The entire manuscript, including quotations, references, figure-caption list, and tables, should be double-spaced.

STYLE

Name of Guide	In general, the journal follows the recommendations of the 2001 *Publication Manual of the American Psychological Association,* and it is suggested that contributors refer to this publication.

Subheadings	Main headings (first level) strongly preferred. Second level subheadings preferred. Third and fourth level headings acceptable.
References	List references alphabetically at the end of the paper and refer to them in the text by name and year in parentheses. References should include (in this order): last names and initials of all authors, year published, title of article, name of publication, volume number, and inclusive pages. The style and punctuation of the references should conform to strict APA style, illustrated by examples provided on the website.
Footnotes	Footnotes should be avoided. When their use is absolutely necessary, footnotes should be numbered consecutively using Arabic numerals and should be typed at the bottom of the page to which they refer. Place a line above the footnote so that it is set off from the text. Use the appropriate superscript numeral for citation in the text.
Tables or Figures	Illustrations (photographs, drawings, diagrams, and charts) are to be numbered in one consecutive series of Arabic numerals and cited in numerical order in the text. Photographs should be high contrast, and drawings should be dark, sharp, and clear. Artwork for each figure should be provided on a separate page. Each figure should have an accompanying caption. The captions for illustrations should be listed on a separate page.
	Tables should be numbered (with Arabic numerals) and referred to by number in the text. Each table should be typed on a separate sheet of paper. Center the title above the table, and type explanatory footnotes (indicated by superscript lowercase letters) below the table.

REVIEW PROCESS

Type of Review	Double-blind peer review usually by three reviewers. The Editor and Associate Editor make the final decision.
Queries	Query letters accepted.
Acknowledgment	The journal uses Editorial Manager, its online manuscript submission and peer review system. Acknowledgments of submission are e-mailed to the contact author.
Review Time	Approximately 3 months.
Revisions	Reviewer comments are supplied to the contact author. The contact author revises the paper accordingly and resubmits the revised version.
Acceptance Rate	Approximately 25%.
Return of Manuscript	N/A. No hard copies are submitted, and therefore none are returned.
Lag Time to Print	Approximately 18 days from acceptance to publication in Online First; published articles are later included in an issue, both online and print.

CHARGES TO AUTHOR

Author Alterations	The journal makes no authors' alterations charges, except under very unusual circumstances. Typographical errors are corrected; authors' alterations are discouraged.

REPRINT, SUBSCRIPTION, AND CONTACT INFORMATION

Reprint Policy	Reprints are available to authors, and order forms with the current price schedule are provided to the contact author upon commencement of typesetting.
Book Reviews	The journal publishes book reviews. The journal does not accept unsolicited book reviews. Books to be considered for review should be sent to the Editor: Thomas K. Kenemore, PhD, Editor, Child and Adolescent Social Work Journal, 160 Spencer Avenue, Wilmette, IL 60091.
Subscriptions	For current pricing and ordering, contact: Journals Customer Service, Spring Science and Business Media, LLC., P.O. Box 2485, Secaucus, NJ 07096, USA. Tel: 800-777-4643.
Affiliation	None.
E-Mail Address	thomas@kenemore.org
Website	www.springer.com/10560

CHILD & FAMILY BEHAVIOR THERAPY

Current Title	*Child & Family Behavior Therapy*
Previous Title	*Child Behavior Therapy*
Editorial Focus	This journal focuses on the practical applications of behavior therapy, sharing the latest developments, extensive case studies, and step-by-step instructions for using these methods in your own practice.
Audience	Teachers, child psychologists, psychiatrists, social workers, school counselors, family therapists, researchers, and other special educators.
Special Themes	Not specified.
Where Indexed/ Abstracted	Criminal Justice Abstracts; Current Contents/Social; EBSCOhost; Education Research Abstracts Online; ERIC; Family Studies Abstracts; PsycINFO; Social Services Abstracts; Sociological Abstracts; Violence & Abuse Abstracts.
Year Established	1978.
Circulation	Not specified.
Frequency	4 times per year.
Months Issued	Not specified.
No. of Articles per Issue	3–5 per issue.

SUBMISSIONS

Postal Mailing Address	Dr. Charles Diament, Co-Editor, 41 Reckless Place, Reb Bank, NJ 07701.
Method for Submission	Either by mail or electronically to drcdiament@comcast.net.
Number of Copies	3.
Disk Submission	If submitting a disk, it should be prepared using MS Word or WordPerfect and should be clearly labeled with the authors names, file name, and software program.
Online or E-mail Submission Allowed or Required	E-mail submission permitted. No online submission.

FORMAT OF MANUSCRIPT

Cover Sheet	Submit a cover page with the manuscript, indicating only the article title (this is used for anonymous refereeing). Include a regular title page (as the second page) as a separate document. Include the title again, plus full authorship; the abstract; the shortened version of the title; page number of total (e.g., pg 2 of 7); and an introductory note with authors' academic degrees, professional titles, affiliations, mailing and e-mail addresses, and any desired acknowledgement of research support or other credit.
Abstract	Each article should be summarized in an abstract of not more than 100 words.
Key Words	Provide 3–10 key words for indexing purposes.
Length	25 pages.
Margins	1 inch.
Spacing	Double-spaced.

STYLE

Name of Guide	*Publication Manual of the American Psychological Association.*
Subheadings	See style guide.
References	See style guide.
Footnotes	Not specified.
Tables or Figures	Tables and figures (illustrations) should not be embedded in the text, but should be included as separate sheets or files. A short descriptive title should appear above each table with a clear legend and any footnotes suitably identified below. All units must be included. Figures should be completely labeled, taking into account necessary size reduction. Captions should be typed, double-spaced, on a separate sheet.

REVIEW PROCESS

Type of Review	Double-blind anonymous peer review.
Queries	Authors are encouraged to read the journal to determine whether their subject matter would be appropriate.
Acknowledgment	Enclose a self-addressed, stamped envelope with submission.

Review Time	Not specified.
Revisions	Not specified.
Acceptance Rate	Not specified.
Return of Manuscript	Only if 9"x12" self-addressed, stamped envelope is enclosed.
Lag Time to Print	Not specified.

REPRINT, SUBSCRIPTION, AND CONTACT INFORMATION

Reprint Policy	Reprints of individual articles are available for order at the time authors review page proofs. A discount on reprints is available to authors who order before print publication. Each corresponding author will receive 3 complete issues in which the article publishes and a complimentary PDF.
Book Reviews	Contact Howard Paul, Book Review Editor.
Subscriptions	Available through the website at: http://www.tandf.co.uk/journals/WCFB.
Affiliation	Not specified.
E-Mail Address	drcdiament@comcast.net
Website	http://www.tandf.co.uk/journals/WCFB

CHILD AND YOUTH CARE FORUM: JOURNAL OF RESEARCH AND PRACTICE IN CHILDREN'S SERVICES

Current Title	*Child and Youth Care Forum: Journal of Research and Practice in Children's Services*
Previous Title	*Child Care Quarterly.*
Editorial Focus	*Child and Youth Care Forum* is a multidisciplinary publication that welcomes submissions—original empirical research papers and theoretical reviews as well as invited commentaries—on the development, implementation, and dissemination of effective practices for children, youth, and families. *CYCF* welcomes submissions from researchers, practitioners, and clinicians in child psychology, early childhood, education, medical anthropology, pediatrics, pediatric psychology, psychiatry, public policy, school/educational psychology, social work, and sociology, as well as government agencies and corporate and nonprofit organizations. Only accepts original manuscripts, written in English. *CYCF* has traditionally aimed to bridge the research-to-practice gap in children's intervention and services, and the current editorial board hopes to build and expand upon this mission by publishing high-quality empirical papers and theoretical reviews that have implications for child and adolescent intervention and services broadly defined. In particular, papers that address the implications of typical and atypical development in effective interventions and youth care practices or that address assessment issues in child care and services are encouraged. Papers that address strategies for helping youth overcome difficulties (e.g., mental health problems) or overcome adversity (e.g., traumatic stress, community violence) are welcome, as well as papers that attempt to help normal children actualize their potential (e.g., positive psychology goals). Methodological papers with implications for child and youth intervention and services are also welcome.
Audience	The journal reaches a broad audience, including researchers, practitioners, and clinicians in social work, clinical child psychology school/educational psychology, pediatric psychology, education, psychiatry, early childhood, public policy, pediatrics, medical anthropology, and sociology, as well as government agencies and corporate and nonprofit organizations.
Special Themes	N/A.
Where Indexed/ Abstracted	British Education Index; CSA Social Services Abstracts; CSA Sociological Abstracts; Family & Society Studies Worldwide; Family Studies Abstracts; PsycINFO; and SCOPUS.
Year Established	1970.
Circulation	Approximately 1,000.
Frequency	6 times per year.
Months Issued	Not specified.
No. of Articles per Issue	3–8.

SUBMISSIONS

Postal Mailing Address	N/A.
Method for Submission	Electronic form via website: http://www.springer.com/psychology/child+&+school+psychology/journal/10566. http://www.editorialmanager.com/ccar/.
Number of Copies	Not specified.
Disk Submission	Not specified.
Online or E-mail Submission Allowed or Required	Electronic form via website: http://www.springer.com/psychology/child+&+school+psychology/journal/10566.

FORMAT OF MANUSCRIPT

Cover Sheet	The electronic submission format does not allow for a separate cover letter. However, you can insert comments to the editor. Simply cut and paste into the provided space what typically would be sent in a cover letter.
Abstract	100 words. See APA style guide.
Key Words	3–5 words.
Length	Most are 12–20 pages, but shorter or even considerably longer ones are considered if appropriate to the content.
Margins	1 inch.
Spacing	Double-spaced.

STYLE

Name of Guide	*Publication Manual of the American Psychological Association* should be used as the style guide for the preparation of manuscripts, particularly with respect to such matters as the order of elements;

citing of references; preparation of the reference list; contents of the Author Note; and the use of headings, abbreviations, numbers, and symbols.

Subheadings	See style guide.
References	See style guide.
Footnotes	See style guide.
Tables or Figures	See style guide.

Thorough coverage: *Child & Youth Care Forum* accepts electronic multimedia files (e.g., animations, movies, audio) and other supplementary files to be published online along with an article. This feature, known as Springer's Electronic Supplementary Material, enables authors to add dimension to the their articles, as certain information cannot be printed or is more convenient in electronic form.

REVIEW PROCESS

Type of Review   Decisions will typically be made after securing the critiques of at least two reviewers from the editorial board or other expert reviewers recruited by the associate editor. My plan will be to make decisions on articles within 3 months of submission. Papers are reviewed first by the Editor-in-Chief for suitability. All submissions will be assigned by the EiC within 2 weeks of submission. Articles will send out for review within 3 weeks from assignment, reviews will be due back in 4 weeks from the agreement to review, with a decision to the author within 3 months. Associate editors will be encouraged to use editorial board members and to self-identify appropriate expert reviewers but will also seek reviewer suggestions from the authors (i.e., authors may suggest individuals with appropriate expertise who do not have conflicts of interest with the author). AE's will handle the paper until it is fully accepted and submit it to the EiC for final approval.

Queries   Welcomed by e-mail.

Acknowledgment   Not specified.

Review Time   Within 3 months of submission.

Revisions   Generally 3 copies required, with cover letter explaining revisions. Revisions are normally read by at least one of the original reviewers and the editor.

Acceptance Rate   Approximately 50%, often subject to revisions, for topically appropriate manuscripts.

Return of Manuscript   With return envelope and postage. Submission warrants that the findings reported in the manuscript have not been published previously and that the manuscript is not being simultaneously submitted elsewhere. The corresponding author warrants that all coauthors agree with the manuscript's content. Before any manuscript can be formally accepted for publication, authors must complete the Consent to Publish and Transfer of Copyright form that reassigns copyright from the authors (or their employers, if they hold the copyright) to Springer. The form can be found on the "Home" page of the Editorial Manager site. Authors in doubt of what constitutes prior publication of their own data or analyses should consult the editor.

Lag Time to Print   Approximately 6 months.

REPRINT, SUBSCRIPTION, AND CONTACT INFORMATION

Reprint Policy   Not specified. *Child & Youth Care Forum* is a multidisciplinary publication that welcomes submissions – original empirical research papers and theoretical reviews as well as invited commentaries – on the development, implementation, and dissemination of effective practices for children, youth, and families broadly defined.

Book Reviews   See website.

Subscriptions   Springer.com.

Affiliation   Editor-in-Chief: Carl Weems, University of New Orleans, Louisiana, USA: sweems@uno.edu.

E-Mail Address   Contact the Editor if you are unable to submit the manuscript electronically or have questions about the submission process.

Associate Editors:

Laura Ferrer-Wreder, Barry University, Florida, USA.

R. Enrique Varela, Tulane University, Louisiana, USA.

Website   http://www.springer.com/psychology/child+&+school+psychology/journal/10566.

CHILD & YOUTH SERVICES

Current Title	*Child & Youth Services*
Previous Title	N/A.
Editorial Focus	Child & Youth Services is devoted to research and theory about the development and care of children and youth in communities, human services, and education. Its readers include researchers, academics, and practitioners. Theme issues allow authors and guest editors the space to survey and critically examine special topics such as work with families, theories of "at-risk" status, civic education, residential care, and street work.
Audience	Practitioners, researchers, clinicians, and academics in the fields of social work, forensic social work, counseling, child development, education, and policy-making as it relates to children and their families and communities.
Special Themes	Special issues have focused on the following topics: pain, normality, and struggle for congruence reinterpreting residential care for children and youth, residential child care staff selection - innovative approaches in working with children and youth, new lessons from the kibbutz street social education in Brazil, transitioning exceptional children and youth into the community-research and practice - family perspectives in child and youth services, helping the youthful offender, individual and group therapies that work, specialist foster family care - a normalizing experience, perspectives in professional child and youth care, America's homeless children, Best practices in child care professions.
Where Indexed/ Abstracted	PsycINFO; Education Research Abstracts; Social Service Abstracts (CSA/ProQuest); Sociological Abstracts (CSA/ProQuest); SOCIndex (EBSCO); CINAHL Information Systems; Criminal Justice Abstracts; Family Index Database; Index Copernicus; Health & Psychological Instruments; International Bulletin of Bibliography on Education; Social Work Abstracts; National Criminal Justice Reference Services; Social Care Institute for Excellence.
Year Established	1978.
Circulation	178.
Frequency	Quarterly.
Months Issued	February, June, August, November.
No. of Articles per Issue	Approximately 6.

SUBMISSIONS

Postal Mailing Address	Doug Magnuson, School of Child & Youth Care, University of Victoria, Box 1700, STN CSC, Victoria, BC, V8W 2Y2, Canada.
Method for Submission	Surface mail, disk, e-mail.
Number of Copies	3.
Disk Submission	Accepted: MS Word format.
Online or E-mail Submission Allowed or Required	Recommended: dougm@uvic.ca.

FORMAT OF MANUSCRIPT

Cover Sheet	Title (50 characters including spaces); Author(s) name, affiliation, contact information.
Abstract	100-word limit.
Key Words	3–10 keywords.
Length	10–50 typed pages.
Margins	Minimum of 1 inch on all sides.
Spacing	Double-spaced.

STYLE

Name of Guide	*Publication Manual of the American Psychological Association.*
Subheadings	See style guide.
References	See style guide.
Footnotes	See style guide.
Tables or Figures	Tables and figures (illustrations) should not be embedded in the text, but should be included as separate sheets or files. A short descriptive title should appear above each table with a clear legend and any footnotes suitably identified below. All units must be included. Figures should be

completely labeled, taking into account necessary size reduction. Captions should be typed, double-spaced, on a separate sheet.

REVIEW PROCESS

Type of Review	All articles in this journal have undergone rigorous peer review, based on initial editor screening and anonymous refereeing by two referees.
Queries	dougm@uvic.ca.
Acknowledgment	Not specified.
Review Time	Not specified.
Revisions	Returned to authors for revision and resubmission; also requested to view final proofs.
Acceptance Rate	Not specified.
Return of Manuscript	Not specified.
Lag Time to Print	Approximately 6–12 months.

CHARGES TO AUTHOR

Author Alterations	N/A.
Page Charges	There are no charges for standard black and white pages. Color illustrations will be considered for publication; however, the author will be required to bear the full cost involved in color art reproduction. Color art can be purchased for online only reproduction or for print and online reproduction. Color reprints can be ordered only if print and online reproduction costs are paid. Rates for color art reproduction are: Online-only reproduction: $225 for the first page of color; $100 per page for the next three pages of color. A maximum charge of $525 applies. Print and online reproduction: $900 for the first page of color; $450 per page for the next three pages of color. A custom quote will be provided for articles with more than four pages of color. Art not supplied at a minimum resolution of 300 dpi will not be considered for print.
Processing	N/A.

REPRINT, SUBSCRIPTION, AND CONTACT INFORMATION

Reprint Policy	Reprints of individual articles are available for order at the time authors review page proofs. A discount on reprints is available to authors who order before print publication. Each corresponding author will receive three complete issues in which the article publishes and a complimentary PDF. This file is for personal use only and may not be copied and disseminated in any form without prior written permission from Taylor and Francis Group, LLC.
Book Reviews	Send books for review to Taylor & Francis, Attn: Child & Youth Services, 325 Chestnut Street, Suite 800, Philadelphia, PA 19106.
Subscriptions	www.tandf.co.uk/journals/wcys or customer.service@taylorandfrancis.com or 1.800.0354.1420, press "4".
Affiliation	N/A.
E-Mail Address	customer.service@taylorandfrancis.com
Website	www.tandf.co.uk/journals/wcys

CHILD MALTREATMENT—OURNAL OF THE AMERICAN PROFESSIONAL SOCIETY ON THE ABUSE OF CHILDREN

Current Title	*Child Maltreatment - Journal of the American Professional Society on the Abuse of Children*
Previous Title	N/A.
Editorial Focus	Reporting current and at-issue scientific information and technical innovations in the field of child abuse and neglect.
Audience	Practitioners and researchers from mental health, child protection, law, law enforcement, medicine, nursing, and allied disciplines.
Special Themes	Treatment outcome research, the decreasing role of the federal government in child protection, medical practice standards, parent training and abuse prevention, legal options with sexual offenders.
Where Indexed/ Abstracted	Cancer Prevention and Control Database; Comprehensive School Health Database; Criminal Justice Abstracts; Health Promotion and Education Database; Linguistics and Language Behavior Abstracts; The Pilot Database: An Electronic Index to the Traumatic Stress Literature; Prenatal Smoking Cessation Database; Social Work Abstracts; Western New England College School of Law.
Year Established	1996.
Circulation	7,000.
Frequency	Quarterly.
Months Issued	February, May, August, November.
No. of Articles per Issue	Approximately 6–9.

SUBMISSIONS

Postal Mailing Address	Online submissions only: http://mc.manuscriptcentral.com/childmaltreatment
Method for Submission	Electronic form via website.
Number of Copies	N/A.
Disk Submission	No.
Online or E-mail Submission Allowed or Required	Online required: http://mc.manuscriptcentral.com/childmaltreatment.

FORMAT OF MANUSCRIPT

Cover Sheet	Yes.
Abstract	Yes.
Key Words	Minimum of 3 words.
Length	30 pages inclusive of references, tables, and figures.
Margins	Normal.
Spacing	Normal.

STYLE

Name of Guide	*Publication Manual of the American Psychological Association.*
Subheadings	Not specified.
References	Separate sheet.
Footnotes	Separate sheet.
Tables or Figures	Separate sheet.

REVIEW PROCESS

Type of Review	Peer reviewed.
Queries	Yes.
Acknowledgment	E-mail.
Review Time	Approximately 30–60 days.
Revisions	Approximately 30–60 days from time of decision.
Acceptance Rate	Approximately 46%.
Return of Manuscript	No.
Lag Time to Print	Approximately 6–12 months.

CHARGES TO AUTHOR

Author Alterations	None.
Page Charges	None.
Processing	None.

REPRINT, SUBSCRIPTION, AND CONTACT INFORMATION

Reprint Policy	Minimum of 50, contact Sage Publications at: http://www.sagepub.com/journalsReprints.nav.
Book Reviews	Yes.
Subscriptions	Online access available through membership in APSAC: www.apsac.org. Print: $135 for individuals: http://www.sagepub.com/journalsSubscribe.nav?prodId=Journal200758.
Affiliation	APSAC: American Professional Society on the Abuse of Children.
E-Mail Address	apsac@apsac.org
Website	http://cmx.sagepub.com/

CHILD PSYCHIATRY AND HUMAN DEVELOPMENT

Current Title	*Child Psychiatry and Human Development*
Previous Title	N/A.
Editorial Focus	The journal publishes research on diagnosis, assessment, treatment, epidemiology, development, advocacy, training, cultural factors, ethics, policy, and professional issues as related to clinical disorders in children, adolescents, and families. The journal publishes peer-reviewed original research, including case studies, in addition to substantive and theoretical reviews.
Audience	*Child Psychiatry and Human Development* is an interdisciplinary international journal serving professionals practicing or training in child and adolescent psychiatry; clinical child; pediatric and family psychology; pediatrics; social science; and human development.
Special Themes	Not specified.
Where Indexed/ Abstracted	Applied Social Sciences Index and Abstracts (ASSIA); CSA Sociological Abstracts; Current Contents/Social & Behavioral Sciences; Educational Research Abstracts Online (ERA); EMBASE; Family & Society Studies Worldwide; LISA (Library and Information Sciences Abstracts); PsycINFO; PubMed/MEDLINE; Science Citation Index Expanded (SciSearch); SCOPUS; Social Science Citation Index.
Year Established	1974.
Circulation	2,000+.
Frequency	Quarterly.
Months Issued	Summer, fall, winter, spring.
No. of Articles per Issue	Approximately 5–6.

SUBMISSIONS

Postal Mailing Address	See website.
Method for Submission	Online submission via web site or surface mail: Springer now offers authors, editors and reviewers of *Child Psychiatry and Human Development* the use of our fully web-enabled online manuscript submission and review system. To keep the review time as short as possible, we request authors to submit manuscripts online to the journal's editorial office. Our online manuscript submission and review system offers authors the option to track the progress of the review process of manuscripts in real time. The online manuscript submission and review system for *Child Psychiatry and Human Development* offers easy and straightforward log-in and submission procedures. This system supports a wide range of submission file formats: for manuscripts, Word, WordPerfect, RTF, TXT and LaTex; for figures, TIFF, GIF, JPEG, EPS, PPT, and Postscript. PDF is not an acceptable file format. Manuscripts should be submitted to: http://chud.edmgr.com. NOTE: In case you encounter any difficulties while submitting your manuscript online, please get in touch with the responsible Editorial Assistant by clicking on CONTACT US from the tool-bar. www.springeronline.com/openchoice.
Number of Copies	See website: http://www.springer.com/psychology/child+%26+school+psychology/journal/10578?detailsPage=contentItemPage&CIPageCounter=142478.
Disk Submission	See website: http://www.springer.com/psychology/child+%26+school+psychology/journal/10578?detailsPage=contentItemPage&CIPageCounter=142478.
Online or E-mail Submission Allowed or Required	Online submission via website preferred. See website for Open Choice program: www.springeronline.com/openchoice.

FORMAT OF MANUSCRIPT

Cover Sheet	Full title; names of authors, including professional degrees, titles, and affiliations; designation of corresponding author with address, phone number, e-mail address, and fax number.
Abstract	6–8 lines.
Key Words	List of salient key words for indexing purposes.
Length	Approximately 17 pages; see website for updated information.
Margins	1 inch on all sides.
Spacing	Double-spaced.

STYLE

Name of Guide	*Index Medicus.*
Subheadings	No heading for introduction. Thereafter as appropriate.

References	In text cited by serially numbered superscript following punctuation. In reference section serially numbered and abbreviated in accordance with *Index Medicus*.
Footnotes	No footnotes.
Tables or Figures	Tables typed double-spaced; figures must be submitted in camera-ready format. Each table and figure must be on a separate page at the end of the manuscript.

REVIEW PROCESS

Type of Review	Peer reviewed.
Queries	Detailed information about submissions is available in each issue.
Acknowledgment	Yes.
Review Time	Approximately 1–3 months; however, see website for changes due to online submission capability.
Revisions	Not specified.
Acceptance Rate	Approximately 40%.
Return of Manuscript	See website: http://www.springer.com/psychology/child+%26+school+psychology/journal/10578?detailsPage=contentItemPage&CIPageCounter=142478.
Lag Time to Print	See website: http://www.springer.com/psychology/child+%26+school+psychology/journal/10578?detailsPage=contentItemPage&CIPageCounter=142478.

REPRINT, SUBSCRIPTION, AND CONTACT INFORMATION

Reprint Policy	See website: http://www.springer.com/psychology/child+%26+school+psychology/journal/10578?detailsPage=contentItemPage&CIPageCounter=142478.
Book Reviews	Submit to editor.
Subscriptions	See website: http://www.springer.com/psychology/child+%26+school+psychology/journal/10578?detailsPage=contentItemPage&CIPageCounter=142478.
Affiliation	American Association of Psychiatric Services for Children.
E-Mail Address	http://chud.edmgr.com
Website	http://www.springer.com/psychology/child+%26+school+psychology/journal/10578?detailsPage=contentItemPage&CIPageCounter=142478

CHILD WELFARE

Current Title	*Child Welfare*
Previous Title	
Editorial Focus	Material that extends knowledge in the field of child and family welfare or related service; on any aspect of administration, supervision, casework, group work, community organization, teaching, and research or interpretation; on any facet of interdisciplinary approaches to the field; or on issues of social policy that bear on the welfare of children, youths, and their families.
Audience	Social workers, administrators, child care workers and paraprofessionals, child day care staff members, board members, volunteers, faculty, students, foster and adoptive parents, librarians, juvenile court personnel, government and legislative officials, social scientists, child psychiatrists, pediatricians, and community leaders.
Special Themes	Past special issues: adoption, disproportionality, mental health, kinship care, children of incarcerated parents. Future special issues: residential care and treatment, recruitment and retention.
Where Indexed/ Abstracted	Applied Social Sciences Index and Abstracts; Criminal Justice Abstracts; Current Abstracts; EBSCOhost; Education Research Index; Education Abstracts Online; ERIC; Exceptional Child Resources; Family Index; Health & Safety Science Abstracts; MEDLINE; Multicultural Education Abstracts; ProQuest; PsycINFO; Risk Abstracts; SCOPUS; Social Services Abstracts; Social Work Abstracts; Sociological Abstracts; Violence & Abuse Abstracts.
Year Established	1922
Circulation	15,000
Frequency	Bimonthly.
Months Issued	January, March, May, July, September, and November.
No. of Articles per Issue	Regular issues, 7; special issues, 10–12.

SUBMISSIONS

Postal Mailing Address	Managing Editor, Child Welfare, c/o CWLA, 2345 Crystal Drive, Suite 250, Arlington, VA 22202.
Method for Submission	Online submission required at www.cwla.org/pubs/authorguidecw.htm
Number of Copies	One online.
Disk Submission	Not required.
Online or E-mail Submission Allowed or Required	Online submission required.

FORMAT OF MANUSCRIPT

Cover Sheet	On a separate sheet, the full title of the manuscript; the full name of each author; each author's academic degree, professional title and affiliation, city, and state. Include a mailing address, phone number, fax, and e-mail address for the corresponding author.
Abstract	Approximately 75 words, on a separate sheet.
Key Words	Not necessary.
Length	Articles should be 3,500–5,000 words in length, or 15–20 double-spaced pages of approximately 250 words each, including references and tables. Text should be in 12-point font.
Margins	1 inch on all sides.
Spacing	Double-spaced throughout, including tables, figures, and references.

STYLE

Name of Guide	*Publication Manual of the American Psychological Association*. A copy of CWLA's *Author's Guide* is available on request at no charge.
Subheadings	*1st level subheadings* should be in bold, upper- and lowercase type. *2nd level subheadings* should be in italic, upper- and lowercase type. *3rd level subheadings* should be set in bold, run into the text paragraph.
References	See style guide. References should be double-spaced throughout.
Footnotes	Avoid the use of footnotes.
Tables or Figures	All tables and figures should be double-spaced on a separate, numbered page at the end of the manuscript. Include reference points used in the creation of charts and graphs.

REVIEW PROCESS

Type of Review	Peer review; 2 anonymous reviewers and the senior editor.
Queries	Not recommended. Authors should check prior issues of *Child Welfare* ad CWLA's *Author's Guide.*
Acknowledgment	By e-mail, with the manuscript number assigned to their submission.
Review Time	6 months.
Revisions	Authors will be notified if revisions are necessary.
Acceptance Rate	30%
Return of Manuscript	Manuscripts are not returned.
Lag Time to Print	12 months.

REPRINT, SUBSCRIPTION, AND CONTACT INFORMATION

Reprint Policy	Authors are expected to fulfill individual requests for reprints of their articles. Reprints may be purchased from *Child Welfare,* or authors may have their own reprints made.
Book Reviews	No book reviews accepted.
Subscriptions	800-407-6273 or order@cwla.org
Affiliation	Child Welfare League of America
E-Mail Address	journal @cwla.org
Website	http://www.cwla.org

CHILDREN AND SCHOOLS

Current Title	*Children and Schools*
Previous Title	*Social Work in Education.*
Editorial Focus	Social work and related services in schools (preschool, elementary, secondary, and post-secondary). Articles on innovation in administration, practice, research, and policy analysis.
Audience	School social workers, students, faculty, health and mental health agencies, educational institutions, the juvenile justice system, libraries, and other organizations.
Special Themes	Evidence-based practice in school settings, prevention and intervention programming, educational policy, working with diverse populations in schools.
Where Indexed/ Abstracted	Caredata; ERIC; PsycINFO; Quality Review Bulletin; Social Work Abstracts; Sociological Abstracts.
Year Established	1978.
Circulation	2,500.
Frequency	Quarterly.
Months Issued	January, April, July, October.
No. of Articles per Issue	Approximately 5.

SUBMISSIONS

Postal Mailing Address	Children & Schools, NASW Press, 750 First Street, NE, Suite 700, Washington, DC 20002-4241.
Method for Submission	Not specified.
Number of Copies	5.
Disk Submission	Authors of accepted manuscripts are asked to submit a disk, preferably in Microsoft Word.
Online or E-mail Submission Allowed or Required	N/A.

FORMAT OF MANUSCRIPT

Cover Sheet	Separate sheet, which does not go out for review. Full title; author names, degrees, and professional titles; designation of one author as corresponding author with full address, phone numbers, e-mail address, and fax number; date of submission.
Abstract	150-word informative abstract.
Key Words	Up to 5 key words or key phrases (2–3 word maximum) describing the article.
Length	20 pages including references and tables.
Margins	1 inch on all sides.
Spacing	Double-spaced for all copy except title page.

STYLE

Name of Guide	*Writing for the NASW Press: Information for Authors* (free) and *Professional Writing for the Human Services* (for purchase from the NASW Press). Contact NASW Press.
Subheadings	Use as needed to guide reader through the article. No more than 3 levels.
References	Author–date citation style; see style guide.
Footnotes	No footnotes preferred; incorporate into text.
Tables or Figures	Type tables double-spaced. Submit camera-ready art (300-dpi resolution or better) for all figures. Place each table or figure on a separate, numbered page at the end of the manuscript.

REVIEW PROCESS

Type of Review	"Double blind" anonymous peer review. Three reviewers plus the editor-in-chief read the manuscript in an anonymous review.
Queries	Query letters are discouraged; authors are encouraged to read the journal and Writing for the NASW Press to determine if their subject matter would be appropriate.
Acknowledgment	The NASW Press sends a letter upon receipt of manuscript.
Review Time	Approximately 3–4 months.
Revisions	Submit 5 copies with a separate cover sheet (not identifying the author) describing the changes made in the manuscript and replying to the reviewers' comments. In general, the original reviewers and the editor-in-chief read revisions.
Acceptance Rate	Approximately 35%.

Return of Manuscript Not returned; author should retain copies.

Lag Time to Print Approximately 6–12 months.

CHARGES TO AUTHOR

Author Alterations NASW Press does not charge authors for alterations.

REPRINT, SUBSCRIPTION, AND CONTACT INFORMATION

Reprint Policy All authors receive 5 complimentary copies of the issue in which the article appears. Authors receive reprint order forms to purchase additional reprinted copies.

Book Reviews By invitation only; send books for review to: Book Review Editor, Children & Schools, NASW Press, 750 First Street, NE, Suite 700, Washington, DC 20002-4241.

Subscriptions Children and Schools, P.O. Box 431, Annapolis JCT, MD 20701.

Affiliation The NASW Press is a division of the National Association of Social Workers.

E-Mail Address press@naswdc.org

Website www.naswpress.org

CHILDREN AND YOUTH SERVICES REVIEW

Current Title	*Children and Youth Services Review*
Previous Title	N/A.
Editorial Focus	This journal is an interdisciplinary forum for critical scholarship regarding service programs for children and youth. The journal will publish full-length articles, current research and policy notes, and book reviews.
Audience	Social workers, sociologists, educators, psychologists.
Special Themes	Foster care, adoption, child poverty, child abuse and neglect.
Where Indexed/ Abstracted	Abstracts in Social Gerontology; Criminal Justice Abstracts; Current Contents; EBSCOhost; Education Research Abstracts Online; Family Studies Abstracts; PsycINFO; Social Services Abstracts; Social Work Abstracts; Sociological Abstracts; Studies on Women and Gender Abstracts.
Year Established	1979.
Circulation	Not specified.
Frequency	12 times per year.
Months Issued	Monthly.
No. of Articles per Issue	12–16 per issue.

SUBMISSIONS

Postal Mailing Address	Duncan Lindsey, Editor-in-Chief, Children and Youth Services Review, School of Public Affairs, University of California, Box 951452, Los Angeles, CA 90095-1452.
Method for Submission	Submission to this journal proceeds totally online and you will be guided stepwise through the creation and uploading of your files. The system automatically converts source files to a single PDF file of the article, which is used in the peer-review process. Please note that even though manuscript source files are converted to PDF files at submission for the review process, these source files are needed for further processing after acceptance.
Number of Copies	No hard copies required.
Disk Submission	No.
Online or E-mail Submission Allowed or Required	Online submission only.

FORMAT OF MANUSCRIPT

Cover Sheet	Title page should indicate manuscript title, authors' names and affiliations, designated corresponding author, and author's present or permanent address.
Abstract	A concise and factual abstract is required. The abstract should state briefly the purpose of the research, the principal results and major conclusions. An abstract is often presented separately from the article, so it must be able to stand alone. For this reason, references should be avoided, but if essential, then cite the author(s) and year(s). Also, nonstandard or uncommon abbreviations should be avoided, but if essential, they must be defined at their first mention in the abstract itself.
Key Words	Immediately after the abstract, provide a maximum of 6 keywords, using American spelling and avoiding general and plural terms and multiple concepts (avoid, for example, "and", "of").
Length	Open.
Margins	1 inch on all sides.
Spacing	Double-spaced.

STYLE

Name of Guide	*Publication Manual of the American Psychological Association.*
Subheadings	See *Guide to Authors* on journal website.
References	See *Guide to Authors* on journal website.
Footnotes	Footnotes should be used sparingly. Number them consecutively throughout the article, using superscript Arabic numbers.
Tables or Figures	See *Guide to Authors* on journal website.

REVIEW PROCESS

Type of Review	Double-blind peer review.
Queries	By e-mail to the Editor-in-Chief, Duncan Linsey at dlcysr@gmail.com.

Acknowledgment	Yes.
Review Time	Not specified.
Revisions	Often required.
Acceptance Rate	Not specified.
Return of Manuscript	Not returned.
Lag Time to Print	Varies.

CHARGES TO AUTHOR

Author Alterations	Not specified.
Page Charges	Not specified.
Processing	Not specified.

REPRINT, SUBSCRIPTION, AND CONTACT INFORMATION

Reprint Policy	The corresponding author, at no cost, will be provided with a PDF file of the article via e-mail. The PDF file is a watermarked version of the published article and includes a cover sheet with the journal cover image and a disclaimer outlining the terms and conditions of use. Additional paper offprints can be ordered by the authors. An order form with prices will be sent to the corresponding author.
Book Reviews	Yes, contact Book Review Editors.
Subscriptions	Available through the website at: http://www.elsevier.com/wps/find/journaldescription.cws_home/556/bibliographic.
Affiliation	Not specified.
E-Mail Address	dlcysr@gmail.com
Website	http://www.elsevier.com/wps/find/journaldescription.cws_home/556/description

CHINA JOURNAL OF SOCIAL WORK

Current Title	*China Journal of Social Work*
Previous Title	N/A.
Editorial Focus	Articles, policy update, book review, research notes.
Audience	Social work researchers, students, educators, practitioners.
Special Themes	Social work, social policy, social development, China.
Where Indexed/ Abstracted	http://www.informaworld.com/smpp/title~content=t777186828~db=all.
Year Established	2008.
Circulation	Not specified.
Frequency	3 issues per year.
Months Issued	April, July, November.
No. of Articles per Issue	5–6.

SUBMISSIONS

Postal Mailing Address	Editor, China Journal of Social Work, Department of Applied Social Sciences, The Hong Kong Polytechnic University, Hung Hom, Kowloon, HKSAR.
Method for Submission	Not specified.
Number of Copies	1.
Disk Submission	Not specified.
Online or E-mail Submission Allowed or Required	Manuscripts sent to sscjsw@inet.polyu.edu.hk.

FORMAT OF MANUSCRIPT

Cover Sheet	The title of the paper; name(s) of author(s); and for each author, academic and/or professional qualifications, main appointment, and address.
Abstract	100–150 words.
Key Words	Up to 10 key words.
Length	Should not exceed 8,000 (English)/ 10,000 (Chinese) words.
Margins	At least 2.5 cm.
Spacing	Double-spaced.

STYLE

Name of Guide	*Harvard Style.*
Subheadings	Not specified.
References	*Harvard Style.*
Footnotes	Accepted.
Tables or Figures	Tables should be typed on separate sheets and should be given Arabic numbers. Their approximate position in the text should be indicated. Units should appear in parentheses in the column heading but not in the body of the table.

REVIEW PROCESS

Type of Review	Anonymous peer review.
Queries	Accept query letters.
Acknowledgment	By electronic acknowledgement letter.
Review Time	Approximately 4 months.
Revisions	Resubmit with minor revisions; resubmit with substantial revisions.
Acceptance Rate	Approximately 36% as of June, 2009.
Return of Manuscript	Not returned.
Lag Time to Print	Approximately 2 months.

REPRINT, SUBSCRIPTION, AND CONTACT INFORMATION

Reprint Policy	All requests to reproduce copyright material should be directed written to Taylor & Francis for permission.
Book Reviews	Both books for review and book review are welcome, by sending to the same person and address as the above.

Subscriptions	Institutional Subscription Rate (print and online): $365; Institutional Subscription Rate (online only): $347; Personal Subscription Rate (print only): $87.
Affiliation	Department of Applied Social Sciences, The Hong Kong Polytechnic University; Department of Sociology, Peking University; Taylor & Francis Group.
E-Mail Address	sscjsw@inet.polyu.edu.hk and tf.enquiries@tfinforma.com
Website	http://www.tandf.co.uk/journals/titles/17525098.asp and http://myweb.polyu.edu.hk/~sscrdn/index.php?option=com_content&task=view&id=13&Itemid=31

CLINICAL GERONTOLOGIST

Current Title	*Clinical Gerontologist*
Previous Title	*Journal of Aged Care*
Editorial Focus	*Clinical Gerontologist* publishes four types of articles: (1) articles reporting original empirically based research; (2) conceptual reviews of the literature, and/or manuscripts presenting new or revised theoretical models, that yield conclusions of direct clinical importance to the mental health care of older adults; (3) case studies and/or "clinical comments"; and (4) papers by new and emerging professionals.
Audience	Psychologists, physicians, nurses, social workers, and counselors (family, pastoral, and vocational) who address the issues commonly found in later life.
Special Themes	
Where Indexed/ Abstracted	Abstracts in Social Gerontology; AgeLine; Current Abstracts; EBSCOhost; Family Studies Abstracts; PsycINFO; Social Services Abstracts; Social Work Abstracts; Sociological Abstracts.
Year Established	1977
Circulation	Not specified.
Frequency	Quarterly
Months Issued	Not specified.
No. of Articles per Issue	6–8 per issue.

SUBMISSIONS

Postal Mailing Address	*Manuscripts should be submitted by e-mail unless other arrangements are made.*
Method for Submission	Manuscripts should be submitted to clinicalgerontologist@yahoo.com. In addition, all manuscripts must be submitted by e-mail to the Editors-in-Chief: Larry W. Thompson, PhD, larrywt@stanford.edu, and Dolores Gallagher-Thompson, PhD, dolorest@stanford.edu. If e-mail submission is impossible, an alternative strategy can be arranged in advance with the editors.
Number of Copies	Online submission to three recipients. No hard copy required.
Disk Submission	No
Online or E-mail Submission Allowed or Required	E-mail submission as noted above.

FORMAT OF MANUSCRIPT

Cover Sheet	The title page should include the authors' full names and their institutions. The corresponding author's complete mailing address, phone and fax numbers, and e-mail address should be included on the title page. (Contact information for all authors should be included on a separate sheet.) A short running head not to exceed 50 characters should be supplied on the title page.
Abstract	A one-paragraph abstract not exceeding 120 words should be supplied on a separate page.
Key Words	3–6 key words.
Length	Original research reports should not exceed 5,000 words, or in unusual circumstances, no more than 6,000 words. Clinical comments should not exceed 2,000 words or three pages.
Margins	1 inch on all sides.
Spacing	Double-spaced.

STYLE

Name of Guide	*Publication Manual of the American Psychological Association.*
Subheadings	Follow style guide.
References	Follow style guide.
Footnotes	Follow style guide.
Tables or Figures	Tables and figures should not be embedded in the text, but should be included on separate sheets or files. A short descriptive title should appear above each table with a clear legend and any footnotes suitably identified below. All units must be included. Figures should be completely labeled, taking into account necessary size reduction. Figure legends should be typed, double-spaced, on a separate sheet.

REVIEW PROCESS

Type of Review	Peer reviewed. Anonymous review is available on request.
Queries	Not specified.

Acknowledgment	Not specified.
Review Time	Not specified.
Revisions	Not specified.
Acceptance Rate	Not specified.
Return of Manuscript	Authors should save an electronic copy of their manuscript.
Lag Time to Print	Not specified.

CHARGES TO AUTHOR

Author Alterations
Page Charges
Processing

REPRINT, SUBSCRIPTION, AND CONTACT INFORMATION

Reprint Policy	Reprints of individual articles are available for order at the time authors review page proofs. A discount on reprints is available to authors who order before print publication. Each corresponding author will receive 3 complete issues in which the article publishes and a complimentary PDF.
Book Reviews	Yes.
Subscriptions	Available through the website at: http://www.informaworld.com/smpp/title~db=all~content=g904300918~tab=subscribe
Affiliation	
E-Mail Address	clinicalgerontologist@yahoo.com
Website	http://www.informaworld.com/smpp/title~content=t792303983~db=all

CLINICAL SOCIAL WORK JOURNAL

Current Title	*Clinical Social Work Journal*
Previous Title	
Editorial Focus	*Clinical Social Work Journal* is an international forum devoted to the advancement of clinical knowledge and acumen of practitioners, educators, researchers, and policymakers. The journal, founded in 1973, publishes leading peer-reviewed original articles germane to contemporary clinical practice with individuals, couples, families, and groups, and welcomes submissions that reflect innovations in theoretical, practice, evidence-based clinical research, and interdisciplinary approaches.
Audience	Practitioners, educators, researchers, policymakers, university libraries and their faculty and student patrons.
Special Themes	*Clinical Social Work Journal* publishes papers on theoretical developments, qualitative research, clinical outcome studies, and clinical case reports based on innovative and contemporary psychoanalytic approaches, all geared toward enhancing practice and clinical education.
Where Indexed/ Abstracted	CSA Social Services Abstracts; CSA Sociological Abstracts; Current Contents/Social & Behavioral Sciences; Family & Society Studies Worldwide; PsycINFO; PsycLIT; SCOPUS; Social Science Citation Index; Social Science Index.
Year Established	1973
Circulation	Available to millions of desktops worldwide via Springer's platform, SpringerLink.
Frequency	Quarterly.
Months Issued	March, June, September, December.
No. of Articles per Issue	12 (average)

SUBMISSIONS

Postal Mailing Address	Not applicable
Method for Submission	Through an online submission system.
Number of Copies	1 through the online system.
Disk Submission	Not required.
Online or E-mail Submission Allowed or Required	Online submission at: http://csow.edmgr.com Acceptable submission file formats include Word, WordPerfect, RTF, TXT, and LaTeX for manuscripts and TIFF, GIF, JPEG, EPS, PPT, and Postscript for figures (artwork). PDF is not an acceptable file format.

FORMAT OF MANUSCRIPT

Cover Sheet	In order to facilitate masked (previously termed "double-blind") review, leave all identifying information off the manuscript, including the title page and the electronic file name. Appropriate identifying information is attached automatically to the electronic file. Upon initial submission, the title page should include only the title of the article. An additional title page should be uploaded as a separate submission item and should include the title of the article, author's name (with degree), and author's affiliation. Academic affiliations of all authors should be included. The affiliation should comprise the department, institution (usually university or company), city, and state (or nation) and should be typed as a footnote to the author's name. This title page should also include the complete mailing address, telephone number, fax number, and e-mail address of the one author designated to review proofs.
Abstract	An abstract is to be provided, preferably no longer than 50–100 words.
Key Words	A list of 3–5 key words is to be provided directly below the abstract. Key words should express the precise content of the manuscript, as they are used for indexing purposes.
Length	Manuscript length, except under unusual circumstances, should not exceed 20 double-spaced pages.
Margins	Type double-spaced on one side of 8½ × 11 inch white paper using generous margins on all sides.
Spacing	The entire manuscript, including quotations, references, figure-caption list, and tables, should be double-spaced.

STYLE

Name of Guide	In general, the journal follows the recommendations of the 2001 *Publication Manual of the American Psychological Association*, and it is suggested that contributors refer to this publication.

Subheadings	Main headings (first level) strongly preferred. Second level subheadings preferred. Third and fourth level headings acceptable.
References	List references alphabetically at the end of the paper and refer to them in the text by name and year in parentheses. References should include (in this order): last names and initials of all authors, year published, title of article, name of publication, volume number, and inclusive pages.
Footnotes	Footnotes should be avoided. When their use is absolutely necessary, footnotes should be numbered consecutively using Arabic numerals and should be typed at the bottom of the page to which they refer. Place a line above the footnote, so that it is set off from the text. Use the appropriate superscript numeral for citation in the text.
Tables or Figures	Illustrations (photographs, drawings, diagrams, and charts) are to be numbered in one consecutive series of Arabic numerals and cited in numerical order in the text. Photographs should be high contrast, and drawings should be dark, sharp, and clear. Artwork for each figure should be provided on a separate page. Each figure should have an accompanying caption. The captions for illustrations should be listed on a separate page. Tables should be numbered (with Arabic numerals) and referred to by number in the text. Each table should be typed on a separate sheet of paper. Center the title above the table, and type explanatory footnotes (indicated by superscript lowercase letters) below the table.

REVIEW PROCESS

Type of Review	Double-blind peer review.
Queries	Query letters accepted.
Acknowledgment	The journal uses Editorial Manager, an online manuscript submission and peer review system. Acknowledgments of submission are e-mailed to contact author.
Review Time	Approximately 2–3 months.
Revisions	Reviewer comments are supplied to contact author. Contact author revises the paper accordingly and resubmits the revised version.
Acceptance Rate	20%
Return of Manuscript	N/A. No hard copies are submitted, and therefore none are returned.
Lag Time to Print	Approximately 23 days from acceptance to publication in Online First; published articles are later included in an issue, both online and print.

REPRINT, SUBSCRIPTION, AND CONTACT INFORMATION

Reprint Policy	Reprints are available to authors, and order forms with the current price schedule are provided to the contact author upon commencement of typesetting.
Book Reviews	The journal publishes book reviews. The journal does not accept unsolicited book reviews. Books to be considered for review should be sent to the CSWJ Book Review Editor, at the following address: Joanna Bettmann, University of Utah College of Social Work, 395 South 1500 East, Room 101, Salt Lake City, UT 84112.
Subscriptions	For current pricing and ordering, contact: journals-ny@springer.com
Affiliation	None.
E-Mail Address	Inquiries regarding journal policy, manuscript preparation, and other such general topics should be sent to the Editor-in-Chief: Carol Tosone, PhD, e-mail: carol.tosone@nyu.edu.
Website	www.springer.com/10615

THE CLINICAL SUPERVISOR

Current Title	*The Clinical Supervisor*
Previous Title	*Journal of Social Work Supervision*
Editorial Focus	An interdisciplinary journal that communicates the ideas, experiences, skills, techniques, concerns, and needs of supervisors in psychotherapy and mental health. Dedicated to the art and science of clinical supervision.
Audience	Not specified.
Special Themes	Not specified.
Where Indexed/ Abstracted	Current Abstracts; EBSCOhost; Education Research Index; Family Index; Human Resources Abstracts; PsycINFO; Social Services Abstracts; Social Work Abstracts; Sociological Abstracts; Violence & Abuse Abstracts.
Year Established	1983.
Circulation	Not specified.
Frequency	Semiannually.
Months Issued	Not specified.
No. of Articles per Issue	6–8 per issue.

SUBMISSIONS

Postal Mailing Address	Carlean Gilbert, DSW, Associate Professor, School of Social Work, Loyola University Chicago, 820 N. Michigan Avenue, Chicago, IL 60611.
Method for Submission	Manuscripts may be mailed; however, authors are strongly encouraged to submit electronically.
Number of Copies	Not specified.
Disk Submission	If submitting a disk, it should be prepared using MS Word and clearly labeled with the authors' names, manuscript file name, and software program.
Online or E-mail Submission Allowed or Required	No online submission available. E-mail manuscripts to Carlean Gilbert at cgilbe2@luc.edu.

FORMAT OF MANUSCRIPT

Cover Sheet	Separate sheet, which does not go out for review. Full title; author names, degrees, and professional titles; designation of 1 author as corresponding author with full address, phone numbers, e-mail address, fax number; date of submission.
Abstract	Each article should be summarized in an abstract of not more than 100 words.
Key Words	5–6 key words that identify article content.
Length	20 pages, including references and abstract. Lengthier manuscripts may be considered, but only at the discretion of the editor. Sometimes, lengthier manuscripts may be considered if they can be divided up into sections for publication in successive issues.
Margins	At least 1 inch on all sides.
Spacing	Double-spaced.

STYLE

Name of Guide	*Publication Manual of the American Psychological Association.*
Subheadings	Use as needed, no more than 4 levels.
References	See style guide.
Footnotes	No footnotes preferred. Incorporate into text.
Tables or Figures	Tables and figures (illustrations) should not be embedded in the text, but should be included as separate sheets or files. A short descriptive title should appear above each table with a clear legend and any footnotes suitably identified below. All units must be included. Figures should be completely labeled, taking into account necessary size reduction. Captions should be typed, double-spaced, on a separate sheet.

REVIEW PROCESS

Type of Review	Peer review, based on initial editor screening and anonymous, double-blind reviews by at least 2 referees.
Queries	Authors are encouraged to read the journal to determine whether their subject matter would be appropriate.
Acknowledgment	Not specified.

Review Time	Not specified.
Revisions	Not specified.
Acceptance Rate	Not specified.
Return of Manuscript	Authors should save a copy of the electronic manuscript.
Lag Time to Print	Not specified.

CHARGES TO AUTHOR

Author Alterations	Not specified.
Page Charges	Not specified.
Processing	Not specified.

REPRINT, SUBSCRIPTION, AND CONTACT INFORMATION

Reprint Policy	Reprints of individual articles are available for order at the time authors review page proofs. A discount on reprints is available to authors who order before print publication. Each corresponding author will receive 3 complete issues in which the article publishes and a complimentary PDF.
Book Reviews	Send to journal editor.
Subscriptions	Available from the journal website at http://www.informaworld.com/smpp/title~db=all~content=g910879641~tab=subscribe
Affiliation	Not specified.
E-Mail Address	journals@routledge.com
Website	http://www.informaworld.com/smpp/title~db=all~content=g910879641~tab=toc

COMMUNITY DEVELOPMENT: JOURNAL OF THE COMMUNITY DEVELOPMENT SOCIETY

Current Title	*Community Development: Journal of the Community Development Society*
Previous Title	N/A.
Editorial Focus	Improving knowledge and practice in the field of purposive community change. The mission is to disseminate information on theory, research and practice, with manuscripts that report research; evaluate theory, techniques and methods; examine community problems; or critically analyze the profession itself.
Audience	Academics and practitioners.
Special Themes	Twice a year, most recent have included youth development, community visioning, integrating tourism into overall community development planning, community development theory, and sustainable agriculture.
Where Indexed/ Abstracted	CIJE; ERIC; International Regional Science Review; Journal of Planning Literature; PAIS Bulletin; PAIS International; Social Planning/Policy and Development Abstracts; Social Work Research and Abstracts; Sociofile; Sociological Abstracts; Ulrich's International Periodicals Directory.
Year Established	1971.
Circulation	Approximately 1,000.
Frequency	Quarterly.
Months Issued	January/February; March/April; July/August; October/November (typical schedule).
No. of Articles per Issue	5–7.

SUBMISSIONS

Postal Mailing Address	www.comm-dev.org.
Method for Submission	Electronic form via website.
Number of Copies	Not specified.
Disk Submission	Not specified.
Online or E-mail Submission Allowed or Required	Required.

FORMAT OF MANUSCRIPT

Cover Sheet	Yes.
Abstract	Yes, up to 150 words.
Key Words	3–5 key words.
Length	No longer than 25 pages, double-spaced.
Margins	Normal.
Spacing	Double-spaced.

STYLE

Name of Guide	*Publication Manual of the American Psychological Association.*
Subheadings	See style guide.
References	See style guide.
Footnotes	None.
Tables or Figures	See style guide.

REVIEW PROCESS

Type of Review	Double-blind peer review.
Queries	Not specified.
Acknowledgment	Not specified.
Review Time	Approximately 3–6 months.
Revisions	Yes.
Acceptance Rate	Approximately 40%–45%.
Return of Manuscript	Not specified.
Lag Time to Print	Production process time is approximately 1–2 months.

CHARGES TO AUTHOR

Author Alterations	Not specified.
Page Charges	Only if space limitations exceeded.
Processing	Not specified.

REPRINT, SUBSCRIPTION, AND CONTACT INFORMATION

Reprint Policy	See Taylor & Francis website: www.tandf.co.uk/journals/rcod.
Book Reviews	Yes.
Subscriptions	Yes, $60 per year.
Affiliation	Community Development Society, www.comm-dev.org.
E-Mail Address	journalcds@gmail.com
Website	Website: www.tandf.co.uk/journals/rcod or www.comm-dev.org

COMMUNITY MENTAL HEALTH JOURNAL

Current Title	*Community Mental Health Journal*
Previous Title	N/A.
Editorial Focus	*Community Mental Health Journal* is devoted to the evaluation and improvement of public sector mental health services for people affected by severe mental disorders, serious emotional disturbances, and/or addictions.
Audience	Not specified.
Special Themes	Not specified.
Where Indexed/ Abstracted	Abstracts in Anthropology; AgeLine; CINAHL; Criminal Justice Abstracts; Educational Research Abstracts Online (ERA); Multicultural Education Abstracts; PsycINFO; PSYCLINE; PubMed/ MEDLINE; SCOPUS; Social Science Index; Special Education Needs Abstracts; Studies on Women and Gender Abstracts.
Year Established	1965.
Circulation	Not specified.
Frequency	Bimonthly.
Months Issued	Not specified.
No. of Articles per Issue	Not specified.

SUBMISSIONS

Postal Mailing Address	Jacqueline M. Feldman, MD, Patrick H. Linton Professor, Department of Psychiatry & Behavioral Neurobiology, University of Alabama at Birmingham, CCB 4th Floor, 1530 3rd Avenue South, Birmingham, AL 35294.
Method for Submission	Authors should submit their manuscripts online at: http://www.editorialmanager.com/comh/.
Number of Copies	Please upload your manuscript only once on to the system.
Disk Submission	Not necessary.
Online or E-mail Submission Allowed or Required	Online submission required.

FORMAT OF MANUSCRIPT

Cover Sheet	The title page should include the names(s) of the author(s); a concise and informative title; the affiliation(s) and address(es) of the author(s); and the e-mail address, telephone, and fax numbers of the corresponding author.
Abstract	Please provide an abstract of 100–150 words. The abstract should not contain any undefined abbreviations or unspecified references.
Key Words	Please provide 4–6 keywords that can be used for indexing purposes.
Length	Limit articles to 16 pages of text, exclusive of references, tables, and figures. Brief Reports should be no longer than 10 pages of text, and should not include any tables or figures.
Margins	1 inch all around.
Spacing	Double-spaced.

STYLE

Name of Guide	*Publication Manual of the American Psychological Association.*
Subheadings	Adhere to journal style and include the following sections: Abstract, Introduction, Methods, Results, Discussion, and References.
References	See style guide.
Footnotes	See style guide.
Tables or Figures	See style guide.

REVIEW PROCESS

Type of Review	Peer reviewed.
Queries	Not specified.
Acknowledgment	Through online submission system.
Review Time	Not specified.
Revisions	Not specified.
Acceptance Rate	Not specified.

Return of Manuscript	Not returned.
Lag Time to Print	Not specified.

CHARGES TO AUTHOR

Author Alterations	Not specified.
Page Charges	Not specified.
Processing	Not specified.

REPRINT, SUBSCRIPTION, AND CONTACT INFORMATION

Reprint Policy	Not specified.
Book Reviews	Not specified.
Subscriptions	Available through the website at: http://www.springer.com/generic/order/journals+subscription?SGWID=0-40514-0-0-0.
Affiliation	American Association of Community Psychiatrists.
E-Mail Address	jfeldman@uabmc.edu
Website	http://springerlink.metapress.com/content/101590/

CONTEMPORARY FAMILY THERAPY: AN INTERNATIONAL JOURNAL

Current Title	*Contemporary Family Therapy: An International Journal*
Previous Title	*International Journal of Family Therapy*
Editorial Focus	*Contemporary Family Therapy: An International Journal* presents the latest developments in theory, research, and practice pertaining to family therapy, with an emphasis on examining families within the broader socioeconomic and ethnic matrices of which families and their members are a part. Demonstrating that the therapeutic relationship is most effective when family, individual, and society are seen as interacting systems, the journal examines essential factors that include family value systems; social class; and racial, religious, and ethnic backgrounds.
Audience	Academic libraries, family therapists, social workers, clinical social workers, clinical psychologists, counselors.
Special Themes	N/A.
Where Indexed/ Abstracted	Academic Search Alumni Edition; Academic Search Complete; Academic Search Premier; AgeLine; CSA Social Services Abstracts; Current Abstracts; Dietrich's Index Philosophicus; Educational Research Abstracts Online (ERA); EMCare; FRANCIS; Google Scholar; International Bibliography of Book Reviews (IBR); Multicultural Education Abstracts; OCLC ArticleFirst Database; OCLC FirstSearch Electronic Collections Online; PsycINFO; PSYCLINE; SCOPUS; Sociology of Education Abstracts; Special Education Needs Abstracts; Studies on Women and Gender Abstracts; Summon by Serial Solutions; TOC Premier.
Year Established	1978.
Circulation	Worldwide electronic circulation reaching at least 1 million desktops.
Frequency	Quarterly.
Months Issued	March, June, September, December.
No. of Articles per Issue	Approximately 6–8.

SUBMISSIONS

Postal Mailing Address	Dorothy S. Becvar, PhD, St. Louis University, School of Social Work, 3550 Lindell Boulevard, Tegeler Hall, Room 214, St. Louis, MO 63108.
Method for Submission	Electronic form via website.
Number of Copies	Submit the original, including title page, and copies of all illustrations and tables.
Disk Submission	N/A.
Online or E-mail Submission Allowed or Required	Online at: http://editorialmanager.com/coft.

FORMAT OF MANUSCRIPT

Cover Sheet	A title page is to be provided and should include the title of the article and author's name (no degrees). Under a dividing line near the bottom of the page, provide each author's name, highest earned degree, current professional position and address, the name and address to which reprint requests should be directed, and any appropriate acknowledgments. The title page should also include the complete mailing address and telephone number of the one author designated to review proofs.
Abstract	An abstract is to be provided, preferably no longer than 100 words.
Key Words	3–5 key words.
Length	25–30 manuscript pages.
Margins	Generous margins on all sides.
Spacing	Double-spaced.

STYLE

Name of Guide	*Publication Manual of the American Psychological Association.*
Subheadings	N/A.
References	See style guide.
Footnotes	No footnotes.
Tables or Figures	Tables should be numbered (with Arabic numerals) and referred to by number in the text. Each

table should be typed on a separate sheet of paper. Center the title above the table, and type explanatory footnotes (if any) below the table.

REVIEW PROCESS

Type of Review	Blind peer review.
Queries	Queries accepted by the editor at becvards@slu.edu.
Acknowledgment	Generated electronically for all submissions.
Review Time	Approximately 1–2 months.
Revisions	Articles may be accepted, accepted with minor revisions, or suggest revise and resubmit.
Acceptance Rate	Approximately 50%.
Return of Manuscript	Original available on website. Also, all manuscripts with editorial comments and suggestions included in track-change mode are e-mailed to the corresponding author regardless of the editor's decision.
Lag Time to Print	Published online within 1–2 weeks of acceptance. Published in hard copy with a maximum of 4 months lag time.

CHARGES TO AUTHOR

Author Alterations	No charges.
Page Charges	No charges.
Processing	No charges.

REPRINT, SUBSCRIPTION, AND CONTACT INFORMATION

Reprint Policy	Reprints are available to authors, and order forms with the current price schedule are sent with proofs. Springer offers two types of reprints: *Hard-copy reprints*: Reproductions of original journal articles and book chapters printed on high-quality paper. Reprints must be ordered in quantities of at least 100. *Electronic reprints*: E-prints are encrypted, electronic copies of works in PDF format that you can easily print yourself, distribute via e-mail, post on a website, or use in e-detailing. E-prints must be ordered in quantities of at least 50. Contact: Victoria Enever, Senior Manager, Corporate Sales, Springer US, 233 Spring Street, New York, NY 10013. Telephone: 212-460-1572; Fax: 212-620-8442; e-mail: victoria.enever@springer.com.
Book Reviews	E-mail to editor at becvards@slul.edu.
Subscriptions	http://www.springer.com/librarians/price+lists?SGWID=0-40585-0-0-0.
Affiliation	N/A.
E-Mail Address	becvards@slu.edu or Assistant Editor, Spring Science and Business Media, LLC, Jennifer.Hadley@Springer.com.
Website	Website: www.springer.com/10591

CRITICAL SOCIAL POLICY: A JOURNAL OF THEORY AND PRACTICE IN SOCIAL WELFARE

Current Title	*Critical Social Policy: A Journal of Theory and Practice in Social Welfare*
Previous Title	*Not specified.*
Editorial Focus	*Critical Social Policy* provides an international forum for advocacy, analysis, and debate on social policy issues. It aims to develop an understanding of welfare from socialist, feminist, anti-racist, and radical perspectives.
Audience	Encouraging contributions from a variety of perspectives and experiences, the journal is tailored to those who are actively involved in welfare issues through pressure groups, consumer groups and community action; practitioners and workers in statutory and voluntary agencies; and teachers and researchers in social welfare issues and social policy.
Special Themes	Not specified.
Where Indexed/ Abstracted	Applied Social Sciences Index & Abstracts (ASSIA); Educational Research Abstracts Online; Family Index Database; International Bibliography of the Social Sciences; Multicultural Education Abstracts; PsycINFO; Social Services Abstracts; SocINFO; Sociological Abstracts; Studies on Women and Gender Abstracts Online; Worldwide Political Science Abstracts.
Year Established	1981.
Circulation	Not specified.
Frequency	Quarterly.
Months Issued	February, May, August, November.
No. of Articles per Issue	6–7 per issue.

SUBMISSIONS

Postal Mailing Address	Shona Hunter, Sociology and Social Policy Department, Social Sciences Building, University of Leeds, Leeds LS2 9JT, UK. s.d.j.hunter@leeds.ac.uk.cc.m.b.ross@leeds.ac.uk
Method for Submission	Surface mail submission.
Number of Copies	4 hard copies.
Disk Submission	Authors will be asked to provide an electronic copy of the final version of their paper following acceptance for publication. The author is responsible for ensuring that the final hard copy and electronic versions of the manuscript are identical.
Online or E-mail Submission Allowed or Required	Not specified.

FORMAT OF MANUSCRIPT

Cover Sheet	On a separate sheet: author's full name, affiliation, address, and e-mail; short biographies (50–100 words) of each author including affiliation, recent publications and e-mail. On the first page: full title of paper (please note that the author's name must not appear on this or any subsequent page).
Abstract	Abstract (100–150 words) covering the key argument(s) and conclusion(s) of the paper should be submitted.
Key Words	Authors should provide up to 5 key words, arranged alphabetically; do not repeat any of the words in the title.
Length	The maximum length for articles inclusive of bibliography, notes, tables, etc. should be 8,000 words, and for Commentary & Issues 4,000 words, including notes and references.
Margins	1 inch all around.
Spacing	Double-spaced.

STYLE

Name of Guide	Harvard-style system.
Subheadings	See style guide.
References	See style guide.
Footnotes	See style guide.
Tables or Figures	Tables and figures should be presented on separate sheets of paper at the end of the article. Their position within the text should be clearly indicated.

REVIEW PROCESS

Type of Review	All submissions to *CSP* are refereed anonymously by 3 members of the editorial collective.
Queries	Members of the *CSP* editorial collective are happy to discuss and offer advice on ideas for papers, particularly for inexperienced and nonacademic contributors.
Acknowledgment	Not specified.
Review Time	Not specified.
Revisions	Please note that resubmitted papers are refereed again and that there is no guarantee that they will be accepted for publication.
Acceptance Rate	Not specified.
Return of Manuscript	Not specified.
Lag Time to Print	Not specified.

CHARGES TO AUTHOR

Author Alterations	Not specified.
Page Charges	Not specified.
Processing	Not specified.

REPRINT, SUBSCRIPTION, AND CONTACT INFORMATION

Reprint Policy	Authors will receive electronic offprints of their article and a complimentary journal copy. A maximum of 5 journal copies will be supplied for multi-authored articles. These will be supplied to the main author.
Book Reviews	Contact: Paul Michael Garrett, Political Science and Sociology, National University of Ireland, Galway, Ireland. pm.garrett@nuigalway.ie.
Subscriptions	Can be obtained through the website at: http://csp.sagepub.com.
Affiliation	Not specified.
E-Mail Address	General correspondence should be sent to Norman Ginsberg at: n.ginsburg@londonment.ac.uk.
Website	http://csp.sagepub.com/

32000

CRITICAL SOCIAL WORK

Current Title	*Critical Social Work*
Previous Title	*N/A.*
Editorial Focus	The journal welcomes manuscripts from authors in all areas that focus upon the issue of social justice. We perceive *Critical Social Work* as an opportunity for constructive dialogue in the interest of achieving social justice. We anticipate the dialogue being wide ranging and welcome manuscripts of a philosophical or theoretical nature, research methods and findings, as well as practical applications. The focus may be on the individual, group, society, or culture.
Audience	Social work educators and practitioners.
Special Themes	Not specified.
Where Indexed/ Abstracted	Not specified.
Year Established	2,000.
Circulation	Not specified.
Frequency	Semiannually.
Months Issued	Not specified.
No. of Articles per Issue	6–9 per issue.

SUBMISSIONS

Postal Mailing Address	G. Brent Angell, PhD, *Critical Social Work,* School of Social Work, University of Windsor, Windsor, Ontario N9B 3P4, Canada.
Method for Submission	A hard copy and an electronic copy in Microsoft Word format should be submitted.
Number of Copies	One hard copy and one electronic copy.
Disk Submission	Electronic copy may be submitted on a disk.
Online or E-mail Submission Allowed or Required	E-mail submissions may be sent to: cswedit@uwindsor.ca; no online submission system.

FORMAT OF MANUSCRIPT

Cover Sheet	Cover sheet data: First page of manuscript: title of manuscript only. Attach cover page: title, author names, academic degrees, professional title, authors' mailing address, any statement of credit or research support.
Abstract	100 word abstract must be submitted.
Key Words	Not required.
Length	5–20 pages.
Margins	1 inch on all sides.
Spacing	Double-spaced.

STYLE

Name of Guide	*Publication Manual of the American Psychological Association.*
Subheadings	See style guide.
References	See style guide.
Footnotes	See style guide.
Tables or Figures	See style guide.

REVIEW PROCESS

Type of Review	Peer review.
Queries	Should be sent to the editor.
Acknowledgment	Not specified.
Review Time	Not specified.
Revisions	Not specified.
Acceptance Rate	Not specified.
Return of Manuscript	Not specified.
Lag Time to Print	Not specified.

REPRINT, SUBSCRIPTION, AND CONTACT INFORMATION

Reprint Policy	Journal is exclusively online.
Book Reviews	Contact the editor.
Subscriptions	*Critical Social Work* is distributed free electronically. Individuals, organizations, and libraries can receive electronically distributed issues of the journal by providing *Critical Social Work* with an e-mail address. Your request should be sent to: cswsub@uwindsor.ca. Subscriptions are for 2 years. Subscribers will be notified electronically of the expiration of their subscription. This registration is solely for the purposes of estimating readership.
Affiliation	University of Windsor, School of Social Work.
E-Mail Address	cswedit@uwindsor.ca
Website	http://www.criticalsocialwork.com/

DEATH STUDIES

Current Title	*Death Studies*
Previous Title	*Suicide*
Editorial Focus	This journal provides refereed papers on significant research, scholarship, and practical approaches in the fast-growing areas of bereavement and loss, grief therapy, death attitudes, suicide, and death education. It provides an international, interdisciplinary forum in which a variety of professionals share results of research and practice, with the aim of better understanding the human encounter with death and assisting those who work with the dying and their families.
Audience	Professionals in a wide variety of settings, including colleges and universities, hospitals, hospices, and counseling centers, who are interested in the major topics in the field of death and dying.
Special Themes	Not specified.
Where Indexed/ Abstracted	AgeLine; CINAHL; EBSCO Academic Search Premier; Educational Research Abstracts Online; ERIC Database/CIJE: Current Index to Journals in Education; Family Index Database; ISI Current Contents/Social & Behavioral Sciences; MEDLINE; Psychological Abstracts; PsycINFO; Violence and Abuse Abstracts; Social Work Abstracts; and Studies on Women and Gender Abstracts.
Year Established	1976.
Circulation	Not specified.
Frequency	10 times per year.
Months Issued	January, February, March, April, May, July, August, September, October, November
No. of Articles per Issue	5–7 per issue

SUBMISSIONS

Postal Mailing Address	Robert A. Neimeyer, PhD, Editor-in-Chief, *Death Studies,* Department of Psychology, University of Memphis, Memphis, TN 38152-6400.
Method for Submission	*Death Studies* uses an online submission and review system, ScholarOne, through which authors submit manuscripts and track their progress up until acceptance for publication.
Number of Copies	No hard copies required.
Disk Submission	Not necessary.
Online or E-mail Submission Allowed or Required	Online submission only.

FORMAT OF MANUSCRIPT

Cover Sheet	Cover letter and title page required.
Abstract	Required, length not specified.
Key Words	Not specified.
Length	Not specified.
Margins	Not specified.
Spacing	Double-spaced.

STYLE

Name of Guide	*Publication Manual of the American Psychological Association.*
Subheadings	Follow style guide.
References	Follow style guide.
Footnotes	Follow style guide.
Tables or Figures	Follow style guide.

REVIEW PROCESS

Type of Review	Anonymous, double-blind peer review.
Queries	Not specified.
Acknowledgment	Manuscript tracking available through online submission system.
Review Time	Not specified.
Revisions	As stipulated in disposition letter.
Acceptance Rate	Not specified.
Return of Manuscript	Not specified.
Lag Time to Print	Not specified.

REPRINT, SUBSCRIPTION, AND CONTACT INFORMATION

Reprint Policy	Reprints of individual articles are available for order at the time authors review page proofs. A discount on reprints is available to authors who order before print publication.
Book Reviews	Contact David E. Balk, PhD, Department of Health and Nutrition Sciences, Brooklyn College, Brooklyn, NY 11210.
Subscriptions	Available online through http://www.informaworld.com.
Affiliation	Not specified.
E-Mail Address	neimeyer@cc.memphis.edu
Website	http://www.tandf.co.uk/journals/journal.asp?issn=0748-1187&linktype=1

DEMENTIA: THE INTERNATIONAL JOURNAL OF SOCIAL RESEARCH AND PRACTICE

Current Title	*Dementia: The International Journal of Social Research and Practice*
Previous Title	N/A.
Editorial Focus	The aim of the journal is to publish original research or original contributions to the existing literature on social research and dementia.
Audience	International audience of dementia researchers and practitioners.
Special Themes	Dementia care.
Where Indexed/ Abstracted	Abstracts in Social Gerontology; AgeInfo on the web; Cravat Abstracts Online; Cumulative Index to Nursing and Allied Health Literature; Educational Research Abstract Online; e-Psyche; Family and Society Studies WorldWide; Family Index; Health and Social Care Abstracts; MEDLINE; PsycINFO; Social Service Abstracts; Sociological Abstracts; WorldWide Political Science Abstracts.
Year Established	2002.
Circulation	International through a number of Sage Publishers on-line Health care packages and hard copy.
Frequency	Because of increasing demand – starting in January will be 6 times a year. Journal started out three times a year.
Months Issued	February, May, August, November; beginning January 2009 will publish every other month.
No. of Articles per Issue	7–8; book review section and every other issue an innovative practice section.

SUBMISSIONS

Postal Mailing Address	Done through e-mail to Pharris@jcu.edu; see http://dem.sagepub.com for more information.
Method for Submission	E-mail.
Number of Copies	1.
Disk Submission	No.
Online or E-mail Submission Allowed or Required	Required.

FORMAT OF MANUSCRIPT

Cover Sheet	Yes, stating it is original work and has not been submitted elsewhere.
Abstract	100–150 words.
Key Words	5 key words.
Length	5,000–8,000 words.
Margins	1 inch.
Spacing	Double-spaced.

STYLE

Name of Guide	*Publication Manual of the American Psychological Association.*
Subheadings	See style guide.
References	See style guide.
Footnotes	See style guide.
Tables or Figures	See style guide.

REVIEW PROCESS

Type of Review	Peer reviewed.
Queries	Not specified.
Acknowledgment	Not specified.
Review Time	Approximately 3 months.
Revisions	Yes, if needed.
Acceptance Rate	Approximately 60%.
Return of Manuscript	Not specified.
Lag Time to Print	Approximately 12 months from final acceptance.

REPRINT, SUBSCRIPTION, AND CONTACT INFORMATION

Reprint Policy	Need to discuss particulars with Sage Publications.
Book Reviews	Not specified.

Subscriptions	Not indicated
Affiliation	Not specified.
E-Mail Address	Pharris@jcu.edu; see http://dem.sagepub.com for more information.
Website	See above.

DEVELOPMENTAL PSYCHOLOGY

Current Title	*Developmental Psychology*
Previous Title	N/A.
Editorial Focus	*Developmental Psychology* publishes articles that advance knowledge and theory about development across the life span. The journal includes significant empirical contributions as well as scholarly reviews and theoretical or methodological articles.
Audience	Researchers and practitioners in the discipline, faculty, libraries.
Special Themes	Not specified.
Where Indexed/ Abstracted	Applied Social Science Index & Abstracts; Biological Abstracts; Child Development Abstracts; Criminal Justice Abstracts; Current Contents; Management Contents; PsycINFO; Sage Family Studies Abstracts; Social Sciences Index; Social Work Abstracts; Studies on Women and Gender Abstracts
Year Established	1969.
Circulation	Not specified.
Frequency	Bimonthly.
Months Issued	January, March, May, July, September, November.
No. of Articles per Issue	15–20 per issue.

SUBMISSIONS

Postal Mailing Address	Cynthia García Coll, *Developmental Psychology,* Center for the Study of Human Development, Brown University, Box 1831, 133 Waterman Street, Providence, RI 02912.
Method for Submission	Manuscripts should be submitted through the online system at http://www.jbo.com/jbo3/submissions/dsp_jbo.cfm?journal_code=dev. A hard copy should also be mailed to the editor.
Number of Copies	1.
Disk Submission	Not necessary.
Online or E-mail Submission Allowed or Required	Online submission required. No e-mail submissions.

FORMAT OF MANUSCRIPT

Cover Sheet	Yes.
Abstract	All manuscripts must include an abstract containing a maximum of 250 words typed on a separate page.
Key Words	Please supply up to five keywords or brief phrases.
Length	Manuscripts must not exceed 10,500 words (approximately 35 double-spaced pages in 12-point Times New Roman font), not including references, tables, and figures. Manuscripts that exceed this limit will not be considered.
Margins	Minimum of 1 inch.
Spacing	Double-spaced all copy.

STYLE

Name of Guide	*Publication Manual of the American Psychological Association.*
Subheadings	See style guide.
References	List references in alphabetical order. Each listed reference should be cited in text, and each text citation should be listed in the References section.
Footnotes	See style guide.
Tables or Figures	See style guide.

REVIEW PROCESS

Type of Review	Masked review.
Queries	General correspondence may be sent to the editor at: developmental_psychology@brown.edu.
Acknowledgment	Not specified.
Review Time	Not specified.
Revisions	Per notification from the editor. Most manuscripts require revision.
Acceptance Rate	Not specified.
Return of Manuscript	Manuscripts not usually returned.
Lag Time to Print	Not specified.

REPRINT, SUBSCRIPTION, AND CONTACT INFORMATION

Reprint Policy	Not specified.
Book Reviews	None.
Subscriptions	Available through the website at: http://www.apa.org/journals/dev/pricing.html.
Affiliation	Published by the American Psychological Association.
E-Mail Address	developmental_psychology@brown.edu
Website	http://www.apa.org/journals/dev/description.html

ETHICS AND SOCIAL WELFARE

Current Title	*Ethics and Social Welfare*
Previous Title	N/A.
Editorial Focus	*Ethics and Social Welfare* publishes articles of a critical and reflective nature concerned with the ethical issues surrounding social welfare practice and policy. It has a particular focus on social work (including practice with individuals, families, and small groups), social care, youth and community work, and related professions. The aim of the journal is to encourage dialogue and debate across social, intercultural, and international boundaries on the serious ethical issues relating to professional interventions into social life. Through this we hope to contribute toward deepening understandings and further ethical practice in the field of social welfare. The journal welcomes material in a variety of formats, including high-quality peer-reviewed academic papers; reflections, debates, and commentaries on policy and practice; book reviews; and review articles. We actively encourage a diverse range of contributions from academic and field practitioners, voluntary workers, service users, carers, and people bringing the perspectives of oppressed groups. Contributions might include reports on research studies on the influence of values and ethics in social welfare practice, education, and organizational structures; theoretical papers discussing the evolution of social welfare values and ethics, linked to contemporary philosophical, social and ethical thought; accounts of ethical issues, problems, and dilemmas in practice; and reflections on the ethics and values of policy and organizational development.
Audience	Primarily professionals and academics in the social professions, with a focus on social work, youth and community work, group workers, and other professionals who work with people.
Special Themes	We are currently (2009) having themed issues on Professional Wisdom, and The Ethics of Control, and plan to have one in 2010 on Feminist Ethics.
Where Indexed/ Abstracted	*Ethics and Social Welfare* is abstracted and indexed in: Social Care Institute for Excellence (SCIE) UK., (website: http://www.scie.org.uk/).
Year Established	2007.
Circulation	Not specified.
Frequency	3 times per year currently, planned to rise to 4 times per year.
Months Issued	April, July, December.
No. of Articles per Issue	4–5 plus a Practice section.

SUBMISSIONS

Postal Mailing Address	USA: Professor Cynthia Bisman, Bryn Mawr College, Graduate School of Social Work and Social Research, Bryn Mawr, PA 19010. UK: Professor Michael Preston-Shoot, Dean, Faculty of Health and Social Sciences, University of Bedfordshire Park Square, Luton, LU1 3JU United Kingdom.
Method for Submission	Submissions should be made online at the *Ethics and Social Welfare* Manuscript Central site. However, the editors will consider material sent by other means.
Number of Copies	2.
Disk Submission	Not required.
Online or E-mail Submission Allowed or Required	Allowed.

FORMAT OF MANUSCRIPT

Cover Sheet	Contributors should also include brief biographical details (not more than three lines) for each author, who may include their institutional affiliation; membership in an organization; and aspects of their biography, including experiences of social difference that they think are important and relevant to their contribution to the journal. These details should be saved as a separate file and defined as "Author Bio."
Abstract	Up to 200 words.
Key Words	3–10 key words.
Length	4,000–7,000 words.
Margins	At least 2.5cm.
Spacing	Double-spaced.

STYLE

Name of Guide	Not specified.
Subheadings	Not specified.

References	Harvard.
Footnotes	Allowed.
Tables or Figures	Allowed.

REVIEW PROCESS

Type of Review	All articles in this journal have undergone editorial screening and peer review.
Queries	To the Editor.
Acknowledgment	Normally automatic acknowledgement of submitted papers through the web-based submissions system.
Review Time	Approximately 6–12 weeks.
Revisions	The editor will inform authors about required revisions in the light of reviewers' comments.
Acceptance Rate	Approximately 60.
Return of Manuscript	Corresponding authors will receive free online access to their article through our website and a complimentary copy of the issue containing their article.
Lag Time to Print	Approximately 3–18 months.

REPRINT, SUBSCRIPTION, AND CONTACT INFORMATION

Reprint Policy	Reprints of articles published in this journal can be purchased through Rightslink® when proofs are received. If you have any queries, please contact our reprints department at reprints@tandf.co.uk.
Book Reviews	Reviews and Commentary Editor: Chris Beckett, Anglia Ruskin University. (c.o.beckett@anglia.ac.uk).
Subscriptions	Print only subscription: Individual £45.00
	Online-only subscription: Any customer type £172.00 plus VAT; Print and online subscription: Any customer type £181.00 plus VAT. * Subscriptions purchased at the personal rate are strictly for personal, noncommercial use only. The reselling of personal subscriptions is prohibited. Personal subscriptions must be purchased with a personal check or credit card. Proof of personal status may be requested.
Affiliation	British Association of Social Workers (BASW) A discount subscription rate is available for BASW members. Please visit the news and offers page for more details.
E-Mail Address	ESW@ljmu.ac.uk
Website	www.informaworld.com/esw

EVALUATION AND PROGRAM PLANNING: AN INTERNATIONAL JOURNAL

Current Title	*Evaluation and Program Planning*
Previous Title	N/A.
Editorial Focus	*Evaluation and Program Planning* is based on the principle that the techniques and methods of evaluation and planning transcend the boundaries of specific fields and that relevant contributions to these areas come from people representing many different positions, intellectual traditions, and interests.
Audience	Planners (e.g., health, mental health, education, development), policy analysts, program developers, management consultants, and social scientists with professional interest in assessing the impact of innovations in government and private sector settings.
Special Themes	"Special issues" (usually a section of an issue), are groups of articles that cover a particular topic in depth. They are organized by "special issue editors" who are willing to conceptualize the topic, find contributors, set up a quality control process, and deliver the material. Often several editors share responsibility for these tasks. Suggestions for special issues are encouraged.
Where Indexed/ Abstracted	AgeLine; Criminal justice Abstracts; EBSCOhost; Education Research Index; Global Health; MEDLINE; PsycINFO; Social Services Abstracts; Sociological Abstracts.
Year Established	1978.
Circulation	Not specified.
Frequency	Quarterly.
Months Issued	January–March, April–June, July–September, October–December
No. of Articles per Issue	7–10 without special half issue, 3–5 with special half issue.

SUBMISSIONS

Postal Mailing Address	Submissions not accepted by mail.
Method for Submission	Authors are requested to submit their papers electronically by using the Evaluation and Program Planning online submission and review web site (http://ees.elsevier.com/epp). Authors who are unable to provide an electronic version or have other circumstances that prevent online submission must contact the Editor prior to submission to discuss alternative options; e-mail: jamorell@jamorell.com. The Publisher and Editor regret that they are not able to consider/ submissions that do not follow these procedures.
Number of Copies	One online submission.
Disk Submission	No.
Online or E-mail Submission Allowed or Required	Online submission only unless alternate option approved by editor.

FORMAT OF MANUSCRIPT

Cover Sheet	Title page should include title, authors' names and affiliations, and corresponding author with all contact information.
Abstract	A concise and factual abstract is required (maximum length 200 words).
Key Words	Immediately after the abstract, provide a list of keywords.
Length	The recommended length for a paper is 5,000–8,000 words, plus illustrations; the preferred length for reviews and conference reports is 2,500 words.
Margins	Wide.
Spacing	Double-spaced.

STYLE

Name of Guide	Journal provides "Guide for Authors" on the website. Name of style guide is not specified; however, format can be found in the "Guide for Authors."
Subheadings	Follow "Guide for Authors."
References	Follow "Guide for Authors."
Footnotes	Footnotes should be used sparingly.
Tables or Figures	Follow "Guide for Authors."

REVIEW PROCESS

Type of Review	Blind peer review.
Queries	Encouraged for prospective authors or those with ideas for special issues.

Acknowledgment	Through the online submission system.
Review Time	Not specified.
Revisions	Managed through the online submission system.
Acceptance Rate	Not specified.
Return of Manuscript	Not returned.
Lag Time to Print	Not specified.

REPRINT, SUBSCRIPTION, AND CONTACT INFORMATION

Reprint Policy	The corresponding author, at no cost, will be provided with a PDF file of the article via e-mail. The PDF file is a watermarked version of the published article and includes a cover sheet with the journal cover image and a disclaimer outlining the terms and conditions of use. Additional paper offprints can be ordered by the authors. An order form with prices will be sent to the corresponding author.
Book Reviews	Suggestions for books and book reviewers are encouraged.
Subscriptions	Available online through: http://www.elsevier.com/wps/find/journaldescription.authors/593/bibliographic.
Affiliation	Not specified.
E-Mail Address	Editor: jamorell@jamorell.com
Website	http://www.elsevier.com/wps/find/journaldescription.authors/593/description

FAMILIES IN SOCIETY: THE JOURNAL OF CONTEMPORARY SOCIAL SERVICES

Current Title	*Families in Society: The Journal of Contemporary Social Services (Print ISSN: 1044-3894). Families in Society Online (Electronic ISSN: 1945-1350).*
Previous Title	*Families in Society: Journal of Contemporary Human Services; Social Casework: The Journal of Contemporary Social Work.*
Editorial Focus	Articles, essays, commentaries, and research- and field-briefs on the art, science, and practice of social work. Topics include practice-related analysis, discussions, and research; agency-based practice; and public and social policy issues.
Audience	Fields include social work, sociology, psychology/psychiatry, and health sciences. Readers include social service professionals in direct practice as well as associates in management, supervision, policy and planning, and education and research.
Special Themes	Direct-practice implications of and applicable recommendations from social work research.
Where Indexed/ Abstracted	Alcohol and Alcohol Science Problems Database (ETOH); Book Review Index; Chicago Psychoanalytic Literature Index; Current Contents; Expanded Academic Index; Hospital Literature Index; Inventory of Marriage and Family Literature; Psychological Abstracts; PsycINFO; Psychiatric Rehabilitation; Sage Family Studies Abstracts; Social Science Citation Index; Social Sciences Index; Social Work Abstracts; and CSA/Sociological Abstracts. In Europe, Applied Social Science Index and Abstracts (ASSIA); Studies on Women Abstracts; and Social Care Online.
Year Established	1920. [The Family (1920–1946), The Journal of Social Casework (1947–1949), Social Casework (1950–1989), and Families in Society (1990 to present)].
Circulation	2,100 (Primarily institution and agency circulation with 20,000-plus readership based on a pass-along average of at least seven readers per issue).
Frequency	Quarterly.
Months Issued	February, April, August, October. Electronic: ongoing.
No. of Articles per Issue	13–16 (print).

SUBMISSIONS

Postal Mailing Address	Families in Society, 11700 West Lake Park Drive, Milwaukee, WI 53224-3099.
Method for Submission	Surface mail, e-mail, electronic form via website.
Number of Copies	Electronic with 2 print copies. Signed publisher agreement required at time of submission.
Disk Submission	No.
Online or E-mail Submission Allowed or Required	Send e-mail to Manuscripts@FamiliesInSociety.org with original and all revisions as MS Word attachments. For most recent instructions, visit www.FamiliesInSociety.org/Writing.

FORMAT OF MANUSCRIPT

Cover Sheet	Indicate the corresponding author with contact information (including an e-mail address) along with the name, position title, and the affiliation of each co-author.
Abstract	120 words.
Key Words	2–3 words or phrases.
Length	The manuscript body must be 20 pages or less in length; the entire page count including abstract; body; references; and accompanying figures, tables, or appendices cannot exceed 28 pages.
Margins	1 inch on all sides.
Spacing	Double-spaced in 12-pt font.

STYLE

Name of Guide	*Publication Manual of the American Psychological Association.*
Subheadings	3 levels, as needed for clarity.
References	See style guide.
Footnotes	Discouraged; up to 5 footnotes if necessary and at journal discretion.
Tables or Figures	Not to exceed 5. Use tables in MS Word or Excel format; tables must be laid out using individual cells for all data. Figures must follow preparation according to section 3.80 in the *Publication Manual.*

REVIEW PROCESS

Type of Review	Double-blind peer review. 2 to 3 reviewers contribute per manuscript.
Queries	Yes, send e-mail to Editor@FamiliesInSociety.org.

Acknowledgment   E-mail sent with manuscript tracking number (to be used with all correspondence).

Review Time   Approximately 3–4 months. Certain manuscripts with complex data or atypical topics may require a review period longer than 4 months. Additionally, at some time periods during the year, such as before or after holidays and academic breaks, it may take longer than usual to secure qualified reviewers.

Revisions   Revised manuscripts should be resubmitted in both electronic and hard copy formats. (See "Submission" section above.) Include a separate document outlining the changes made from original manuscript. Final disposition within 1 month after the resubmission date; deadline of 4 months for revised manuscripts to be resubmitted after the initial disposition.

Acceptance Rate   Approximately 28%.

Return of Manuscript   No.

Lag Time to Print   Approximately 11–15 months. Manuscripts are not strictly scheduled for publication in the order in which they are accepted. Instead, the editor selects manuscripts based on focus or topic, and a desired editorial balance within an issue.

CHARGES TO AUTHOR

Author Alterations $15 per galley page having corrections; galley sent to author as a PDF file.

Page Charges   No.

Processing   No.

REPRINT, SUBSCRIPTION, AND CONTACT INFORMATION

Reprint Policy   Author(s) provided 2 print copies of the issue in which the article is published and a PDF of the electronic version.

Book Reviews   Invited only; send inquiry to Reviews@FamiliesInSociety.org. Publisher review/complimentary copies can be sent to editorial office.

Subscriptions   Print and electronic options available. Visit Web site (www.FamiliesInSociety.org/Subscriptions) or inquire at Subs@FamiliesInSociety.org.

Affiliation   Alliance for Children and Families (www.Alliance1.org) in association with Families International, Inc.

E-Mail Address   Manuscripts@FamiliesInSociety.org for all manuscript-related inquiries.

Website   http://www.FamiliesInSociety.org

FAMILY PRESERVATION JOURNAL

Current Title	*Family Preservation Journal*
Previous Title	N/A.
Editorial Focus	The Journal is devoted to presenting theoretical, research, and practice articles on family preservation and support, thereby assisting professionals to develop and implement the best possible programs.
Audience	Practitioners, administrators, researches, and educators.
Special Themes	Family preservation, unities, and practice.
Where Indexed/ Abstracted	Social Services Abstracts; Social Work Abstracts.
Year Established	1995.
Circulation	Not specified.
Frequency	Annual.
Months Issued	Not specified.
No. of Articles per Issue	Not specified.

SUBMISSIONS

Postal Mailing Address	Family Preservation Journal, Family Preservation Institute, School of Social Work, New Mexico State University, 1335 International Mall, Las Cruces, NM 88003-8001.
Method for Submission	Manuscripts should be mailed.
Number of Copies	3.
Disk Submission	One electronic copy acceptable.
Online or E-mail Submission Allowed or Required	No.

FORMAT OF MANUSCRIPT

Cover Sheet	The title page should list only the author's name, affiliation, address, and telephone number.
Abstract	An abstract of approximately 100 words should be submitted.
Key Words	Not specified.
Length	18–25 pages, excluding tables and figures.
Margins	1 inch on all sides.
Spacing	Double-spaced.

STYLE

Name of Guide	*Publication Manual of the American Psychological Association.*
Subheadings	See style guide.
References	See style guide.
Footnotes	See style guide.
Tables or Figures	See style guide.

REVIEW PROCESS

Type of Review	Peer reviewed.
Queries	Can be sent using same address as manuscript submission.
Acknowledgment	Yes.
Review Time	Approximately 1–3 months.
Revisions	Approximately 1 month.
Acceptance Rate	Approximately 20%.
Return of Manuscript	Not returned.
Lag Time to Print	Approximately 3–6 months.

REPRINT, SUBSCRIPTION, AND CONTACT INFORMATION

Reprint Policy	Request permission from publisher.
Book Reviews	By invitation.
Subscriptions	Through the publisher at: eddiebowerspub@aol.com or 800-747-2411.
Affiliation	Family Preservation Institute, New Mexico State University.
E-Mail Address	fpi@nmsu.edu
Website	http://fpi.nmsu.edu/?go=journal.html

FAMILY PROCESS

Current Title	*Family Process*
Previous Title	N/A.
Editorial Focus	*Family Process* is a multidisciplinary international journal that publishes clinical research, training, and theoretical contributions in the broad area of family therapy.
Audience	Family therapists, social workers, counselors, educators, researchers.
Special Themes	Family therapy theory and practice, multiculturalism, family therapy outcome research, systems theory.
Where Indexed/ Abstracted	AgeLine; Criminal Justice Abstracts; EBSCOhost; Family Studies Abstracts; MEDLINE; ProQuest; PsycINFO; Social Services Abstracts; Sociological Abstracts; Violence and Abuse Abstracts.
Year Established	1962.
Circulation	Not specified.
Frequency	Quarterly
Months Issued	March, June, September, December.
No. of Articles per Issue	8–10 per issue.

SUBMISSIONS

Postal Mailing Address	All correspondence will be through e-mail.
Method for Submission	All submissions are electronic. Authors should submit manuscripts to the Family Process submissions website (http://mc.manuscriptcentral.com/fp).
Number of Copies	Online submission only.
Disk Submission	Online submission only.
Online or E-mail Submission Allowed or Required	Online submission required

FORMAT OF MANUSCRIPT

Cover Sheet	A separate cover page should be used to provide identifying information about the authors.
Abstract	Abstract of 200–250 words should be provided.
Key Words	Not specified.
Length	Manuscripts should not exceed 6,000 words (including tables and references).
Margins	1 inch on all sides.
Spacing	Double-spaced.

STYLE

Name of Guide	*Publication Manual of the American Psychological Association.*
Subheadings	The journal uses a bi-column format; headings must be short. Within the text, three levels of headings are used.
References	See style guide.
Footnotes	See style guide.
Tables or Figures	Use a separate sheet of paper for each table.

REVIEW PROCESS

Type of Review	Blind peer review.
Queries	Query letters are discouraged.
Acknowledgment	Managed through the online submission system.
Review Time	Approximately 3–4 months.
Revisions	Managed through the online submission system.
Acceptance Rate	Approximately 25%.
Return of Manuscript	Not returned.
Lag Time to Print	Approximately 6–12 months.

REPRINT, SUBSCRIPTION, AND CONTACT INFORMATION

Reprint Policy	Not specified.
Book Reviews	None.
Subscriptions	Through the publisher's website at: http://www.wiley.com/bw/subs.asp?ref=0014-7370.
Affiliation	The Family Process Institute.
E-Mail Address	editor@FamilyProcess.org
Website	http://www.familyprocess.org/about.asp

FAMILY RELATIONS: INTERDISCIPLINARY JOURNAL OF APPLIED FAMILY STUDIES

Current Title	*Family Relations: Interdisciplinary Journal of Applied Family Studies*
Previous Title	N/A.
Editorial Focus	High-quality, scholarly research with a particular emphasis on relationships across the life cycle and the implications of the research for practitioners. Content areas within the broad field of family studies are open, but all submissions should have a strong theoretical/conceptual framework.
Audience	Scholars and practitioners interested in family life education, intervention, law, and policy.
Special Themes	An applied journal of family studies, *Family Relations* is mandatory reading for family scholars and all professionals who work with families, including family practitioners, educators, marriage and family therapists, researchers, and social policy specialists. The journal's content emphasizes family research with implications for intervention, education, and public policy, always publishing original, innovative, and interdisciplinary works with specific recommendations for practice.
Where Indexed/ Abstracted	Adolescent Mental Health Abstracts; Book Review Index; Child Development Abstracts; Current Index to Journals in Education; International Bibliography of Sociology; Inventory of Marriage and Family Literature; Psychological Abstracts; Sage Family Studies Abstracts; Social Sciences Citation Index.
Year Established	1951.
Circulation	5,000.
Frequency	5 per year.
Months Issued	January, April, July, October, December.
No. of Articles per Issue	Approximately 10–12.

SUBMISSIONS

Postal Mailing Address	Articles are submitted Electronically. Authors should feel free to contact the Editor: Ronald M. Sabatelli, Editor, Family Relations, University of Connecticut, Human Development and Family Studies, Box U-2058, Storrs, CT 06269-2058. E-mail address: Ronald.sabatelli@uconn.edu.
Method for Submission	Electronic form via Website.
Number of Copies	N/A.
Disk Submission	N/A.
Online or E-mail Submission Allowed or Required	Articles are submitted online and using the following website address: http://mc.manuscriptcentral.com/fr.

FORMAT OF MANUSCRIPT

Cover Sheet	Title followed by a starred footnote indicating any acknowledgment for grant or individual assistance and any previous presentations of the paper. Corresponding author with a double-starred footnote after his or her name indicating his or her contact information. Because articles are reviewed anonymously, only the title should appear on the first page of the manuscript proper. Titles should be a maximum of 15 words.
Abstract	For every article of 6 pages or longer, an abstract of no more than 75 words that introduces the topic, method of study, and implications or conclusions should precede the article. Double-space and underline.
Key Words	No more than 5 key words, underlined and in alphabetical order, to assist investigators who use computer retrieval systems to review literature.
Length	No longer than 30 pages, including references.
Margins	Lines of text should not exceed 6 inches in length, and margins should not be less than 1 inch all around. The right-hand margin should not be justified.
Spacing	Double-space the entire manuscript.

STYLE

Name of Guide	*Publication Manual of the American Psychological Association.*
Subheadings	Follow style guide.
References	Follow style guide.
Footnotes	Follow style guide.
Tables or Figures	Follow style guide.

REVIEW PROCESS

Type of Review	Blind, typically 3 reviewers.
Queries	Editor welcomes query letters.
Acknowledgment	Acknowledgement of the manuscript occurs immediately following online submission.
Review Time	Approximately 2 months.
Revisions	Within 60 days.
Acceptance Rate	Approximately 20%.
Return of Manuscript	Not returned.
Lag Time to Print	Approximately 6 months.

CHARGES TO AUTHOR

Author Alterations	Minimal changes allowed at proof stage.
Page Charges	Not indicated.
Processing	$15 processing fee; check payable to the National Council on Family Relations. Manuscripts submitted without fee will not be reviewed. No addition fee for manuscripts invited to be revised and resubmitted.

REPRINT, SUBSCRIPTION, AND CONTACT INFORMATION

Reprint Policy	Must order before publication. Purchase reprints in multiples of 100 (minimum).
Book Reviews	Book reviews are not routinely included in the journal.
Subscriptions	Contact National Council on Family Relations to subscribe. Individual $45 in US; $57 outside US; student $20 in US; $32 outside US; organizations $85 in US; $97 outside US.
Affiliation	National Council on Family Relations.
E-Mail Address	Ronald.sabatelli@uconn.edu
Website	www.ncfr.org

FEDERAL PROBATION: A JOURNAL OF PHILOSPHY AND PRACTICE

Current Title	*Federal Probation: A Journal of Philosophy and Practice*
Previous Title	N/A.
Editorial Focus	All aspects of corrections and criminal justice including community corrections, sentencing, and treatment.
Audience	Community corrections professionals at federal, state, and local levels; educators, researchers, students.
Special Themes	Yearly special issue on themes such as prisoner reentry, community corrections, risk assessment, evidence-based practices.
Where Indexed/ Abstracted	Westlaw.
Year Established	1937.
Circulation	7,000.
Frequency	3 times per year.
Months Issued	June, September, December.
No. of Articles per Issue	Approximately 8.

SUBMISSIONS

Postal Mailing Address	Editor, Federal Probation, Administrative Office of the U.S. Courts, Washington, DC 20544.
Method for Submission	Online or e-mail submission strongly recommended.
Number of Copies	N/A.
Disk Submission	No (they are damaged by mail-handling irradiation process).
Online or E-mail Submission Allowed or Required	Strongly recommended.

FORMAT OF MANUSCRIPT

Cover Sheet	Not specified.
Abstract	Not specified.
Key Words	Not specified.
Length	3,000–6,000 words.
Margins	1 inch all sides.
Spacing	Double-spaced.

STYLE

Name of Guide	*Publication Manual of the American Psychological Association.*
Subheadings	Not specified.
References	See style guide.
Footnotes	See style guide.
Tables or Figures	Tables and figures should be used sparingly.

REVIEW PROCESS

Type of Review	Review by editors, advisory board members.
Queries	Permitted.
Acknowledgment	On request by e-mail.
Review Time	Approximately 2–5 months.
Revisions	Minor or style edits made by editor; additions, clearing up ambiguity, citation issues directed to author.
Acceptance Rate	Approximately 40%.
Return of Manuscript	No.
Lag Time to Print	Approximately 4–6 months.

REPRINT, SUBSCRIPTION, AND CONTACT INFORMATION

Reprint Policy	Upon request, no charge, proper identification and credit for original publication required.
Book Reviews	Yes. Reviews assigned by editor, but unsolicited ones are accepted. E-mail to the Editor at Ellen_Fielding@ao.uscourts.gov.

Subscriptions	$16.50 yearly for US; $22.40 yearly foreign.
Affiliation	Published by The Administrative Office of the US Courts.
E-Mail Address	Ellen_Fielding@ao.uscourts.gov
Website	www.uscourts.gov

GENDER & SOCIETY

Current Title	*Gender & Society*
Previous Title	N/A.
Editorial Focus	*Gender & Society* focuses on the social and structural study of gender as a basic principle of the social order and as a primary social category. Emphasizing theory and research from micro- and macrostructural perspectives, the journal features original research, reviews, international perspectives, and book reviews from diverse social science disciplines, including anthropology, economics, history, political science, sociology and social psychology.
Audience	Social science disciplines.
Special Themes	Occasionally. For example, August 2009 is a special issue: Heteronormativity and Sexualities.
Where Indexed/ Abstracted	This is an extensive list; please see our website at http://www.sagepub.com/journalsProdAbsIdx.nav?prodId=Journal200793.
Year Established	1987.
Circulation	Please contact Sage Publications for this information.
Frequency	6 times per year.
Months Issued	February, April, June, August, October, December.
No. of Articles per Issue	5–6, plus book reviews.

SUBMISSIONS

Postal Mailing Address	204 Waters Hall, Manhattan, KS 66506 (However, contact via e-mail is preferred. The e-mail address is gendsoc@ksu.edu. Note, this changes when the journal transitions editors. Check the website for the most current information: http://gas.sagepub.com/.
Method for Submission	Electronic form via website.
Number of Copies	1.
Disk Submission	N/A.
Online or E-mail Submission Allowed or Required	Yes.

FORMAT OF MANUSCRIPT

Cover Sheet	Yes.
Abstract	150 words or less.
Key Words	Yes.
Length	8,500 word limit for manuscripts.
Margins	1 inch.
Spacing	Double-spaced.

STYLE

Name of Guide	*Chicago Manual of Style.*
Subheadings	See style guide at http://www.sagepub.com/upm-data/19433_Style_Guide.pdf or http://www.sagepub.com/journalsProdManSub.nav?prodId=Journal200793.
References	See style guide at http://www.sagepub.com/upm-data/19433_Style_Guide.pdf or http://www.sagepub.com/journalsProdManSub.nav?prodId=Journal200793.
Footnotes	See style guide at http://www.sagepub.com/upm-data/19433_Style_Guide.pdf or http://www.sagepub.com/journalsProdManSub.nav?prodId=Journal200793.
Tables or Figures	See style guide at http://www.sagepub.com/upm-data/19433_Style_Guide.pdf or http://www.sagepub.com/journalsProdManSub.nav?prodId=Journal200793.

REVIEW PROCESS

Type of Review	Anonymous review process.
Queries	Via e-mail at gendsoc@ksu.edu.
Acknowledgment	Permitted.
Review Time	Approximately 60–90 days for the initial review; there are usually 2 rounds of reviews.
Revisions	As needed, but generally 1 major and 1 minor revision permitted.
Acceptance Rate	Approximately 9%.
Return of Manuscript	Not specified.
Lag Time to Print	Approximately 4 months.

CHARGES TO AUTHOR

Author Alterations There is a fee for significant rewriting at the proof stage but no other fee for author alterations. Please see Sage Publications for more information.

Page Charges No other charges to the author.

Processing No other charges to the author.

REPRINT, SUBSCRIPTION, AND CONTACT INFORMATION

Reprint Policy Current information available at http://www.sagepub.com/journalsReprints.nav

Book Reviews Book Reviews: Books for review should be sent to Dr. Martha McCaughey, *Gender & Society* Book Review Editor, Women's Studies, Living Learning Center, Appalachian State University, Boone, NC 28608; gendsoc@appstate.edu. Please note that the journal does not accept or consider unsolicited book reviews but instead invites appropriate scholars to review books germane to the scope and mission of *Gender & Society*. This journal does not review text books.

Subscriptions Please see this information at http://www.sagepub.com/journalsProdDesc.nav?prodId= Journal200793. Free subscription to members of Sociologists for Women in Society (for more information, please see http://www.socwomen.org/).

Affiliation Sociologists for Women in Society (http://www.socwomen.org/).

E-Mail Address gendsoc@ksu.edu

Website http://gas.sagepub.com/

THE GERONTOLOGIST

Current Title	*The Gerontologist*
Previous Title	N/A.
Editorial Focus	*The Gerontologist* is a bimonthly journal of The Gerontological Society of America that provides a multidisciplinary perspective on human aging through the publication of research and analysis in gerontology, including social policy, program development, and service delivery. It reflects and informs the broad community of disciplines and professions involved in understanding the aging process and providing service to older people. Articles, including those in applied research, should report concepts and research findings, with implications for policy or practice. Contributions from social and psychological sciences, biomedical and health sciences, political science and public policy, economics, education, law, and the humanities are welcome. Brief descriptions of innovative practices and programs are appropriate in the Practice Concepts section.
Audience	Multidisciplinary.
Special Themes	Special issues twice a year.
Where Indexed/ Abstracted	Index Medicus; MEDLINE; PubMed; Current Contents; and Social Index.
Year Established	1961.
Circulation	Approximately 10,000.
Frequency	Bimonthly.
Months Issued	February, April, June, August, October, December.
No. of Articles per Issue	15.

SUBMISSIONS

Postal Mailing Address	Postal mailing address: Authors are strongly encouraged to submit all manuscripts online at http://mc.manuscriptcentral.com/tg.
Method for Submission	Electronic form via website.
Number of Copies	Prior to submission, corresponding authors should gather the following information: (a) complete contact information for themselves and each contributing author; at a minimum, this should include mailing address, e-mail address, and phone number; (b) a copy of the manuscript, in a Word-compatible format, including title page, key words, acknowledgments, abstract, text, and references. This journal requires authors to submit 2 versions of the article file, anonymous and non-anonymous. Please do not submit PDF versions of your manuscript submission materials. These files will be combined into a single PDF document for the double-blind peer review process.
Disk Submission	N/A.
Online or E-mail Submission Allowed or Required	Manuscripts should be submitted online at http://mc.manuscriptcentral.com/tg.

FORMAT OF MANUSCRIPT

Cover Sheet	A cover letter (optional) may be included explaining how the manuscript is innovative, provocative, timely, and of interest to a broad audience, and other information authors wish to share with editors. Note: The cover letter for manuscripts will not be shared with reviewers.
Abstract	On a separate page, each manuscript must include a brief abstract, double-spaced. Abstracts for Research Articles, Brief Reports, and Practice Concepts submissions should be approximately 200 words (the Web-based system will not accept an abstract of more than 250 words), and must include the following headings: Purpose of the study, Design and Methods, Results, and Implications. Forum manuscripts must also include an abstract of about 200 words, but the headings are not necessary.
Key Words	Authors should supply three to five key words that are NOT in the title. (Please avoid elders, older adults, or other words that would apply to all manuscripts submitted to The Gerontologist).
Length	Research Articles: Most articles present the results of original research. These manuscripts may be no longer than 6,000 words. The text is usually divided into sections with the headings: Introduction, Design and Methods, Results, and Discussion. Subheads may also be needed to clarify content. Qualitative manuscripts may be no longer than 7,000 words. Please refer to the following editorial for further information about qualitative submissions: Schoenberg, N. & McAuley, W. J. (2007).

Promoting qualitative research. The Gerontologist, 47(5), 576-577. The Forum: Timely scholarly review articles or well-documented arguments presenting a viewpoint on a topical issue are published in this section. Total length should be no more than 5,000 words. Practice Concepts: A Practice Concepts manuscript describes, in 4,000 words or fewer, an innovative practice amenable to replication. Authors must clearly specify the following information about the practice: (a) uniqueness or innovation, (b) theoretical or conceptual basis, (c) essential components or features, and (d) evidence that supports replication or suggests modifications. The article should be structured to highlight these points (the structure of a research article does not necessarily apply). An important goal is to provide enough information about the practice to allow its replication. Please refer to the following editorial for further information about Practice Concept submissions: Morrow-Howell, N. & Noelker L. (2006). Raising the Bar to Enhance the Research–Practice Link. The Gerontologist, 46, 315-316. Letters to the Editor: Letters related to content in recent issues are published as space permits. Letters should reference the original article (if applicable) and be no more than 900 words. Letters are subject to review, editing, and rebuttal. Guest Editorials: Upon occasion, the Editor-in-Chief will invite guest editorials. Unsolicited editorials are not accepted. Brief Reports: Emergent and provocative reports of research, especially discoveries requiring rapid publication and policy/practice-related conceptual frameworks with broad implications are examples of articles published in this section. Manuscripts should be no more than 2,500 words.

The Gerontologist does not publish obituaries, speeches, poems, announcements of programs, or new product information.

Margins	1 inch.
Spacing	Double-spaced, including references and tables. Number pages consecutively for the abstract, text, references, tables, and figures (in this order).

STYLE

Name of Guide	*The Gerontologist* uses APA style. General guidelines follow; for more detailed information, consult the *Publication Manual of the American Psychological Association* .
Subheadings	APA style.
References	Refer to the *Publication Manual of the American Psychological Association* for style. References in text are shown by citing in parentheses the author's surname and the year of publication. Example: " . . . a recent study (Jones, 1987) has shown. . . . " If a reference has 2 authors, the citation includes the surnames of both authors each time the citation appears in the text. When a reference has more than 2 authors and fewer than 6 authors, cite all authors the first time the reference occurs. In subsequent citations, and for all citations having six or more authors, include only the surname of the first author followed by "et al." Multiple references cited at the same point in the text are in alphabetical order by author's surname. Reference list: Type double-spaced and arrange alphabetically by author's surname; do not number. The reference list includes only references cited in the text and in most cases should not exceed 50 entries. Do not include references to private communications or submitted work. Consult the *Publication Manual of the American Psychological Association* for correct form.
Footnotes	Place table footnotes immediately below the table, using superscript letters (a, b, c) as reference marks. Asterisks are used only for probability levels of tests of significance (*p < .05).
Tables or Figures	Tables are to be double-spaced, numbered consecutively with Arabic numbers, and have a brief title for each. Place table footnotes immediately below the table, using superscript letters (a, b, c) as reference marks. Asterisks are used only for probability levels of tests of significance (*p < .05). Please upload your figures either embedded in the word processing file or as separate high-resolution images in any of the following file formats: .jpg, .tif, .gif or .eps. For line drawings, the resolution should be 1200 dpi and for color and half-tone artwork, the resolution should be 300 dpi. For useful information on preparing figures, visit http://dx.sheridan.com, where you can also test whether your figures are suitable for production by using the Proflight tool at http://dx.sheridan.com/onl/.

REVIEW PROCESS

Type of Review	Double-blind peer review process.
Queries	Online.
Acknowledgment	Online.
Review Time	Approximately 17 days.
Revisions	Online.
Acceptance Rate	Approximately 16.17%.

Return of Manuscript	Online.
Lag Time to Print	Approximately 10 months.

CHARGES TO AUTHOR

Author Alterations	None.
Page Charges	None.
Processing	None.

REPRINT, SUBSCRIPTION, AND CONTACT INFORMATION

Reprint Policy	Reprints available; contact publisher for pricing.
Book Reviews	Book reviews are published in essay form. Reviews are prepared at the request of the Book Review Editor and are not guaranteed acceptance prior to submission. Unsolicited book review essays are not accepted.
Subscriptions	http://www.oxfordjournals.org/our_journals/geront/access_purchase/price_list.html.
Affiliation	The Gerontological Society of America.
E-Mail Address	http://gerontologist.oxfordjournals.org/cgi/feedback/
Website	http://gerontologist.oxfordjournals.org/

GLOBAL SOCIAL POLICY

Current Title	*Global Social Policy*
Previous Title	N/A.
Editorial Focus	*Global Social Policy* advances the understanding of the impact of globalization processes upon social policy and social development on the one hand, and the impact of social policy upon globalization processes on the other hand. The journal analyzes the contributions of a range of national and international actors, both governmental and nongovernmental, to global social policy and social development discourse and practice. *Global Social Policy* publishes scholarly policy-oriented articles and reports that focus on aspects of social policy and social and human development as broadly defined in the context of globalization, be it in contemporary or historical contexts. The editors welcome articles and contributions from a variety of disciplines, fields of study that address social issues, politics, and policies using a global and transnational analytical framework. The editors welcome articles and contributions from a wide range of theoretical and political perspectives.
	Global Social Policy is multidisciplinary, publishing work from all disciplines, including anthropology, economics, history, law, political science, and sociology. The journal also publishes work from a wide variety of fields of study including childhood studies, criminology, cultural studies, demography, development studies, education studies, 'race' and ethnicity studies, food studies, gender studies, health studies, housing studies, labor studies, labor market studies, international relations, international sociolegal studies, migration studies, public policy studies, political economy, refugee studies, regional studies, social gerontology, social security (protection) studies, social work, social policy, and urban studies.
Audience	The journal is designed to appeal to scholars in the disciplines and fields mentioned above, policymakers and professionals involved in government and international governmental organizations, members of NGOs and social movements, as well as international consultants in social development and social policy. It is important to stress that the journal serves both academic, policymaker and policy advocacy audiences.
Special Themes	Not specified.
Where Indexed/ Abstracted	Academic Search Premier; Cumulative Index to Nursing and Allied Health Literature CINAHL; EconLit; e-JEL; Family & Society Studies Worldwide; Family Index; Geo Abstracts: Human Geography; International Bibliography of the Social Sciences; International Political Science Abstracts; JEL on CD; Journal of Economic Literature; Journal of Social Work Practice; Sociological Abstracts; Worldwide Political Science Abstracts.
Year Established	2,000.
Circulation	Not specified.
Frequency	3 issues per year.
Months Issued	April, August, December.
No. of Articles per Issue	A minimum of 4 full-length research articles.

SUBMISSIONS

Postal Mailing Address	c/o Editorial Office, 2176 Lindsay Street, Regina, Saskatchewan, S4N 3B9 Canada.
Method for Submission	E-mail.
Number of Copies	1.
Disk Submission	Not required.
Online or E-mail Submission Allowed or Required	Yes, preferred.

FORMAT OF MANUSCRIPT

Cover Sheet	Full contact/affiliation details, title, and confirmation that manuscript is not currently being considered for publication elsewhere.
Abstract	Required.
Key Words	5 alphabetized key words.
Length	9,000 words as working maximum.
Margins	Not specified.
Spacing	Double-spaced.

STYLE

Name of Guide	Refer to publisher's website: http://www.sagepub.com/journalsPermissions.nav.
Subheadings	Refer to publisher's website: http://www.sagepub.com/journalsPermissions.nav.
References	Required; refer to website guidelines.
Footnotes	Endnotes, plain text.
Tables or Figures	Accepted, yet copyright permission remains author's responsibility.

REVIEW PROCESS

Type of Review	Double-blind peer review.
Queries	Address to Managing Editor at gsp@mcmaster.ca.
Acknowledgment	Not specified.
Review Time	Variable.
Revisions	Not specified.
Acceptance Rate	Not specified.
Return of Manuscript	Not returned.
Lag Time to Print	Varied.

REPRINT, SUBSCRIPTION, AND CONTACT INFORMATION

Reprint Policy	Refer to publisher's website: http://www.sagepub.com/journalsPermissions.nav.
Book Reviews	Refer to publisher's website: http://www.sagepub.com/journalsPermissions.nav.
Subscriptions	http://www.sagepub.com/journalsProdAbsIdx.nav?prodId=Journal200964.
Affiliation	McMaster University (Hamilton, Canada); Sage Publications, UK.
E-Mail Address	gsp@mcmaster.ca
Website	http://www.sagepub.com/journalsProdDesc.nav?prodId=Journal200964

GROUPWORK

Current Title	*Groupwork*
Previous Title	N/A.
Editorial Focus	Social Groupwork.
Audience	Social workers, health and education personnel, and academics interested in groupwork.
Special Themes	Special issues from time to time. Subjects including groupwork and older people, groupwork and management, groupwork and research.
Where Indexed/ Abstracted	Applied Social Sciences Index; Bibliographies Zeitschriftenliteratur aller Gebieten des Wissens; Social Care Update; Social Work Abstracts; Sociological Abstracts; and Studies on Women and Gender Abstracts.
Year Established	1988.
Circulation	Not specified.
Frequency	3 per year.
Months Issued	April, August, December.
No. of Articles per Issue	6–8.

SUBMISSIONS

Postal Mailing Address	c/o Whiting and Birch Ltd, 90 Dartmouth Road, London SE23 3HZ, England.
Method for Submission	E-mail.
Number of Copies	1.
Disk Submission	E-mail is preferred.
Online or E-mail Submission Allowed or Required	Preferred.

FORMAT OF MANUSCRIPT

Cover Sheet	Yes.
Abstract	Less than 200 words.
Key Words	Up to 8 words.
Length	2,500–6,000 words.
Margins	No requirement.
Spacing	Single or Double-spaced.

STYLE

Name of Guide	See notes for contributors in journal, or publisher's website for more detail. Refer to *American Psychological Association Publication Manual* for points of detail.
Subheadings	3 levels or less. Minimize capitalization.
References	Harvard.
Footnotes	Endnotes permitted only if absolutely essential.
Tables or Figures	See publisher's website (www.whitingbirch.net) for full details. Graphics for figures and charts must be supplied to at least 300 dpi in tiff or pdf format. Charts and figures must work in monochrome.

REVIEW PROCESS

Type of Review	Double anonymous.
Queries	Editors welcome queries.
Acknowledgment	By e-mail.
Review Time	Approximately 3 months.
Revisions	Material may be accepted subject to minor revisions; rejected; or more substantial revision required, in which case resubmission may be required.
Acceptance Rate	Approximately 40%.
Return of Manuscript	Not relevant, as submissions should be by e-mail.
Lag Time to Print	Approximately 12 months or less (target 1 year or less).

CHARGES TO AUTHOR

Author Alterations	US $10 per page for significant and foreseeable alterations.
Page Charges	None.
Processing	None.

REPRINT, SUBSCRIPTION, AND CONTACT INFORMATION

Reprint Policy	Two free copies of journal and a pdf file. Offprint's can be provided at cost for those who want them.
Book Reviews	Published.
Subscriptions	Whiting & Birch Ltd, 90 Dartmouth Road, London SE23 3HZ. www.whitingbirch.net. North America rates: US $250.00 for libraries, US $60.00 for individuals.
Affiliation	None.
E-Mail Address	enquiries@whitingbirch.net
Website	www.whitingbirch.net

HASTINGS CENTER REPORT

Current Title	*Hastings Center Report*
Previous Title	N/A.
Editorial Focus	Articles (general theoretical, analysis of particular topics, rarely reports of empirical research), reflective essays, and case studies (approximately 20% solicited, remainder unsolicited); letters to the editor, book reviews (solicited only), and "In Brief" news features.
Audience	Health care professionals, educators, academics (medicine, law, philosophy, social sciences), students (undergraduate, graduate/professional), libraries, interested lay readers.
Special Themes	Ethical issues in medicine and the life sciences, public policy relating to health care, environmental ethics (limited).
Where Indexed/ Abstracted	Current Contents; EBSCO; Information Access; Sociological Abstracts.
Year Established	1971.
Circulation	4,000.
Frequency	Bimonthly.
Months Issued	January, March, May, July, September, November.
No. of Articles per Issue	3–6 per issue, depending on the length.

SUBMISSIONS

Postal Mailing Address	Editor, The Hastings Center, 21 Malcolm Gordon Rd., Garrison, NY 10524.
Method for Submission	E-mail.
Number of Copies	3.
Disk Submission	Unnecessary for review purposes.
Online or E-mail Submission Allowed or Required	Not specified.

FORMAT OF MANUSCRIPT

Cover Sheet	Contact name, address, phone number and fax number.
Abstract	None.
Key Words	None.
Length	20–25 pages, including references (5,000–6,000 words for main text).
Margins	1 inch on all sides.
Spacing	Double-spaced.

STYLE

Name of Guide	*Chicago Manual of Style.*
Subheadings	Not specified.
References	See style guide.
Footnotes	Not accepted.
Tables or Figures	Prefer no tables or figures.

REVIEW PROCESS

Type of Review	Blind peer reviewed.
Queries	Potential contributors are encouraged to submit letters of inquiry or descriptions of possible articles.
Acknowledgment	By postcard on receipt of manuscript.
Review Time	Approximately 8–10 weeks.
Revisions	Not specified.
Acceptance Rate	Approximately 20%.
Return of Manuscript	Not returned.
Lag Time to Print	Varied.

REPRINT, SUBSCRIPTION, AND CONTACT INFORMATION

Reprint Policy	Center provides 2 bound copies of journal and 5 copies of tear sheets of article. Contributors may purchase reprints; information provided along with bound copies and tear sheets after publication.
Book Reviews	Solicited only.

Subscriptions	Membership Department, The Hastings Center, 255 Elm Road, Briarcliff Manor, NY 10510; (914) 762-8500 ext 234 or 235. $55 individuals, $70 institutions, $42 full-time students/seniors.
Affiliation	The Hastings Center.
E-Mail Address	Not specified.
Website	Not specified.

HEALING MINISTRY

Current Title	*Healing Ministry*
Previous Title	N/A.
Editorial Focus	*Healing Ministry* considers articles in fields related to the spiritual, administrative, and social aspects of health care ministering that are of value and interest to professional and lay people involved in healing ministry.
Audience	Professionals and lay people working in the healing ministry.
Special Themes	None.
Where Indexed/ Abstracted	Not specified.
Year Established	1995.
Circulation	Not specified.
Frequency	Quarterly.
Months Issued	Not specified.
No. of Articles per Issue	3–5 plus regular features.

SUBMISSIONS

Postal Mailing Address	Editor, *Healing Ministry*, 470 Boston Post Road, Weston, MA 02493.
Method for Submission	Electronic manuscript submission is preferred over regular mail. E-mail submissions should be sent to healingministry@pnpco.com.
Number of Copies	1 if submitted in hard copy.
Disk Submission	Required if paper submitted in hard copy.
Online or E-mail Submission Allowed or Required	E-mail submission preferred. Online submission not available.

FORMAT OF MANUSCRIPT

Cover Sheet	Article's title; author's full names; highest pertinent academic degrees; affiliations; current address of each author; the author handling all correspondence; telephone number; and if the manuscript was orally presented, the name of the organization, place, and date presented.
Abstract	Authors are asked to provide a 1-paragraph (125 words) abstract summarizing the main points of the article.
Key Words	A list of keywords is required.
Length	Approximately 12–15 pages.
Margins	Wide.
Spacing	Double-spaced.

STYLE

Name of Guide	*MLA Handbook.*
Subheadings	Insert at suitable intervals.
References	References should be cited in the text in numerically consecutive order.
Footnotes	No footnotes.
Tables or Figures	Tables may be included at the end of the manuscript file.

REVIEW PROCESS

Type of Review	Peer review by 2 reviewers.
Queries	The editorial staff is pleased to process and reply to any inquiries received, as well as to advise authors in the preparation of manuscripts.
Acknowledgment	All submissions are acknowledged.
Review Time	Efforts are made to review manuscripts within 60 days of receipt.
Revisions	*Healing Ministry* reserves the right to make editorial revisions prior to publication.
Acceptance Rate	Approximately 60%.
Return of Manuscript	Returned if not published.
Lag Time to Print	Approximately 3–8 months

REPRINT, SUBSCRIPTION, AND CONTACT INFORMATION

Reprint Policy	Available through the website at: http://www.alzheimersjournal.com/pn04000.html.
Book Reviews	Unsolicited reviews rarely used.
Subscriptions	Available by mail at: *Healing Ministry*, Attention Subscription Department, 470 Boston Post Road, Weston, MA 02493.
Affiliation	Not specified.
E-Mail Address	healingministry@pnpco.com
Website	http://www.alzheimersjournal.com/pn04000.html

HEALTH AFFAIRS

Current Title	*Health Affairs*
Previous Title	N/A.
Editorial Focus	*Health Affairs* is a multidisciplinary, peer-reviewed journal dedicated to the serious exploration of domestic and international health policy issues.
Audience	Policymakers, health services researchers, health care executives, students of health care administration, media.
Special Themes	Health insurance, Medicare, Medicaid, health spending, managed care, pharmaceutical industry, hospitals, consumers, global health, mental health care, health law, philanthropy.
Where Indexed/ Abstracted	Health Affairs is indexed and/or abstracted in EBSCO EJS; EBSCOhost; ISI's Current Contents/ Health Sciences and Behavioral Sciences; Lexis-Nexis; MEDLINE; ProQuest; Pubmed; SwetsWise Online Content.
Year Established	1981.
Circulation	10,000 domestic and international subscribers. Readership: 3 readers per issue copy (Beta Research Corp. independent survey) or 30,000 readers per printed copy.
Frequency	Number of issues per year is 6 with additional supplements. Online peer-reviewed papers of a timely nature are published weekly on average as Web Exclusives.
Months Issued	January, March, May, July, September, and November.
No. of Articles per Issue	20–25.

SUBMISSIONS

Postal Mailing Address	Susan Dentzer, *Health Affairs*, 7500 Old Georgetown Road, Suite 600, Bethesda, MD 20814.
Method for Submission	Electronic form via website.
Number of Copies	Online submission at http://mc.manuscriptcentral.com/ha.
Disk Submission	N/A.
Online or E-mail Submission Allowed or Required	Yes. Microsoft Word preferred.

FORMAT OF MANUSCRIPT

Cover Sheet	No cover sheet, but online submission forms require working title, name, affiliations, complete addresses and telephone numbers of all authors, whether the paper has been presented at a meeting, funding, and acknowledgements.
Abstract	100 words.
Key Words	Not required.
Length	2,500–5,000 words (including endnotes).
Margins	Not specified.
Spacing	Double-spaced.

STYLE

Name of Guide	*Chicago Manual of Style* (reference and endnote style is Vancouver style).
Subheadings	As needed to guide reader through the paper.
References	First and last name of author.
Footnotes	Endnotes only, Vancouver style.
Tables or Figures	Should be placed at the end of the manuscript, 1 exhibit per page. Authors must provide numerical data for all graphs, and sources for all data presented must be included in a footnote.

REVIEW PROCESS

Type of Review	Anonymous peer review; 2–3 peer reviewers, plus *Health Affairs* editors.
Queries	Queries are permitted, but full submission is preferred.
Acknowledgment	All papers are acknowledged by e-mail.
Review Time	Approximately 6 weeks to 4 months (time-sensitive papers are expedited).
Revisions	Via online processing system.
Acceptance Rate	Approximately 10%–15% (unsolicited manuscripts).
Return of Manuscript	N/A.
Lag Time to Print	Approximately 2 weeks to 6 months.

REPRINT, SUBSCRIPTION, AND CONTACT INFORMATION

Reprint Policy Our reprint policy can be found at http://www.healthaffairs.org/1340_reprints.php.

Book Reviews Send books to be reviewed to Sue Driesen, Senior Editor, *Health Affairs*, 7500 Old Georgetown Road, Suite 600, Bethesda, MD 20814. We consider unsolicited book reviews, but encourage authors to query first.

Subscriptions *Health Affairs*, P.O. Box 148, Congers, NY 10920; phone: 800-765-7514, fax: 914-267-3479. 1997 1-year prices (US and Canada): $79 individuals, $129 institutions.

Affiliation Health Affairs is published by Project HOPE.

E-Mail Address dmetz@projecthope.org

Website http://www.projecthope.org

HEALTH & SOCIAL WORK

Current Title	*Health & Social Work*
Previous Title	
Editorial Focus	*Health & Social Work* is a professional journal committed to improving social work practice and expanding knowledge in health care. Health is defined broadly to include both physical and mental health. The editorial board welcomes manuscripts on all aspects of health that are of professional concern to social workers. The journal carries articles on practice, social policy and planning, legislative issues, innovations in health care, and research.
Audience	Health care practitioners including social workers and other professionals, researchers, students, libraries, organizations.
Special Themes:	
Where Indexed/ Abstracted	Applied Social Sciences Index and Abstracts; Abstracts in Anthropology; AgeLine; Current Abstracts; EBSCOhost; Education Research Index; ERIC; Family & Society Studies Worldwide; Family Index; Health & Safety Science Abstracts; MEDLINE; ProQuest; PsycINFO; Risk Abstracts; SCOPUS; Social Services Abstracts; Social Work Abstracts; Sociological Abstracts; Studies on Women and Gender Abstracts.
Year Established	1976
Circulation	Not specified.
Frequency	Quarterly.
Months Issued	February, May, August, November.
No. of Articles per Issue	Generally 8.

SUBMISSIONS

Postal Mailing Address	*Health & Social Work,* NASW Press, 750 First Street NE, Suite 700, Washington, DC 20002-4241
Method for Submission	All submissions must be made by postal mail.
Number of Copies	5 copies should be sent.
Disk Submission	Authors of accepted manuscripts are asked to submit a disk in Microsoft Word.
Online or E-mail Submission Allowed or Required	No electronic submission available at this time.

FORMAT OF MANUSCRIPT

Cover Sheet	The cover sheet should contain the following: full title of the article, complete author information, and date of submission.
Abstract	A journal abstract should be written as a single paragraph of between 150 and 200 words.
Key Words	An article should be accompanied by 3 to 5 key words, carefully selected on the basis of how well they describe its content.
Length	Manuscripts for full-length articles should not exceed 20 pages, including references and tables. Manuscripts exceeding 25 pages will be returned without review.
Margins	1 inch on all sides.
Spacing	Double-spaced.

STYLE

Name of Guide	*Publication Manual of the American Psychological Association.* See also *NASW Press Author Guidelines* on the website at http://www.naswpress.org/authors/guidelines/00-contents.html.
Subheadings	See style guide.
References	See style guide.
Footnotes	See style guide.
Tables or Figures	See style guide.

REVIEW PROCESS

Type of Review	The entire review process is anonymous. At least 3 reviewers critique each manuscript; then the editor-in-chief makes a decision, taking those reviews into consideration.
Queries	Query letters are discouraged; authors are encouraged to read the journal and *Writing for the NASW Press* to determine whether their subject matter would be appropriate.

Acknowledgment	The NASW Press sends a letter on receipt of manuscripts.
Review Time	3-4 months.
Revisions	Per editor instruction.
Acceptance Rate	Not specified.
Return of Manuscript	Not returned. Author should retain a copy.
Lag Time to Print	Approximately 6 months to 1 year.

REPRINT, SUBSCRIPTION, AND CONTACT INFORMATION

Reprint Policy	All authors receive 5 complimentary copies of the issue in which the article appears. Authors receive a reprint order form to purchase additional reprinted copies.
Book Reviews	By invitation only; send book for review to: Book Review Editor, *Health & Social Work,* NASW Press, 750 First Street NE, Suite 700, Washington, DC 20002-4241.
Subscriptions	Available online through www.naswpressonline.org.
Affiliation	National Association of Social Workers.
E-Mail Address	press@naswdc.org
Website	www.naswpress.org.

HEALTH CARE FINANCING REVIEW

Current Title	*Health Care Financing Review*
Previous Title	N/A.
Editorial Focus	The *Review* seeks to contribute to an improved understanding of the Medicare and Medicaid Programs and the U.S. health care system by presenting information and analyses on a broad range of health care financing and delivery issues.
Audience	Health care policymakers, planners, administrators, insurers, researchers, and health care providers.
Special Themes	Managed care, vulnerable populations, rural health, health care reform, quality of care.
Where Indexed/ Abstracted	Abstracts in Social Gerontology; AgeLine; EBSCOhost; Family Index; MEDLINE; ProQuest; PsycINFO; Social Work Abstracts; U.S. Government Periodicals Index.
Year Established	1979.
Circulation	Not specified.
Frequency	Quarterly.
Months Issued	Seasonally: spring, summer, fall, winter.
No. of Articles per Issue	8–12 per issue

SUBMISSIONS

Postal Mailing Address	*Health Care Financing Review,* 7500 Security Boulevard, C3-24-07, Baltimore, MD 21244-1850.
Method for Submission	All manuscripts should be submitted electronically by the submission date to: HCFR_Submissions@cms.hhs.gov. You may obtain a copy of "Information for Authors and Electronic Submission Guidelines" at www.cms.hhs.gov/HealthCareFinancingReview/.
Number of Copies	Electronic submission; no hard copies required.
Disk Submission	Disk submission not required.
Online or E-mail Submission Allowed or Required	E-mail submissions accepted at HCFR_Submissions@cms.hhs.gov. Online submission not available.

FORMAT OF MANUSCRIPT

Cover Sheet	The cover page must include the title of the manuscript (10 words or less); names, formal titles, academic degrees, affiliations; complete addresses (including e-mail), and telephone/FAX numbers of all authors, date of submission; and word count including footnotes.
Abstract	Include a 100-word abstract acquainting the prospective reader with the essence of the text.
Key Words	None.
Length	Word count should be 5,000 or less, excluding references, tables, and figures.
Margins	1 inch margin on all sides.
Spacing	Double-spaced.

STYLE

Name of Guide	*U.S. Government Printing Office Style Manual.*
Subheadings	3 levels.
References	References must be limited to 30 or fewer.
Footnotes	Footnotes must be cited in the text with a superscript number and must be numbered sequentially throughout the manuscript.
Tables or Figures	Place all tables and figures (10 maximum in combination) at the end of the article. Each table must be on a separate sheet and specifically cited within the text.

REVIEW PROCESS

Type of Review	All manuscripts are acknowledged upon receipt and are submitted for discussion to the *Review* Committee for their policy relevancy and/or implications to the health care financing field. Manuscripts of interest are referred to subject-matter experts for peer review.
Queries	For questions regarding journal content, general information about editorial policy, and to inquire about the status of a manuscript under review, please contact linda.wolf@cms.hhs.gov.
Acknowledgment	All manuscripts are acknowledged upon receipt.
Review Time	Not specified.

Revisions   Manuscripts under consideration for publication are subject to the peer reviewer's critiques, and authors will be required to make revisions based on those comments or delineate in a cover letter why specific comments have not be addressed.

Acceptance Rate   Not specified.

Return of Manuscript   Rejected manuscripts will be returned to the author; the *Review* accepts no responsibility for lost manuscripts.

Lag Time to Print   Approximately 6–12 months.

REPRINT, SUBSCRIPTION, AND CONTACT INFORMATION

Reprint Policy   Once the manuscript has been published, the lead author will receive a printed copy and an electronic file for reprint requests.

Book Reviews   Not specified.

Subscriptions   Available online at: http://bookstore.gpo.gov.

Affiliation   Centers for Medicare & Medicaid Services (CMS).

E-Mail Address   linda.wolf@cms.hhs.gov

Website   http://www.cms.hhs.gov/HealthCareFinancingReview/01_Overview.asp#TopOfPage

HEALTH PSYCHOLOGY

Current Title	*Health Psychology*
Previous Title	N/A.
Editorial Focus	*Health Psychology* is a scholarly journal devoted to furthering an understanding of scientific relationships between behavioral principles on the one hand and physical health and illness on the other. The major type of paper being solicited for Health Psychology is the report of empirical research. Such papers should have significant theoretical or practical import for an understanding of relationships between behavior and physical health. Integrative papers that address themselves to a broad constituency are particularly welcome.
Audience	The readership has a broad range of backgrounds, interests, and specializations, often interdisciplinary in nature.
Special Themes	Not specified.
Where Indexed/ Abstracted	Addiction Abstracts; AgeLine; EBSCOhost; Education Research Abstracts Online; Health and Safety Science Abstracts; MEDLINE; Multicultural Education Abstracts (print); PsycINFO; Social Work Abstracts; Studies on Women and Gender Abstracts.
Year Established	1982.
Circulation	Not specified.
Frequency	Bimonthly.
Months Issued	January, March, May, July, September, November.
No. of Articles per Issue	Not specified.

SUBMISSIONS

Postal Mailing Address	Robert M. Kaplan, Editor, Department of Health Services, UCLA School of Public Health, 650 Charles E. Young Drive, Room 31-293C, Los Angeles, CA 90095-1772.
Method for Submission	Online submission at: http://www.jbo.com/jbo3/submissions/dsp_jbo.cfm?journal_code=hea.
Number of Copies	Single online submission.
Disk Submission	Not required.
Online or E-mail Submission Allowed or Required	Online submission required.

FORMAT OF MANUSCRIPT

Cover Sheet	Refer to Instructions for Authors on the website.
Abstract	All manuscripts must include an abstract containing a maximum of 250 words typed on a separate page.
Key Words	Please supply up to 5 keywords or brief phrases.
Length	Manuscripts should not exceed 30 pages (including references, notes, tables, captions, and figures).
Margins	See style guide.
Spacing	Double-spaced.

STYLE

Name of Guide	*Publication Manual of the American Psychological Association.*
Subheadings	See style guide.
References	See style guide.
Footnotes	Please avoid footnotes when possible.
Tables or Figures	See style guide.

REVIEW PROCESS

Type of Review	All submissions receive masked review unless requested by the author. Include this request in the submission letter.
Queries	General correspondence may be directed to the Editor's Office at: jmMcBride@ph.ucla.edu.
Acknowledgment	Acknowledgement through online system.
Review Time	Not specified.
Revisions	Editor will notify author if revision is necessary.
Acceptance Rate	Not specified.

| Return of Manuscript | Authors are encouraged to keep a copy of the manuscript to guard against loss. Manuscripts not usually returned. |
| Lag Time to Print | Not specified. |

REPRINT, SUBSCRIPTION, AND CONTACT INFORMATION

Reprint Policy	Not specified.
Book Reviews	None.
Subscriptions	May be obtained online from: http://www.apa.org/journals/hea/pricing.html.
Affiliation	Published by the American Psychological Association.
E-Mail Address	jmMcBride@ph.ucla.edu
Website	http://www.apa.org

HOME HEALTH CARE SERVICES QUARTERLY

Current Title	*Home Health Care Services Quarterly.*
Previous Title	N/A.
Editorial Focus	Important research on the cutting edge of home care and alternatives to long-term institutional care for elderly, disabled, and other population groups that use in-home health care services. Aimed toward service providers and health care specialists involved with health care financing, evaluation of services, organization of services, and public policy issues. New insights into delivery and management of home health care related community services.
Audience	Audience: Service providers, health care specialists, business people, professors, researchers.
Special Themes	Not specified.
Where Indexed/ Abstracted	Abstracted/indexed in Academic Search Premier, British Library Inside: Cambridge Scientific Abstracts; CINAHL; Elsevier SCOPUS; Family & Society Studies Worldwide; MEDLINE; PsycINFO; PSYCLINE; PubMed; Social Services Abstracts; Social Work Abstracts; Thompson Scientific.
Year Established	1981.
Circulation	Less than 1,000.
Frequency	Quarterly.
Months Issued	February, May, August, November.
No. of Articles per Issue	Not specified.

SUBMISSIONS

Postal Mailing Address	Maria P. Aranda, PhD, LCSW, Associate Professor, Editor, School of Social Work, University of Southern California, 699 West 34th Street, Los Angeles, CA, 90089.
Method for Submission	E-mail and electronic form via Website.
Number of Copies	2 (one to Maria P. Aranda, PhD, Editor, School of Social Work, University of Southern California, at aranda@usc.edu. Additional copy should be send to Anschion Maiden, Coordinator, at amaiden@usc.edu.
Disk Submission	If electronic submission cannot be done.
Online or E-mail Submission Allowed or Required	Preferred.

FORMAT OF MANUSCRIPT

Cover Sheet	Title page to include complete authors name(s); affiliations; mailing address; and phone, fax and e-mail information (for multiple author papers, provide complete information for each author and indicate the corresponding author). Authors should also supply a shortened version of the title suitable for the running head, not exceeding 50 character spaces.
Abstract	100 words on a separate sheet of paper.
Key Words	3–10 keywords below the abstract.
Length	20 pages (Lengthier manuscripts may be considered, but only at the discretion of the editor).
Margins	1 inch margin on all sides.
Spacing	Double-spaced.

STYLE

Name of Guide	*Publication Manual of the American Psychological Association.*
Subheadings	As needed.
References	Should be double-spaced, placed in alphabetical order, and listed on separate pages following the text.
Footnotes	The use of footnotes is discouraged
Tables or Figures	Tables and figures should not be embedded in the text but should be included on separate sheets or files. A short descriptive title should appear above each table with a clear legend and any foot-notes suitably identified below. All units must be included. Figures should be completely labeled, taking into account necessary size reduction. Figure legends should be typed, double-spaced, on a separate sheet.

REVIEW PROCESS

Type of Review	Blind review by at least 2 reviewers as well as the editor.
Queries	Not specified.

Acknowledgment	By letter or e-mail on receipt of manuscript.
Review Time	Approximately 4–6 weeks.
Revisions	Submit 4 copies with a separate cover sheet (not identifying the author) describing the changes made in the manuscript and replying to the reviewers' comments.
Acceptance Rate	Approximately 21%–30%.
Return of Manuscript	Manuscripts will not be returned.
Lag Time to Print	Approximately 4–6 months.

REPRINT, SUBSCRIPTION, AND CONTACT INFORMATION

Reprint Policy	The senior author will receive 2 copies of the journal issue and 10 complimentary reprints. The junior author will receive 2 copies of the journal issue. Reprints may be ordered.
Book Reviews	By invitation only.
Subscriptions	*Home Health Care Quarterly*, Taylor & Francis Group, LLC, 325 Chestnut Street, Suite 800, Philadelphia, PA 19106.
Affiliation	Not specified.
E-Mail Address	aranda@usc.edu, amaiden@usc.edu
Website	http://www.tandf.co.uk/journals/titles/01621424.asp

INTERNATIONAL JOURNAL OF AGING AND HUMAN DEVELOPMENT

Current Title	*International Journal of Aging and Human Development*
Previous Title	N/A.
Editorial Focus	Psychological, social, anthropological, and humanistic studies of aging and the aged; observations from other fields that illuminate the human side of gerontology, or use gerontological observations to illuminate problems in other fields.
Audience	Not specified.
Special Themes	Not specified.
Where Indexed/ Abstracted	Aged Care and Services Review; Applied Social Sciences Index & Abstracts; Bibliographical Index of Health Education Periodicals; Current Index to Journals in Education (CIJE); Excerpta Medica; Family Abstracts; PREY; Social Work Abstracts; Sociological Abstracts.
Year Established	1970.
Circulation	1,700.
Frequency	8 times per year.
Months Issued	Not specified.
No. of Articles per Issue	6.

SUBMISSIONS

Postal Mailing Address	Dr. Robert Kastenbaum, Department of Communications, Arizona State University, P.O. Box 871205, Tempe, AZ 85287-1205.
Method for Submission	Not specified.
Number of Copies	3.
Disk Submission	No.
Online or E-mail Submission Allowed or Required	Not specified.

FORMAT OF MANUSCRIPT

Cover Sheet	Not required.
Abstract	100–150 words.
Key Words	Not specified.
Length	22 pages, but depends on content.
Margins	Wide.
Spacing	Double-spaced.

STYLE

Name of Guide	*Publication Manual of the American Psychological Association.*
Subheadings	Yes.
References	Should relate only to material cited in text and be listed numerically according to appearance within text. Consult editor for more details on reference style.
Footnotes	Place at the bottom of page where referenced. Number using superscript Arabic numbers without parentheses or brackets. Footnotes should be brief, with an average length of 3 lines. Keep to a minimum.
Tables or Figures	Tables: Cite tables in text in numerical sequence. Give each a descriptive title. Superscript lower-case letters for footnotes to tables, if any. Type tables on separate pages and indicate their approximate placement in text. Figures: Number figure callouts in text in numerical sequence. Line art must be original drawings in black ink, proportionate to the journal's page size, and suitable for photographing. Indicate top and bottom of figure where confusion may exist. Label using 8-point type. Clearly identify all figures. Draw figures on separate pages and indicate their placement in text.

REVIEW PROCESS

Type of Review	Anonymous by a minimum of 2 reviewers.
Queries	Not specified.
Acknowledgment	Within 48 hours.
Review Time	Approximately 6–10 weeks.

Revisions	Authors receive detailed suggestions from reviewers. Manuscripts requiring minor revisions are reviewed again by editorial staff. Manuscripts with major revisions are re-read by reviewers.
Acceptance Rate	Approximately 20% after first submission, 30%–35% after revision.
Return of Manuscript	Include a self-addressed, stamped envelope when submitting manuscript.
Lag Time to Print	Approximately 12 months, but usually within 1 year.

REPRINT, SUBSCRIPTION, AND CONTACT INFORMATION

Reprint Policy	Authors receive 20 free reprints and an information form for ordering additional copies.
Book Reviews	Contact editor. Indicate areas of expertise and interests, and include a vita.
Subscriptions	Baywood Publishing Company, Inc., 26 Austin Avenue, P.O. Box 33, Amityville, NY 11701. Individuals $54; Institutions $135.
Affiliation	Not specified.
E-Mail Address	Not specified.
Website	Not specified.

INTERNATIONAL JOURNAL OF CULTURE AND MENTAL HEALTH

Current Title	*International Journal of Culture and Mental Health*
Previous Title	N/A.
Editorial Focus	*International Journal of Culture and Mental Health* provides an innovative forum, both international and multidisciplinary, for addressing cross-cultural issues and mental health. Culture as it comes to bear on mental health is a rapidly expanding area of inquiry and research within psychiatry and psychology, and other related fields such as social work, with important implications for practice in the global context. The journal will be divided into three main sections: (i) The first section will deal with invited review papers on a specific topic. These will be subject to peer review. (ii) The second section will deal with empirical research papers. These will be peer reviewed. (iii) There will be a miscellaneous section including book reviews and a single article presenting the "Current State of Psychiatry in . . . [a country]."
Audience	The journal is an essential resource for health care professionals working in the field of cross-cultural mental health, including psychiatrists, psychologists, medical anthropologists, medical sociologists, psychiatric nurses and social workers, general practitioners, and other mental health professionals interested in this area.
Special Themes	Cross-cultural psychiatry, cross-cultural psychology, medical anthropology, medical sociology, clinical psychiatry, mental health.
Where Indexed/ Abstracted	Cabell's Directory of Publishing Opportunities in Psychology and Psychiatry (3rd edition).
Year Established	2008.
Circulation	Not specified.
Frequency	Twice a year.
Months Issued	June and December.
No. of Articles per Issue	Approximately 5 plus book reviews.

SUBMISSIONS

Postal Mailing Address	E-mail submissions to dinesh.bhugra@iop.kcl.ac.uk. Books for review only to be sent to Professor Dinesh Bhugra, Institute of Psychiatry (KCL), De Crespigny Park, London, SE5 8AF, United Kingdom.
Method for Submission	E-mail.
Number of Copies	1 electronic copy.
Disk Submission	N/A.
Online or E-mail Submission Allowed or Required	Authors are encouraged to submit manuscripts electronically. Electronic submissions should be sent as e-mail attachments using a standard word processing program, such as Microsoft Word or PDF. Books for review should be sent to the Editor, Professor Dinesh Bhugra, Institute of Psychiatry (KCL), De Crespigny Park, London, SE5 8AF, United Kingdom.

FORMAT OF MANUSCRIPT

Cover Sheet	The first page should include the title of the paper; first name, middle initial(s), and last name of the author(s); for each author a short institutional address; and an abbreviated title (for running headlines within the article). At the bottom of the page give the full name and address (including telephone and fax numbers and e-mail address if possible) of the author to whom all correspondence (including proofs) should be sent.
Abstract	The second page should repeat the title and no more than 200 words.
Key Words	4–6 key words.
Length	Empirical articles, no longer than 4,000 words; Review papers, no longer than 6,000 words; Theoretical articles no longer than 5,000 words.
Margins	At least 2.5 cm (1 inch).
Spacing	Double spacing required throughout.

STYLE

Name of Guide	Please refer to the following website for the journal style guide: http://www.tandf.co.uk/journals/authors/style/layout/tf_1.pdf.
Subheadings	A. Bold initial cap only; B. Bold italic initial cap only; C. Italic initial cap only; D. Italic initial cap only. Text runs on.
References	Please use the *Publication Manual of the American Psychological Association* (APA) for points of detail: http://www.tandf.co.uk/journals/authors/style/reference/tf_A.pdf

Footnotes	Footnotes are not normally permitted, but endnotes may be used if necessary.
Tables or Figures	Tables should be laid out clearly and supplied on separate pages, with an indication within the text of their approximate location. Vertical lines should be omitted and horizontal lines limited to those indicating the top and bottom of the table, below column headings and above summed totals. Totals and percentages should be labeled clearly.

REVIEW PROCESS

Type of Review	Double anonymous peer review.
Queries	Please direct queries to dinesh.bhugra@iop.kcl.ac.uk.
Acknowledgment	Not specified.
Review Time	Not specified.
Revisions	Material may be accepted subject to minor or major revisions, rejected, or rejected with the option to resubmit.
Acceptance Rate	Not specified.
Return of Manuscript	N/A.
Lag Time to Print	Not specified.

REPRINT, SUBSCRIPTION, AND CONTACT INFORMATION

Reprint Policy	Corresponding authors can receive free online access to their article through our website (www.informaworld.com) and a complimentary copy of the issue containing their article. Additional reprints can be ordered through Rightslink when proofs are received or alternatively on our journals website. If you have any queries, please contact our reprints department at reprints@tandf.co.uk.
Book Reviews	Not specified.
Subscriptions	T&F Customer Services, Sheepen Place, Colchester, Essex, CO3 3LP, UK; Tel: +44 (0) 20 7017 5544; Fax: +44 (0) 20 7017 5198; E-mail: subscriptions@tandf.co.uk
Affiliation	Not specified.
E-Mail Address	Editor, Dinesh Bhugra: dinesh.bhugra@iop.kcl.ac.uk
Website	www.tandf.co.uk/journals

INTERNATIONAL JOURNAL OF MENTAL HEALTH

Current Title	*International Journal of Mental Health*
Previous Title	N/A.
Editorial Focus	The official journal of the World Association for Psychosocial Rehabilitation, the *International Journal of Mental Health* features in-depth articles on research, clinical practice, and the organization and delivery of mental health services around the world. Covering both developed and developing countries, it provides vital information on important new ideas and trends in community mental health, social psychiatry, psychiatric epidemiology, prevention, treatment, and psychosocial rehabilitation.
Audience	Mental health professionals, planners, and researchers.
Special Themes	There are 2–3 commissioned thematic issues by guest editors per year.
Where Indexed/ Abstracted	Applied Social Sciences Index and Abstracts; EMCare; Health Economic Evaluation Database (HEED); PsycINFO; SCOPUS.
Year Established	1970.
Circulation	1,200.
Frequency	Quarterly.
Months Issued	March, June, September, December.
No. of Articles per Issue	5–6.

SUBMISSIONS

Postal Mailing Address	IJMH, Dr. Martin Gittelman, M.E. Sharpe Publishing, 80 Business Park Drive, Armonk, NY 10504.
Method for Submission	E-mail.
Number of Copies	1.
Disk Submission	Prefer e-mail submission, but if a disk sent with 1 copy of the article, Word is requested.
Online or E-mail Submission Allowed or Required	Required. Please use Word and send attachment to Lynn Taylor at ltaylor@mesharpe.com.

FORMAT OF MANUSCRIPT

Cover Sheet	Article title, author name, affiliation and title, full mailing address and e-mail address.
Abstract	150 words.
Key Words	Maximum of 5 words.
Length	5,000–7,000 words included references.
Margins	N/A.
Spacing	Double-spaced.

STYLE

Name of Guide	Please e-mail Lynn Taylor at ltaylor@mesharpe.com for Contributor Guidelines.
Subheadings	Not specified.
References	Not specified.
Footnotes	Not specified.
Tables or Figures	Not specified.

REVIEW PROCESS

Type of Review	Anonymous review by 2 reviewers.
Queries	Not specified.
Acknowledgment	E-mail only
Review Time	Approximately 3–12 months.
Revisions	Not specified.
Acceptance Rate	Approximately 90% are invited; of the 10% remaining, 40% are accepted.
Return of Manuscript	No.
Lag Time to Print	After acceptance 3–9 months (depending upon the number of commissioned thematic issues scheduled for publication).

REPRINT, SUBSCRIPTION, AND CONTACT INFORMATION

Reprint Policy	Contributors can purchase reprints.
Book Reviews	Commissioned only.
Subscriptions	www.mesharpe.com
Affiliation	World Association for Psychosocial Rehabilitation.
E-Mail Address	ltaylor@mesharpe.com
Website	www.mesharpe.com

THE INTERNATIONAL JOURNAL OF PSYCHIATRY IN MEDICINE

Current Title	*International Journal of Psychiatry in Medicine*
Previous Title	N/A.
Editorial Focus	Limit submissions to biopsychosocial aspects of disease and patient care.
Audience	Researchers and clinicians in psychiatry.
Special Themes	The goal of the *International Journal of Psychiatry in Medicine* is to address the complex relationships among biological, psychological, social, religious, and cultural systems in patient care. The aim of the journal is to provide a forum where researchers and clinicians in psychiatry and primary care from around the world can educate each other and advance knowledge concerning biological, psychological, and social theory, methods, and treatment as they apply to patient care. Topics of interest include but are not limited to: psychobiological, psychological, social, religious, and cultural modifiers of illness; mental disorders seen and treated in outpatient practice; doctor–patient interactions; ethical issues in medicine; biomedical etiologies of mental symptoms; research from successful multidisciplinary collaborative models, and health services research.
Where Indexed/ Abstracted	Abstracts on Criminology and Penology; Adolescent Mental Health Abstracts; Annals of Behavioral Medicine; Biosciences Information Service of Biological Abstracts; Cambridge Scientific Abstracts; Clinical Medicine; Combined Health Information Database (CHID); Current Contents/Social and Behavioral Sciences; Current Science; DataTRAQ international, Inc.; Digest of Neurology and Psychiatry; EBSCO Publishing Database; Educational Administration Abstracts/EAA; EMBASE/Excerpta Medica; Index Medicus; Health and Psychosocial Instruments (HaPI); Human Resources Abstracts/HRA; International Review of Psychiatry; Medical Socioeconomic Research Sources; Mental Health Abstracts; Mental Health Book Review Index; Modern Medicine; Psychological Abstracts; Psychosocial Rehabilitation Journal; Sage Public Administration Abstracts/SPAA; Sage Urban Studies Abstracts/SUSA; Selected List of Tables of Contents of Psychiatric Periodicals and Social Science Citation Index; Social Work Research and Abstracts; Violence and Abuse Abstracts/VAA.
Year Established	1970.
Circulation	Not specified
Frequency	4 times per year.
Months Issued	Not specified
No. of Articles per Issue	Not specified.

SUBMISSIONS

Postal Mailing Address	Dana E. King, MD, MS, Editor, International Journal of Psychiatry in Medicine, Department of Family Medicine, Medical University of South Carolina, 295 Calhoun Street, Charleston, SC 29425.
Method for Submission	Surface mail, e-mail.
Number of Copies	5 copies if not by e-mail.
Disk Submission	Not specified.
Online or E-mail Submission Allowed or Required	E-mail preferred; paper allowed.

FORMAT OF MANUSCRIPT

Cover Sheet	The title page should have a title which is informative, declarative, and concise.
Abstract	Abstract should be a single paragraph no longer than 250 words, structured with headings: Objective, Method, Results, Conclusions.
Key Words	After abstract include 3–10 index words* and "(Int'l. J. Psychiatry in Medicine 200x; 30:000-000)". *(from MeSH list of *Index Medicus*).
Length	3,000 words.
Margins	1 inch.
Spacing	Double-spaced starting with title page.

STYLE

Name of Guide	Instructions are in accordance with the *Uniform Requirements for Manuscripts Submitted to Biomedical Journals: Writing and Editing for Biomedical Publication*, International Committee of Medical Journal Editors. www.icmje.org

Subheadings	Not specified.
References	References are to be cited in text in numerical order [1], with brackets [2]. References are to be listed in numerical order at the end of the article.
Footnotes	Footnotes are placed at the bottom of the page where referenced.
Tables or Figures	Tables must be cited in text in numbered sequence starting with Table 1 (even if only 1 table). Figures should be referenced in text and appear in numerical sequence starting with Figure 1 (even if only 1 figure).

REVIEW PROCESS

Type of Review	Authors may suggest 3 potential unbiased reviewers, but their use is not guaranteed.
Queries	Not specified.
Acknowledgment	Authors will be notified of the receipt of their paper and a number that has been assigned to it. This number should be included in all further correspondence. Reviewed manuscripts will not be returned except upon special request made in the original submission letter and if a self-addressed, postage-paid envelope is included.
Review Time	Not specified.
Revisions	Not specified.
Acceptance Rate	Not specified.
Return of Manuscript	Reviewed manuscripts will not be returned except upon special request made in the original submission letter and if a self-addressed, postage-paid envelope is included.
Lag Time to Print	Not specified.

REPRINT, SUBSCRIPTION, AND CONTACT INFORMATION

Reprint Policy	Authors will receive 20 complimentary reprints of their published article.
Book Reviews	No.
Subscriptions	Yes; see website: http://baywood.com/journals/PreviewJournals.asp?Id=0091-2174.
Affiliation	Not specified.
E-Mail Address	ijpm@musc.edu
Website	http://baywood.com/journals/PreviewJournals.asp?Id=0091-2174

INTERNATIONAL JOURNAL OF SEXUAL HEALTH

Current Title	*International Journal of Sexual Health*
Previous Title	*Journal of Psychology & Human Sexuality.*
Editorial Focus	As the official journal of the World Association for Sexual Health, *IJSH* promotes sexual health as a state of physical, emotional, mental, and social well-being through a positive approach to sexuality and sexual rights.
Audience	Academia.
Special Themes	Sexual health.
Where Indexed/ Abstracted	Academic Search Premier (EBSCO); Academic Source Premier (EBSCO); All-Russian Scientific and Technical Information Institute; Gender Watch CSA/ProQuest); Google Scholar; Health and Psychosocial Instruments (HaPI); Higher Education Abstracts; Index Copernicus; Psychological Abstracts/PsycINFO; Risk Abstracts (ProQuest CSA); Sociedad Iberoamericana de Informacion Cientifica (SIIC); Web of Science (Thomson Scientific).
Year Established	1988.
Circulation	500.
Frequency	Quarterly.
Months Issued	Varies.
No. of Articles per Issue	Varies.

SUBMISSIONS

Postal Mailing Address	E-mail only (see attached PDF for all other submission info).
Method for Submission	E-mail.
Number of Copies	1.
Disk Submission	E-mail only.
Online or E-mail Submission Allowed or Required	Required: e-mail only.

FORMAT OF MANUSCRIPT

Cover Sheet	Separation sheet, which does not go out for review. Full title, author names, degrees, professional titles; designation of one author as corresponding author with full address, phone numbers; e-mail address, and fax number; date of submission.
Abstract	Approximately 100 words.
Key Words	5 or 6 key words that identify article content.
Length	25 pages, including references and abstract. Lengthier manuscripts may be considered, but only at the discretion of the editor. Sometimes, lengthier manuscripts may be considered if they can be divided into sections for publication in successive issues.
Margins	1 inch on all sides.
Spacing	Double-spaced for all copy, except title page.

STYLE

Name of Guide	*Publication Manual of the American Psychological Association.*
Subheadings	Use as needed to guide the reader through the article. No more than 4 levels.
References	Author–date citation style; see style guide.
Footnotes	No footnotes preferred; incorporate into text.
Tables or Figures	Type tables double-spaced. Submit camera-ready art (300 dpi printer or better) for all figures. Place each table or figure on a separate, numbered page at the end of the manuscript.

REVIEW PROCESS

Type of Review	"Double-blind" anonymous peer review. 3 reviewers plus editor-in-chief read the manuscript in an anonymous review.
Queries	Authors are encouraged to read the journal to determine whether their subject would be appropriate.
Acknowledgment	Enclose a regular self-addressed, stamped envelope with submission.
Review Time	Approximately 3–4 months.
Revisions	See journal.
Acceptance Rate	Not specified.

Return of Manuscript   Only if 9" × 12" self-addressed, stamped envelope is enclosed.

Lag Time to Print   Approximately 6–12 months.

REPRINT, SUBSCRIPTION, AND CONTACT INFORMATION

Reprint Policy   All authors receive 2 complimentary copies of the issue in which the article appears. Authors receive a reprint order forms to purchase additional reprinted copies.

Book Reviews   Send to journal editor.

Subscriptions   The Haworth Press, Inc., 10 Alice Street, Binghamton, NY 13904-1580. Individuals $40; Institutions $120; Libraries $225.

Affiliation   Not specified.

E-Mail Address   Not specified.

Website   Not specified.

INTERNATIONAL JOURNAL OF SOCIAL WELFARE

Current Title	*International Journal of Social Welfare*
Previous Title	*Scandinavian Journal of Social Welfare.*
Editorial Focus	Comparative research and practice pertaining to welfare issues.
Audience	Worldwide.
Special Themes	Yes, special issues, mini-symposia and supplements.
Where Indexed/ Abstracted	PsycINFO; Research Alert; Social & Behavioural Sciences; Social Care Online; Social Sciences Citation Index; Social Services Abstracts.
Year Established	1991.
Circulation	Approximately 60,000 article downloads a year; access to approximately 6,000 libraries worldwide.
Frequency	Quarterly.
Months Issued	January, April, July, October.
No. of Articles per Issue	10–12.

SUBMISSIONS

Postal Mailing Address	SE-106 91 Stockholm Sweden.
Method for Submission	E-mail and electronic submission via the website.
Number of Copies	1.
Disk Submission	Possible for global south submissions.
Online or E-mail Submission Allowed or Required	Required.

FORMAT OF MANUSCRIPT

Cover Sheet	As separate file.
Abstract	Maximum 150 words.
Key Words	5–8 key words.
Length	Maximum approximately 6,000 words.
Margins	2.5 cm all round.
Spacing	Double-spaced.

STYLE

Name of Guide	*Publication Manual of the American Psychological Association.*
Subheadings	3
References	*Publication Manual of the American Psychological Association.*
Footnotes	Maximum 5–6.
Tables or Figures	Maximum 5–6.

REVIEW PROCESS

Type of Review	Anonymous peer review.
Queries	To be addressed to Editorial Office.
Acknowledgment	Allowed.
Review Time	Approximately 8–10 weeks.
Revisions	Allowed.
Acceptance Rate	Approximately 50%.
Return of Manuscript	No, but accessible through the online submission system.
Lag Time to Print	Approximately 12 months.

CHARGES TO AUTHOR

Author Alterations	For more than 10% changes.
Page Charges	None.
Processing	None.

REPRINT, SUBSCRIPTION, AND CONTACT INFORMATION

Reprint Policy	Author access through the Internet.
Book Reviews	Yes.

Subscriptions	Not specified.
Affiliation	None.
E-Mail Address	sven.hessle@socarb.su.se/noella.bickham@socarb.su.se
Website	socarb.su.se/IJSW

THE INTERNATIONAL JOURNAL OF VOLUNTEER ADMINISTRATION

Current Title	*The International Journal of Volunteer Administration*
Previous Title	*Journal of Volunteer Administration*
Editorial Focus	*The International Journal of Volunteer Administration* (*IJOVA*) seeks to publish original manuscripts that provide for an exchange of ideas and sharing of knowledge and insights about volunteerism and volunteer management and administration.
Audience	Professional volunteer administrators and other not-for-profit managers.
Special Themes	Not planned specifically; some occur spontaneously. The spring issue usually is devoted in its entirety to proceedings of the annual International Conference on Volunteer Administration sponsored by the Association for Volunteer Administration.
Where Indexed/ Abstracted	Hospital Literature Index; Human Resources Abstracts; Philanthropic Studies Index.
Year Established	1982.
Circulation	2,200.
Frequency	Quarterly.
Months Issued	January, April, July, October.
No. of Articles per Issue	Approximately 6.

SUBMISSIONS

Postal Mailing Address	Department of 4-H Youth Development and Family and Consumer Sciences, North Carolina State University, Campus Box 7606, Raleigh, NC 27695-7606.
Method for Submission	Submit manuscripts as Microsoft Word 5.0 for Windows or Word Perfect 5.2 or higher as an electronic file attachment via e-mail to the Editor at dale_safrit@ncsu.edu.
Number of Copies	Not specified.
Disk Submission	Not specified.
Online or E-mail Submission Allowed or Required	Dr. R. Dale Safrit, Professor, Editor-In-Chief, The *IJOVA*. E-mail: dale_safrit@ncsu.edu.

FORMAT OF MANUSCRIPT

Cover Sheet	The title page must contain each of the following for each author: full name and professional credentials, complete postal/mailing address, both telephone and fax contact numbers, e-mail address, the title page should contain (1) an abstract of no more than 250 words and (2) 3–5 key. words descriptive of the manuscript, which may be used to index and retrieve the manuscript electronically.
Abstract	Included in cover sheet not more than 250 words.
Key Words	Included in cover sheet = 3–5 words.
Length	Not specified.
Margins	1 inch.
Spacing	Double-spaced between sections.

STYLE

Name of Guide	*Publication Manual of the American Psychological Association.*
Subheadings	Not specified.
References	All in-text citations are included in the reference list; all references have in-text citations.
Footnotes	Not specified.
Tables or Figures	Figures are camera-ready and sent as electronic files; they appear exactly as they should in the finished article, except for sizing.

REVIEW PROCESS

Type of Review	Peer; Feature Article (reviewed by 3 external reviewers): Ideas That Work (reviewed by 1 reviewer): Tools of the Trade and Commentary (each reviewed by the Editor)
Queries	Not specified.
Acknowledgment	Not specified.
Review Time	Within 6 months of receipt.
Revisions	If a manuscript is returned for major revisions and the author(s) rewrite(s) the manuscript, the second submission will be entered into the regular review process as a new manuscript.

Acceptance Rate	Not specified.
Return of Manuscript	Not specified.
Lag Time to Print	Not specified.

REPRINT, SUBSCRIPTION, AND CONTACT INFORMATION

Reprint Policy	Not specified.
Book Reviews	Not specified.
Subscriptions	Not specified.
Affiliation	Department of 4-H Youth Development and Family & Consumer Sciences at North Carolina State University in Raleigh, NC, USA.
E-Mail Address	dale_safrit@ncsu.edu
Website	http://www.ijova.org/

INTERNATIONAL SOCIAL WORK

Current Title	*International Social Work*
Previous Title	N/A.
Editorial Focus	*International Social Work* is a scholarly refereed journal designed to extend knowledge and promote international exchange in the fields of social work, social welfare and community development. It is the official journal of the International Association of Schools of Social Work (IASSW), the International Council on Social Welfare (ICSW) and the International Federation of Social Workers (IFSW).
Audience	Academics, students, practitioners, managers and policy-makers in social work and related fields, as well as anyone concerned with the development of services in the social welfare sector.
Special Themes	The major focus of *International Social Work* is on the interaction between processes of globalization and the development of social welfare at national level, as well as social work and community development locally. It aims to examine the meaning of international social work in practice and theory, and to explore how those concerned with social work and community development can engage with international issues. In addition, the journal aims to promote dissemination of material from cross-national research.
Where Indexed/ Abstracted	Academic Search Elite; Academic Search Premier; AgeInfo; Applied Social Sciences Index & Abstracts (ASSIA); British Education Index; Business Source Corporate; Cab Abstracts; Caredata Abstracts and Information Bulletin; International Bibliography of Book Reviews of Scholarly Literature on the Humanities and Social Sciences; International Bibliography of Periodical Literature on the Humanities and Social Sciences; Cumulative Index to Nursing and Allied Health Literature CINAHL; Current Contents/Social and Behavioral Sciences; e-Psyche; Family Index; Health Source; IBZ: International Bibliography of Periodical Literature; International Bibliography of the Social Sciences; Journal of Social Work Practice; Middle East Abstracts & Index; New Literature on Old Age; Periodical Abstracts; Psychological Abstracts/PsycINFO; Research Alert; Science Direct Navigator; Social Sciences Citation Index; Social Sciences Index; Social SciSearch; Social Services Abstracts; Social Work Abstracts; SocINFO; Sociofile; Sociological Abstracts; Southeast Asia Abstracts & Index; Violence & Abuse Abstracts; Vocational Search.
Year Established	1957
Circulation	Approximately 2,000.
Frequency	6 issues per year.
Months Issued	January, March, May, July, September, November.
No. of Articles per Issue	7–8 full length articles plus Brief Notes articles, Regional Perspectives articles, News and Views from member organizations (see below), International Legal Notes, book reviews.

SUBMISSIONS

Postal Mailing Address	Karen Lyons, Editor in Chief, *International Social Work*. London Metropolitan University, Department of Applied Social Sciences, Ladbroke House, 62-66, Highbury Grove, London, N5 2AD, UK. (Please note that editorship will change in 2009, please consult journal website for updates on address details).
Method for Submission	E-mail.
Number of Copies	1.
Disk Submission	Not required.
Online or E-mail Submission Allowed or Required	E-mail submission required; moving to Sage Track in Autumn 2009.

FORMAT OF MANUSCRIPT

Cover Sheet	1 page with the name, position and contact details (postal address, telephone including international dialing code, and e-mail address) of the author(s).
Abstract	50 words (for full-length papers only).
Key Words	4–6 words (for full-length papers only).
Length	Up to 5,000 words including references for full length papers; up to 2,500 words (including references) for Brief Notes submissions.
Margins	3 cm on each side.
Spacing	Double-spaced.

STYLE

Name of Guide   Available inside journal cover (back) and on website: http://isw.sagepub.com/
Subheadings   Not specified.
References   Harvard style system: (Author, date) in the text and full references list at the end of the article.
Footnotes   Preferably as endnotes, used for explanations and comments rather than citations, and kept to a necessary minimum.
Tables or Figures   Camera ready; preferably provided in a separate file with indication of location in the article text.

REVIEW PROCESS

Type of Review   'Double-blind' peer review by 2–3 referees from an international panel.
Queries   Welcomed.
Acknowledgment   By e-mail, within 10 working days (from autumn 2009 automated via Sage Track).
Review Time   Approximately 3–4 months.
Revisions   Resubmission by e-mail upon invitation, with a letter indicating how reviewers' concerns and suggestions have been addressed.
Acceptance Rate   Approximately 50%.
Return of Manuscript   Not applicable (e-mail submission).
Lag Time to Print   Approximately 6–7 months on average.

REPRINT, SUBSCRIPTION, AND CONTACT INFORMATION

Reprint Policy   1 hard copy of printed issue per contributing author and access to PDF.
Book Reviews   Queries and reviews should be sent to: Silvia Fargion, Book Review Editor, International Social Work, Universita degli studi di Trento, Trento, P.zza Venezia, 41-38100 Trento, Italy (silvia.fargion@soc.unitn.it).
Subscriptions   See journal website: www.sagepub.com/journalsSubscribe.nav?prodId=Journal200781; individual subscription $109 (concessions for members of affiliated organizations, see below).
Affiliation   International Association of Schools of Social Work (IASSW), International Council on Social Welfare (ICSW), and International Federation of Social Workers (IFSW).
E-Mail Address   isw@londonmet.ac.uk (Please note that editorship will change in 2009, please consult journal website for updates on e-mail address details).
Website   http://isw.sagepub.com/

JOURNAL FOR SPECIALISTS IN GROUP WORK

Current Title	*Journal for Specialists in Group Work*
Previous Title	N/A.
Editorial Focus	The journal publishes articles in the following categories: Research, Practice, Training, Reflection, and Commentary.
Audience	The readers include counselors in all settings, psychologists, therapists, researchers, social workers, and university instructors.
Special Themes	All topics related to group work are welcomed.
Where Indexed/ Abstracted	ASSIA: Applied Social Sciences Index & Abstracts; CINAHL: Cumulative Index to Nursing and Allied Health Literature, CSA Risk Abstracts; CSA Social Services Abstracts; CSA Sociological Abstracts; CSA Worldwide Political Science Abstracts; EBSCO SocINDEX; ERIC Database/CIJE: Current Index to Journals in Education; Family Index Database; Higher Education Abstracts; NISC Family & Society Studies Worldwide Database; OCLC ArticleFirst; OCLC Electronic Collections Online; Psychological Abstracts/PsycINFO; Social Work Abstracts; and Windows Live Academic..
Year Established	Continuously since 1976.
Circulation	Approximately 2,100.
Frequency	Quarterly.
Months Issued	March, June, September, December.
No. of Articles per Issue	Approximately 5–6.

SUBMISSIONS

Postal Mailing Address	http://mc.manuscriptcentral.com/usgw
Method for Submission	All submissions are electronic via website. See URL above.
Number of Copies	All submissions are electronic via website. See URL above.
Disk Submission	No disks are requested. Documents should in Microsoft Word 2003. At present, Manuscript Central does not handle documents in Microsoft Word 2007.
Online or E-mail Submission Allowed or Required	Only. All submissions are electronic via website. See URL above.

FORMAT OF MANUSCRIPT

Cover Sheet	Title and running head only. Manuscripts are blind reviewed.
Abstract	Abstracts should be 100 words or less.
Key Words	3–5 keywords are required.
Length	Generally, manuscripts should be less than 35 double-spaced pages including reference list, tables, and figures. Longer manuscripts are considered if space is available.
Margins	1 inch on all sides.
Spacing	Double-spaced.

STYLE

Name of Guide	*Publication Manual of the American Psychological Association*
Subheadings	Authors discretion, adhere to style.
References	See style guide.
Footnotes	Only essential footnotes should be used, placed at the bottom of the page and numbered consecutively using Arabic numerals.
Tables or Figures	Illustrations submitted (line drawings, halftones, photos, photomicrographs, etc.) should be clean originals or digital files. Digital files are recommended for highest quality reproduction and should follow these guidelines: 300 dpi or higher; sized to fit on journal page; EPS, TIFF, or PSD format only; submitted as separate files; not embedded in text files.

REVIEW PROCESS

Type of Review	Manuscripts are blind peer-reviewed.
Queries	Queries are welcome if the information is not included in author guidelines.
Acknowledgment	Receipt of manuscript is acknowledged electronically.
Review Time	Average time to first decision is 66 days.

Revisions
If revisions are invited, instructions for submission via the journal's website are included in the decision letter.

Acceptance Rate
25%–30% of manuscripts are eventually accepted.

Return of Manuscript
N/A.

Lag Time to Print
Approximately 3–6 months.

CHARGES TO AUTHOR

Author Alterations
No charge for minor editorial corrections to proofs.

Page Charges
There are no page charges. Color Reproduction. Color illustrations will be considered for publication; however, the author will be required to bear the full cost involved in color art reproduction. Color art can be purchased for online only conversion and reproduction or for print and online reproduction. Color reprints can only be ordered if print and online reproduction costs are paid. Rates for color art reproduction are: Online-Only Reproduction: $225 for the first page of color; $100 per page for the next three pages of color. A maximum charge of $525 applies. Print and Online Reproduction. $900 for the first page of color; $450 per page for the next three pages of color. A custom quote will be provided for articles with more than 4 pages of color.

Processing
There are no processing charges.

REPRINT, SUBSCRIPTION, AND CONTACT INFORMATION

Reprint Policy
Authors receive complementary copies of the journal in which their article appears. Reprints can be purchased as well. Reprint information is available at http://www.informaworld.com/smpp/journals_reprints~db=all.

Book Reviews
No book reviews are published in this journal.

Subscriptions
Subscriptions are a benefit of membership in the Association for Specialists in Group Work. Individual print subscriptions are $94.00 per year. Subscription information is available at: http://www.informaworld.com/smpp/title~content=t713658627~tab=subscribe~db=all.

Affiliation
Association for Specialists in Group Work.

E-Mail Address
The editor can be contacted at sherib@u.arizona.edu.

Website
http://www.tandf.co.uk/journals/titles/01933922.asp

JOURNAL OF ABNORMAL PSYCHOLOGY

Current Title	*Journal of Abnormal Psychology*
Previous Title	*Journal of Abnormal and Social Psychology.*
Editorial Focus	Most of the articles published in *Journal of Abnormal Psychology* are reports of original research, but other types of articles are acceptable. Short Reports of replications or of failures to replicate previously reported results are given serious consideration; Comments on articles published in the journal are also considered, Case studies from either a clinical setting or a laboratory will be considered if they raise or illustrate important questions that go beyond the single case and have heuristic value. Manuscripts that present or discuss theoretical formulations of psychopathology, or that evaluate competing theoretical formulations on the basis of published data, may also be accepted.
	Journal of Abnormal Psychology publishes articles on basic research and theory in the broad field of abnormal behavior, its determinants, and its correlates.
	The following general topics fall within its area of major focus: psychopathology—its etiology, development, symptomatology, and course; normal processes in abnormal individuals; pathological or atypical features of the behavior of normal persons; experimental studies, with human or animal subjects, relating to disordered emotional behavior or pathology; sociocultural effects on pathological processes, including the influence of gender and ethnicity; and tests of hypotheses from psychological theories that relate to abnormal behavior. Thus, studies of patient populations, analyses of abnormal behavior and motivation in terms of modern behavior theories, case histories, and theoretical papers of scholarly substance on deviant personality and emotional abnormality would all fall within the boundaries of the journal's interests. Each article should represent an addition to knowledge and understanding of abnormal behavior in its etiology, description, or change. In order to improve the use of journal resources, it has been agreed by the two Editors concerned that *Journal of Abnormal Psychology* will not consider articles dealing with diagnosis or treatment of abnormal behavior, and *Journal of Consulting and Clinical Psychology* will not consider articles dealing with the etiology or descriptive pathology of abnormal behavior. Therefore, a study that focuses primarily on treatment efficacy should be submitted to *Journal of Consulting and Clinical Psychology.* However, a longitudinal study focusing on developmental influences or origins of abnormal behavior should be submitted to *Journal of Abnormal Psychology.* Articles will be published in five different sections of journal: Brief Reports, Regular Articles, Extended Articles, Case Studies, and Commentaries:
Audience	Researchers and practitioners in the discipline, faculty, libraries
Special Themes	*Journal of Abnormal Psychology* presents the best cutting-edge research and scholarly thought on abnormal psychology. The journal features articles about the nature of depression and other mood disorders, anxiety disorders, personality disorders, eating disorders, schizophrenia, addictive disorders, childhood disorders, somatoform disorders, and special states of consciousness, including hypnosis and sleep. Readers will find research in psychopathology, normal processes in abnormal individuals, and pathological or atypical features of the behavior of normal persons. Coverage includes cognitive, behavioral, biological, and psychodynamic perspectives.
Where Indexed/ Abstracted	Academic Index; Addiction Abstracts; Applied Social Science Index & Abstracts; Biological Abstracts; Criminal Justice Abstracts; Current Contents; Exceptional Child Education Resources; EMBASE/Excerpta Medica; Health Index; Index Medicus; Management Contents; PsycINFO; Sage Family Studies Abstracts; Social Sciences Citation Index; Social Sciences Index; Social Work Research & Abstracts; Studies on Women and Gender Abstracts.
Year Established	1906.
Circulation	Not specified.
Frequency	Quarterly.
Months Issued	February, May, August, November.
No. of Articles per Issue	18

SUBMISSIONS

Postal Mailing Address	http://www.jbo.com/jbo3/submissions/dsp_jbo.cfm?journal_code=ab2
Method for Submission	Electronic form via website.
Number of Copies	N/A.
Disk Submission	N/A.
Online or E-mail Submission Allowed or Required	Required.

FORMAT OF MANUSCRIPT

Cover Sheet Components of all cover letters will contain the following: the full postal and e-mail address of the corresponding author; the complete telephone and fax numbers of the same; the proposed category under which the manuscript was submitted; a request for masked review, if desired, along with a statement ensuring that the manuscript was prepared in accordance with the guidelines above. Authors should also specify the overall length of the manuscript (in words) and indicate the number of tables and figures that are included in the manuscript.

Abstract All manuscripts must include an abstract containing a maximum of 180 words typed on a separate page.

Key Words Please supply up to 5 keywords or brief phrases.

Length Brief Reports must not exceed 5,000 words in overall length. This limit includes all aspects of the manuscript (title page, abstract, text, references, tables, author notes and footnotes, appendices, figure captions) except figures. Brief Reports also may include a maximum of 2 figures. For Brief Reports, the length limits are exact and must be strictly followed. Regular Articles typically should not exceed 9,000 words in overall length (excluding figures). Extended Articles are published within regular issues of the journal (they are not free standing) and are reserved for manuscripts that require extended exposition beyond the normal length restrictions of a Regular Article. Typically, Extended Articles will report multiple experiments, multifaceted longitudinal studies, cross-disciplinary investigations, or studies that are extraordinarily complex in terms of methodology or analysis. Any submission that exceeds a total of 12,000 words in length automatically will be considered for publication as an Extended Article. Case Studies and Commentaries have the same length requirements as Brief Reports.

Margins *Publication Manual of the American Psychological Association* (APA, 5th edition or latest).

Spacing *Publication Manual of the American Psychological Association* (APA, 5th edition or latest).

STYLE

Name of Guide *Publication Manual of the American Psychological Association.*

Subheadings *Publication Manual of the American Psychological Association.*

References *Publication Manual of the American Psychological Association.*

Footnotes *Publication Manual of the American Psychological Association.*

Tables or Figures *Publication Manual of the American Psychological Association*; Graphics files are welcome if supplied as TIF, EPS, or PowerPoint files. The minimum line weight for line art is 0.5 point for optimal printing.

REVIEW PROCESS

Type of Review Masked review optional, by request of author.

Queries No query letters.

Acknowledgment By e-mail.

Review Time Approximately 60–90 days.

Revisions Editor will notify author if revision is desired (most manuscripts are initially rejected; most published manuscripts have gone through 1 or 2 revisions).

Acceptance Rate Approximately 19%.

Return of Manuscript N/A.

Lag Time to Print Approximately 6 months.

CHARGES TO AUTHOR

Author Alterations Authors are charged for alterations in excess of $25.

Page Charges None.

Processing None.

REPRINT, SUBSCRIPTION, AND CONTACT INFORMATION

Reprint Policy Authors may purchase reprints of their articles (order form accompanies proofs).

Book Reviews None.

Subscriptions http://www.apa.org/journals/abn/pricing.html

Affiliation Published by the American Psychological Association.

E-Mail Address Journals@apa.org

Website http://www.apa.org/journals/abn/

JOURNAL OF ADDICTIVE DISEASES

Current Title	*Journal of Addictive Disease*
Previous Title	*Advances in Alcohol and Substance Abuse.*
Editorial Focus	Epidemiological and clinical studies pertaining to chemical dependency as well as well-constructed reviews of same.
Audience	All health professionals in the field of chemical dependency.
Special Themes	Special issues are published based on editorial decision.
Where Indexed/ Abstracted	Over 30 services including Academic Abstracts; Addiction Abstracts; Current Contents; Excerpta Medica; Index Medicus/Medicine; Mental Health Abstracts; Sage Family Studies; Sage Urban Studies; Social Work Abstracts; Sociological Abstracts; Studies on Women and Gender Abstracts.
Year Established	1980.
Circulation	5,000.
Frequency	Quarterly.
Months Issued	March, June, September, December.
No. of Articles per Issue	5–7.

SUBMISSIONS

Postal Mailing Address	Barry Stimmer, MD, Editor, Dean, Graduate Medical Education, Mt. Sinai School of Medicine, 1 Gustave Levy Place, New York, NY 10029.
Method for Submission	Not specified.
Number of Copies	3.
Disk Submission	Yes.
Online or E-mail Submission Allowed or Required	Not specified.

FORMAT OF MANUSCRIPT

Cover Sheet	Not specified.
Abstract	Yes.
Key Words	Yes.
Length	15–20 pages.
Margins	1 inch on all sides.
Spacing	Double-spaced.

STYLE

Name of Guide	*Index Medicus.*
Subheadings	Not specified.
References	See style guide.
Footnotes	None.
Tables or Figures	Type tables double-spaced. Submit camera-ready art. Place each table or figure on a separate numbered page at end of manuscript.

REVIEW PROCESS

Type of Review	2 reviewers and the editor read all papers.
Queries	To editor.
Acknowledgment	Enclose a regular self-addressed, stamped envelope with submission.
Review Time	Approximately 3 months.
Revisions	3 copies with cover letter noting changes made.
Acceptance Rate	Approximately 30%.
Return of Manuscript	Not returned.
Lag Time to Print	Approximately 6–12 months.

REPRINT, SUBSCRIPTION, AND CONTACT INFORMATION

Reprint Policy	Reprint order forms sent.
Book Reviews	None.
Subscriptions	The Haworth Press, Inc., 10 Alice Street, Binghamton, NY 13904-1580. Individual $45;

Institutions $120; Libraries $275.

Affiliation The journal is sponsored by the American Society of Addiction Medicine.

E-Mail Address Not specified.

Website Not specified.

JOURNAL OF AGGRESSION, MALTREATMENT, AND TRAUMA (JAMT)

Current Title	*Journal of Aggression, Maltreatment, and Trauma (JAMT)*
Previous Title	N/A.
Editorial Focus	Research, treatment, and prevention programs surrounding aggression, maltreatment, and trauma. Experts in the field present findings on how to prevent these behaviors, how to help victims, and how to intervene in abusive or violent situations using the latest research in these areas.
Audience	Interdisciplinary professionals involved in any aspect of working with aggression, maltreatment, and trauma issues, victims, or offenders.
Special Themes	Varies.
Where Indexed/ Abstracted	CINAHL Database; Criminal Justice Abstracts; Family Index Database; National Criminal Justice Abstract Service; PILOTS Database; PsycINFO; SafetyLit; SOCIndex; Social Service Abstracts; Social Work Abstracts.
Year Established	1997.
Circulation	299.
Frequency	Eight issues per year.
Months Issued	Every 1–2 months.
No. of Articles per Issue	6–9.

SUBMISSIONS

Postal Mailing Address	*Journal of Aggression, Maltreatment, and Trauma*, Institute on Violence, Abuse, and Trauma. 10065 Old Grove Road, San Diego, CA 92131.
Method for Submission	E-mail.
Number of Copies	2 (1 original with identifying names, etc., and 1 copy without this information).
Disk Submission	Not required.
Online or E-mail Submission Allowed or Required	E-mail submission in MS Word, Works, or Excel format.

FORMAT OF MANUSCRIPT

Cover Sheet	Title; authors; brief biography of author's including degrees, positions, affiliations, and 1-sentence background; address for reprint requests.
Abstract	Required, no longer than 120 words.
Key Words	Required, 4–8 key words.
Length	No longer than 35 pages including references, abstract, and tables.
Margins	1 inch on all sides.
Spacing	Double-spaced.

STYLE

Name of Guide	*Publication Manual of the American Psychological Association;* instructions for authors available from publisher's website (Taylor & Francis).
Subheadings	See style guide.
References	See style guide.
Footnotes	Not suggested unless absolutely needed; see style guide.
Tables or Figures	See style guide.

REVIEW PROCESS

Type of Review	Anonymous review by editorial board or ad hoc reviewers.
Queries	Editor welcomes query letters, e-mails, or phone calls.
Acknowledgment	On receipt of manuscript, copyright form sent to corresponding author to sign original.
Review Time	Approximately 3–5 months.
Revisions	Feedback is given to authors for making revisions. *JAMT* encourages revisions and resubmissions, with a cover letter by the author explaining what has been done to address the concerns.
Acceptance Rate	Approximately 20%–25% initially; additional after revisions.
Return of Manuscript	If requested.
Lag Time to Print	Approximately 8–12 months.

CHARGES TO AUTHOR

Author Alterations | None if done ahead of time.
Page Charges | None.
Processing | None.

REPRINT, SUBSCRIPTION, AND CONTACT INFORMATION

Reprint Policy | All authors receive a complimentary copy as well as a free PDF of their article. If they would like to order additional reprints, they may do so at prepublication prices by placing an order BEFORE the article is published ("offprint order"). NOTE: If reprints are ordered after the issue has gone to press, the price doubles. The minimum reprint order is 50, and prices for quantities of reprints vary by the length of the article.

Book Reviews | No.

Subscriptions | Order through Taylor & Francis Inc., 325 Chestnut Street, Suite 800, Philadelphia, PA 19106.

Affiliation | Institute on Violence, Abuse, and Trauma at Alliant International University.

E-Mail Address | journals@alliant.edu

Website | www.tandf.co.uk/journals/wamt/ivatcenters.org

JOURNAL OF AGING STUDIES

Current Title	*Journal of Aging Studies*
Previous Title	N/A.
Editorial Focus	*Journal of Aging Studies* features scholarly papers offering new interpretations that challenge existing theory and empirical work.
Audience	Sociologists, psychologists, social workers, political scientists, anthropologists.
Special Themes	Contact editor for details.
Where Indexed/ Abstracted	Abstracts in Social Gerontology; AgeLine; Current Contents/Arts & Humanities; Current Contents/Social & Behavioral Sciences; Family Resources; Psychological Abstracts/PsycINFO; Research Alert; SCOPUS; Social Planning/Policy and Development Abstracts; Social Sciences Citation Index; Sociological Abstracts.
Year Established	1986.
Circulation	Not specified.
Frequency	Quarterly.
Months Issued	January, April, August, December.
No. of Articles per Issue	6.

SUBMISSIONS

Postal Mailing Address	Editor, *Journal of Aging Studies*, Department of Sociology, University of Florida, Gainesville, FL 32611-7330.
Method for Submission	E-mail.
Number of Copies	Not specified.
Disk Submission	No.
Online or E-mail Submission Allowed or Required	gubriumj@missouri.edu Subject line should read JAS Submission.

FORMAT OF MANUSCRIPT

Cover Sheet	Provide the following information in the order given below.
Abstract	This is a page of its own following the title page. Repeat the full title of the article at the top of the abstract page. A concise and factual abstract is required (maximum length 150 words), headed "Abstract." References should be avoided, but if essential, they must be cited in full, without reference to the reference list.
Key Words	No.
Length	No specific length.
Margins	1 inch.
Spacing	Double-spaced.

STYLE

Name of Guide	*Publication Manual of the American Psychological Association.*
Subheadings	Divide your article into clearly defined sections with concise subheadings.
References	Consult editorial office for reference style.
Footnotes	Responsibility for the accuracy of bibliographic citations lies entirely with the authors.
Tables or Figures	Footnotes should be used sparingly. Number them consecutively throughout the article, using superscript Arabic numbers. Do not include footnotes in the reference list. Present tables and figure captions at the end of the manuscript.

REVIEW PROCESS

Type of Review	
Queries	Yes.
Acknowledgment	For inquiries relating to the submission of articles (including electronic submission where available) please visit this journal's homepage at: www.elsevier.com/locate/jaging.
Review Time	Approximately 4–6 weeks.
Revisions	Please list your corrections quoting line number. If, for any reason, this is not possible, then mark the corrections and any other comments (including replies to the Query Form) on a printout of your proof and return by fax, or scan the pages and e-mail, or by post.
Acceptance Rate	Not specified.

Return of Manuscript	Accepted papers will be copyedited and returned to the corresponding author for approval prior to typesetting.
Lag Time to Print	Not specified.

CHARGES TO AUTHOR

Author Alterations	Not specified.
Page Charges	Not specified.
Processing	Not specified.

REPRINT, SUBSCRIPTION, AND CONTACT INFORMATION

Reprint Policy	Anne Rosenthal: reprints@elsevier.com, 212 633 3812.
Book Reviews	None.
Subscriptions	http://www.elsevier.com/wps/find/journaldescription.cws_home/620198/bibliographic.
Affiliation	Not specified.
E-Mail Address	Not specified.
Website	http://www.elsevier.com/wps/find/journaldescription.cws_home/620198/description#description

JOURNAL OF AGING & SOCIAL POLICY

Current Title	*Journal of Aging & Social Policy*
Previous Title	N/A.
Editorial Focus	Thought and discussion about the pressing policy issues faced by a rapidly changing and aging society.
Audience	All professionals engaged in policy and program development for the elderly.
Special Themes	Public policy, probing the history of contemporary issues, exploring the evolution of policy, and examining the literature in related policy areas to make a point relevant to the aging society and the systems that deliver programs or services.
Where Indexed/ Abstracted	Medline Academic Abstracts/CD-ROM; ALCONLINE Database; Biology Digest; Brown University Digest of Addiction Theory and Application (DATA Newsletter); Cambridge Scientific Abstracts; Child Development Abstracts & Bibliography; CINAHL (Cumulative Index to Nursing & Allied Health Literature); CNPIEC Reference Guide: Chinese National Directory of Foreign Periodicals; Criminal Justice Abstracts, Current Contents; Educational Administration Abstracts (EAA); ERIC Clearinghouse on Counseling and Student Services (ERIC/CASS); Exceptional Child Education Resources (ECER); Family Life Educator "Abstracts Section"; Family Studies Database (online and CD-ROM); Health Source: Indexing & Abstracting of 160 selected health related journals, updated monthly; Health Source Plus; Index to Periodical Articles Related to Law; Institute for Scientific Information; International Bulletin of Bibliography on Education; INTERNET ACCESS (and additional networks) Bulletin Board for Libraries ("BUBL"), coverage of information resources on INTERNET, JANET, and other networks; Medication Use Studies (MUST) DATABASE; MEDLINE; Mental Health Abstracts (online through DIALOG); National Criminal Justice Reference Service; NIAAA Alcohol and Alcohol Problems Science Database (ETOH); Psychological Abstracts/PsycINFO; Refcrativnyi Zhurnal (Abstracts Journal of the Institute of Scientific Information of the Republic of Russia); Sage Family Studies Abstracts (SFSA); Sage Urban Studies Abstracts (SUSA); Social Planning/Policy & Development Abstracts (SOPODA); Social Sciences Citation Index; Social Work Abstracts; Sociological Abstracts (SA); Special Educational Needs Abstracts; Studies on Women Abstracts; Violence and Abuse Abstracts (VAA).
Year Established	1989.
Circulation	400.
Frequency	Quarterly.
Months Issued	Not specified.
No. of Articles per Issue	6–10.

SUBMISSIONS

Postal Mailing Address	Editor: Francis Caro, PhD. Managing Editor, Robert Geary. Gerontology Institute, 100 Morrissey Boulevard, Boston, MA 02125.
Method for Submission	E-mail.
Number of Copies	4.
Disk Submission	Microsoft Word.
Online or E-mail Submission Allowed or Required	Required.

FORMAT OF MANUSCRIPT

Cover Sheet	Separate sheet, which does not go out for review. Full title; author names; degrees; professional titles; designation of one author as corresponding author with full address, phone numbers, e-mail address, and fax number; date of submission.
Abstract	Approximately 100 words.
Key Words	5–6 key words to identify article content.
Length	20 pages, including references and abstract. Lengthier manuscripts may be considered, but only at the discretion of the editor. Sometimes, lengthier manuscripts may be considered if they can be divided into sections for publication in successive issues.
Margins	1 inch all sides.
Spacing	Double-spaced for all copy except title page.

STYLE

Name of Guide	*Publication Manual of the American Psychological Association.*
Subheadings	Use as needed to guide reader through the article. No more than 4 levels.
References	Author–date citation style; see style guide.
Footnotes	No footnotes preferred; incorporate into text.
Tables or Figures	Type tables double-spaced. Submit camera-ready art (300 dpi printer or better) for all figures. Please each table or figure on a separate, numbered page at the end of the manuscript.

REVIEW PROCESS

Type of Review	Double-blind anonymous peer review. 3 reviewers plus editor-in-chief reads the manuscript in an anonymous review.
Queries	Authors are encouraged to read the journal to determine whether their subject matter would be appropriate.
Acknowledgment	Managing Editor will acknowledge receipt of manuscript via e-mail.
Review Time	3–4 months.
Revisions	See journal.
Acceptance Rate	Approximately 57%.
Return of Manuscript	N/A because all submissions are electronic.
Lag Time to Print	6–12 months.

REPRINT, SUBSCRIPTION, AND CONTACT INFORMATION

Reprint Policy	All authors receive 2 complimentary copies of the issue in which the article appears. Authors receive reprint order forms to purchase additional reprinted copies.
Book Reviews	Send to journal editors.
Subscriptions	Taylor & Francis, 325 Chestnut Street, Philadelphia, PA 19106. Individuals (print and online), $120; Institutions (online only), $591; Institutions (print and online), $622.
Affiliation	Not specified.
E-Mail Address	robert.geary@umb.edu
Website	www.informaworld.com/WASP

JOURNAL OF APPLIED RESEARCH IN INTELLECTUAL DISABILITIES

Current Title	*Journal of Applied Research in Intellectual Disabilities*
Previous Title	*Mental Handicap Research before 1996 volume 9.*
Editorial Focus	*Journal of Applied Research in Intellectual Disabilities* is an international, peer-reviewed journal that draws together findings derived from original applied research in intellectual disabilities. The journal is an important forum for the dissemination of ideas to promote valued lifestyles for people with intellectual disabilities. It reports on research from the United Kingdom and overseas by authors from all relevant professional disciplines. It is aimed at an international, multi-disciplinary readership.
	The topics it covers include community living, quality of life, challenging behavior, communication, sexuality, medication, aging, supported employment, family issues, mental health, physical health, autism, economic issues, social networks, staff stress, staff training, epidemiology, and service provision. Theoretical papers are also considered provided the implications for therapeutic action or enhancing quality of life are clear. Both quantitative and qualitative methodologies are welcomed. All original and review articles continue to undergo a rigorous, peer-refereeing process.
Audience	Psychiatrists, psychologists, educationalists, doctors, researchers, health care workers.
Special Themes	Proceedings of the IASSMD Conference, intellectual disabilities and the criminal justice system, challenging behavior, biobehavioral factors, sexuality.
Where Indexed/ Abstracted	By PsycINFO and Medicine and other abstracting services.
Year Established	1987.
Circulation	525.
Frequency	6 per year.
Months Issued	January, March, May, July, September, December.
No. of Articles per Issue	Approximately 10.

SUBMISSIONS

Postal Mailing Address	74 White Lund Road, Heaton with Oxcliffe, Morecambe, Lancashire LA3 3DU.
Method for Submission	E-mail.
Number of Copies	1.
Disk Submission	N/A.
Online or E-mail Submission Allowed or Required	E-mail submission requested.

Conflict of Interest: Authors are required to disclose any possible conflict of interest. These include financial (for example patent ownership, stock ownership, consultancies, speaker's fee). Author's conflict of interest (or information specifying the absence of conflict of interest) will be published under a separate heading. *Journal of Applied Research in Intellectual Disabilities* requires that sources of institutional, private, and corporate financial support for the work within the manuscript must be fully acknowledged, and any potential conflict of interest noted. As of March 1, 2007, this information is a requirement for all manuscripts submitted to the journal and will be published in a highlighted box on the title page of the article. Please include this information under the separate headings of "Source of Funding" and "Conflict of Interest" at the end of the manuscript. If the author does not include a conflict of interest statement in the manuscript, then the following statement will be included by default: "No conflict of interest has been declared".

FORMAT OF MANUSCRIPT

Cover Sheet	A short title of not more than 50 characters, including spaces, should be provided. The title page should include title, name of authors, and address for correspondence.
Abstract	All papers should be divided into a structured summary (150 words) and the main text with appropriate subheadings. A structured summary should be given at the beginning of each article, incorporating the following headings: Background, Materials and Methods, Results, Conclusions. These should outline the questions investigated, the design, essential findings, and main conclusions of the study. The text should proceed through sections of Abstract, Introduction, Materials and Methods, Results, and Discussion.
Key Words	Up to 6 key words to aid indexing should also be provided.
Length	The paper should not exceed 7,000 words. Brief Reports should not exceed 2,000 words.

Margins	Manuscripts should be formatted with a wide margin. Include all parts of the text of the paper in a single file, but do not embed figures. Please note the following points, which will help us to process your manuscript successfully: Include all figure legends, and tables with their legends if available. Do not use the carriage return (enter) at the end of lines within a paragraph. Turn the hyphenation option off. In the cover e-mail, specify any special characters used to represent non-keyboard characters. Take care not to use l (ell) for 1 (one), O (capital o) for 0 (zero) or ß (German esszett) for (beta). Use a tab, not spaces, to separate data points in tables. If you use a table editor function, ensure that each data point is contained within a unique cell, that is, do not use carriage returns within cells.
Spacing	Double-spaced.

STYLE

Name of Guide	*Publication Manual of the American Psychological Association.*
Subheadings	Background, Materials and Methods, Results, Conclusions.
References	Journal titles should be in full. References in text with more than 2 authors should be abbreviated to (Brown et al. 1977). Authors are responsible for the accuracy of their references. The reference list should be in alphabetic order.
Footnotes	No special requirements.
Tables or Figures	These are not included in the word count. Tables/figures should be submitted as a separate file. Tables should include only essential data. Each table must be typewritten on a separate sheet and should be numbered consecutively with Arabic numerals, e.g. Table 1, and given a short caption. Figures should be referred to in the text as Figures using Arabic numbers, for example, Fig.1, Fig.2 etc, in order of appearance. Figures should be clearly labeled with the name of the first author and the appropriate number. Each figure should have a separate legend; these should be grouped on a separate page at the end of the manuscript. All symbols and abbreviations should be clearly explained. In the full-text online edition of the journal, figure legends may be truncated in abbreviated links to the full screen version. Therefore, the first 100 characters of any legend should inform the reader of key aspects of the figure.

REVIEW PROCESS

Type of Review	Should follow the referee guidelines supplied. All articles submitted to the journal are assessed by at least 2 anonymous reviewers with expertise in that field. The Editors reserve the right to edit any contribution to ensure that it conforms to the requirements of the journal.
Queries	Queries should be addressed to the Editorial Assistant, Pat Clelland, by e-mail
Acknowledgment	Contributors to the article other than the authors accredited should be specified. Specifications of the source of funding for the study should also be specified and any potential conflict of interest if appropriate. Suppliers of materials should be named and their location (town, state/county, country) included.
Review Time	Approximately 3 months.
Revisions	References returned to reviewer.
Acceptance Rate	51 in 2007 (out of 114).
Return of Manuscript	Not returned.
Lag Time to Print	Approximately 6–12 months.

REPRINT, SUBSCRIPTION, AND CONTACT INFORMATION

Reprint Policy	Not specified.
Book Reviews	Accepted.
Subscriptions	Interscience.wiley.com; for support, contact the nearest office.
Affiliation	BILD
E-Mail Address	patclelland@wightcablenorth.net
Website	http://www.wiley.com/bw/submit.asp?ref=1360-2322

JOURNAL OF APPLIED SCHOOL PSYCHOLOGY

Current Title	*Journal of Applied School Psychology*
Previous Title	N/A.
Editorial Focus	Reflect psychological applications that pertain to individual students, groups of students, teachers, parents, and administrators. The journal also seeks, over time, novel and creative ways in which to disseminate information about practically sound and empirically supported school psychology practice.
Audience	Individual students, groups of students, teachers, parents, and administrators.
Special Themes	*Journal of Applied School Psychology* will continue to publish articles and periodic thematic issues in 2009.
Where Indexed/ Abstracted	Academic Search Premier (EBSCO); Academic Source Premier (EBSCO); Advanced Polymers Abstracts (ProQuest CSA); Aluminum Industry Abstracts (ProQuest CSA); British Library Inside (The British Library); International Bibliography of Book Reviews on the Humanities and Social Sciences (IBR); International Bibliography of Periodical Literature on the Humanities and Social Sciences (IBZ); LISA: Library and Information Science Abstracts (ProQuest CSA); MasterFILE Premier (EBSCO).
Year Established	Not specified.
Circulation	Not specified.
Frequency	2 times per year.
Months Issued	Not specified.
No. of Articles per Issue	Not specified.

SUBMISSIONS

Postal Mailing Address	Manuscripts should be submitted electronically to David L. Wodrich, PhD, ABPP, Editor, Journal of Applied School Psychology, at jasp@asu.edu.
Method for Submission	Manuscripts should be submitted electronically to David L. Wodrich, PhD, ABPP, Editor, *Journal of Applied School Psychology*, at jasp@asu.edu.
Number of Copies	The manuscript should be sent as an attachment (preferably with MS Word) and labeled with the first author's last name and the manuscript's running heading.
Disk Submission	N/A.
Online or E-mail Submission Allowed or Required	Electronic submission via website.

FORMAT OF MANUSCRIPT

Cover Sheet	Each manuscript must be accompanied by a statement that it has not been published elsewhere and that it has not been submitted simultaneously for publication elsewhere. Indication for IRB approval should be made in all studies involving human subjects.
Abstract	120 words.
Key Words	Not specified.
Length	Not specified.
Margins	1 inch.
Spacing	Double-spaced.

STYLE

Name of Guide	*Publication Manual of the American Psychological Association.*
Subheadings	See style guide.
References	References, citations, and general style of manuscripts should be prepared in accordance with the *APA Publication Manual*, 5th ed. Cite in the text by author and date (Smith, 1983) and include an alphabetical list at the end of the article.
Footnotes	Not specified.
Tables or Figures	Tables and figures (illustrations) should not be embedded in the text, but should be included as separate sheets or files. A short descriptive title should appear above each table with a clear legend and any footnotes suitably identified below. All units must be included. Figures should be completely labeled, taking into account necessary size reduction. Captions should be typed, double-spaced, on a separate sheet.

REVIEW PROCESS

Type of Review Each manuscript is read by the Editor and 2 or more reviewers from the Editorial Board or individuals appointed on an ad hoc basis. At times, student editorial board members may also review and comment on manuscripts, but their evaluations are not considered in editorial decisions. Each reviewer judges manuscripts on the following dimensions: Are research questions (hypothesis/hypotheses) clearly stated and presented in the context of the current literature?, Are research questions, as stated, important (i.e., ones that if answered would advance knowledge, test a theory, or guide practice)?, Was a suitable methodology, including statistical techniques if warranted, used to answer the research questions?, Was an adequate sample collected to answer the research questions?, Were data analyses correctly conducted and results properly interpreted?, Did the study's findings turned out to be important?, Was information presented clearly and in a manner that readily promoted the reader's understanding?, Should the manuscript be accepted for publication? Literature reviews, conceptual and theoretical articles, and other manuscripts that are nonempirical in nature may not be evaluated on each of these dimensions. Moreover, because some reviewers are selected because of their methodological expertise but may not possess school practice backgrounds (or vice versa), some of the dimensions listed above are unrated by some reviewers. Summary judgment about acceptance is provided in prompt manner (target 2 months) via e-mail correspondence from the Editor. For manuscripts accepted for publication, authors receive additional (hardcopy) correspondence from the Editor.

Queries Not specified.

Acknowledgment Not specified.

Review Time Not specified.

Revisions Not specified.

Acceptance Rate Not specified.

Return of Manuscript Not specified.

Lag Time to Print Not specified.

CHARGES TO AUTHOR

Author Alterations Page proofs are sent to the designated author using Taylor & Francis' Central Article Tracking System (CATS). They must be carefully checked and returned within 48 hours of receipt.

Page Charges Color Illustrations. Color illustrations will be considered for publication; however, the author will be required to bear the full cost involved in color art reproduction. Color art can be purchased for online only reproduction or for print and online reproduction. Color reprints can only be ordered if print and online reproduction costs are paid. Rates for color art reproduction are: Online-Only Reproduction: $225 for the first page of color; $100 for the next three pages of color. A custom quote will be provided for articles with more than four pages of color. Print and Online Reproduction: $900 for the first page of color; $450 for the next three pages of color. A custom quote will be provided for articles with more than four pages of color.

Processing Not specified.

REPRINT, SUBSCRIPTION, AND CONTACT INFORMATION

Reprint Policy Reprints of individual articles are available for order at the time authors review page proofs. A discount on reprints is available to authors who order before print publication. Each corresponding author will receive 3 complete issues in which the article publishes and a complimentary PDF. This file is for personal use only and may not be copied and disseminated in any form without prior written permission from Taylor and Francis Group, LLC.

Book Reviews Not specified.

Subscriptions See website: http://www.informaworld.com/smpp/title~db=all~content=g910941382~tab=subscribe.

Affiliation Not specified.

E-Mail Address jasp@asu.edu

Website http://www.informaworld.com/smpp/title~db=all~content=t792303966

JOURNAL OF AUTISM AND DEVELOPMENTAL DISORDERS

Current Title	*Journal of Autism and Developmental Disorders*
Previous Title	N/A.
Editorial Focus	*JADD* is committed to advancing the understanding of autism, including potential causes and prevalence (e.g., genetic, immunological, environmental); diagnosis advancements; and effective clinical care, education, and treatment for all individuals. Studies of diagnostic reliability and validity, psychotherapeutic and psychopharmacological treatment efficacy, and mental health services effectiveness are encouraged. *JADD* also seeks to promote the well-being of children and families by publishing scholarly papers on such subjects as health policy, legislation, advocacy, culture and society, and service provision as they pertain to the mental health of children and families.
Audience	Authors and readers of the *Journal of Autism and Developmental Disorders* include scholars, researchers, professionals, policy makers, and graduate students from a broad range of cross-disciplines, including developmental, clinical child, and school psychology; pediatrics; psychiatry; education; social work and counseling; speech, communication, and physical therapy; medicine and neuroscience; and public health.
Special Themes	Autism and pervasive developmental disorders.
Where Indexed/ Abstracted	Biological Abstracts; Cumulative Index to Nursing & Allied Health Literature; Current Abstracts; EBSCOhost; Education Research Index; Family & Society Studies Worldwide; Family Index; Linguistics and Language Behavior Abstracts; MEDLINE; PsycINFO; SCOPUS; Social Work Abstracts; Studies on Women and Gender Abstracts.
Year Established	1971.
Circulation	Not specified.
Frequency	Monthly.
Months Issued	Monthly.
No. of Articles per Issue	14–16.

SUBMISSIONS

Postal Mailing Address	*Manuscript will not be accepted through the mail.*
Method for Submission	Manuscripts should be submitted online at: http://www.editorialmanager.com/jadd/.
Number of Copies	1 copy submitted online.
Disk Submission	Not necessary.
Online or E-mail Submission Allowed or Required	Online submission required.

FORMAT OF MANUSCRIPT

Cover Sheet	The title page is page 1 and should contain: (1) a full title, (2) the authors' full names and institutional affiliations, and (3) a running head for publication. (see below). The preferred form for author's name is first name, middle initial (s), and last name. Omit titles and degrees. The institutional affiliation is the location where the study was conducted. Full address for the corresponding author, location of the institutions, and current affiliations (if changed since the time of the study) belong in the Author Note.
Abstract	Abstracts should not exceed 120 words.
Key Words	6 or fewer key words should appear one line below the abstract.
Length	3 types of submissions are accepted. Preferably, an Article is 20–23 manuscript pages or 4,500 words. Editors can approve up to 40 pages (references, tables, and figures included in the page count) if required to convey the information. A Brief Report is approximately 8 double-spaced pages or 2,000 words with the words "Brief Report:" typed before the title. A Case Report is a kind of brief report. 12-point font should be used.
Margins	1 inch on all sides.
Spacing	Double-spaced.

STYLE

Name of Guide	*Publication Manual of the American Psychological Association.*
Subheadings	Follow style guide.
References	Follow style guide.

Footnotes	Center the label "Footnotes" at the top of a separate page. Type all content footnotes and copyright permission footnotes together, double-spaced, and numbered consecutively in the order they appear in the article. Indent the first line of each footnote 5–7 spaces.
Tables or Figures	Tables should be numbered sequentially in the order that they are first mentioned in the text and referred to by number in the text. Each table is identified with the word "Table" and an Arabic numeral and a descriptive title. Each table should be inserted on a separate page at the back of the manuscript in the order noted above.

REVIEW PROCESS

Type of Review	Open, peer review.
Queries	Welcomed.
Acknowledgment	Through the online system.
Review Time	Not specified.
Revisions	Specified by reviewers and editor.
Acceptance Rate	Not specified.
Return of Manuscript	Not returned.
Lag Time to Print	Not specified.

CHARGES TO AUTHOR

Author Alterations	Not specified.
Page Charges	The journal makes no page charges.
Processing	Not specified.

REPRINT, SUBSCRIPTION, AND CONTACT INFORMATION

Reprint Policy	Reprints and electronic reprints are available to authors, and order forms with the current price schedule are sent with proofs.
Book Reviews	Contact the editor.
Subscriptions	Available through the website at: http://www.springer.com/generic/order/journals+subscription?SGWID=0-40514-0-0-0.
Affiliation	Not specified.
E-Mail Address	Not specified.
Website	http://www.springerlink.com/content/104757/.

JOURNAL OF BACCALAUREATE SOCIAL WORK

Current Title	*Journal of Baccalaureate Social Work*
Previous Title	N/A.
Editorial Focus	Not specified.
Audience	Baccalaureate/graduate social work faculty, students and practitioners; libraries; schools of social work; and human services organizations.
Special Themes	Human diversity, innovations in baccalaureate social work education and practice, values and ethics, social and economic justice.
Where Indexed/ Abstracted	Social Work Abstracts.
Year Established	1995.
Circulation	Approximately 900.
Frequency	Semiannually.
Months Issued	April and October.
No. of Articles per Issue	8–10.

SUBMISSIONS

Postal Mailing Address	BPD, Association Manager, 1725 Duke Street, Suite 500, Alexandria, VA 22314.
Method for Submission	Electronic via website.
Number of Copies	1.
Disk Submission	Online submission only.
Online or E-mail Submission Allowed or Required	Required.

FORMAT OF MANUSCRIPT

Cover Sheet	All author identifying information. Cover sheet is removed before the manuscript is sent out for review.
Abstract	150 words.
Key Words	5–6 words.
Length	15–20 pages.
Margins	1 inch on all sides.
Spacing	Double-spaced.

STYLE

Name of Guide	*Publication Manual of the American Psychological Association.*
Subheadings	Encouraged for clarity and organization.
References	See style guide.
Footnotes	Not preferred unless absolutely necessary.
Tables or Figures	Tables: at end of text file or in separate file (do not position in text). Figures: separate file in TIFF, EPS, or PDF with embedded fonts.

REVIEW PROCESS

Type of Review	Anonymous peer review by 2 consulting editors. Third review or editor review when reviews are widely divergent.
Queries	E-mail preferred.
Acknowledgment	Letter acknowledging receipt sent to first author.
Review Time	Approximately 3 months.
Revisions	Depends on reviewer recommendations. Accept, Accept with Minor Revisions: Revisions made and manuscript resubmitted with a list of changes made in response to reviewers. Reject, Revise, Resubmit: Resubmit for second review by reviewers. Include thorough details of changes. Reject: Not appropriate for *JBSW*.
Acceptance Rate	Approximately 20%–25%.
Return of Manuscript	Not returned.
Lag Time to Print	Approximately 6 months.

CHARGES TO AUTHOR

Author Alterations	Not specified.
Page Charges	Not specified.
Processing	Not specified.

REPRINT, SUBSCRIPTION, AND CONTACT INFORMATION

Reprint Policy	All authors receive 2 complimentary copies of the issue in which the article appears.
Book Reviews	Murali Nair, *JBSW* Book Review Editor, Cleveland State University, Department of Social Work, 1983 E. 24th Street, Cleveland, OH 44115.
Subscriptions	Free with all categories of BPD membership. Contact 1725 Duke Street • Suite 500.
Affiliation	Alexandria, VA 22314 or visit www.bpdonline.org
E-Mail Address	JBSW@CSWE.org
Website	www.bpdonline.org

JOURNAL OF BISEXUALITY

Current Title	*Journal of Bisexuality*
Previous Title	N/A.
Editorial Focus	This journal is intended for more than the academic audience. While articles are published after a peer-reviewed process, other sections of the journal cover bisexual topics in a more popular and nonacademic style. Book and movie reviews cover bisexual lead characters from every era. Articles come from inter- and intradisciplinary perspectives.
Audience	Academic and public audience .
Special Themes	Bisexual Women in the Twenty-First Century, Current Research on Bisexuality, Bisexuality and Transgenderism, Plural Loves: Designs for Bi and Poly Living, Bisexuality in the Lives of Men, Women and Bisexuality: A Global Perspective, Bi Men Coming out Every Which Way, Affirmative Psychotherapy with Bisexual Women and Bisexual Men, Bisexual Men in Culture and Society, Kinsey Zero through Sixty: Bisexual Perspectives on Kinsey, Bisexuality, and Same-Sex Marriage.
Where Indexed/ Abstracted	www.tandf.co.uk/journals/WJBI.
Year Established	2001.
Circulation	Contact Taylor & Francis.
Frequency	4 issues per year.
Months Issued	January, April, July, October.
No. of Articles per Issue	575 typeset pages.

SUBMISSIONS

Postal Mailing Address	Jonathan Alexander, PhD, Editor, University of California, Irvine, 435 Humanities Instructional Bldg, Irvine, CA 92697-7397.
Method for Submission	Surface mail, disk, e-mail, electronic submission via website. jamma@fuse.net.
Number of Copies	1.
Disk Submission	1.
Online or E-mail Submission Allowed or Required	Yes.

FORMAT OF MANUSCRIPT

Cover Sheet	Yes.
Abstract	Yes, up to 100 words.
Key Words	Yes.
Length	Up to 50 pages.
Margins	1 inch.
Spacing	Double-spaced.

STYLE

Name of Guide	*Publication Manual of the American Psychological Association.*
Subheadings	Author instruction: www.tandf.co.uk/journals/WJBI.
References	Double-spaced, alphabetical order.
Footnotes	See author instructions.
Tables or Figures	Included as separate sheets or files.

REVIEW PROCESS

Type of Review	Peer review.
Queries	Yes.
Acknowledgment	Yes.
Review Time	Approximately 1 month.
Revisions	Approximately 1 month.
Acceptance Rate	Approximately 25%.
Return of Manuscript	Approximately 2 weeks.
Lag Time to Print	Not specified.

CHARGES TO AUTHOR

Author Alterations N/A.

Page Charges N/A.

Processing N/A.

REPRINT, SUBSCRIPTION, AND CONTACT INFORMATION

Reprint Policy Contact: Taylor and Francis.

Book Reviews Not specified.

Subscriptions Taylor & Francis Attn: Journals Customer Service, 325 Chestnut Street, Philadelphia, PA 19106.

Affiliation Not specified.

E-Mail Address customerservice@taylorandfrancis.com

Website http://www.tandf.co.uk/journals/online.asp

JOURNAL OF BLACK STUDIES

Current Title	*Journal of Black Studies.*
Previous Title	N/A.
Editorial Focus	The scholarship inside *Journal of Black Studies* covers a wide range of subject areas, including: society, social issues, Afrocentricity, economics, culture, media, literature, language, heritage, and biology.
Audience	Not specified.
Special Themes	Several thematic issues per year.
Where Indexed/ Abstracted	Abstract Journal of the Educational Resources Information Center (ERIC), America: History Life; Applied Social Sciences Index & Abstracts (ASSIA); Asia Pacific Database; Biological and Sciences Abstracts; Central Asia: Abstracts & Index; Corporate ResourceNET – EBSCO; Current Citations Express; Current Contents: Social & Behavioral Sciences; ERIC Current Index to Journals in Education (CIJE); Expanded Academic Index – Gale; Family & Society Studies Worldwide (NISC); Health & Safety Sciences Abstracts; Higher Education Abstracts; Historical Abstracts; Humanities Source; Index to Black Periodicals; International Bibliography of the Social Sciences; International Index of Black Periodicals (ProQuest); International Political Science Abstracts; ISI Basic Social Sciences Index; MAS FullTEXT; MasterFILE – EBSCO; Middle East: Abstracts & Index; Military Library FullTEXT; NISC; North Africa: Abstracts & Index; PAIS International; Periodical Abstracts – ProQuest; Political Science Abstracts; Political Science Complete; ProQuest Education Complete; ProQuest Education Journals; Psychological Abstracts/PsycINFO; PsychLIT; Race Relations Abstracts; Risk Abstracts; Safety Science & Risk Abstracts; SCOPUS; Social Science Source; Social Sciences Citation Index (Web of Science); Social Sciences Index Full Text; Social SciSearch; Social Services Abstracts; Social Work Abstracts; Sociological Abstracts; Southeast Asia: Abstracts & Index; Standard Periodical Directory (SPD); TOPICsearch – EBSCO; Urban Affairs Abstracts; Wilson OmniFile V; Wilson Social Sciences Index/Abstracts.
Year Established	Not specified.
Circulation	2,200.
Frequency	6 times per year.
Months Issued	January, March, May, July, September, November.
No. of Articles per Issue	6–8.

SUBMISSIONS

Postal Mailing Address	Molefi K. Asante, Editor, *Journal of Black Studies*, Department of African American Studies, Temple University, Gladfelter Hall, Philadelphia, PA 19122.
Method for Submission	Surface mail and disk.
Number of Copies	1 disk.
Disk Submission	Yes, with surface mail
Online or E-mail Submission Allowed or Required	Not specified

FORMAT OF MANUSCRIPT

Cover Sheet	Title of manuscript; author's name and affiliation; number of pages; brief bibliographic paragraph describing each author's current affiliation, research interests, and recent publications.
Abstract	Not specified.
Key Words	Not specified.
Length	25' including all pages.
Margins	1 inch.
Spacing	Double-spaced.

STYLE

Name of Guide	*Publication Manual of the American Psychological Association.*
Subheadings	Include.
References	See style guide.
Footnotes	Avoid using footnotes.
Tables or Figures	Submit camera-ready.

REVIEW PROCESS

Type of Review	Anonymous review by 2 reviewers minimum, occasionally 3.
Queries	Not specified.
Acknowledgment	Include self-addressed, stamped postcard when submitting manuscript.
Review Time	Approximately 2–3 months.
Revisions	Not specified.
Acceptance Rate	Approximately 20%–25%.
Return of Manuscript	Include self-addressed, stamped envelope when submitting manuscript.
Lag Time to Print	Approximately 12–18 months.

CHARGES TO AUTHOR

Author Alterations	Not specified.
Page Charges	Not specified.
Processing	Not specified.

REPRINT, SUBSCRIPTION, AND CONTACT INFORMATION

Reprint Policy	Not specified.
Book Reviews	Review essays and bibliographic articles and compilations are sought; contact editor. Send books for review and annotation to: Molefi Kete Asante, Editor, Department of African American Studies, Temple University, Philadelphia, PA 19122.
Subscriptions	Not specified.
Affiliation	Not specified.
E-Mail Address	masante@temple.edu
Website	http://www.sagepub.com/journalsProdManSub.nav?prodId=Journal200876

JOURNAL OF CHILD AND ADOLESCENT GROUP THERAPY

Current Title	*Journal of Child and Adolescent Group Therapy*
Previous Title	N/A.
Editorial Focus	Application of theoretical concepts in child and adolescent group therapy; reports on clinical methods and results; innovation on group methods and treatment; manuscripts on techniques, theoretical concepts, and research information; brief observation and book review; comments to the editor.
Audience	Not specified.
Special Themes	Special issues considered by invitation or need and interest.
Where Indexed/ Abstracted	Not specified.
Year Established	1990.
Circulation	Not specified.
Frequency	Quarterly.
Months Issued	March, June, September, December.
No. of Articles per Issue	3–6.

SUBMISSIONS

Postal Mailing Address	Edward S. Soo, Editor, P. O. Box 427, Tenafly, NJ 07670.
Method for Submission	Surface mail.
Number of Copies	4 (quadruplicate).
Disk Submission	No.
Online or E-mail Submission Allowed or Required	Not specified.

FORMAT OF MANUSCRIPT

Cover Sheet	Title page: title of manuscript, author's name (with degree), author's affiliation, suggested running head, complete mailing address and phone number of the one author designated to review proofs. Affiliation: department, institution (usually university or company), city and state (or nation) typed as a numbered footnote to the author's name. Running head: Fewer than 80 characters (including spaces), comprising the title of an abbreviated version thereof.
Abstract	100–150 words maximum.
Key Words	3–5 key words listed directly below the abstract.
Length	Approximately 20 pages.
Margins	Wide.
Spacing	Double-spaced.

STYLE

Name of Guide	*Publication Manual of the American Psychological Association.*
Subheadings	Use as needed.
References	List references alphabetically at the end of the paper and refer to them in the text by name and year in parentheses. References should include (in this order): last names and initials of all authors, year published, title of article, name of publication, volume number, and inclusive pages.
Footnotes	Footnotes should be avoided. When their use is absolutely necessary, footnotes should be numbered consecutively using Arabic numerals and should be typed at the bottom of the page to which they refer. Place a line above the footnote, so that it is set off from the text. Use the appropriate superscript numeral for citation in the text.
Tables or Figures	Tables should be numbered and referred to by number in the text. Each table should be typed on a separate sheet of paper. Center the title above the table, and type explanatory footnotes (indicated by superscript lowercase letters) below the table.

REVIEW PROCESS

Type of Review	Anonymous review by 2 reviewers minimum.
Queries	Editor welcomes and accepts queries.
Acknowledgment	Editor sends postcard on manuscript receipt.
Review Time	Within weeks.

Revisions	Criticisms and comments.
Acceptance Rate	Not specified.
Return of Manuscript	Include self-addressed, stamped envelope when submitting manuscript.
Lag Time to Print	Approximately 4 months.

CHARGES TO AUTHOR

Author Alterations	After a manuscript has been accepted for publication and after all revisions have been incorporated, manuscripts should be submitted to the Editor's Office as hard copy accompanied by electronic files on disk. Label the disk with identifying information: software, journal name, and first author's last name. The disk must be the one from which the accompanying manuscript (finalized version) was printed out. The Editor's Office cannot accept a disk without its accompanying, matching hard-copy manuscript.
Page Charges	The journal makes no page charges.
Processing	Not specified.

REPRINT, SUBSCRIPTION, AND CONTACT INFORMATION

Reprint Policy	Order forms with the current price schedule are sent with proofs.
Book Reviews	Send reviews to: B.W Maclennan, PhD, 6307 Crathie Lane, Bethesda, MD 20816.
Subscriptions	Human Sciences Press, 233 Spring Street, New York, NY 10013-1578. Individual $42 (within U.S.), Institutions $145 (within U.S.), Individual $49 (outside of U.S.), Institution $170 (outside of U.S.).
Affiliation	Not specified.
E-Mail Address	plenum@panix.com
Website	http://www.springer.com/journal/10821

JOURNAL OF CHILD AND ADOLESCENT SUBSTANCE ABUSE

Current Title	*Journal of Child and Adolescent Substance Abuse*
Previous Title	N/A.
Editorial Focus	Current, useful information regarding state-of-the-art approaches to the strategies and issues in the assessment, prevention, and treatment of adolescent substance abuse.
Audience	All professionals who work with children and adolescents on a daily basis, chemical dependency clinicians, and prevention/treatment specialists.
Special Themes	Surveys of clinical strategies, treatment modalities, and specific applications.
Where Indexed/ Abstracted	CAB International; Criminal Justice Abstracts; Cumulative Index to Nursing and Allied Health Literature (CINAHL); Current Contents/Social & Behavioral Sciences; EBSCOhost Products; Education Research Abstracts; Journal Citation Report/Social Sciences Edition; PILOTS Database; Psychological Abstracts/PsycINFO; Social Sciences Citation Index; Social Scisearch; Social Service Abstracts.
Year Established	1990.
Circulation	287.
Frequency	Quarterly.
Months Issued	Not specified.
No. of Articles per Issue	6.

SUBMISSIONS

Postal Mailing Address	Vincent B. Van Hasselt, PhD, Center of Psychological Studies, Nova Southeastern University, 33101 College Avenue, Ft. Lauderdale, FL 33314 or Brad Donohue, PhD, University of Nevada, Las Vegas, Department of Psychology, 4505 Maryland Parkway, Box 455030, Las Vegas, NV 89154-5030.
Method for Submission	Not specified.
Number of Copies	3 (triplicate).
Disk Submission	Authors of accepted manuscripts area asked to submit a disk, preferably in Microsoft Word.
Online or E-mail Submission Allowed or Required	Not specified.

FORMAT OF MANUSCRIPT

Cover Sheet	Separate sheet, which does not go out for review. Full title, author names, degrees, professional titles; designation of one author as corresponding author with full address, phone numbers, e-mail address, fax number, and date of submission.
Abstract	100 words.
Key Words	Not specified.
Length	Not specified.
Margins	1 inch.
Spacing	Double-spaced.

STYLE

Name of Guide	*Publication Manual of the American Psychological Association.*
Subheadings	Use as needed to guide reader through the article. No more than 4 levels.
References	References, citations, and general style of manuscripts should be prepared in accordance with the *APA Publication Manual*. Cite in the text by author and date (Smith, 1983) and include an alphabetical list at the end of the article.
Footnotes	No footnotes preferred; incorporate into text.
Tables or Figures	Tables and figures (illustrations) should not be embedded in the text, but should be included as separate sheets or files. A short descriptive title should appear above each table with a clear legend and any footnotes suitably identified below. All units must be included. Figures should be completely labeled, taking into account necessary size reduction. Captions should be typed, double-spaced, on a separate sheet.

REVIEW PROCESS

Type of Review	"Double-blind" anonymous peer review. 3 reviewers plus editor-in-chief read the manuscript in an anonymous review.

Queries	Authors are encouraged to read the journal to determine whether their subject matter would be appropriate.
Acknowledgment	Enclose a regular self-addressed, stamped envelope with submission.
Review Time	Approximately 3–4 months.
Revisions	See journal.
Acceptance Rate	Not specified.
Return of Manuscript	Only if 9" × 12" self-addressed, stamped envelope is enclosed.
Lag Time to Print	Approximately 6–12 months.

REPRINT, SUBSCRIPTION, AND CONTACT INFORMATION

Reprint Policy	Reprints of individual articles are available for order at the time authors review page proofs. A discount on reprints is available to authors who order before print publication. Each corresponding author will receive 3 complete issues in which the article publishes and a complimentary PDF. This file is for personal use only and may not be copied and disseminated in any form without prior written permission from Taylor and Francis Group, LLC.
Book Reviews	Send to journal co-editors.
Subscriptions	The Hawthorn Press, Inc., 10 Alice Street, Binghamton, NY 13904-1580. Individuals $36; Institutions $75; Libraries $105.
Affiliation	Not specified.
E-Mail Address	Editorial Assistant: vjournal@nova.edu
Website	http://www.informaworld.com/smpp/title~db=all~content=t792303974~tab=submit~mode=paper_submission_instructions

JOURNAL OF CHILD AND ADOLESCENT TRAUMA

Current Title	*Journal of Child and Adolescent Trauma (JCAT)*
Previous Title	None.
Editorial Focus	Presents original research, prevention, and treatment strategies and techniques for dealing with symptoms and disorders related to the effects of trauma in children and adolescents.
Audience	Practitioners, policymakers, researchers, and academics who work with children or adolescents exposed to traumatic events.
Special Themes	Varies.
Where Indexed/ Abstracted	Academic Search Complete; Academic Source Complete; PILOTS Database; Social Work Abstracts.
Year Established	2007.
Circulation	92.
Frequency	Quarterly.
Months Issued	March, June, September, December.
No. of Articles per Issue	6–9.

SUBMISSIONS

Postal Mailing Address	*Journal of Child and Adolescent Trauma*, Institute on Violence, Abuse, and Trauma. 10065 Old Grove Road, San Diego, CA 92131.
Method for Submission	E-mail
Number of Copies	2 (1 original with identifying names, etc., and 1 copy without this information).
Disk Submission	Not required.
Online or E-mail Submission Allowed or Required	E-mail submission in MS Word, Works, or Excel format.

FORMAT OF MANUSCRIPT

Cover Sheet	Title; authors; brief biography of author's including degrees, positions, affiliations, and 1-sentence background; address for reprint requests.
Abstract	Required, no longer than 120 words.
Key Words	Required, 4–8 key words.
Length	No longer than 35 pages including references, abstract, and tables.
Margins	1 inch on all sides.
Spacing	Double-spaced.

STYLE

Name of Guide	*Publication Manual of the American Psychological Association;* Instructions for authors available from publisher's website (Taylor & Francis).
Subheadings	See style guide.
References	See style guide.
Footnotes	Not suggested unless absolutely needed; see style guide.
Tables or Figures	See style guide.

REVIEW PROCESS

Type of Review	Anonymous review by editorial board or ad hoc reviewers.
Queries	Editor welcomes query letters, e-mails, or phone calls.
Acknowledgment	On receipt of manuscript, copyright form sent to corresponding author to sign original.
Review Time	Approximately 3–5 months.
Revisions	Feedback is given to authors for making revisions. *JCAT* encourages revisions and resubmissions, with a cover letter by the author explaining what has been done to address the concerns.
Acceptance Rate	Approximately 37% based on initial submission, 67% on resubmission (sometimes 2–3 revisions are needed before publishing).
Return of Manuscript	If requested.
Lag Time to Print	Approximately 8–11 months.

CHARGES TO AUTHOR

Author Alterations None if done ahead of time.

Page Charges None.

Processing None.

REPRINT, SUBSCRIPTION, AND CONTACT INFORMATION

Reprint Policy All authors receive a complimentary copy as well as a free PDF of their article. If they would like to order additional reprints, they may do so at prepublication prices by placing an order BEFORE the article is published ("offprint order"). NOTE: If reprints are ordered after the issue has gone to press, the price doubles. The minimum reprint order is 50, and prices for quantities of reprints vary by the length of the article.

Book Reviews Yes.

Subscriptions Order through Taylor & Francis Inc., 325 Chestnut Street, Suite 800, Philadelphia, PA 19106.

Affiliation Institute on Violence, Abuse, and Trauma at Alliant International University.

E-Mail Address journals@alliant.edu

Website www.tandf.co.uk/journals/wcat/ivatcenters.org

JOURNAL OF CHILD PSYCHOLOGY AND PSYCHIATRY

Current Title	*Journal of Child Psychology and Psychiatry*
Previous Title	*Journal of Child Psychology and Psychiatry & Allied Disciplines*
Editorial Focus	*Journal of Child Psychology and Psychiatry (JCPP)* is internationally recognized to be the leading journal covering both child and adolescent psychology and psychiatry. *JCPP* publishes the highest quality clinically relevant research in psychology, psychiatry, and related disciplines. With a large and expanding global readership, its coverage includes studies on epidemiology, diagnosis, psychotherapeutic and psychopharmacological treatments, behavior, cognition, neuroscience, neurobiology, and genetic aspects of childhood disorders. Articles published include experimental, longitudinal, and intervention studies, especially those that advance our understanding of developmental psychopathology and that inform both theory and clinical practice. An important function of the journal is to bring together empirical research, clinical studies, and reviews of high quality that arise from different points of view, different theoretical perspectives, and different disciplines.
Audience	Psychologists, psychiatrists, social workers, and related disciplines.
Special Themes	Epidemiology, diagnosis, psychotherapeutic and psychopharmacological treatments, behavior, cognition, neuroscience, neurobiology, and genetic aspects of childhood disorders.
Where Indexed/ Abstracted	AMED (Allied and Complimentary Medicine Database); ASSIA (Applied Social Sciences Index & Abstracts); AgeLine; Biological Abstracts; BIOSIS Previews; British Nursing Index; Cumulative Index to Nursing and Allied Health Literature (CINAHL); Current Contents; Education Index; Education Resources Information Center (ERIC); Environmental Sciences and Pollution Management; Exceptional Child Education Resources (Online Edition); Excerpta Medica; Abstract Journals; Family Index; Health and Safety Science Abstracts (Online Edition); Indian Psychological Abstracts and Reviews; Linguistics and Language Behavior Abstracts; MEDLINE; PASCAL; Periodicals Contents Index; Personal Alert; Psychological Abstracts/PsycINFO; PsycSCAN: Developmental Psychology; SCOPUS; Social Sciences Citation Index; Social Sciences Index; Social Services Abstracts; Sociological Abstracts.
Year Established	1959
Circulation	Over 6,000 institutions with access to current content.
Frequency	Monthly.
Months Issued	Each month.
No. of Articles per Issue	Approximately 12.

SUBMISSIONS

Postal Mailing Address	N/A
Method for Submission	Online submission only.
Number of Copies	N/A
Disk Submission	Not required.
Online or E-mail Submission Allowed or Required	Online submission required via http://mc.manuscriptcentral.com/jcpp-camh

FORMAT OF MANUSCRIPT

Cover Sheet	Title, authors' names and affiliations, address of corresponding author.
Abstract	Maximum 300 words.
Key Words	Yes, 4–6 key words.
Length	6,000 words including title page, abstracts, references, table and figures.
Margins	Minimum 1 inch on all sides.
Spacing	Double-spaced.

STYLE

Name of Guide	See Notes for Contributors. The journal follows the style of the *Publication Manual of the American Psychological Association.*
Subheadings	Not specified.
References	Not specified.
Footnotes	Not specified.
Tables or Figures	Should be clearly drawn on a separate page, with legends for figures and headings for tables on separate sheets, clearly labeled.

REVIEW PROCESS

Type of Review	Anonymous peer review by at least 2 referees. Processing editor reads manuscript. "Blind" review available if requested by author.
Queries	Authors should read the Notes for Contributors carefully to determine whether their subject matter is appropriate, but if still in doubt, editors will advise.
Acknowledgment	By e-mail to corresponding author.
Review Time	4–5 months.
Revisions	Revisions are not always re-reviewed by referees; this depends on the nature and extent of revisions requested. Revisions are always read by the Editors.
Acceptance Rate	20%–25%.
Return of Manuscript	N/A
Lag Time to Print	6–10 months.

CHARGES TO AUTHOR

Author Alterations	No charges unless alterations are extensive.
Page Charges:	
Processing:	

REPRINT, SUBSCRIPTION, AND CONTACT INFORMATION

Reprint Policy	First author receives 50 free reprints automatically, and an order form is sent with proofs, on which extra reprints (at author's expense) can be ordered.
Book Reviews	By invitation only. Published in all issues except No. 1 (Annual Research Review). Books for review should be sent to: The Books Review Editors (Professor Lionel Hersov), *Journal of Child Psychology and Psychiatry,* ACPP, St. Saviour's House, 39-41 Union Street, London SE1 1SD, England.
Subscriptions	Available by e-mail at: cs-journals@wiley.com.
Affiliation	The *Journal of Child Psychology and Psychiatry* is published on behalf of the Association for Child and Adolescent Mental Health.
E-Mail Address	ingrid.king@acamh.org.uk
Website	www.blackwellpublishing.com/JCPP

JOURNAL OF CHILD SEXUAL ABUSE (JCSA)

Current Title	*Journal of Child Sexual Abuse (JCSA)*
Previous Title	N/A.
Editorial Focus	*JCSA* covers research issues, clinical issues, legal issues, prevention programs, case studies, and brief reports, focusing on three subject groups: child and adolescent victims of sexual abuse or incest, adult survivors of childhood sexual abuse or incest, and sexual abuse or incest offenders. Research, treatment approaches and techniques, prevention, intervention, and other programs concerning any of these groups are general categories of the published articles and brief reports. The articles emphasize applying research, treatment, and interventions to practical situations so the importance of the results will be clear.
Audience	Interdisciplinary professionals involved in any aspect of working with child sexual abuse issues, victims, or offenders.
Special Themes	Varies.
Where Indexed/ Abstracted	Abstracts in Anthropology; CINAHL Plus Full Text; Criminal Justice Abstracts; Education Research Abstracts; MEDLINE; PILOTS Database; PsycINFO; Social Service Abstracts; Social Work Abstracts; SOCIndex with Full Text; Sociological Abstracts.
Year Established	1990.
Circulation	381.
Frequency	6 per year.
Months Issued	Every 2 months.
No. of Articles per Issue	6–9.

SUBMISSIONS

Postal Mailing Address	*Journal of Child Sexual Abuse*, Institute on Violence, Abuse, and Trauma. 10065 Old Grove Rd, San Diego, CA 92131.
Method for Submission	E-mail.
Number of Copies	2 (1 original with identifying names, etc., and 1 copy without this information).
Disk Submission	Not required.
Online or E-mail Submission Allowed or Required	E-mail submission in MS Word, Works, or Excel format.

FORMAT OF MANUSCRIPT

Cover Sheet	Title; authors; brief biography of author's including degrees, positions, affiliations, and 1-sentence background; address for reprint requests.
Abstract	Required, no longer than 120 words.
Key Words	Required, 4–8 key words.
Length	No longer than 35 pages including references, abstract, and tables.
Margins	1 inch on all sides.
Spacing	Double-spaced.

STYLE

Name of Guide	*Publication Manual of the American Psychological Association;* Instructions for authors available from publisher's website (Taylor & Francis).
Subheadings	See style guide.
References	See style guide.
Footnotes	Not suggested unless absolutely needed; see style guide.
Tables or Figures	See style guide.

REVIEW PROCESS

Type of Review	Anonymous review by editorial board or ad hoc reviewers.
Queries	Editor welcomes query letters, e-mails, or phone calls.
Acknowledgment	On receipt of manuscript, copyright form sent to corresponding author to sign original.
Review Time	Approximately 3–5 months.
Revisions	Feedback is given to authors for making revisions. *JCSA* encourages revisions and resubmissions, with a cover letter by the author explaining what has been done to address the concerns.
Acceptance Rate	Approximately 20% initially; additional increase after revisions made.

Return of Manuscript	If requested.
Lag Time to Print	Approximately 8–12 months.

CHARGES TO AUTHOR

Author Alterations	None if done ahead of time.
Page Charges	None.
Processing	None.

REPRINT, SUBSCRIPTION, AND CONTACT INFORMATION

Reprint Policy	All authors receive a complimentary copy as well as a free PDF of their article. If they would like to order additional reprints, they may do so at pre-publication prices by placing an order BEFORE the article is published ("offprint order"). NOTE: If reprints are ordered after the issue has gone to press, the price doubles. The minimum reprint order is 50, and prices for quantities of reprints vary by the length of the article.
Book Reviews	No.
Subscriptions	Order through Taylor & Francis Inc., 325 Chestnut St., Suite 800, Philadelphia, PA 19106.
Affiliation	Institute on Violence, Abuse, and Trauma at Alliant International University.
E-Mail Address	journals@alliant.edu
Website	http://www.tandf.co.uk/journals/wcsa/ivatcenters.org

JOURNAL OF CHILDREN AND POVERTY

Current Title	*Journal of Children and Poverty*
Previous Title	N/A.
Editorial Focus	A forum for the presentation of research and policy initiatives in the areas of education, health, public policy, and the socioeconomic causes and effects of poverty, the *Journal of Children & Poverty* seeks to promote intellectual debate and new ideas that will impact policy and practice in the field of child and family welfare. The journal invites critical analyses to further the understanding of global issues affecting the quality of life for children and families.
Audience	Targets a cross-disciplinary audience that includes policy makers, academics, service providers, advocates, educators, philanthropists, and community leaders.
Special Themes	Not specified.
Where Indexed/ Abstracted	Current Abstracts; EBSCOhost; Family Index; Race Relations Abstracts; SCOPUS; Social Services Abstracts; Sociological Abstracts.
Year Established	1995.
Circulation	Not specified.
Frequency	Semiannually.
Months Issued	March and September
No. of Articles per Issue	4–6 per issue.

SUBMISSIONS

Postal Mailing Address	E-mail submission required.
Method for Submission	Please submit manuscripts to jcp@icpny.org with separate files for tables and graphs.
Number of Copies	E-mail one copy.
Disk Submission	Not necessary.
Online or E-mail Submission Allowed or Required	E-mail submission. No online submission system available.

FORMAT OF MANUSCRIPT

Cover Sheet	Templates provided through the journal's website at: http://www.tandf.co.uk/journals/journal.asp?issn=1079-6126&linktype=44.
Abstract	Required; see template.
Key Words	See template.
Length	See template.
Margins	See template.
Spacing	See template.

STYLE

Name of Guide	See journal style guide online at http://www.tandf.co.uk/journals/authors/style/layout/tf_1.pdf.
Subheadings	See style guide.
References	If you have any questions about references or formatting your article, please contact authorqueries@tandf.co.uk (please mention the journal title in your e-mail).
Footnotes	See style guide.
Tables or Figures	See style guide.

REVIEW PROCESS

Type of Review	All research articles in this journal have undergone rigorous peer review, based on initial editor screening and refereeing by 2 anonymous referees.
Queries	If you have any questions about references or formatting your article, please contact authorqueries@tandf.co.uk (please mention the journal title in your e-mail).
Acknowledgment	Not specified.
Review Time	Not specified.
Revisions	Based on editor's recommendation.
Acceptance Rate	Not specified.
Return of Manuscript	Manuscripts not returned.
Lag Time to Print	Not specified.

CHARGES TO AUTHOR

Author Alterations   Not specified.

Page Charges   Not specified.

Processing   Not specified.

REPRINT, SUBSCRIPTION, AND CONTACT INFORMATION

Reprint Policy   Corresponding authors will receive free online access to their article through our website (www.informaworld.com) and a complimentary copy of the issue containing their article. Reprints of articles published in this journal can be purchased through Rightslink® when proofs are received. If you have any queries, please contact our reprints department at reprints@tandf.co.uk.

Book Reviews   Journal prints book reviews. Contact editor for information.

Subscriptions   Available through e-mail at: subscriptions@tandf.co.uk.

Affiliation   Institute for Children and Poverty.

E-Mail Address   info@icpny.org

Website   http://www.icpny.org

JOURNAL OF COMMUNITY PRACTICE

Current Title	*Journal of Community Practice*
Previous Title	N/A.
Editorial Focus	As the only journal focusing on community practice, it covers research, theory, practice, and curriculum strategies for the full range of work with communities and organizations.
Audience	Practitioners and academics.
Special Themes	Social work, city and regional planning, social and economic development, community organizing, social planning and policy analysis, urban and rural sociology, public administration, and nonprofit management.
Where Indexed/ Abstracted	Academic Search Complete; Academic Search Premier; Academic Source Premier; ASSIA: Applied Social Science Index and Abstracts; CAB International Abstracts; CINAHL Database; Family Index Database; MegaFile; Social Work Abstracts; SOCIndex; TOCPremier; Violence and Abuse Abstracts.
Year Established	1994.
Circulation	569.
Frequency	Quarterly.
Months Issued	Not specified.
No. of Articles per Issue	6–10 issues.

SUBMISSIONS

Postal Mailing Address	Editor, Dr. Marie Weil, Professor, School of Social Work, CB#3550, University of North Carolina, Chapel Hill, Chapel Hill, NC 27599-3550.
Method for Submission	Not specified.
Number of Copies	4.
Disk Submission	Ok.
Online or E-mail Submission Allowed or Required	E-mail preferred.

FORMAT OF MANUSCRIPT

Cover Sheet	Separate sheet, which does not go out for review. Full title; author names; degrees; professional titles; designation of 1 author as corresponding author with full address, phone numbers, e-mail address, fax number; and date of submission.
Abstract	100 words.
Key Words	5–6 key words that identify article content.
Length	15–18 pages, including references and abstract. Lengthier manuscripts may be considered, but only at the discretion of the editor. Sometimes, lengthier manuscripts may be considered if they can be divided s for up into sections for publication in successive issues.
Margins	1 inch on all sides.
Spacing	Double-spaced for all copy except title page.

STYLE

Name of Guide	*Publication Manual of the American Psychological Association.*
Subheadings	Use as needed to guide reader through the article. No more than 4 levels.
References	References, citations, and general style of manuscripts should be prepared in accordance with the *APA Publication Manual*, 5th ed. Cite in the text by author and date (Smith, 1983) and include an alphabetical list at the end of the article.
Footnotes	No footnotes preferred; incorporate into text.
Tables or Figures	Tables and figures (illustrations) should not be embedded in the text, but should be included as separate sheets or files. A short descriptive title should appear above each table with a clear legend and any footnotes suitably identified below. All units must be included. Figures should be completely labeled, taking into account necessary size reduction. Captions should be typed, double-spaced, on a separate sheet.

REVIEW PROCESS

Type of Review	"Double-blind" anonymous peer review. 3 reviewers plus editor-in-chief read the manuscript in an anonymous review.

Queries	Authors are encouraged to read the journal to determine whether their subject matter would be appropriate.
Acknowledgment	Enclose a regular self-addressed, stamped envelope with submission.
Review Time	Approximately 3–4 months.
Revisions	See journal.
Acceptance Rate	Not specified.
Return of Manuscript	All accepted manuscripts, artwork, and photographs become the property of the publisher.
Lag Time to Print	Approximately 6–12 months.

REPRINT, SUBSCRIPTION, AND CONTACT INFORMATION

Reprint Policy	Reprints of individual articles are available for order at the time authors review page proofs. A discount on reprints is available to authors who order before print publication. Each corresponding author will receive 3 complete issues in which the article publishes and a complimentary PDF. This file is for personal use only and may not be copied and disseminated in any form without prior written permission from Taylor and Francis Group, LLC.
Book Reviews	Send to journal editor.
Subscriptions	The Haworth Press, Inc., 10 Alice Street, Binghamton, NY 13904-1580. Individuals $36, Institutions $48, Libraries 475. ACOSA members receive reduced rates.
Affiliation	Association for Community Organization and Association (ACOSA).
E-Mail Address	jcp@acosa.org
Website	http://www.informaworld.com/smpp/title~db=all~content=t792303986~tab=submit~mode=paper_submission_instructions

JOURNAL OF COMPARATIVE SOCIAL WELFARE

Current Title	*Journal of Comparative Social Welfare*
Previous Title	*New Global Development & J. of Int'l and Comparative Social Welfare.*
Editorial Focus	Board of Editors; International Consultants.
Audience	Social policy/welfare researchers and students with an interest in comparative and international studies.
Special Themes	Not specified
Where Indexed/ Abstracted	Extensively indexed.
Year Established	1981.
Circulation	Global.
Frequency	3 issues per year.
Months Issued	March, June, December.
No. of Articles per Issue	6–8.

SUBMISSIONS

Postal Mailing Address	325 School of Social Work; Louisiana State University, Baton Rouge, LA 70803.
Method for Submission	E-mail. Submissions from Europe should be sent to: Mark Drakeford, Co-Editor (Europe), *JCSW*, Cardiff School of Social Sciences, Glamorgan Bldg., King Edward Avenue, Cardiff, CF10 3WT, United Kingdom. E-mail: drakeford@cf.ac.uk. Submissions from the rest of the world should be sent to: Brij Mohan, Editor-in-Chief, *JCSW*, 325 School of Social Work, Louisiana State University, Baton Rouge, LA 70803, USA. E-mail: swmoha@lsu.edu, or dialog@cox.net.
Number of Copies	Authors are asked to submit 3 doubled-spaced manuscripts and one electronic version, either on disc or via e-mail.
Disk Submission	See above.
Online or E-mail Submission Allowed or Required	E-mail preferred, see above.

FORMAT OF MANUSCRIPT

Cover Sheet	Yes.
Abstract	Approximately 100 words.
Key Words	4–6 key words.
Length	Not exceeding 4,000 words.
Margins	Not specified.
Spacing	Double-spaced.

STYLE

Name of Guide	If you have any questions about formatting your article or references, please contact authorqueries@tandf.co.uk (please mention the journal title in your e-mail).
Subheadings	Short and relevant subtitles are encouraged.
References	*Publication Manual of the American Psychological Association* (APA) references are used in the social sciences, education, engineering and business. For detailed information, please see the *APA Publication Manual,* 5th edition. See also http://apastyle.apa.org/.
Footnotes	See website: http://www.tandf.co.uk/journals/authors/style/layout/tf_2.pdf.
Tables or Figures	These should be comprehensible without reference to the text. Each must appear on a separate sheet, with the desired position indicated in the text and numbered continuously (for example, Table 1, Table 2; Figure 1, Figure 2, etc.). Where various shadings are used within 1 figure, please ensure that it is easy to differentiate between them. See website: http://www.tandf.co.uk/journals/authors/style/layout/tf_2.pdf.

REVIEW PROCESS

Type of Review	*Journal of Comparative Social Welfare* is a refereed forum. All articles and papers have undergone careful editorial screening and peer review.
Queries	Not specified.
Acknowledgment	Not specified.

Review Time	Not specified.
Revisions	1 allowed.
Acceptance Rate	Approximately 40%.
Return of Manuscript	N/A.
Lag Time to Print	Approximately 4 months.

REPRINT, SUBSCRIPTION, AND CONTACT INFORMATION

Reprint Policy	20 electronic reprints allowed without any charge.
Book Reviews	Yes.
Subscriptions	http://www.informaworld.com/smpp/title~content=t725304179~tab=subscribe~db=all.
Affiliation	Louisiana State University.
E-Mail Address	dialog@Cox.net; swmoha@lsu.edu
Website	http://www.tandf.co.uk/journals/titles/17486831.asp

JOURNAL OF CONSULTING AND CLINICAL PSYCHOLOGY

Current Title	*Journal of Consulting and Clinical Psychology*
Previous Title	N/A.
Editorial Focus	The development, validity, and use of techniques of diagnosis and treatment of disordered behavior; studies of a variety of populations that have clinical interest, including but not limited to medical patients, ethnic minorities, persons with serious mental illness, and community samples; studies that have a cross-cultural or demographic focus and are of interest for treating behavior disorders; studies of personality and of its assessment and development where these have a clear bearing on problems of clinical dysfunction and treatment; studies of gender, ethnicity, or sexual orientation that have a clear bearing on diagnosis, assessment, and treatment; studies of psychosocial aspects of health behaviors; and methodologically sound case studies pertinent to the preceding topics.
Audience	Researchers in the discipline, faculty, and libraries.
Special Themes	Not specified.
Where Indexed/ Abstracted	Addiction Abstracts; Applied Social Science Index & Abstracts; Biological Abstracts; Communications Abstracts; Current Contents; Current Index to Journals in Education; Exceptional Child Education Resources; EMBASE/Excerpta Medica; Health Index; Index Medicus; Management Contents; PsycINFO; Rehabilitation Literature; Risk Abstracts; Sage Family Studies Abstracts; Social Sciences Citation Index; Social Sciences Index; Social Work Research & Abstracts.
Year Established	1937.
Circulation	11,700.
Frequency	Bimonthly.
Months Issued	February, April, June, August, October, December.
No. of Articles per Issue	14.

SUBMISSIONS

Postal Mailing Address	Electronic form via website.
Method for Submission	Not specified.
Number of Copies	Not specified.
Disk Submission	Not specified.
Online or E-mail Submission Allowed or Required	Online Portal required.

FORMAT OF MANUSCRIPT

Cover Sheet	This journal uses a masked reviewing system for all submissions. The first page of the manuscript should omit the authors' names and affiliations but should include the title of the manuscript and the date it is submitted.
Abstract	125–180 words.
Key Words	5 key words.
Length	35 pages, all parts.
Margins	1 inch.
Spacing	Double-spaced.

STYLE

Name of Guide	*Publication Manual of the American Psychological Association.*
Subheadings	See style guide.
References	List references in alphabetical order. Each listed reference should be cited in text, and each text citation should be listed in the References section.
Footnotes	Footnotes containing information pertaining to the authors' identities or affiliations should not be included in the manuscript, but may be provided after a manuscript is accepted.
Tables or Figures	Graphics files are welcome if supplied as TIFF, EPS, or PowerPoint files. The minimum line weight for line art is 0.5 point for optimal printing. When possible, please place symbol legends below the figure instead of to the side. Original color figures can be printed in color at the editor's and publisher's discretion provided the author agrees to pay ($255 for 1 figure, $425 for 2 figures, $575 for 3 figures, $675 for 4 figures, $55 for each additional figure).

REVIEW PROCESS

Type of Review	Masked review optional.
Queries	No query letters.
Acknowledgment	Editors acknowledge submission by mail.
Review Time	Approximately 60–90 days.
Revisions	Editor will notify author if revision is desired (most manuscripts are initially rejected; most published manuscripts have gone through 1 or 2 revisions).
Acceptance Rate	Approximately 29%.
Return of Manuscript	Manuscripts are not usually returned.
Lag Time to Print	Approximately 9 months.

CHARGES TO AUTHOR

Author Alterations	Authors are billed for alterations in proofs.
Page Charges	Not specified.
Processing	Not specified.

REPRINT, SUBSCRIPTION, AND CONTACT INFORMATION

Reprint Policy	Authors may purchase reprints of their articles (order form accompanies proofs).
Book Reviews	None.
Subscriptions	http://www.apa.org/journals/ccp/pricing.html.
Affiliation	American Psychological Association.
E-Mail Address	Not specified.
Website	http://www.apa.org/journals/ccp/

JOURNAL OF COUNSELING PSYCHOLOGY

Current Title	*Journal of Counseling Psychology*
Previous Title	N/A.
Editorial Focus	Empirical research in the areas of counseling activities, career development and vocational psychology, diversity and underrepresented populations in relation to counseling activities, the development of new measures to be used in counseling activities, and professional issues in counseling psychology.
Audience	PhD psychologists.
Special Themes	Empirical research in the areas of counseling activities, career development and vocational psychology, diversity and underrepresented populations in relation to counseling activities, the development of new measures to be used in counseling activities, and professional issues in counseling psychology.
Where Indexed/ Abstracted	PsycINFO; SSCI.
Year Established	1953.
Circulation	4,200 individual, 1,200 institutional.
Frequency	4 times per year.
Months Issued	January, April, July, October.
No. of Articles per Issue	10–14.

SUBMISSIONS

Postal Mailing Address	N/A.
Method for Submission	Electronic via website.
Number of Copies	N/A.
Disk Submission	N/A.
Online or E-mail Submission Allowed or Required	Required.

FORMAT OF MANUSCRIPT

Cover Sheet	Yes.
Abstract	180 words or less.
Key Words	5 key words.
Length	See: http://www.apa.org/journals/cou/submission.html.
Margins	See: http://www.apa.org/journals/cou/submission.html.
Spacing	See: http://www.apa.org/journals/cou/submission.html.

STYLE

Name of Guide	*Publication Manual of the American Psychological Association.*
Subheadings	See style guide.
References	See style guide.
Footnotes	See style guide.
Tables or Figures	See style guide.

REVIEW PROCESS

Type of Review	Masked, peer reviewed.
Queries	Send to: jcp@utk.edu.
Acknowledgment	Yes.
Review Time	Approximately 60 days.
Revisions	Usually 3 cycles until acceptance.
Acceptance Rate	Approximately 20%.
Return of Manuscript	No.
Lag Time to Print	Approximately 4 months.

CHARGES TO AUTHOR

Author Alterations	None if completed as part of peer review.
Page Charges	None.
Processing	None.

REPRINT, SUBSCRIPTION, AND CONTACT INFORMATION

Reprint Policy	May be purchased at time of initial publication.
Book Reviews	No.
Subscriptions	Yes.
Affiliation	American Psychological Association.
E-Mail Address	jcp@utk.edu
Website	http://www.apa.org/journals/cou/

JOURNAL OF DIVORCE & REMARRIAGE

Current Title	*Journal of Divorce and Remarriage*
Previous Title	N/A.
Editorial Focus	Clinical studies and research in family therapy, family mediation, family studies, and family law.
Audience	Professionals working with family dissolution.
Special Themes	Understanding of the divorce process, thereby to improve therapeutic, legal, and community services to those who are divorcing.
Where Indexed/ Abstracted	SFSA); Social Planning/Policy & Development Abstracts (SOPODA); Social Sciences Citation Index; Social Work Abstracts; Sociological Abstracts (SA); Studies on Women and Gender Abstracts; Violence and Abuse Abstracts: A Review of Current Literature on Interpersonal Violence (VAA).
Year Established	1977.
Circulation	Approximately 525.
Frequency	Quarterly.
Months Issued	Not specified.
No. of Articles per Issue	6–10.

SUBMISSIONS

Postal Mailing Address	2200 East River Road, Suite 124, Tucson, AZ 85719.
Method for Submission	Mail.
Number of Copies	4.
Disk Submission	Authors of accepted manuscripts are asked to submit a disk, preferably in Microsoft Word.
Online or E-mail Submission Allowed or Required	Not specified.

FORMAT OF MANUSCRIPT

Cover Sheet	Separate sheet, which does not go out for review. Full title, author names, degrees, professional titles; designation of one author as corresponding author with full address, phone numbers, e-mail address, fax number and date of submission.
Abstract	Approximately 100 words.
Key Words	5–6 words that identify article content.
Length	20 pages, including references and abstract. Lengthier manuscripts may be considered, but only at the discretion of the editor. Sometimes lengthier manuscripts may be considered if they can be divided up into sections for publication in successive issues.
Margins	1 inch on all sides.
Spacing	Double-spaced on all copy, except for title page.

STYLE

Name of Guide	*Publication Manual of the American Psychological Association.*
Subheadings	Use as needed to guide reader through the article. No more than 4 levels.
References	Author-date citation style; see style guide.
Footnotes	No footnotes preferred; incorporate into text.
Tables or Figures	Type tables Double-spaced. Submit camera-ready art (300 dpi printer or better) for all figures. Place each table or figure on a separate, numbered page at the end of the manuscript.

REVIEW PROCESS

Type of Review	"Double-blind" anonymous peer review. 3 reviewers plus editor-in-chief read the manuscript in an anonymous review.
Queries	Authors are encouraged to read the journal to determine if their subject matter would be appropriate.
Acknowledgment	Enclose a regular self addressed, stamped envelope with submission.
Review Time	Approximately 3–4 months.
Revisions	See journal.
Acceptance Rate	Not specified.
Return of Manuscript	Only if 9" × 12" self addressed, stamp envelope is enclosed.
Lag Time to Print	Approximately 6–12 months.

CHARGES TO AUTHOR

Author Alterations	Not specified.
Page Charges	Not specified.
Processing	Not specified.

REPRINT, SUBSCRIPTION, AND CONTACT INFORMATION

Reprint Policy	All authors receive 2 complimentary copies of the issue in which the article appears. Authors receive reprint order forms to purchase additional reprinted copies.
Book Reviews	Send to journal editor.
Subscriptions	The Haworth Press, Inc. 10 Alice Street, Binghamton, NY 13904-1508. Individuals $45, Institutions $180, Libraries $325.
Affiliation	Not specified.
E-Mail Address	Not specified.
Website	Not specified.

JOURNAL OF DRUG ISSUES

Current Title	*Journal of Drug Issues*
Previous Title	N/A.
Editorial Focus	Empirical research, theoretical analysis, policy analysis, clinical developments, theme issues, and book digests.
Audience	All who are interested in drug issues in their varied aspects.
Special Themes	Varied and topical.
Where Indexed/ Abstracted	Abstracts on Criminology and Penology; Addiction Abstracts; Alcohol and Alcohol Problems Science Database; Alcohol, Drugs and Traffic Safety; Applied Social Sciences Index and Abstracts; Criminology Abstracts; Current Contents: Social and Behavioral Sciences; Excerpta Medica; Expanded Academic Index; Family Abstracts; Family Resources Database; International Bibliography of Periodical Literature; International Bibliography of Book Reviews; Pharmaceutical Abstracts; Psychological Abstracts/PsycINFO; Research Alert; Social Planning/Policy and Development Abstracts; Social Sciences Citation Index; Sociological Abstracts.
Year Established	1971.
Circulation	1,100.
Frequency	Quarterly.
Months Issued	Winter, spring, summer, fall.
No. of Articles per Issue	10–14 per issue.

SUBMISSIONS

Postal Mailing Address	Florida State University, College of Criminology and Criminal Justice, 325 John Knox Road, Bldg L, Suite 102, MC 7809, Tallahassee, FL 32303.
Method for Submission	Surface mail and e-mail.
Number of Copies	4.
Disk Submission	N/A.
Online or E-mail Submission Allowed or Required	Allowed.

FORMAT OF MANUSCRIPT

Cover Sheet	Name, address, fax number, and e-mail address of contact author.
Abstract	Required. No more than 100 words.
Key Words	2–3 key words required.
Length	15–40 pages.
Margins	1 inch on all sides.
Spacing	Double-spaced, including references.

STYLE

Name of Guide	*Chicago Manual of Style.*
Subheadings	See style guide.
References	See style guide.
Footnotes	See style guide.
Tables or Figures	Must be camera-ready and suitable for page size of 4.5" × 7.5".

REVIEW PROCESS

Type of Review	Anonymous.
Queries	Accepted.
Acknowledgment	Provide a self-addressed, stamped postcard.
Review Time	Approximately 6–8 weeks.
Revisions	Author provided with reviewer comments as guide to revision.
Acceptance Rate	Approximately 20%.
Return of Manuscript	Provide a self-addressed, stamped envelope.
Lag Time to Print	Approximately 12 months.

CHARGES TO AUTHOR

Author Alterations	$2.50 per line for galley corrections if due to author error.
Page Charges	N/A.
Processing	N/A.

REPRINT, SUBSCRIPTION, AND CONTACT INFORMATION

Reprint Policy	Reprints may be purchased by author at time of publication.
Book Reviews	Book digests published once a year. Book reviews seldom published.
Subscriptions	$95 per year domestic. E-mail jdi@garnet.fsu.edu
Affiliation	College of Criminology and Criminal Justice, Florida State University.
E-Mail Address	jdi@garner.fsu.edu
Website	http://www2.criminology.fsu.edu/~jdi/

JOURNAL OF DUAL DIAGNOSIS

Current Title	*Journal of Dual Diagnosis*
Previous Title	*Journal of Chemical Dependency Treatment*
Editorial Focus	*Journal of Dual Diagnosis* examines the latest research in the co-occurrence of mental health disorders and substance abuse disorders. This publication publishes articles on current trends in research and practice as well as case studies from treatment programs internationally.
Audience	This journal serves clinicians, research neuroscientists, mental health services researchers, and health service administrators, as well as junior colleagues in training who are encouraged to contribute articles for publication.
Special Themes	Not specified.
Where Indexed/ Abstracted	Addiction Abstracts; Current Abstracts; EBSCOhost; Education Research Index; Family & Society Studies Worldwide; Family Index; SCOPUS; Social Services Abstracts; Social Work Abstracts; Toxicology Abstracts; Violence & Abuse Abstracts.
Year Established	1987.
Circulation	Not specified.
Frequency	Quarterly.
Months Issued	Not specified.
No. of Articles per Issue	8–9.

SUBMISSIONS

Postal Mailing Address	Manuscripts should be sent electronically. Signed, original release forms should be sent to: Karen LaFontaine, 844 Chafee Avenue, Augusta, GA 30912.
Method for Submission	Electronic submission of the manuscript and cover letter are to be sent directly to the Editorial Assistant, Ms. Karen LaFontaine, at klafontaine@mcg.edu.
Number of Copies	1 electronic copy.
Disk Submission	Not required.
Online or E-mail Submission Allowed or Required	E-mail submission required.

FORMAT OF MANUSCRIPT

Cover Sheet	Manuscripts should be prepared in accordance with the guidelines of the International Committee of Medical Journal Editors (http://www.icmje.org/).
Abstract	The abstract, up to 200 words, should state specifically the main purposes, procedures, findings, and conclusions of the study, emphasizing what is new or important.
Key Words	Include 3–10 keywords.
Length	5–25 pages, Times New Roman 12 point font. Longer manuscripts may be considered at the editor's discretion.
Margins	1 inch all around.
Spacing	Double-spaced

STYLE

Name of Guide	*Publication Manual of the American Psychological Association.*
Subheadings	Follow style guide.
References	Timely references should highlight the study's relevance within the past 5 years.
Footnotes	Follow style guide.
Tables or Figures	Tables and figures (illustrations) should not be embedded in the text, but should be included as separate sheets or files. A short descriptive title should appear above each table with a clear legend and any footnotes suitably identified below. All units must be included. Figures should be completely labeled, taking into account necessary size reduction. Captions should be typed, double-spaced, on a separate sheet.

REVIEW PROCESS

Type of Review	All papers are subject to peer review by a Review Editor (member of the Editorial Board of Review Editors) the Editor, and/or 1–3 invited referees.
Queries	Direct queries to the editor.
Acknowledgment	Not specified.

Review Time	Not specified.
Revisions	Per editor instruction.
Acceptance Rate	Not specified.
Return of Manuscript	Not specified.
Lag Time to Print	Not specified.

REPRINT, SUBSCRIPTION, AND CONTACT INFORMATION

Reprint Policy	Reprints of individual articles are available for order at the time authors review page proofs. A discount on reprints is available to authors who order before print publication. Each corresponding author will receive 3 complete issues in which the article publishes and a complimentary PDF. This file is for personal use only and may not be copied and disseminated in any form without prior written permission from Taylor and Francis Group, LLC.
Book Reviews	Journal publishes book reviews. Contact editor.
Subscriptions	Available through the website at www. informaworld.com.
Affiliation	Not specified.
E-Mail Address	klafontaine@mcg.edu.
Website	www.informaworld.com.

JOURNAL OF ELDER ABUSE & NEGLECT

Current Title	*Journal of Elder Abuse & Neglect*
Previous Title	N/A.
Editorial Focus	Study of the causes, treatment, effect, and prevention of the abuse and neglect of older people and disabled adults.
Audience	Practitioners, researchers, academics, administrators, policymakers, and educators in the fields of aging, health, social services, domestic violence, law, criminal justice, law enforcement, and other human services.
Special Themes	Not specified.
Where Indexed/ Abstracted	Ageinfo CD-ROM; AgeLine Database; Behavioral Medicine Abstracts; Brown University Geriatric Research Application Digest "Abstracts Section"; Cambridge Scientific Abstracts; Bulletin Board for Libraries ("BUBL"); Caredata CD: The Social and Community Care Database; CNPIEC Reference Guide: Chinese National Director of Foreign Periodicals; Communication Abstracts; coverage of information resources on INTERNET, JANET, and other networks; Criminal Justice Abstracts; Criminal Justice Periodical Index; Current Contents; Current Literature on Aging; Educational Administration Abstracts (EAA); Family Studies Database (online and CD-ROM); Family Violence & Sexual Assault Bulletin; Human Resources Abstracts (HRA); IBZ International Bibliography of Periodical Literature; Index to Periodical Articles Related to Law; Institute for Scientific Information; INTERNET ACCESS (& additional networks); MEDLINE; New Literature on Old Age; PsycINFO; Pubmed; Sage Family Studies Abstracts (SFSA); Sage Urban Studies Abstracts (SUSAP): Social Planning/Policy & Development Abstracts (SOPODA); Social Work Abstracts; Sociological Abstracts (SA); Violence and Abuse Abstracts: A Review of Current Literature on Interpersonal Violence (VAA).
Year Established	1989.
Circulation	800.
Frequency	Quarterly.
Months Issued	Spring, summer, fall and winter.
No. of Articles per Issue	5–6.

SUBMISSIONS

Postal Mailing Address	Georgia J. Anetzberger, PhD, Editor, *Journal of Elder Abuse & Neglect*, 1105 Hillrock Drive, South Euclid, OII 44121 USA E-mail: JofElderAbuse@aol.com.
Method for Submission	E-mail.
Number of Copies	Submissions should be sent by e-mail attachment with follow-up surface mail hard copy and accompanying cover letter.
Disk Submission	N/A.
Online or E-mail Submission Allowed or Required	See above.

FORMAT OF MANUSCRIPT

Cover Sheet	Separate sheet with title and abstract.
Abstract	Approximately 100 words.
Key Words	5–6 key words that identify article content.
Length	20–30 pages including references and tables; lengthier manuscripts considered at the discretion of the editor.
Margins	1 inch on all sides.
Spacing	Double-spaced for all copy.

STYLE

Name of Guide	*Publication Manual of the American Psychological Association.*
Subheadings	Use as needed to guide the reader through the article.
References	Author–date citation style; see style guide.
Footnotes	No footnotes; endnotes can be used.
Tables or Figures	All tables, figures, illustrations, etc., must be camera ready; prepare on separate sheets of paper using black ink and professional drawing instruments.

REVIEW PROCESS

Type of Review	External review by at 2 anonymous peers and internal review by 2 editorial staff.
Queries	Query letters are encouraged.
Acknowledgment	On receipt of the manuscript, a letter is sent to the senior author.
Review Time	Approximately 3 months.
Revisions	Resubmit 4 copies with a separate cover sheet describing the changes made in the manuscript and replying to the reviewers' comments.
Acceptance Rate	Approximately 5% accepted outright, 60% accepted subject to rewriting or revision, 35% rejected.
Return of Manuscript	Not returned.
Lag Time to Print	Approximately 12 months.

REPRINT, SUBSCRIPTION, AND CONTACT INFORMATION

Reprint Policy	Senior author receives 2 copies of the journal issue and 10 complimentary reprints several weeks after the issue is published. The junior author will receive 2 copies of the journal issue.
Book Reviews	Send to Bridget Penhale, MSc, CQSW, Associate International Editor and Book Review Editor, Center for Health and Social Care Studies and Service Development, University of Sheffield, Samuel Fox House, Northern General Hospital, Herries Road, Sheffield S5 7AU, United Kingdom.
Subscriptions	Included in memberships to the National Committee for the Prevention of Elder Abuse ($60 individual membership) and through the publisher, Taylor and Francis ($120 personal subscriptions, $693 institutional subscriptions).
Affiliation	Taylor and Francis Group, LLC, 325 Chestnut Street, Philadelphia, PA 19106.
E-Mail Address	Not specified.
Website	www.taylorandfrancis.com

JOURNAL OF ETHNIC & CULTURAL DIVERSITY IN SOCIAL WORK

Current Title	*Journal of Ethnic & Cultural Diversity in Social Work*
Previous Title	*Journal of Multicultural Social Work.*
Editorial Focus	*Journal of Ethnic & Cultural Diversity in Social Work* is dedicated to the examination of multicultural social issues as they relate to social work policy, research, theory, and practice. The journal helps readers develop knowledge and promote understanding of the impact of culture, ethnicity, and class on the individual, group, organization, and community in the delivery of human services.
Audience	Faculty; researchers; and professionals in the fields of social work; human services; psychology; counseling; mental health; and related social sciences who are interested in multicultural social issues.
Special Themes	Multicultural social issues as they relate to social work policy; research; theory; and practice.
Where Indexed/ Abstracted	Academic Search Alumni Edition (EBSCO); Academic Search Complete (EBSCO); Academic Search Premier (EBSCO); CINAHL: Cumulative Index to Nursing & Allied Health Literature (EBSCO); Educational Research Abstracts (T&F); Education Research Complete (EBSCO); ERIC: Educational Resources Information Center; IBZ: Internationale Bibliographie der Zeitschriftenliteratur (Germany); Index Copernicus/Google Scholar; PsycINFO, SOC Index (EBSCO); Social Services Abstracts (CSA/ProQuest); Social Work Abstracts; TOC Premier (EBSCO); VINITI: All Russian Scientific and Technical Information.
Year Established	1991.
Circulation	Approximately 400, more than 95% institutional subscription.
Frequency	4 per year.
Months Issued	March, June, September, and December
No. of Articles per Issue	Approximately 5 articles.

SUBMISSIONS

Postal Mailing Address	Editor, Mo Yee Lee, PhD, Professor, College of Social Work, Ohio State University, 1947 College Road, Room 325W, Stillman Hall, Columbus, OH 43210, USA.
Method for Submission	Surface mail and e-mail.
Number of Copies	2.
Disk Submission	N/A.
Online or E-mail Submission Allowed or Required	Yes.

FORMAT OF MANUSCRIPT

Cover Sheet	Required. Include title, name and contact information of authors.
Abstract	100 words.
Key Words	Required, 4–6 keywords.
Length	25 pages including content, tables, and figures.
Margins	1 inch.
Spacing	Double-spaced.

STYLE

Name of Guide	*Publication Manual of the American Psychological Association.*
Subheadings	Use as needed to guide reader through the article. No more than 4 levels.
References	Author–date citation style; see style guide.
Footnotes	No footnotes preferred; incorporate into text.
Tables or Figures	Type tables double-spaced. Submit camera-ready art (300-dpi printer or better) for all figures. Place each table or figure on a separate, numbered page at the end of the manuscript.

REVIEW PROCESS

Type of Review	Double-blind anonymous peer review. 3 reviewers plus editor-in-chief read the manuscript in an anonymous review.
Queries	Authors are encouraged to read the journal to determine whether their subject matter would be appropriate.
Acknowledgment	Not specified.
Review Time	3–4 months.
Revisions	See journal.

Acceptance Rate	Not specified.
Return of Manuscript	Only if 9" × 12" self-addressed, stamped envelope is enclosed.
Lag Time to Print	6–12 months.

REPRINT, SUBSCRIPTION, AND CONTACT INFORMATION

Reprint Policy	All authors receive 2 complimentary copies of the issue in which the article appears. Authors receive reprint order forms to purchase additional reprinted copies.
Book Reviews	Book reviews should be sent to: Editor, Mo Yee Lee, PhD, Professor, College of Social Work, Ohio State University, 1947 College Road, Room 325W, Stillman Hall, Columbus, OH 43210, USA.
Subscriptions	The Haworth Press, Inc, 10 Alice Street, Binghamton, NY 13904-1580. Individuals $32; institutions $60; libraries $125.
Affiliation	Not specified.
E-Mail Address	Not specified.
Website	Not specified.

JOURNAL OF EVIDENCE-BASED SOCIAL WORK

Current Title	*Journal of Evidence-Based Social Work*
Previous Title	N/A.
Editorial Focus	*Journal of Evidence-Based Social Work* examines the fast-growing use of evidence-based practice in everyday care, identifying and evaluating cutting-edge theory, techniques, and strategies. The journal content will help sharpen the reader's evaluation skills and diagnostic techniques, and help them design effective treatment procedures as they work to develop longitudinal studies, systematic reviews, qualitative studies, cause-and-effect reviews, and comparison studies.
Audience	Practitioners, researchers, clinicians, and academics in the fields of social work, public health, counseling, mental health, and psychology.
Special Themes	Not specified.
Where Indexed/ Abstracted	Academic Search Complete (EBSCO); CINAHL Database (EBSCO); CINAHL Database - Full Text (EBSCO); Family Index Database; Family Studies Abstracts (EBSCO); IBZ: Internationale Bibliographie der Zeitschriftenliteratur (Germany); Index Copernicus - Google Scholar; National Criminal Justice Reference Services Abstracts Database; Social Services Abstracts (CSA/ProQuest); SOCindex (EBSCO); SOCindex Full Text (EBSCO); Studies on Women and Gender Abstracts (Informaworld); VINITI: All Russian Scientific and Technical Information.
Year Established	2004.
Circulation	131.
Frequency	4 in 2009/ 5 in 2010.
Months Issued	January, April, July, October.
No. of Articles per Issue	Approximately 6.

SUBMISSIONS

Postal Mailing Address	Marvin D. Feit, PhD, Professor, Social Work, Norfolk State University, Ethelyn R. Strong School of Social Work, 700 Park Avenue, Norfolk, VA 23504 USA – or – John S. Wodarski, PhD, Professor of Social Work, College of Social Work, University of Tennessee, 324 Henson Hall, Knoxville, TN 37996 USA.
Method for Submission	Surface mail, disk, e-mail.
Number of Copies	3.
Disk Submission	Accepted.
Online or E-mail Submission Allowed or Required	Recommended. Send to: mdfeit@nsu.edu.

FORMAT OF MANUSCRIPT

Cover Sheet	Required.
Abstract	Included as part of the submission.
Key Words	3–5.
Length	Depends on author and topic, usually 20–25 written pages, but could be more.
Margins	1 inch.
Spacing	Not specified.

STYLE

Name of Guide	*Publication Manual of the American Psychological Association.*
Subheadings	See style guide.
References	See style guide.
Footnotes	See style guide.
Tables or Figures	Tables and figures (illustrations) should not be embedded in the text, but should be included as separate sheets or files. A short descriptive title should appear above each table with a clear legend and any footnotes suitably identified below. All units must be included. Figures should be completely labeled, taking into account necessary size reduction. Captions should be typed, double-spaced, on a separate sheets.

REVIEW PROCESS

Type of Review	Blind.
Queries	Accepted.
Acknowledgment	Not specified.

Review Time	Approximately 3 months.
Revisions	To be expected.
Acceptance Rate	We work extensively with author regarding revisions to assist in publication.
Return of Manuscript	If needed, as requested.
Lag Time to Print	Approximately 12 months after submission to publisher.

CHARGES TO AUTHOR

Author Alterations	N/A.
Page Charges	There are no charges for standard black and white pages. Color illustrations will be considered for publication; however, the author will be required to bear the full cost involved in color art reproduction. Color art can be purchased for online-only reproduction or for print and online reproduction. Color reprints can only be ordered if print + online reproduction costs are paid. Rates for color art reproduction are: Online-Only Reproduction: $225 for the first page of color; $100 per page for the next three pages of color. A maximum charge of $525 applies. Print and Online Reproduction: $900 for the first page of color; $450 per page for the next 3 pages of color. A custom quote will be provided for articles with more than 4 pages of color. Art not supplied at a minimum of 300 dpi will not considered for print.
Processing	N/A.

REPRINT, SUBSCRIPTION, AND CONTACT INFORMATION

Reprint Policy	Reprints of individual articles are available for order at the time authors review page proofs. A discount on reprints is available to authors who order before print publication. Each corresponding author will receive 3 complete issues in which the article publishes and a complimentary PDF. This file is for personal use only and may not be copied and disseminated in any form without prior written permission from Taylor and Francis Group, LLC.
Book Reviews	Not specified.
Subscriptions	www.tandf.co.uk/journals/webs or customer.service@taylorandfrancis.com or 1.800..0354.1420, press 4.
Affiliation	N/A.
E-Mail Address	customer.service@taylorandfrancis.com
Website	www.tandf.co.uk/journals/webs

JOURNAL OF FAMILY AND ECONOMIC ISSUES

Current Title	*Journal of Family and Economic Issues*
Previous Title	*Lifestyles: Family and Economic Issues.*
Editorial Focus	Family economic issues.
Audience	Researchers and practitioners who care about family economic well-being.
Special Themes	Not specified.
Where Indexed/ Abstracted	ABI/INFORM; EconLit; Family & Society Studies Worldwide; International Bibliography of the Social Sciences (IBSS); Journal of Economic Literature; PsycINFO; Research Papers in Economics (RePEc); SCOPUS.
Year Established	1978; new title as of 1992.
Circulation	Not specified.
Frequency	4 per year.
Months Issued	March, June, September, December.
No. of Articles per Issue	8.

SUBMISSIONS

Postal Mailing Address	Use e-submission only.
Method for Submission	Electronic form via the website.
Number of Copies	1.
Disk Submission	Not required.
Online or E-mail Submission Allowed or Required	Required.

FORMAT OF MANUSCRIPT

Cover Sheet	Paper title, author name, affiliation, e-mail, phone and brief bio.
Abstract	120 words.
Key Words	3–5 words.
Length	35 pages.
Margins	1 inch.
Spacing	Double-spaced.

STYLE

Name of Guide	*Publication Manual of the American Psychological Association.*
Subheadings	See style guide.
References	See style guide.
Footnotes	See style guide.
Tables or Figures	See style guide.

REVIEW PROCESS

Type of Review	Double-blind.
Queries	Allowed.
Acknowledgment	Yes.
Review Time	Approximately 3 months.
Revisions	Depends. Most papers are revised at least once.
Acceptance Rate	Approximately 32%.
Return of Manuscript	N/A.
Lag Time to Print	Usually within 6 months.

CHARGES TO AUTHOR

Author Alterations	None.
Page Charges	None.
Processing	None.

REPRINT, SUBSCRIPTION, AND CONTACT INFORMATION

Reprint Policy	Available by fee.
Book Reviews	Occasionally.

Subscriptions   Available.
Affiliation   Springer.
E-Mail Address   jfei.editor@gmail.com
Website   http://www.springerlink.com/content/104904/

JOURNAL OF FAMILY ISSUES

Current Title	*Journal of Family Issues*
Previous Title	N/A.
Editorial Focus	The journal is devoted to contemporary social issues and social problems related to marriage and family life and to theoretical and professional issues of current interest to those who work with and study families.
Audience	Practitioners, researchers, and academics encompassing such areas as: family studies, family violence, gender studies, psychology, social work, and sociology.
Special Themes	Family studies, family violence, gender studies, psychology, social work, and sociology.
Where Indexed/ Abstracted	Applied Social Sciences Index & Abstracts; Criminal Justice Abstracts; Current Abstracts; EBSCOhost; Education Research Index; ERIC; Family & Society Studies Worldwide; Family Index; PsycINFO; Race Relations Abstracts; SCOPUS; Social Services Abstracts; Social Work Abstracts; Sociological Abstracts; Studies on Women and Gender Abstracts; Violence & Abuse Abstracts.
Year Established	1980.
Circulation	Not specified.
Frequency	Monthly.
Months Issued	January, February, March, April, May, June, July, August, September, October, November, December.
No. of Articles per Issue	5–9.

SUBMISSIONS

Postal Mailing Address	Constance Shehan, Editor, *Journal of Family Issues,* Department of Sociology, University of Florida, 3219 Turlington Hall, P.O. Box 117330, Gainesville, FL 32611.
Method for Submission	Mail to the editor with an electronic copy on CD.
Number of Copies	Manuscripts should be submitted in quadruplicate — 1 file copy for our records (1-sided, double-spaced) and 3 copies (double-sided, double-spaced) to be sent out for review.
Disk Submission	Required with hard copies.
Online or E-mail Submission Allowed or Required	Currently, all manuscripts must be sent by postal service.

FORMAT OF MANUSCRIPT

Cover Sheet	Each manuscript should be accompanied by a cover sheet giving title, author(s), affiliation(s), acknowledgments, along with the full mailing address, phone and fax numbers, and e-mail address for the corresponding author.
Abstract	Authors should include an abstract of approximately 150 words.
Key Words	Not specified.
Length	Manuscripts should not exceed 30 typewritten double-spaced pages (including footnotes, references, tables, and figures).
Margins	1 inch all on each side.
Spacing	Double-spaced.

STYLE

Name of Guide	*Publication Manual of the American Psychological Association.*
Subheadings	Follow style guide.
References	Follow style guide.
Footnotes	Follow style guide.
Tables or Figures	Follow style guide.

REVIEW PROCESS

Type of Review	Peer review.
Queries	For further questions regarding submissions, please contact Diane Buehn at buehnd@ufl.edu.
Acknowledgment	Not specified.
Review Time	Not specified.
Revisions	Per editor instruction.
Acceptance Rate	Not specified.

Return of Manuscript	Manuscripts cannot be returned to authors.
Lag Time to Print	Not specified.

REPRINT, SUBSCRIPTION, AND CONTACT INFORMATION

Reprint Policy	Reprints of articles from all Sage journals are available for purchase for educational and marketing opportunities. If you are interested in ordering reprints, please contact us as specified below and we will provide you with a price quote.
Book Reviews	*Journal of Family Issues* does not publish book reviews.
Subscriptions	Available through the website at www.sagepub.com/journals.
Affiliation	Not specified.
E-Mail Address	journals@sagepub.com.
Website	www.sagepub.com/journals.

JOURNAL OF FAMILY PSYCHOLOGY

Current Title	*Journal of Family Psychology.*
Previous Title	N/A.
Editorial Focus	*Journal of Family Psychology* offers cutting-edge, ground-breaking, state-of-the-art, and innovative empirical research with real-world applicability in the field of family psychology. This premiere family research journal is devoted to the study of the family system, broadly defined, from multiple perspectives and to the application of psychological methods to advance knowledge related to family research, patterns and processes, and assessment and intervention, as well as to policies relevant to advancing the quality of life for families. Coverage includes empirical research in the areas of: couple and family patterns and processes, life stages, transitions, and stress and coping; health and illness across the family life cycle; couple and family diagnosis; couple and family assessment; couple and family intervention studies; family-focused prevention programs; families in transition (separation, divorce, and single parenting; remarriage and the stepfamily; adoption; death); family violence; employment and the family; family and other systems; diversity – ethnicity/race, social class, gender, sexual orientation, and disability; methodological and statistical advances in qualitative and quantitative research; policies related to families; theories related to families and systems; family psychology education and training; and professional issues in family psychology.
Audience	Researchers in the discipline, family therapists, faculty, students, libraries.
Special Themes	See editorial focus.
Where Indexed/ Abstracted	MEDLINE; PsycINFO.
Year Established	1987.
Circulation	2,400.
Frequency	Bimonthly.
Months Issued	February, April, June, August, October, December.
No. of Articles per Issue	10–14.

SUBMISSIONS

Postal Mailing Address	N/A.
Method for Submission	Electronic form via Web – http://www.apa.org/journals/fam/.
Number of Copies	N/A.
Disk Submission	N/A.
Online or E-mail Submission Allowed or Required	Online submission required.

FORMAT OF MANUSCRIPT

Cover Sheet	Refer to instructions to authors.
Abstract	180 word maximum typed on a separate page.
Key Words	5 key words.
Length	25–30 pages maximum for regular article and 12 pages maximum for brief report.
Margins	1 inch.
Spacing	Double-spaced.

STYLE

Name of Guide	*Publication Manual of the American Psychological Association.*
Subheadings	See style guide.
References	See style guide.
Footnotes	See style guide.
Tables or Figures	See style guide.

REVIEW PROCESS

Type of Review	Masked.
Queries	Query letters.
Acknowledgment	Editor acknowledges submission by e-mail via the Journal Back Office (JBO) system.
Review Time	60–90 days.
Revisions	Editor will notify author if revision is desired.

Acceptance Rate	Approximately 24%.
Return of Manuscript	No.
Lag Time to Print	Approximately 6 months.

REPRINT, SUBSCRIPTION, AND CONTACT INFORMATION

Reprint Policy	Authors may purchase reprints of their articles.
Book Reviews	None.
Subscriptions	Subscriptions Department, 750 First St. NE, Washington, DC 20022-4242.
Affiliation	Published by the American Psychological Association.
E-Mail Address	subscriptions@apa.org
Website	http://www.apa.org

JOURNAL OF FAMILY PSYCHOTHERAPY

Current Title	*Journal of Family Psychotherapy*
Previous Title	N/A.
Editorial Focus	Omnibus journal with a focus on family therapy and family studies.
Audience	Family therapy practitioners and academics, with a large international readership.
Special Themes	N/A.
Where Indexed/ Abstracted	Psychological Abstracts/PsycINFO.
Year Established	1989.
Circulation	Not specified.
Frequency	Quarterly.
Months Issued	March, June, September, December.
No. of Articles per Issue	7–10.

SUBMISSIONS

Postal Mailing Address	Terry S. Trepper, PhD, Editor, *Journal of Family Psychotherapy*, Department of Behavioral Sciences, Purdue University Calumet, 2200 169th Street, Hammond, IN 46323.
Method for Submission	Surface mail, e-mail.
Number of Copies	3.
Disk Submission	Yes.
Online or E-mail Submission Allowed or Required	Allowed.

FORMAT OF MANUSCRIPT

Cover Sheet	Yes.
Abstract	Yes.
Key Words	Yes.
Length	20 pages.
Margins	1 inch.
Spacing	Double-spaced.

STYLE

Name of Guide	*Publication Manual of the American Psychological Association.*
Subheadings	Yes.
References	Yes.
Footnotes	Yes.
Tables or Figures	Yes.

REVIEW PROCESS

Type of Review	Peer reviewed.
Queries	Yes.
Acknowledgment	Yes.
Review Time	Approximately 3 months.
Revisions	Yes.
Acceptance Rate	Approximately 38%.
Return of Manuscript	No.
Lag Time to Print	Not specified.

REPRINT, SUBSCRIPTION, AND CONTACT INFORMATION

Reprint Policy	Contact Patrick Dunn (Patrick.dunn@taylorandfrancis.com).
Book Reviews	Contact Terry Trepper (trepper@calumet.purdue.edu).
Subscriptions	Contact Les Anderson (les.anderson@taylorandfrancis.com).
Affiliation	Not specified.
E-Mail Address	Not specified.
Website	http://www.tandf.co.uk/journals/wjfp

JOURNAL OF FAMILY SOCIAL WORK

Current Title	*Journal of Family Social Work*
Previous Title	*Journal of Social Work and Human Sexuality*
Editorial Focus	*Journal of Family Social Work* examines the fast-growing use of evidence-based practice in everyday care, identifying and evaluating cutting-edge theory, techniques, and strategies. The journal presents literature from practitioners, researchers, and academics that collates and analyzes research findings relative to practice issues and intervention approaches over a given period of time.
Audience	Social work practitioners, clinicians and educators, mental health professionals, and counselors.
Special Themes	Not specified.
Where Indexed/ Abstracted	Criminal Justice Abstracts; Current Abstracts; EBSCOhost; Education Research Index; Family & Society Studies Worldwide; Family Index; Risk Abstracts (Online); SCOPUS; Social Services Abstracts; Social Work Abstracts, Sociological Abstracts; Studies on Women and Gender Abstracts; Violence & Abuse Abstracts.
Year Established	1981.
Circulation	Not specified.
Frequency	Quarterly.
Months Issued	Not specified.
No. of Articles per Issue	5–7.

SUBMISSIONS

Postal Mailing Address	Pat Conway, PhD, LCSW, 501 N. Columbia Road, Stop 9037, Grand Forks, ND 58202.
Method for Submission	Authors are strongly encouraged to submit manuscripts electronically.
Number of Copies	3.
Disk Submission	If submitting a disk, it should be prepared using MS Word or WordPerfect and should be clearly labeled with the authors' names, file name, and software program.
Online or E-mail Submission Allowed or Required	E-mail submissions to jfsw@medicine.nodak.edu.

FORMAT OF MANUSCRIPT

Cover Sheet	Follow style guide.
Abstract	Each article should be summarized in an abstract of not more than 100 words. Avoid abbreviations, diagrams, and reference to the text in the abstract.
Key Words	Not specified.
Length	Not specified.
Margins	1 inch on all sides.
Spacing	Double-spaced

STYLE

Name of Guide	*Publication Manual of the American Psychological Association.*
Subheadings	Follow style guide.
References	Follow style guide.
Footnotes	Follow style guide.
Tables or Figures	Tables and figures (illustrations) should not be embedded in the text, but should be included as separate sheets or files. A short descriptive title should appear above each table with a clear legend and any footnotes suitably identified below. All units must be included. Figures should be completely labeled, taking into account necessary size reduction. Captions should be typed, double-spaced, on a separate sheet.

REVIEW PROCESS

Type of Review	Peer review.
Queries	Contact editors.
Acknowledgment	Not specified.
Review Time	Not specified.
Revisions	Per editor instruction.
Acceptance Rate	Not specified.

Return of Manuscript	Not specified.
Lag Time to Print	Not specified.

CHARGES TO AUTHOR

Author Alterations	Not specified.
Page Charges	Not specified.
Processing	Not specified.

REPRINT, SUBSCRIPTION, AND CONTACT INFORMATION

Reprint Policy	Reprints of individual articles are available for order at the time authors review page proofs. A discount on reprints is available to authors who order before print publication. Each corresponding author will receive 3 complete issues in which the article publishes and a complimentary PDF. This file is for personal use only and may not be copied and disseminated in any form without prior written permission from Taylor and Francis Group, LLC.
Book Reviews	Contact editor.
Subscriptions	Available through the website at www.informaworld.com.
Affiliation	Not specified.
E-Mail Address	jfsw@medicine.nodak.edu
Website	www.informaworld.com

JOURNAL OF FAMILY VIOLENCE

Current Title	*Journal of Family Violence*
Previous Title	N/A.
Editorial Focus	The journal focuses on investigations utilizing group comparisons and single-case experimental strategies. It features case studies of special clinical relevance or that describe innovative evaluation and intervention techniques, reviews, and theoretical discussions that substantially contribute to understanding of family violence. This interdisciplinary forum presents information on clinical and investigative efforts concerning all forms of family violence and its precursors, including spouse-battering, child abuse, sexual abuse of children, incest, abuse of the elderly, marital rape, domestic homicide, the alcoholic marriage, and general family conflict.
Audience	The journal publishes clinical and research reports spanning a broad range of disciplines, including clinical and counseling psychology, sociology, psychiatry, public health, criminology, law, marital counseling, and social work.
Special Themes	Not specified.
Where Indexed/ Abstracted	AgeLine; Criminal Justice Abstracts; Current Contents/Social & Behavioral Sciences; EBSCOhost; Family & Society Studies Worldwide; PsycINFO; SCOPUS; Social Services Index; Sociological Abstracts.
Year Established	1986.
Circulation	Not specified.
Frequency	Bimonthly.
Months Issued	January, February, April, May, July, August, October, November.
No. of Articles per Issue	Usually 6 per issue.

SUBMISSIONS

Postal Mailing Address	Dr. Vincent B. Van Hasselt, Coeditor, Center for Psychological Studies, Nova Southeastern University, 3301 College Avenue, Fort Lauderdale, FL 33314 or Dr. Michel Hersen, PhD, ABPP, HPC/School of Professional Psychology, Pacific University, 222 SE 8th Avenue, Suite 563, Hillsboro, OR 97123-4218.
Method for Submission	Manuscripts, in American English, should be submitted to the Editor's Office via the journal's web-based online manuscript submission and peer-review system: www.jofv.edmgr.com.
Number of Copies	Submit 1 copy online.
Disk Submission	Not necessary.
Online or E-mail Submission Allowed or Required	Online submission required. No e-mail submissions.

FORMAT OF MANUSCRIPT

Cover Sheet	A title page should be uploaded as the first page of the manuscript and should include the title of the article, author's name (no degrees), and author's affiliation. Academic affiliations of all authors should be included. The affiliation should comprise the department, institution (usually university or company), city, and state (or nation) and should be typed as a footnote to the author's name. The suggested running head should be fewer than 80 characters (including spaces) and should comprise the article title or an abbreviated version thereof. This title page should also include the complete mailing address, telephone number, fax number, and e-mail address of the one author designated to review proofs.
Abstract	An abstract is to be provided, preferably no more than 150 words.
Key Words	A list of 4–5 key words is to be provided directly below the abstract. Key words should express the precise content of the manuscript, as they are used for indexing purposes.
Length	Not specified.
Margins	Not specified.
Spacing	Double-spaced.

STYLE

Name of Guide	Not specified. See journal website for style guidelines.
Subheadings	Not specified. See journal website for style guidelines.
References	Not specified. See journal website for style guidelines.
Footnotes	Footnotes should be avoided. When their use is absolutely necessary, footnotes should be numbered consecutively using Arabic numerals and should be typed at the bottom of the page to which they

refer. Place a line above the footnote, so that it is set off from the text. Use the appropriate superscript numeral for citation in the text.

Tables or Figures   Tables should be numbered (with Roman numerals) and referred to by number in the text. Each table should be typed on a separate sheet of paper. Center the title above the table, and type explanatory footnotes (indicated by superscript lowercase letters) below the table.

REVIEW PROCESS

Type of Review   Peer reviewed.

Queries   Inquiries regarding journal policy, manuscript preparation, and other such general topics can be sent to either Co-Editor's editorial managers at Amy Angleman: vjournal@nova.edu or Carole L. Londerée: londerec@pacificu.edu.

Acknowledgment   Managed through online submission system.

Review Time   Not specified.

Revisions   Managed through online submission system.

Acceptance Rate   Not specified.

Return of Manuscript   Manuscript not returned.

Lag Time to Print   Not specified.

REPRINT, SUBSCRIPTION, AND CONTACT INFORMATION

Reprint Policy   Reprints are available to authors, and order forms with the current price schedule are sent with proofs.

Book Reviews   Not specified.

Subscriptions   Available online through: http://www.springer.com/generic/order/journals+subscription?SGWID=0-40514-0-0-0.

Affiliation   Not specified.

E-Mail Address   service-ny@springer.com

Website   http://www.springerlink.com/content/104903/

JOURNAL OF FEMINIST FAMILY THERAPY

Current Title	*Journal of Feminist Family Therapy*
Previous Title	N/A.
Editorial Focus	*Journal of Feminist Family Therapy* provides an international forum to further explore the relationship between feminist theory and family therapy theory and practice. The journal presents thought-provoking and insightful articles of a theoretical nature, as well as articles focusing on empirical research and clinical application. *Journal of Feminist Family Therapy* critiques family therapy concepts from a feminist perspective with careful attention to cultural, class, and racial differences; applies a feminist-sensitive perspective to the treatment issues particular to women such as depression, agoraphobia, eating disorders, incest, and domestic abuse; explores the implications of a feminist approach to training and supervision in family therapy; examines the field of family therapy and its organization and institutional structure from a feminist perspective; and describes clinical applications of feminist-informed treatment in family therapy.
Audience	Social workers, psychologists, counselors, other related practitioners, researchers, and academics.
Special Themes	Incest, eating disorders, and domestic abuse; implications of a feminist approach to training and supervision in family therapy, its organizations, and institutional structure from a feminist perspective.
Where Indexed/ Abstracted	Applied Social Science Abstracts; Current Abstracts; EBSCOhost; Education Research Index; Family & Society Studies Worldwide; Family Index; Gender Watch; PsycINFO; SCOPUS; Social Services Abstracts; Social Work Abstracts; Sociological Abstracts; Violence & Abuse Abstracts; Women's Studies Abstracts.
Year Established	1989.
Circulation	Not specified.
Frequency	Quarterly.
Months Issued	January, April, July, October.
No. of Articles per Issue	3–5.

SUBMISSIONS

Postal Mailing Address	Manuscripts should not be sent by mail.
Method for Submission	Authors are strongly encouraged to submit manuscripts electronically. Manuscripts should be prepared using MS Word and should be clearly labeled.
Number of Copies	1 copy electronically.
Disk Submission	Not specified.
Online or E-mail Submission Allowed or Required	Please e-mail manuscripts to Anne M. Prouty Lyness, PhD, LMFT, at JFFT@antiochne.edu.

FORMAT OF MANUSCRIPT

Cover Sheet	Follow style guide.
Abstract	Each article should be summarized in an abstract of not more than 100 words. Avoid abbreviations, diagrams, and reference to the text in the abstract.
Key Words	Not specified.
Length	Not specified.
Margins	1 inch on all sides.
Spacing	Double-spaced.

STYLE

Name of Guide	*Publication Manual of the American Psychological Association.*
Subheadings	Follow style guide.
References	Follow style guide.
Footnotes	Follow style guide.
Tables or Figures	Tables and figures (illustrations) should not be embedded in the text, but should be included as separate sheets or files. A short descriptive title should appear above each table with a clear legend and any footnotes suitably identified below. All units must be included. Figures should be completely labeled, taking into account necessary size reduction. Captions should be typed, double-spaced, on a separate sheet.

REVIEW PROCESS

Type of Review	Peer reviewed.
Queries	Contact editor.
Acknowledgment	Not specified.
Review Time	Not specified.
Revisions	Per editor instruction.
Acceptance Rate	Not specified.
Return of Manuscript	Not specified.
Lag Time to Print	Not specified.

REPRINT, SUBSCRIPTION, AND CONTACT INFORMATION

Reprint Policy	Reprints of individual articles are available for order at the time authors review page proofs. A discount on reprints is available to authors who order before print publication. Each corresponding author will receive 3 complete issues in which the article publishes and a complimentary PDF. This file is for personal use only and may not be copied and disseminated in any form without prior written permission from Taylor and Francis Group, LLC.
Book Reviews	Journal publishes book reviews. Contact editor prior to submission.
Subscriptions	Available online through the website at www.informaworld.com.
Affiliation	Not specified.
E-Mail Address	JFFT@antiochne.edu.
Website	www.informaworld.com.

JOURNAL OF FORENSIC SOCIAL WORK

Current Title	*Journal of Forensic Social Work*
Previous Title	N/A.
Editorial Focus	Original articles that are theoretical, empirical, practice-oriented, or based on comprehensive reviews of the literature; letters to the editors; book reviews; opinion articles.
Audience	Practitioners, faculty, libraries, hospitals, courts, government agencies, nonprofit organizations and others involved in social work, law, psychiatry, psychology, sociology, etc.
Special Themes	N/A.
Where Indexed/ Abstracted	None yet.
Year Established	2010.
Circulation	TBD.
Frequency	2 times per year.
Months Issued	TBD.
No. of Articles per Issue	Approximately 6.

SUBMISSIONS

Postal Mailing Address	460 Smith Street, Suite K, Middletown, CT 06457.
Method for Submission	Surface mail, disk, or e-mail.
Number of Copies	1.
Disk Submission	Yes, in Microsoft Word submitted by disk or e-mail.
Online or E-mail Submission Allowed or Required	Allowed, in Microsoft Word submitted by disk or e-mail.

FORMAT OF MANUSCRIPT

Cover Sheet	Please include a separate title page with the submission that provides the author(s)' name(s) and affiliation(s); identifying information should not appear elsewhere on the submission.
Abstract	All manuscripts must include an abstract containing a maximum of 100–150 words on a separate page.
Key Words	List up to 6 key words on the same page immediately below the abstract.
Length	Manuscripts for full-length articles should not exceed 20 pages, including all references and tables.
Margins	See style guide.
Spacing	See style guide.

STYLE

Name of Guide	Author(s) should prepare manuscripts according to the latest edition of *Publication Manual of the American Psychological Association*.
Subheadings	Subheadings:
References	See style guide.
Footnotes	See style guide.
Tables or Figures	See style guide.

REVIEW PROCESS

Type of Review	Manuscripts will be reviewed anonymously.
Queries	Accepted at *JFSW*, 460 Smith Street, Ste K, Middletown, CT 06457 or e-mail pbrady@nofsw.org.
Acknowledgment	By e-mail or mail.
Review Time	Approximately 4–6 months.
Revisions	Authors will be e-mailed or mailed recommendations for revisions by reviewers.
Acceptance Rate	New journal.
Return of Manuscript	No.
Lag Time to Print	Approximately 6–12 months.

REPRINT, SUBSCRIPTION, AND CONTACT INFORMATION

Reprint Policy	TBD.
Book Reviews	Book Reviews: yes, solicited or unsolicited. Contact *JFSW* at 460 Smith Street, Ste K, Middletown, CT 06457 or e-mail pbrady@nofsw.org.

Subscriptions   http://www.tandf.co.uk/journals/subscription.asp
Affiliation   National Organization of Forensic Social Work.
E-Mail Address   pbrady@nofsw.org
Website   www.nofsw.org

JOURNAL OF GAY AND LESBIAN MENTAL HEALTH

Current Title	*Journal of Gay and Lesbian Mental Health*
Previous Title	*Journal of Gay and Lesbian Psychotherapy.*
Editorial Focus	This timely quarterly resource covers topics such as psychotherapy issues in LGBT people, mental health problems in LGBT people such as substance abuse and suicide, diversity within the LGBT community, and the needs of ethnic minority LGBT people. The journal provides a unique opportunity for researchers or anyone writing in the field of LGBT mental health to gather, develop, and explore their knowledge in the field.
Audience	The *Journal of Gay & Lesbian Mental Health* is the scientific resource for psychiatrists, psychologists, psychoanalysts, social workers, psychiatric nurses and nurse practitioners, educators, and mental health professionals in training.
Special Themes	
Where Indexed/ Abstracted	ABI/INFORM Global; Abstracts in Anthropology; Abstracts of Research in Pastoral Care & Counseling; Academic Index; Bulletin Board for Libraries (BUBL), coverage of information resources on INTERNET, JANET, and other networks; Cambridge Scientific Abstracts; CNPIEC Reference Guide: Chinese National Directory of Foreign Periodicals; Digest of Neurology and Psychiatry; Expanded Academic Index; Family Violence & Sexual Assault Bulletin; HOMODOK/"Relevant" Bibliographic database; Index to Periodical Articles Related to Law; INTERNET ACCESS (and additional networks), Inventory of Marriage and Family Literature (online and CD-ROM); Leeds Medical Information; Mental Health Abstracts (online through DIALOG); MLA International Bibliography; Periodical Abstracts, Research II; PsychNet; Psychological Abstracts/PsycINFO; Referativnyi Zhurnal (Abstracts Journal of the Institute of Scientific Information of the Republic of Russia); Sage Family Studies Abstracts (SFSA); Social Planning/Policy & Development Abstracts (SOPODA); Social Work Abstracts; Sociological Abstracts (SA); Studies on Women and Gender Abstracts; Violence and Abuse Abstracts: A Review of Current Literature on Interpersonal Violence (VAA).
Year Established	1987.
Circulation	Not specified.
Frequency	Quarterly.
Months Issued	Varies
No. of Articles per Issue	Varies

SUBMISSIONS

Postal Mailing Address	Association of Gay and Lesbian Psychiatrists (AGLP), Roy Harker, Executive Director, 4514 Chester Avenue, Philadelphia, PA 19143.
Method for Submission	Surface mail, disk, e-mail or electronic form via website.
Number of Copies	3 copies if submitted in hard copy.
Disk Submission	1
Online or E-mail Submission Allowed or Required	Submit to rharker@AGLP.org.

FORMAT OF MANUSCRIPT

Cover Sheet	Yes.
Abstract	1 page or less.
Key Words	20 words or less.
Length	Varies.
Margins	N/A.
Spacing	Double-spaced (if hard copy).

STYLE

Name of Guide	*Publication Manual of the American Psychological Association.*
Subheadings	Use as needed to guide reader through the article. No more than 4 levels.
References	Author-date citation style; see style guide.
Footnotes	No footnotes preferred, incorporate into text.
Tables or Figures	Type tables double-spaced. Submit camera ready art (300-dpi printer or better) for all figures. Place each table or figure on a separate, numbered page at the end of the manuscript.

REVIEW PROCESS

Type of Review	Double-blind anonymous peer review. 3 reviewers plus editor-in-chief read the manuscript in an anonymous review.
Queries	Authors are encouraged to read the journal to determine whether their subject matter would be appropriate.
Acknowledgment	Enclose a regular self-addressed, stamped envelope with submission.
Review Time	Approximately 3–4 months.
Revisions	See journal.
Acceptance Rate	Not specified.
Return of Manuscript	Only if 9" × 12" self-addressed, stamped envelope is enclosed.
Lag Time to Print	Approximately 6–12 months.

REPRINT, SUBSCRIPTION, AND CONTACT INFORMATION

Reprint Policy	All authors receive 2 complimentary copies of the issue in which the article appears. Authors receive reprint order forms to purchase additional reprinted copies.
Book Reviews	Journal editor.
Subscriptions	The Haworth Press, Inc., 10 Alice Street, Binghamton, NY 13904-1580.
Affiliation	Association of Gay and Lesbian Psychiatrists.
E-Mail Address	rharker@AGLP.org
Website	http://www.aglp.org/

JOURNAL OF GAY AND LESBIAN SOCIAL SERVICES

Current Title	*The Journal of Gay and Lesbian Social Services*
Previous Title	N/A.
Editorial Focus	GLBT issues and interventions.
Audience	Researchers and academics interested in GLBT issues.
Special Themes	LBGT.
Where Indexed/ Abstracted	See website.
Year Established	1988
Circulation	Not specified.
Frequency	Quarterly
Months Issued	Not specified.
No. of Articles per Issue	6.

SUBMISSIONS

Postal Mailing Address	No.
Method for Submission	E-mail.
Number of Copies	1.
Disk Submission	No.
Online or E-mail Submission Allowed or Required	Yes.

FORMAT OF MANUSCRIPT

Cover Sheet	Yes.
Abstract	Yes.
Key Words	Yes.
Length	25–30 pages.
Margins	1 inch.
Spacing	Double-spaced.

STYLE

Name of Guide	*Publication Manual of the American Psychological Association.*
Subheadings	See Web site.
References	See Web site.
Footnotes	See Web site.
Tables or Figures	See style guide.

REVIEW PROCESS

Type of Review	Blind peer review.
Queries	Not specified.
Acknowledgment	Not specified.
Review Time	Approximately 4–8 weeks.
Revisions	Not specified.
Acceptance Rate	Approximately 50%.
Return of Manuscript	No.
Lag Time to Print	Approximately 18–24 months.

REPRINT, SUBSCRIPTION, AND CONTACT INFORMATION

Reprint Policy	Yes.
Book Reviews	Yes.
Subscriptions	Not specified.
Affiliation	Official publication of the GLBT Caucus.
E-Mail Address	Michael.sullivan@lamar.edu
Website	Taylor & Francis has a website for this journal.

JOURNAL OF GENERAL PSYCHOLOGY

Current Title	*Journal of General Psychology*
Previous Title	N/A.
Editorial Focus	The journal covers traditional topics such as physiological and comparative psychology, sensation, perception, learning, and motivation, as well as more diverse topics such as cognition, memory, language, aging, and substance abuse, or mathematical, statistical, methodological, and other theoretical investigations.
Audience	Researchers and professors in the field, libraries.
Special Themes	Human and animals studies, mathematical and theoretical investigations, technical reports.
Where Indexed/ Abstracted	Abstracts for Social Workers; Academic Abstracts; Child Development Abstracts & Bibliographies; Current Contents: Social & Behavioral Sciences; Directory of Title Pages, Indexes, and Contents Pages; Exceptional Child Education Resources; Health and Psychosocial Instrument; Index Medicus; Linguistic and Language Behavior Abstracts; PsycINFO; Research Alert; Social Planning/Policy and Development Abstracts; Social Science Source; Social Sciences Citation Index; Social Sciences Index; Sociological Abstracts.
Year Established	1927.
Circulation	1035.
Frequency	Quarterly.
Months Issued	January, April, July, October.
No. of Articles per Issue	6–8 per issues.

SUBMISSIONS

Postal Mailing Address	Managing Editor, *The Journal of General Psychology,* 1319 18th Street, NW, Washington, DC 20036-1802.
Method for Submission	Electronic: http://mc.manuscriptcentral.com/heldref/gen.
Number of Copies	Not specified.
Disk Submission	Not specified.
Online or E-mail Submission Allowed or Required	Electronic required.

FORMAT OF MANUSCRIPT

Cover Sheet	Submission letter stating that it is not under consideration elsewhere.
Abstract	Yes, 100–125 words.
Key Words	3–4 keywords.
Length	Short reports to articles shorter than monograph length.
Margins	1 inch on all sides.
Spacing	Double-spaced and Times or Times New Roman.

STYLE

Name of Guide	*Publication Manual of the American Psychological Association.*
Subheadings	See style guide.
References	See style guide.
Footnotes	See style guide.
Tables or Figures	Please include all tables and figures in a separate document when submitting the manuscript. Electronic versions of figures as tiff or eps files or as original files in Excel, Illustrator, or PhotoShop are required for accepted manuscripts.

REVIEW PROCESS

Type of Review	Blind peer reviewed.
Queries	Welcomed.
Acknowledgment	By postcard.
Review Time	Approximately 2 months or less.
Revisions	Re-reviewed; submit with original copy
Acceptance Rate	Approximately 50%.
Return of Manuscript	Yes, no need to send self-addressed stamped envelope.
Lag Time to Print	Approximately 2–6 months.

CHARGES TO AUTHOR

Author Alterations   Not specified.

Page Charges   Not specified.

Processing   Charges for setting tables and scanning figures.

REPRINT, SUBSCRIPTION, AND CONTACT INFORMATION

Reprint Policy   Each author receives complimentary online access to the issue in which his or her article appears and permission to reproduce additional copies of that article. Contributors may order reprints at their own expense through Heldref Publications.

Book Reviews   Not specified.

Subscriptions   *Journal of General Psychology,* 1319 18th Street, NW, Washington, DC 20036; phone: 800-365-9753. $99.50 per year.

Affiliation   Not specified.

E-Mail Address   gen@heldref.org (for author/editor correspondence after manuscript acceptance).

Website   www.heldref.org

JOURNAL OF GENETIC PSYCHOLOGY

Current Title	*Journal of Genetic Psychology*
Previous Title	N/A.
Editorial Focus	*Journal of Genetic Psychology* is devoted to research and theory in developmental psychology across the life span.
Audience	Psychology researchers.
Special Themes	Not specified.
Where Indexed/ Abstracted	Abstracts for Social Workers; Biological Abstracts; BIOSIS; Child Development Abstracts & Bibliography; Current Contents: Social & Behavioral Sciences; Directory of Title Pages, Indexes and Contents Pages; Exceptional Child Education Resources; Health & Psychosocial Instruments; Index Medicus; Linguistic and Language Behavior Abstracts; Mental Health Abstracts; Psychological Abstracts/PsycINFO; Research Alert; Social Planning/Policy & Development Abstracts; Social Sciences Citation Index; Social Sciences Index; Sociological Abstracts; Sociology of Education Abstracts; Special Needs Abstracts.
Year Established	1981/1925.
Circulation	1,000+.
Frequency	Quarterly.
Months Issued	March, June, Sept, December.
No. of Articles per Issue	10–12.

SUBMISSIONS

Postal Mailing Address	Not specified.
Method for Submission	Electronic: http://mc.manuscriptcentral.com/heldref/gnt.
Number of Copies	Not specified.
Disk Submission	Not specified.
Online or E-mail Submission Allowed or Required	Electronic: http://mc.manuscriptcentral.com/heldref/gnt.

FORMAT OF MANUSCRIPT

Cover Sheet	Manuscript Central will prompt you to provide a submission letter, with a statement that the manuscript is not under concurrent consideration elsewhere and that you can vouch that the article is based on original research. In addition, the letter must state, where applicable, that (a) APA and IRB guidelines were followed in the treatment of participants, and (b) informed consent was granted by the participants and that they were debriefed. Each manuscript undergoes a blind review, a process that may require 2 to 3 months
Abstract	See style guide.
Key Words	See style guide.
Length	40 pages
Margins	See style guide.
Spacing	Double-spaced.

STYLE

Name of Guide	*Publication of the American Psychological Association.*
Subheadings	See style guide.
References	See style guide.
Footnotes	See style guide.
Tables or Figures	Figures (graphs and charts) must also be submitted through Manuscript Central. Tables should be prepared exactly as they are to appear in the journal. Accepted manuscripts will be edited for clarity and adherence to APA and Heldref style rules.

REVIEW PROCESS

Type of Review	Blind peer reviewed.
Queries	Not specified.
Acknowledgment	Not specified.
Review Time	Approximately 2–3 months.
Revisions	Not specified.

Acceptance Rate	Approximately 60% after revisions.
Return of Manuscript	Not specified.
Lag Time to Print	Approximately 10–12 months.

REPRINT, SUBSCRIPTION, AND CONTACT INFORMATION

Reprint Policy	Each author receives complimentary online access to the issue in which his or her article appears and permission to reproduce copies of that article. Contributors may order reprints at their own expense through Heldref Publications.
Book Reviews	Yes.
Subscriptions	Not specified.
Affiliation	Not specified.
E-Mail Address	Not specified.
Website	Not specified.

JOURNAL OF GERONTOLOGICAL SOCIAL WORK

Current Title	*Journal of Gerontological Social Work*
Previous Title	N/A.
Editorial Focus	Work and conceptual pieces related to social and health issues affecting older adults, with a focus on work with direct relevance to social work practice and social or health policy.
Audience	Academics in social work and gerontology, as well as policymakers, social work administrators, practitioners, consultants, and supervisors in long-term care facilities, acute-treatment and psychiatric hospitals, mental health centers, family service agencies, community and senior citizen centers, and public health and welfare agencies.
Special Themes	Emerging issues and cutting-edge research in gerontology are featured in Policy, Practice, and Research Forums and a section called "Brief Reports." Book reviews with clear policy and/or practice implications are also featured.
Where Indexed/ Abstracted	Abstracts in Social Gerontology; Academic Search Series; Ageline; Applied Social Science Index and Abstracts; CINAHL Database; PsycINFO; Social Service Abstracts; SocIndex; TOCPremier.
Year Established	1979.
Circulation	649 (includes libraries and individuals).
Frequency	8 times a year.
Months Issued	January, February, April, May, July, August, October, November.
No. of Articles per Issue	Approximately 10.

SUBMISSIONS

Postal Mailing Address	N/A.
Method for Submission	Electronically via website available at: www.agesocialwork.org.
Number of Copies	N/A.
Disk Submission	N/A.
Online or E-mail Submission Allowed or Required	Online submission required.

FORMAT OF MANUSCRIPT

Cover Sheet	Anonymous title page, as well as a title page with authors' names, titles, affiliations, addresses and acknowledgements.
Abstract	Approximately 100 words.
Key Words	3–10 words with abstract.
Length	15–20 pages; lengthier manuscripts considered at discretion of the editor.
Margins	1 inch all sides.
Spacing	Double-spaced.

STYLE

Name of Guide	*Publication Manual of the American Psychological Association.*
Subheadings	See style guide.
References	See style guide.
Footnotes	Discouraged; incorporate into text.
Tables or Figures	Professional quality in APA format.

REVIEW PROCESS

Type of Review	Anonymous peer review.
Queries	Direct queries to Editor at: JGeroSW@gmail.com.
Acknowledgment	Automated acknowledgement provided via e-mail by online system.
Review Time	2–4 months.
Revisions	Revisions requested within 4 weeks, subject to additional review.
Acceptance Rate	Approximately 20–30%.
Return of Manuscript	No.
Lag Time to Print	6 months.

REPRINT, SUBSCRIPTION, AND CONTACT INFORMATION

Reprint Policy	Senior author receives 1 copy of journal issue and 10 reprints of the article. Junior authors receive 1 copy of journal. Reprint order forms are provided to all authors.

Book Reviews	Proposals are welcome; please send to Book Review Editor.
Subscriptions	Individual: $218 v. Library: $1,298
Affiliation	*JGSW* is the official journal of the Association for Gerontology Education in Social Work (AGE-SW).
E-Mail Address	JGeroSW@gmail.com
Website	www.agesocialwork.org and www.tandf.co.uk/journals/wger

JOURNAL OF GLOBAL SOCIAL WORK PRACTICE

Current Title	*Journal of Global Social Work Practice*
Previous Title	N/A.
Editorial Focus	Forum for the publication, dissemination, and discussion of all aspects of developing a common base of global social work practice.
Audience	Scholars, practitioners, and students.
Special Themes	Community development/macro issues, immigration/resettlement, empowerment practice, grass roots organizing, administration/international program evaluation; micro work in international practice, international group work practice, technology, and global social work practice; micro finance/economic development; human trafficking work. We invite articles on any topic concerning global social work practice throughout the world. The journal aims to provide exemplars in international social work practice at all levels of practice. The journal seeks to give social workers around the world an opportunity to tell their story in how they provide change to individuals, groups, communities, villages and nations. Scholars, practitioners, and graduate students are invited to submit their manuscripts for publications. The journal is dedicated to international social workers and social work agencies, government organizations, and nongovernmental organizations to encourage mutual scholarly exchanges about practice methods, skills building, theoretical framework development, tactics, and techniques. The journal also offers opportunity to discuss the application of the IFSW Code of Ethics to all levels of international social work practice.
Where Indexed/ Abstracted	Working on SW Abstracts, Open Access Journals (OAJ), APA Database.
Year Established	2008
Circulation	Open access online.
Frequency	Twice a year.
Months Issued	May, June and November, December.
No. of Articles per Issue	8–15.

SUBMISSIONS

Postal Mailing Address	Jan A. Rodgers MSW, LCSW, BCD, MLIS, Editor-in-Chief, Dominican University, 7200 West Division Street, River Forest, IL 60305.
Method for Submission	Surface mail and e-mail.
Number of Copies	Surface mail (5) e-mail (1).
Disk Submission	Not specified.
Online or E-mail Submission Allowed or Required	Yes.

FORMAT OF MANUSCRIPT

Cover Sheet	Place the title of the paper at the top of the first page of the manuscript. Follow the title by the full name of all authors, their professional titles or positions, institutional affiliations, and e-mail addresses. If one author should function as the point of contact for questions or comments, please indicate this with the phrase "direct comments to" followed by the author's e-mail address. Do not include the author(s) name anywhere else in the document, except the title page. This way, anonymity can be maintained when your manuscript is reviewed by our editorial staff. Title and author information should appear on the first page as follows: Title, Author, Professional Title/ Position, Institutional Affiliation(s), E-mail Address(es), Direct comments to: E-mail address. All readers will better understand your message through simple explanations and less complex sentences. Shorter sentences and paragraphs are best suited to electronic publications. Refer to the Writing Tips section for further information on creating concise text for a diverse international audience.
Abstract	All papers submitted to *Journal of Global Social Work Practice* for consideration must include an abstract, or a brief summary of the paper's fundamental findings and conclusions. A well-written abstract will pique the interest of readers by succinctly presenting the facts and ideas that build a paper. Follow these guidelines: Place the abstract before the formal contents of the paper and after the title and author information, Limit the abstract to between 3 and 5 sentences of 100–150 words on the second page of the manuscript, State the main ideas of the paper only, avoiding unnecessary details and explanations that are addressed in the body of the paper, Do not include references or notes in the abstract, Use proper grammar, punctuation, and English language conventions. See: http://www.globalsocialwork.org/authors.html#style.

Key Words	3–4 key words. See: http://www.globalsocialwork.org/authors.html#style.
Length	Material of any length will be considered. In certain cases, articles may be edited into "research summaries" or divided into parts over more than 1 issue. This will be done only with the author's permission, however.
Margins	1 inch all around
Spacing	The entire document should be accurately typed and double-spaced. All pages should be numbered, starting with the title page. Use only a basic, widely available font like Courier or Times New Roman, 12 point. Do not justify or break words at the right margin.

STYLE

Name of Guide	*Publication Manual of the American Psychological Association.* See http://www.globalsocialwork.org/authors.html#style.
Subheadings	APA style guide. See http://www.globalsocialwork.org/authors.html#style.
References	APA style guide. See http://www.globalsocialwork.org/authors.html#style. Manuscripts should be prepared using the current edition of *Publication Manual of the American Psychological Association.* Because *Journal of Global Social Work Practice* is an online journal, authors should review the electronic publication format appendix in the APA style guide, which is online at ehttp://www.apastyle.org/ Additional APA citation resources can be found at http://owl.english.purdue.edu/owl/resource/560/01/ If you have any questions concerning reference format, send an e-mail to jrodgers@dom.edu.
Footnotes	See APA style guide. See http://www.globalsocialwork.org/authors.html#style.
Tables or Figures	See APA style guide. See http://www.globalsocialwork.org/authors.html#style. Illustrations, figures, and tables should be included as separate .GIF or .JPG files, named simply as figure1.gif, figure2.gif, etc. They should be embedded in their proper place in the document with captions or marked in the manuscript in this fashion: Insert figure1.gif here, caption. Additional data, illustrations, commentary, and complicated or long tables should be placed in consecutively numbered appendices at the end of the manuscript.

REVIEW PROCESS

Type of Review	Peer reviewed.
Queries	Dialogue with the author is encouraged.
Acknowledgment	Acknowledgement is given when the article is submitted by the Editor.
Review Time	Can be between 3–6 months.
Revisions	After the initial review (peer), authors can be asked to revise the article. The article is then resubmitted and then peer reviewed again if there are many changes. The author reviews one last time before publication. The flow of a typical article, from author to publication is as follows: An author is contacted by an editor to write an article or an author submits an article to the editors, The Editorial Office reviews the article, The author is asked to complete any revisions, The revised paper is reviewed and accepted for publication, The article is submitted to the production team, The production team performs editing, markup, and layout design, A draft version is prepared, Authors, editors and production staff review the contents of the draft, Authors, editors and production staff make corrections as necessary, The final approved article is published to the Journal of Global Social Work Practice Website.
Acceptance Rate	Approximately 50%.
Return of Manuscript	Not specified.
Lag Time to Print	Approximately 1–2 months.

REPRINT, SUBSCRIPTION, AND CONTACT INFORMATION

Reprint Policy	Must receive written permission to reprint. See http://www.globalsocialwork.org/authors.html#style.
Book Reviews	Book Reviews are peer reviewed. Unsolicited book reviews will not be accepted. Book reviews are initiated directly by the Editor, who asks a specific person to review a particular book.
Subscriptions	Free.
Affiliation	Dominican University Graduate School of Social Work, 7200 West Division Street, River Forest, Illinois 60305.
E-Mail Address	jrodgers@dom.edu or globalsocialwork@dom.edu
Website	www.globalsocialwork.org

JOURNAL OF HIV/AIDS & SOCIAL SERVICES

Current Title	*Journal of HIV/AIDS & Social Services*
Previous Title	N/A.
Editorial Focus	*Journal of HIV/AIDS & Social Services* provides a forum in which social workers and other professionals in the field of HIV/AIDS work can access the latest research and techniques in order to provide effective social, educational, and clinical services to all individuals affected by HIV/AIDS. From best practices and advice on case management to evaluations of the impact of various legislation and social policy decisions, this journal will keep you at the forefront of the field.
Audience	Social workers and other professionals in the field of HIV/AIDS work.
Special Themes	Not specified.
Where Indexed/ Abstracted	Abstracts on Hygiene & Communicable Diseases; Current Abstracts; EBSCOhost; Education Research Abstracts Online; Family Index; Global Health; PsycINFO; Social Services Abstracts; Social Work Abstracts; Sociological Abstracts.
Year Established	2002.
Circulation	Not specified.
Frequency	Quarterly.
Months Issued	Not specified.
No. of Articles per Issue	5–6.

SUBMISSIONS

Postal Mailing Address	Nathan L. Linsk, PhD, Professor, Jane Addams College of Social Work, Midwest AIDS Education & Training Center, University of Illinois at Chicago, 1040 W Harrison Street, M/C 309 EPASW4256, Chicago, IL 60607-7134, E-mail: Nlinsk@uic.edu.
Method for Submission	Manuscripts should be submitted (6 copies) to the Coeditors c/o Nathan L. Linsk, PhD.
Number of Copies	6.
Disk Submission	Not specified.
Online or E-mail Submission Allowed or Required	Discuss with editor.

FORMAT OF MANUSCRIPT

Cover Sheet	Submit a cover page with the manuscript, indicating only the article title (this is used for anonymous referencing). Second "title page": Include a regular title page as a separate document. Include the title again, plus full authorship.
Abstract	An abstract of approximately 100 words is required.
Key Words	3–10 key words should be provided for indexing purposes.
Length	15–25 pages.
Margins	1 inch on all sides.
Spacing	Double-spaced.

STYLE

Name of Guide	*Publication Manual of the American Psychological Association.*
Subheadings	See style guide.
References	See style guide.
Footnotes	See style guide.
Tables or Figures	Tables and figures (illustrations) should not be embedded in the text, but should be included as separate sheets or files. A short descriptive title should appear above each table with a clear legend and any footnotes suitably identified below. All units must be included. Figures should be completely labeled, taking into account necessary size reduction. Captions should be typed, double-spaced, on a separate sheet.

REVIEW PROCESS

Type of Review	Anonymous peer review.
Queries	Send queries to coeditor.
Acknowledgment	Not specified.
Review Time	Not specified.
Revisions	Per editor instructions.

Acceptance Rate	Not specified.
Return of Manuscript	Not specified.
Lag Time to Print	Not specified.

REPRINT, SUBSCRIPTION, AND CONTACT INFORMATION

Reprint Policy	Reprints of individual articles are available for order at the time authors review page proofs. A discount on reprints is available to authors who order before print publication. Each corresponding author will receive 3 complete issues in which the article publishes and a complimentary PDF.
Book Reviews	Contact editor.
Subscriptions	Available online through www.informaworld.com.
Affiliation	Incorporates *Journal of HIV/AIDS Infection in Children & Youth*.
E-Mail Address	Nlinsk@uic.edu.
Website	www.informaworld.com.

JOURNAL OF HOMOSEXUALITY

Current Title	*Journal of Homosexuality*
Previous Title	N/A.
Editorial Focus	*Journal of Homosexuality* is devoted to scholarly research on homosexuality, including sexual practices and gender roles and their cultural, historical, interpersonal, and modern social contexts.
Audience	Allied disciplinary and professional groups represented by anthropology, art, history, the law, literature, philosophy, politics, religion, and sociology, as well as research in the biological sciences, medicine, psychiatry, and psychology.
Special Themes	Not specified.
Where Indexed/ Abstracted	Abstracts in Anthropology, AgeLine, Criminal Justice Abstracts, Current Contents/Social and Behavioral Sciences, EBSCOhost Products, Education Research Abstracts, IGLSS Abstracts, INIST, Journal Citation Report/Social Sciences Edition, Lesbian Information Services, MEDLINE, PsycINFO/Psychological Abstracts, Social Sciences Citation Index, Social Scisearch, Sociological Abstracts, Studies on Women and Gender Abstracts
Year Established	1974
Circulation	Not specified.
Frequency	8 times per year.
Months Issued	Not specified.
No. of Articles per Issue	6–10 issues.

SUBMISSIONS

Postal Mailing Address	Address manuscripts to the Editor: John P. Elia: jpelia@sfsu.edu; San Francisco State University, College of Health & Human Services, 1600 Holloway Avenue, San Francisco, CA 94132-4161.
Method for Submission	Manuscripts should be submitted both electronically and in hard copy to the Editor
Number of Copies	1
Disk Submission	Disks should be prepared using MS Word or WordPerfect and should be clearly labeled with the authors' names, file name, and software program.
Online or E-mail Submission Allowed or Required	E-mail manuscripts to the editor: John P. Elia: jpelia@sfsu.edu;

FORMAT OF MANUSCRIPT

Cover Sheet	Statement saying the manuscript is not being considered elsewhere.
Abstract	100 words.
Key Words	Not specified.
Length	5–50 pages; Title and running head of not > 50 characters
Margins	1 inch.
Spacing	Double-spaced for all copy except title page.

STYLE

Name of Guide	*Publication Manual of the American Psychological Association* (APA).
Subheadings	Use as needed to guide reader through article. No more than 4 levels.
References	References, citations, and general style of manuscripts should be prepared in accordance with the *APA Publication Manual*, 4th ed.
Footnotes	Not footnotes preferred. Incorporate into text.
Tables or Figures	Tables and figures (illustrations) should not be embedded in the text, but should be included as separate sheets or files. A short descriptive title should appear above each table with a clear legend and any footnotes suitably identified below. All units must be included. Figures should be completely labeled, taking into account necessary size reduction. Captions should be typed, double-spaced, on a separate sheet.

REVIEW PROCESS

Type of Review	Peer reviewed.
Queries	Authors are encouraged to read the journal to determine whether their subject matter would be appropriate.
Acknowledgment	Enclose a regular self addressed stamped envelope with submission.
Review Time	Approximately 3–4 months.
Revisions	See journal.

Acceptance Rate	Not specified.
Return of Manuscript	Only if 9" × 12" self addressed stamped envelope is enclosed.
Lag Time to Print	Approximately 6–12 months.

REPRINT, SUBSCRIPTION, AND CONTACT INFORMATION

Reprint Policy	Reprints of individual articles are available for order at the time authors review page proofs. A discount on reprints is available to authors who order before print publication. Each corresponding author will receive 3 complete issues in which the article publishes and a complimentary PDF. This file is for personal use only and may not be copied and disseminated in any form without prior written permission from Taylor and Francis Group, LLC.
Book Reviews	Send book reviews directly to Dr. John P. Elia, Associate Editor and book Review Editor, at jpelia@sfsu.edu. Book reviews of single books should not exceed 6 pages (approximately 1,800 words) (double-spaced, in Times Roman 12 font, 1 inch margins (top/bottom and left/right). Composite book reviews (a review of 2 of more books in a single review) may include additional pages, which should be negotiated with the book review editor. Book reviewers should present a "balanced review" (of the strengths and weaknesses of a book) whenever possible.
Subscriptions	Haworth Press Inc.
Affiliation	Haworth Press Inc.
E-Mail Address	Not specified.
Website	http://www.informaworld.com/smpp/title~db=all~content=t792306897~tab=summary

JOURNAL OF HUMAN BEHAVIOR IN THE SOCIAL ENVIRONMENT

Current Title	*Journal of Human Behavior in the Social Environment*
Previous Title	*N/A.*
Editorial Focus	*Journal of Human Behavior in the Social Environment* helps social workers firmly grasp developing issues in human behavior theories. It provides an outlet for empirically based articles about human behavior theory that facilitate social workers' practice goals. This innovative journal is the first to address the complexities of human behavior in relation to social work and its relevancy to practice. This makes it an essential resource for classes in human behavior in the social environment. Articles provide you with groundbreaking, up-to-date information on developments in empirically based human behavior theory. They address conceptual and empirical foci that study human behavior as a complex phenomenon. Supported theories target specific behaviors for change, possess clarity by describing in detail the intended change(s), predict the change(s), and facilitate the desired behavioral change(s) through implementation of the model theory.
Audience	Practitioners, researchers, clinicians, and academics in the fields of social work, public health, counseling, mental health, sociology, anthropology, and psychology.
Special Themes	Not specified.
Where Indexed/ Abstracted	Abstracts Database; Abstracts in Anthropology; Academic Search Complete (EBSCO); CINAHL: Cumulative Index to Nursing and Allied Health Literature Database (EBSCO); CINAHL Database Full-Text (EBSCO); CINAHL Pus (EBSCO); Education Research Complete (EBSCO); HaPI -Health and Psychosocial Instruments (Ovid); Humanities International Complete (EBSCO); Humanities International Index (EBSCO); Index Copernicus - Google Scholar; IBZ: Internationale Bibliographie der Zeitschriftenliteratur (Germany); National Criminal Justice Reference Services, PsycINFO; Social Service Abstracts (CSA/ProQuest); SOCIndex (EBSCO); SOCIndex Full Text (EBSCO); Sociological Abstracts (CSA/ProQuest); VINITI: All Russian Scientific and Technical Information.
Year Established	1998.
Circulation	172.
Frequency	8.
Months Issued	February, March, April, June, August, September, November, December.
No. of Articles per Issue	6 (average).

SUBMISSIONS

Postal Mailing Address	Marvin D. Feit, PhD, Professor, Social Work, Norfolk State University, Ethelyn R. Strong School of Social Work, 700 Park Avenue, Norfolk, VA 23504 USA - or - John S. Wodarski, PhD, Professor of Social Work, College of Social Work, University of Tennessee, 324 Henson Hall, Knoxville, TN 37996 USA
Method for Submission	Surface mail, disk, e-mail.
Number of Copies	3.
Disk Submission	Accepted.
Online or E-mail Submission Allowed or Required	Recommended: mdfeit@nsu.edu.

FORMAT OF MANUSCRIPT

Cover Sheet	Needed.
Abstract	To be included as part of the submission.
Key Words	Usually 3–5 key words.
Length	Depends on the author and the topic. Length will vary, usually 20–25 pages written.
Margins	1 inch.
Spacing	Not specified.

STYLE

Name of Guide	*Publication Manual of the American Psychological Association.*
Subheadings	See style guide.
References	See style guide.
Footnotes	See style guide.
Tables or Figures	Tables and figures (illustrations) should not be embedded in the text, but should be included as separate sheets or files. A short descriptive title should appear above each table with a clear legend

and any footnotes suitably identified below. All units must be included. Figures should be completely labeled, taking into account necessary size reduction. Captions should be typed, double-spaced, on a separate sheet.

REVIEW PROCESS

Type of Review	Blind.
Queries	Accepted.
Acknowledgment	Not specified.
Review Time	Approximately 3 months.
Revisions	To be expected.
Acceptance Rate	We work with the author to assist in revisions.
Return of Manuscript	Yes, as requested.
Lag Time to Print	Approximately 12 months when forwarded to publisher.

CHARGES TO AUTHOR

Author Alterations	N/A.
Page Charges	There are no charges for standard black and white pages. Color illustrations will be considered for publication; however, the author will be required to bear the full cost involved in color art reproduction. Color art can be purchased for online only reproduction or for print and online reproduction. Color reprints can only be ordered if print and online reproduction costs are paid. Rates for color art reproduction are: Online-Only Reproduction: $225 for the first page of color; $100 per page for the next three pages of color. A maximum charge of $525 applies. Print and Online Reproduction: $900 for the first page of color; $450 per page for the next 3 pages of color. A custom quote will be provided for articles with more than 4 pages of color. Art not supplied at a minimum of 300 dpi will not considered for print.
Processing	N/A.

REPRINT, SUBSCRIPTION, AND CONTACT INFORMATION

Reprint Policy	Reprints of individual articles are available for order at the time authors review page proofs. A discount on reprints is available to authors who order before print publication. Each corresponding author will receive 3 complete issues in which the article publishes and a complimentary PDF. This file is for personal use only and may not be copied and disseminated in any form without prior written permission from Taylor and Francis Group, LLC.
Book Reviews	Not specified.
Subscriptions	www.tandf.co.uk/journals/webs or customer.service@taylorandfrancis.com or 1 800 0354.1420, press 4.
Affiliation	N/A.
E-Mail Address	customer.service@taylorandfrancis.com
Website	www.tandf.co.uk/journals/webs

JOURNAL OF IMMIGRANT AND REFUGEE STUDIES

Current Title	*Journal of Immigrant and Refugee Studies*
Previous Title	*Journal of Immigrant & Refugee Services*
Editorial Focus	Conceptual, empirical, review, also book reviews and brief notes.
Audience	Researchers, practitioners, policy makers interested in migration worldwide.
Special Themes	International and interdisciplinary focus on human migration.
Where Indexed/ Abstracted	Academic Search Premier (EBSCO); Academic Source Premier (EBSCO); The British Library; Cambridge Scientific Abstracts; Child Development Abstracts; Current Abstracts (EBSCO); Current Citation Express (EBSCO); DH-Data; EBSCOhost Electronic Journals Service (EJS); Education Research Complete; Educational Research Index (EBSCO); Electronic Collections Online (OCLC); Elsevier Eflow-D; Elsevier SCOPUS; ERCOMER Virtual Library; Family & Society Studies Worldwide (NISC); Family Index Database; GEOBASE; Index to Periodical Articles Related to Law; IndexCopernicus; Information for Practice; International Bibliography of Book Reviews on the Humanities & Social Sciences (IBR); International Bibliography of Periodical Literature on the Humanities and Social Sciences (IBZ); Intute; JournalSeek; Labordoc; Links@Ovid; MasterFILE Premier (EBSCO); NewJour; OCLC ArticleFirst; Ovid Linksolver; Peace Research Abstracts (Sage); Public Affairs Information Service (PAIS); Recent References (CSA); Social Care Online; Social Services Abstracts (CSA); SocIndex (EBSCO); Sociological Abstracts (CSA); Special Educational Needs Abstracts; TOC Premier (EBSCO).
Year Established	2000.
Circulation	Not specified.
Frequency	Quarterly.
Months Issued	March, June, September, December.
No. of Articles per Issue	5–7.

SUBMISSIONS

Postal Mailing Address	School of Social Work & Center for International Studies, 366 Social Sciences and Business Building, University of Missouri–St. Louis, One University Boulevard, St. Louis, MO 63121-4400, USA.
Method for Submission	E-mail. Manuscripts must be submitted electronically as an attached Word document to ijirs@umsl.edu.
Number of Copies	N/A.
Disk Submission	N/A.
Online or E-mail Submission Allowed or Required	Required, submission requested in Word format (no pdf).

FORMAT OF MANUSCRIPT

Cover Sheet	Yes.
Abstract	Each article should be summarized in an abstract of not more than 100–150 words. Avoid abbreviations, diagrams, and reference to the text in the abstract.
Key Words	4–6 key words.
Length	20 pages. Brief notes are 5–6 pages, Book reviews are 2–3 pages.
Margins	1 inch.
Spacing	Double-spaced.

STYLE

Name of Guide	*Publication Manual of the American Psychological Association* (APA).
Subheadings	Not specified.
References	References, citations, and general style of manuscripts should be prepared in accordance with the *APA Publication Manual*, 5th ed.
Footnotes	None.
Tables or Figures	Tables and figures (illustrations) should not be embedded in the text, but should be included as separate sheets or files. A short descriptive title should appear above each table with a clear legend and any footnotes suitably identified below. All units must be included. Figures should be completely labeled, taking into account necessary size reduction. Captions should be typed, double-spaced, on a separate sheet.

REVIEW PROCESS

Type of Review	Double-blind peer review of manuscripts that are each sent to 3 reviewers. Book reviews are reviewed by Book Editor; Brief Notes are not blind reviewed and are reviewed by editorial staff.
Queries	Yes.
Acknowledgment	E-mailed acknowledgement within 5 working days.
Review Time	Approximately 8 weeks.
Revisions	Must be completed within 3 weeks of notification.
Acceptance Rate	Approximately 55%.
Return of Manuscript	N/A.
Lag Time to Print	Approximately 6–12 months.

CHARGES TO AUTHOR

Author Alterations	Not specified.
Page Charges	Color illustrations will be considered for publication; however, the author will be required to bear the full cost involved in color art reproduction. Color art can be purchased for online only reproduction or for print and online reproduction. Color reprints can only be ordered if print and online reproduction costs are paid. Rates for color art reproduction are: Online-Only Reproduction: $225 for the first page of color; $100 per page for the next three pages of color. A maximum charge of $525 applies. Print and Online Reproduction: $900 for the first page of color; $450 per page for the next 3 pages of color. A custom quote will be provided for articles with more than 4 pages of color.
Processing	Not specified.

REPRINT, SUBSCRIPTION, AND CONTACT INFORMATION

Reprint Policy	http://www.informaworld.com/smpp/title~db=all~content=g912372509~tab=submit~mode=paper_submission_instructions.
Book Reviews	Yes, both invited and unsolicited, but are subject to review. Submit by e-mail to ijirs@umsl.edu.
Subscriptions	http://www.informaworld.com/smpp/title~db=all~content=g912372509~tab=subscribe.
Affiliation	University of Missouri – St. Louis, School of Social Work & Center for International Studies.
E-Mail Address	ijirs@umsl.edu
Website	http://www.informaworld.com/smpp/title~db=all~content=t792306878~tab=summary; http://www.tandf.co.uk/journals/titles/1556-2948.asp

JOURNAL OF INTERPERSONAL VIOLENCE

Current Title	*Journal of Interpersonal Violence*
Previous Title	N/A.
Editorial Focus	*Journal of Interpersonal Violence* is devoted to the study and treatment of victims and perpetrators of interpersonal violence. It provides a forum of discussion of the concerns and activities of professionals and researchers working in domestic violence, child sexual abuse, rape and sexual assault, physical child abuse, and violent crime. With its dual focus on victims and victimizers, the journal will publish material that addresses the causes, effects, treatment, and prevention of all types of violence.
Audience	Not specified.
Special Themes	Domestic violence, child sexual abuse, rape and sexual assault, physical child abuse, and violent crime focusing on both victims and victimizers.
Where Indexed/ Abstracted	Abstract Journal of the Educational Resources Information Center (ERIC); Academic Search – EBSCO; Applied Social Sciences Index & Abstracts (ASSIA); Biological Sciences Abstracts; CINAHL; Corporate ResourceNET – EBSCO; Criminal Justice Abstracts; Criminal Justice Periodical Index – ProQuest; Current Citations Express; Current Contents: Social & Behavioral Sciences; ERIC Current Index to Journals in Education (CIJE); Expanded Academic Index – Gale; Family & Society Studies Worldwide (NISC); Family Studies Abstracts (EBSCO); Health & Safety Sciences Abstracts; ISI Basic Social Sciences Index; MasterFILE – EBSCO; NCJRS Abstracts Database; NISC; Periodical Abstracts – ProQuest; PILOTS Database; Prevention Evaluation Research Registry for Youth (PERRY); Psychological Abstracts/PsycINFO; PsycLIT; Risk Abstracts; Safety Science & Risk Abstracts; SCOPUS; Sexual Diversity Studies (formerly Gay & Lesbian Abstracts); Social Care Online (formerly CareData); Social Science Source; Social Sciences Citation Index (Web of Science); Social Sciences Index Full Text; Social SciSearch; Social Services Abstracts; Social Work Abstracts; Sociological Abstracts; Standard Periodical Directory (SPD); Studies on Women and Gender Abstracts; TOPICsearch – EBSCO; Urban Studies Abstracts; Violence & Abuse Abstracts; Wilson OmniFile V; Wilson Social Sciences Index/Abstracts.
Year Established	1986.
Circulation	Not specified.
Frequency	Bimonthly.
Months Issued	February, April, June, August, October, December
No. of Articles per Issue	8–10.

SUBMISSIONS

Postal Mailing Address	Not necessary.
Method for Submission	Online only: Manuscripts should be submitted electronically to http://mc.manuscriptcentral.com/jiv, where authors will be required to set up an online account on the SageTrack system powered by ScholarOne.
Number of Copies	1 through online submission.
Disk Submission	Not specified.
Online or E-mail Submission Allowed or Required	Yes, online via website.

FORMAT OF MANUSCRIPT

Cover Sheet	Name, affiliation, mailing address, and phone number.
Abstract	Yes and biographical statement.
Key Words	None.
Length	22 pages including figures and references.
Margins	1 inch.
Spacing	Double-spaced.

STYLE

Name of Guide	*Publication Manual of the American Psychological Association.*
Subheadings	Not specified.
References	Separate pages.

Footnotes	Separate pages.
Tables or Figures	Separate pages.

REVIEW PROCESS

Type of Review	Peer reviewed.
Queries	Not specified.
Acknowledgment	Through online submission system.
Review Time	Not specified.
Revisions	Not specified.
Acceptance Rate	Not specified.
Return of Manuscript	Manuscripts not returned.
Lag Time to Print	Not specified.

REPRINT, SUBSCRIPTION, AND CONTACT INFORMATION

Reprint Policy	If you are seeking 1 copy of an article that was published in a SAGE journal, please purchase the article through the pay-per-view function (PPV) on the journal's online platform. Your PPV purchase will allow you to access, download, and print a copy of the article. To locate the journal article you are interested in, start here: http://online.sagepub.com
Book Reviews	Not specified.
Subscriptions	SAGE provides reprints for orders with a minimum quantity of 50. Orders for 49 or fewer copies will be fulfilled as permission.
Affiliation	Not specified.
E-Mail Address	jiv@u.washington.edu
Website	http://jiv.sagepub.com/

JOURNAL OF LESBIAN STUDIES

Current Title	*Journal of Lesbian Studies*
Previous Title	N/A.
Editorial Focus	*Journal of Lesbian Studies* examines the cultural, historical, and interpersonal impact of the lesbian experience on society, keeping all readers—professional, academic, or general—informed and up to date on current findings, resources, and community concerns.
Audience	Independent scholars, professors, students and lay people.
Special Themes	3 issues a year will be thematic; contact the editor for upcoming themes.
Where Indexed/ Abstracted	Not specified.
Year Established	1997.
Circulation	Not specified.
Frequency	Quarterly.
Months Issued	Not specified.
No. of Articles per Issue	7–10.

SUBMISSIONS

Postal Mailing Address	Editor, Esther D. Rothblum, PhD, San Diego State University, Women's Studies Department, 5500 Campanile Drive, San Diego, CA 92182-8138.
Method for Submission	Surface mail.
Number of Copies	Triplicate.
Disk Submission	Final manuscript only.
Online or E-mail Submission Allowed or Required	No.

FORMAT OF MANUSCRIPT

Cover Sheet	Statement not published or reviewed elsewhere.
Abstract	100 words; title with 50 characters for running head.
Key Words	None.
Length	Up to 15 pages.
Margins	1 inch.
Spacing	Double-spaced.

STYLE

Name of Guide	Not specified.
Subheadings	Open, but must be consistent.
References	References should be double-spaced and placed in alphabetical order. The use of footnotes within the text is discouraged. Words should be underlined only when it is intended that they be typeset in italics. If an author wishes to submit a paper that has been already prepared in another style, he or she may do so. However, if the paper is accepted (with or without reviewer's alterations), the author is fully responsible for retyping the manuscript in the correct style as indicated above. Neither the Editor nor the Publisher is responsible for re-preparing the manuscript copy to adhere to the journal's style.
Footnotes	Optional.
Tables or Figures	Tables and figures (illustrations) should not be embedded in the text, but should be included as separate sheets or files. A short descriptive title should appear above each table with a clear legend and any footnotes suitably identified below. All units must be included. Figures should be completely labeled, taking into account necessary size reduction. Captions should be typed, double-spaced, on a separate sheet.

REVIEW PROCESS

Type of Review	Peer reviewed.
Queries	Welcomed.
Acknowledgment	By letter.
Review Time	Approximately 3 months.
Revisions	Approximately 3 months.

Acceptance Rate	Not specified.
Return of Manuscript	Yes.
Lag Time to Print	Approximately 12–18 months.

REPRINT, SUBSCRIPTION, AND CONTACT INFORMATION

Reprint Policy	Reprints of individual articles are available for order at the time authors review page proofs. A discount on reprints is available to authors who order before print publication. Each corresponding author will receive 3 complete issues in which the article publishes and a complimentary PDF. This file is for personal use only and may not be copied and disseminated in any form without prior written permission from Taylor and Francis Group, LLC.
Book Reviews	Yes.
Subscriptions	See website.
Affiliation	Taylor and Francis.
E-Mail Address	e_rothbl@dewey.uvm.edu
Website	http://www.informaworld.com/smpp/title~db=all~content=g910383942~tab=toc

JOURNAL OF LGBT HEALTH RESEARCH

Current Title	*Journal of LGBT Health Research*
Previous Title	*Journal of Neuro-AIDS*
Editorial Focus	This journal provides an innovative forum for LGBT health issues and highlights the best of social-, psycho-behavioral and biologically based public health research and health services access/utilization evaluation. This top-notch scientific journal presents the leading researchers in LGBT health research from multiple disciplines discussing the finest quality research findings on topics previously lacking adequate study. Each issue examines the health disparities and public health problems of the LGBT community while focusing on population- and community-level health-related research designed to be useful in clinical practice. Featured reports include leading scientific research that identifies health-seeking behaviors in the LGBT community, and findings on the etiologies of positive health outcomes.
Audience	Physicians, psychologists, social workers, nurses, counselors, academic researchers and students in the schools of public health, medicine, allied health professions, sociology, psychology, and social work.
Special Themes	
Where Indexed/ Abstracted	Current Abstracts; EBSCOhost; Excerpta Medica, Abstract Journals; MEDLINE; Reactions Weekly; SCOPUS.
Year Established	2007
Circulation	Not specified.
Frequency	Quarterly.
Months Issued	Not specified.
No. of Articles per Issue	Varies, usually around 6.

SUBMISSIONS

Postal Mailing Address	Not applicable.
Method for Submission	Manuscripts should be submitted electronically (in MS Word format) to the Editor at slwelles@bu.edu.
Number of Copies	1
Disk Submission	Not required.
Online or E-mail Submission Allowed or Required	E-mail submission required.

FORMAT OF MANUSCRIPT

Cover Sheet	Follow style guide.
Abstract	Each article should be summarized in an abstract of not more than 100 words. Avoid abbreviations, diagrams, and reference to the text in the abstract.
Key Words	Not specified.
Length	Pages should be numbered. Length not specified.
Margins	1 inch on all sides.
Spacing	Double-spaced.

STYLE

Name of Guide	*Publication Manual of the American Psychological Association.*
Subheadings	Follow style guide.
References	References, citations, and general style of manuscripts should be prepared in accordance with the *APA Publication Manual*, 4th ed. Cite in the text by author and date (Smith, 1983) and include an alphabetical list at the end of the article.
Footnotes	Follow style guide.
Tables or Figures	Tables and figures (illustrations) should not be embedded in the text, but should be included as separate sheets or files. A short descriptive title should appear above each table with a clear legend and any footnotes suitably identified below. All units must be included. Figures should be completely labeled, taking into account necessary size reduction. Captions should be typed, double-spaced, on a separate sheet.

REVIEW PROCESS

Type of Review	Peer reviewed.
Queries	All editorial inquiries should be directed to the Editor.
Acknowledgment	Not specified.
Review Time	Not specified.
Revisions	Per editor instruction.
Acceptance Rate	Not specified.
Return of Manuscript	Manuscript not returned.
Lag Time to Print	Not specified.

REPRINT, SUBSCRIPTION, AND CONTACT INFORMATION

Reprint Policy	Reprints of individual articles are available for order at the time authors review page proofs. A discount on reprints is available to authors who order before print publication. Each corresponding author will receive 3 complete issues in which the article publishes and a complimentary PDF. This file is for personal use only and may not be copied and disseminated in any form without prior written permission from Taylor and Francis Group, LLC.
Book Reviews	Books and other materials for review purposes should be submitted to the Editor.
Subscriptions	Available online at: http://www.informaworld.com/smpp/title~db=all~content=g911839392~tab=subscribe
Affiliation	Not specified.
E-Mail Address	slwelles@bu.edu
Website	http://www.informaworld.com

JOURNAL OF LGBT YOUTH

Current Title	*Journal of LGBT Youth*
Previous Title	*Journal of Gay and Lesbian Issues in Education*
Editorial Focus	*Journal of LGBT Youth* is the interdisciplinary forum dedicated to improving the quality of life for lesbian, gay, bisexual, transgender, and questioning youth. This quarterly journal presents peer-reviewed scholarly articles, practitioner-based essays, policy analyses, and revealing narratives from young people. This invaluable resource is committed to advancing knowledge about, and support of, LGBT youth. The wide-ranging topics include formal and nonformal education; family; peer culture; the media, arts, and entertainment industry; religious institutions and youth organizations; health care; and the workplace.
Audience	Researchers, educators, social workers, and others working with GLBT youth.
Special Themes	Not specified.
Where Indexed/ Abstracted	Current Abstracts; EBSCOhost; Education Research Abstracts Online; Multicultural Education Abstracts; SCOPUS; Sociology of Education Abstracts; Studies on Women and Gender Abstracts.
Year Established	2003.
Circulation	Not specified.
Frequency	Quarterly.
Months Issued	Not specified.
No. of Articles per Issue	5–6.

SUBMISSIONS

Postal Mailing Address	Articles should be submitted by e-mail.
Method for Submission	Authors are strongly encouraged to submit manuscripts electronically to journal@jtsears.com.
Number of Copies	1 attached to e-mail.
Disk Submission	Not specified.
Online or E-mail Submission Allowed or Required	Yes, e-mail submission encouraged.

FORMAT OF MANUSCRIPT

Cover Sheet	Follow style guide.
Abstract	Each article should be summarized in an abstract of not more than 100 words.
Key Words	Not specified.
Length	Not specified.
Margins	1 inch on all sides.
Spacing	Double-spaced.

STYLE

Name of Guide	*Publication Manual of the American Psychological Association.*
Subheadings	Follow style guide.
References	Follow style guide.
Footnotes	Follow style guide.
Tables or Figures	Tables and figures (illustrations) should not be embedded in the text, but should be included as separate sheets or files. A short descriptive title should appear above each table with a clear legend and any footnotes suitably identified below. All units must be included. Figures should be completely labeled, taking into account necessary size reduction. Captions should be typed, double-spaced, on a separate sheet.

REVIEW PROCESS

Type of Review	All research articles in this journal have undergone rigorous peer review, based on initial editor screening and anonymous refereeing by 2 referees.
Queries	Contact editor.
Acknowledgment	Not specified.
Review Time	Not specified.
Revisions	Per editor instruction.
Acceptance Rate	Not specified.

Return of Manuscript	Not specified.
Lag Time to Print	Not specified.

REPRINT, SUBSCRIPTION, AND CONTACT INFORMATION

Reprint Policy	Reprints of individual articles are available for order at the time authors review page proofs. A discount on reprints is available to authors who order before print publication. Each corresponding author will receive 3 complete issues in which the article publishes and a complimentary PDF.
Book Reviews	Contact editor.
Subscriptions	Available through the website at www.informaworld.com.
Affiliation	American Education Research Association Queer Studies SIG.
E-Mail Address	journal@jtsears.com
Website	http://www.naea-reston.org/olc/pub/NAEA/home/

JOURNAL OF MARRIAGE & THE FAMILY

Current Title	*Journal of Marriage and Family*
Previous Title	N/A.
Editorial Focus	Original research and theory concerning families, broadly defined, from all disciplines of social sciences.
Audience	Family scholars, policy analysts.
Special Themes	None.
Where Indexed/ Abstracted	All major social science abstracting services.
Year Established	1939.
Circulation	6,200.
Frequency	5 issues a year.
Months Issued	February, May, August, November, December.
No. of Articles per Issue	Varies.

SUBMISSIONS

Postal Mailing Address	*Journal of Marriage and Family*, 248 Stone Building 319 College Avenue Greensboro, NC 27412.
Method for Submission	Electronic submission via website.
Approximately Number of Copies	N/A.
Disk Submission	No; electronic submission via website.
Online or E-mail Submission Allowed or Required	Required. Electronic submission via website.

FORMAT OF MANUSCRIPT

Cover Sheet	See website: http://www.ncfr.org/journals/marriage_family/submit/prep.asp.
Abstract	See website above.
Key Words	See website above.
Length	See website above.
Margins	See website above.
Spacing	See website above.

STYLE

Name of Guide	*Publication Manual of the American Psychological Association.*
Subheadings	See website: http://www.ncfr.org/journals/marriage_family/submit/prep.asp.
References	See website: http://www.ncfr.org/journals/marriage_family/submit/prep.asp.
Footnotes	See website: http://www.ncfr.org/journals/marriage_family/submit/prep.asp.
Tables or Figures	See website: http://www.ncfr.org/journals/marriage_family/submit/prep.asp.

REVIEW PROCESS

Type of Review	Anonymous blind review.
Queries	Yes.
Acknowledgment	E-mail from online submission website.
Review Time	Approximately 12 weeks.
Revisions	Typically required as per instructions from the editor.
Acceptance Rate	Approximately 14%.
Return of Manuscript	Not returned.
Lag Time to Print	Approximately 6 months.

CHARGES TO AUTHOR

Author Alterations	None.
Page Charges	None.
Processing	$25.00

REPRINT, SUBSCRIPTION, AND CONTACT INFORMATION

Reprint Policy	Available on order directly from the printer.
Book Reviews	Yes.

Subscriptions	Price varies. See website: https://secure.ncfr.com/membership.asp.
Affiliation	National Council on Family Relations.
E-Mail Address	jmf@uncg.edu
Website	http://www.ncfr.org/journals/marriage_family/home.asp

JOURNAL OF NONPROFIT & PUBLIC SECTOR MARKETING

Current Title	*Journal of Nonprofit & Public Sector Marketing*
Previous Title	N/A.
Editorial Focus	*Journal of Nonprofit & Public Sector Marketing* is devoted to the study of the adaptation of traditional marketing principles for use by nonprofit organizations.
Audience	Marketing professionals, scholars, and researchers from such disciplines as leisure services—parks, recreation, tourism; public relations; higher education administration; and health care.
Special Themes	Guest editors periodically develop thematic special issues.
Where Indexed/ Abstracted	ABSCAN, Inc; CNPIEC Reference Guide: Chinese National Directory of Foreign Periodicals; Communication Abstracts; Digest of Neurology and Psychiatry; Health Care Literature Information Network/HECLINET; Human Resources Abstracts (HRA); IBZ International Bibliography of Periodical Literature; INTERNET ACCESS (and additional networks) Bulletin Board for Libraries ("BUBL"), coverage of information resources on INTERNET.JANET; Journal of Academic Librarianship: Guide to Professional Literature; Journal of Health Care Marketing (Abstracts section); Management & Marketing Abstracts; Marketing Executive Report; Mental Health Abstracts (online through DIALOG); Operations Research/Management Science; OT BibSys, American Occupational Therapy Foundation; Political Science Abstracts; Public Affairs Information Bulletin (PAIS); Social Work Abstracts; Sport Database/Discus.
Year Established	1990
Circulation	Not specified.
Frequency	Quarterly.
Months Issued	Not specified.
No. of Articles per Issue	6–8.

SUBMISSIONS

Postal Mailing Address	Manuscripts should be submitted electronically to Professor Walter Wymer, Center for Socially Responsible Marketing, Faculty of Management, University of Lethbridge, 4401 University Drive, Lethbridge, Alberta, T1K 3M4, Canada.
Method for Submission	Electronic: walter.wymer@uleth.ca.
Number of Copies	Submit 2 versions: 1 with identifying information and 1 without.
Disk Submission	Not specified.
Online or E-mail Submission Allowed or Required	Electronic.

FORMAT OF MANUSCRIPT

Cover Sheet	Statement indicating author is not submitting elsewhere. Enclose a regular title page that includes the title plus full authorship, an abstract of approximately 100 words, and an introductory footnote with authors' academic degrees, professional titles, affiliations, mailing addresses, and any desired acknowledgement of research support or other credit.
Abstract	150 words.
Key Words	Yes, number not specified.
Length	10–30 pages including references and abstracts. Longer manuscripts may be considered.
Margins	1 inch.
Spacing	Double-spaced and in 12-point font.

STYLE

Name of Guide	*Publication Manual of the American Psychological Association.*
Subheadings	No more than 3 levels. See style guide.
References	Cite in the text by author and date (Smith, 1983) and include an alphabetical list at the end of the article.
Footnotes	No footnotes preferred; incorporate into text.
Tables or Figures	Tables and figures (illustrations) should not be embedded in the text, but should be included as separate sheets or files. A short descriptive title should appear above each table with a clear legend and any footnotes suitably identified below. All units must be included. Figures should be completely labeled, taking into account necessary size reduction. Captions should be typed, double-spaced, on a separate sheet.

REVIEW PROCESS

Type of Review	Peer reviewed.
Queries	To editor.
Acknowledgment	Enclose a regular self-addressed, stamped envelope with submission.
Review Time	Approximately 2–3 months.
Revisions	Not specified.
Acceptance Rate	Approximately 21%–30$.
Return of Manuscript	Not returned; author should retain copies.
Lag Time to Print	Approximately 6–12 months.

CHARGES TO AUTHOR

Author Alterations	Page proofs are sent to the designated author using Taylor & Francis' Central Article Tracking System (CATS). They must be carefully checked and returned within 48 hours of receipt.
Page Charges	Color illustrations will be considered for publication; however, the author will be required to bear the full cost involved in color art reproduction. Color art can be purchased for online-only reproduction or for print and online reproduction. Color reprints can only be ordered if print and online reproduction costs are paid. Rates for color art reproduction are: Online-Only Reproduction: $225 for the first page of color; $100 per page for the next 3 pages of color. A maximum charge of $525 applies. Print and Online Reproduction: $900 for the first page of color; $450 per page for the next 3 pages of color. A custom quote will be provided for articles with more than 4 pages of color.
Processing	Not specified.

REPRINT, SUBSCRIPTION, AND CONTACT INFORMATION

Reprint Policy	Reprints of individual articles are available for order at the time authors review page proofs. A discount on reprints is available to authors who order before print publication. Each corresponding author will receive 3 complete issues in which the article publishes and a complimentary PDF. This file is for personal use only and may not be copied and disseminated in any form without prior written permission from Taylor and Francis Group, LLC.
Book Reviews	Yes.
Subscriptions	See website: http://www.informaworld.com/smpp/title~db=all~content=t792306939~tab=subscribe.
Affiliation	Taylor & Francis, Inc., 325 Chestnut Street, Suite 800, Philadelphia, PA 19106.
E-Mail Address	Dself@Monk.Aum.Edu
Website	http://www.informaworld.com/smpp/title~content=t792306939~db=all

JOURNAL OF NUTRITION FOR THE ELDERLY

Current Title	*Journal of Nutrition for the Elderly*
Previous Title	N/A.
Editorial Focus	*Journal of Nutrition for the Elderly* invites papers on a broad array of topics in the nutrition and aging field, including but not limited to studies of preventive nutrition, nutritional interventions for chronic disease, aging effects on nutritional requirements, nutritional status and dietary intake behaviors, nutritional frailty and functional status, usefulness of supplements, programmatic interventions, transitions in care and long term care, and community nutrition issues.
Audience	Health care professionals who work with older adults: physicians, nurses, nutritionists, public health workers.
Special Themes	Newly Added Editorial Guidelines: Recognizing that the journal title runs counter to this concept, the incoming editors are nonetheless trying to move away from using the term "elderly" as a noun. Instead of "the elderly," the use of terms such as "older persons," "older adults," and "in later life," is suggested. "Elderly persons" or "elderly individuals" can also be used. In the past, the people enrolled in medical research studies have been referred to as "subjects" and this term has been broadly institutionalized. However, recognizing that individuals are not just passively observed but contribute actively to clinical and translational research, we recommend the terminology change from "subjects" to "participants".
Where Indexed/ Abstracted	Abstracts in Anthropology; AgeInfo; AgeLine; Biological Abstracts; BIOSIS Previews; CAB International; Cumulative Index to Nursing and Allied Health Literature (CINAHL); EBSCOhost Products; GeroLit; MEDLINE; Psychological Abstracts/PsycINFO.
Year Established	1981
Circulation	1,000+.
Frequency	Quarterly.
Months Issued	Spring, summer, fall, winter.
No. of Articles per Issue	3–7.

SUBMISSIONS

Postal Mailing Address	Editor-In-Chief: Connie W. Bales, PhD, RD, *Journal of Nutrition for the Elderly,* Box 3003, Center for Aging, Duke University Medical Center, Durham, NC 27710.
Method for Submission	Electronic strongly encouraged; bales001@mc.duke.edu.
Number of Copies	4.
Disk Submission	If submitting a disk, it should be prepared using MS Word or WordPerfect and should be clearly labeled with the authors' names, file name, and software program.
Online or E-mail Submission Allowed or Required	Electronic strongly encouraged; bales001@mc.duke.edu.

FORMAT OF MANUSCRIPT

Cover Sheet	Note that a new feature of "Take Away Points" has been added at the end of the manuscript. These points can replace or partially replace a concluding paragraph or simply restate the conclusions of the article. They should represent the important points that a reader should come away with after reading the article.
Abstract	150 words.
Key Words	5–10 key words.
Length	10–30 pages.
Margins	1 inch.
Spacing	Double-spaced with 12-point font in New Times Roman.

STYLE

Name of Guide	*Annals of Internal Medicine.*
Subheadings	See website
References	References, citations, and general style of manuscripts should be prepared in accordance with the style of the *Annals of Internal Medicine.* That is, references should be numbered, using numbers in parentheses, in order of which they appear in the text.
Footnotes	Not specified.
Tables or Figures	Tables and figures (illustrations) should not be embedded in the text, but should be included as separate sheets or files. A short descriptive title should appear above each table with any footnotes

suitably identified below. All units must be included. Figures should be completely labeled, taking into account necessary size reduction. Figure headings should be typed, double-spaced, on a separate sheet. Illustrations submitted (line drawings, halftones, photos, photomicrographs, etc.) should be clean originals or digital files. Digital files are recommended for highest quality reproduction and should follow these guidelines: 300 dpi or higher, sized to fit on journal page, EPS, TIFF, or PSD format only and submitted as separate files, not embedded in text files.

REVIEW PROCESS

Type of Review	Anonymous peer reviewed.
Queries	Accepted.
Acknowledgment	Not specified.
Review Time	Not specified.
Revisions	Not specified.
Acceptance Rate	Not specified.
Return of Manuscript	Each manuscript must be accompanied by a statement that it has not been published elsewhere and that it has not been submitted simultaneously for publication elsewhere. Authors are responsible for obtaining permission to reproduce copyrighted material from other sources and are required to sign an agreement for the transfer of copyright to the publisher. All accepted manuscripts, artwork, and photographs become the property of the publisher.
Lag Time to Print	Not specified.

CHARGES TO AUTHOR

Author Alterations	Page proofs are sent to the designated author using Taylor & Francis' Central Article Tracking System (CATS). They must be carefully checked and returned within 48 hours of receipt
Page Charges	See website.
Processing	Color illustrations will be considered for publication; however, the author will be required to bear the full cost involved in color art reproduction. Color art can be purchased for online-only reproduction or for print and online reproduction. Color reprints can only be ordered if print and online reproduction costs are paid. Rates for color art reproduction are: Online-Only Reproduction: $225 for the first page of color; $100 per page for the next three pages of color. A maximum charge of $525 applies. Print and Online Reproduction: $900 for the first page of color; $450 per page for the next 3 pages of color. A custom quote will be provided for articles with more than 4 pages of color. Art not supplied at a minimum of 300 dpi will not be considered for print.

REPRINT, SUBSCRIPTION, AND CONTACT INFORMATION

Reprint Policy	Reprints of individual articles are available for order at the time authors review page proofs. A discount on reprints is available to authors who order before print publication. Each corresponding author will receive 3 complete issues in which the article publishes and a complimentary PDF. This file is for personal use only and may not be copied and disseminated in any form without prior written permission from Taylor and Francis Group, LLC.
Book Reviews	Not specified.
Subscriptions	See website: http://www.informaworld.com/smpp/title~db=all~content=t792306906~tab=subscribe.
Affiliation	Haworth Inc.
E-Mail Address	bales001@mc.duke.edu
Website	http://www.informaworld.com/smpp/title~db=all~content=t792306906~tab=summary

JOURNAL OF OFFENDER REHABILITATION

Current Title	*Journal of Offender Rehabilitation*
Previous Title	*Journal of Offender Counseling Services Rehabilitation.*
Editorial Focus	A multidisciplinary journal of innovation in research, services, and programs in criminal justice and corrections. Original research using qualitative or quantitative methodology, theoretical discussions, evaluations of program outcomes, and state of the science reviews will be considered. A primary journal focus is the use of research to improve practice, with articles clearly defining the theoretical and empirical basis for program models and establishing connections between research findings and needed interventions and services. Programs and services for correctional populations residing in prison, as well as in the community, are examined.
	The range of topics included in the journal is broad and encompasses alternatives to incarceration; community reentry and reintegration; alcohol, substance abuse and mental health treatment interventions; services for correctional populations with special needs; recidivism prevention strategies; educational and vocational programs; families and incarceration; and culturally appropriate practice and probation and parole services.
Audience	Not specified.
Special Themes	Not specified.
Where Indexed/ Abstracted	Academic Search Premiere; Criminal Justice Abstracts; Expanded Academic ASAP; Family Index Database; Family Justice; Family & Society Studies Worldwide; H.W. Wilson-Social Sciences Index; IBZ; PsycINFO; PYSCLINE; Referativnyi Zhurnal; SCOPUS; Social Services Abstracts; Social Work Abstracts; Sociological Abstracts.
Year Established	Established in 1976 as *Journal of Offender Counseling Services Rehabilitation.* Published as *Journal of Offender Rehabilitation* since 1990.
Circulation	Not specified.
Frequency	8 times per year.
Months Issued	Not specified.
No. of Articles per Issue	Averages 5 per issue.

SUBMISSIONS

Postal Mailing Address	Creasie Finney Hairston, PhD; Jane Addams College of Social Work; University of Illinois at Chicago; 1040 W. Harrison Street, MC309; Room 4010, EPASW; Chicago, IL 60607-7134.
Method for Submission	E-mail.
Number of Copies	1 copy.
Disk Submission	Disk or e-mailed electronic version required.
Online or E-mail Submission Allowed or Required	Yes.

FORMAT OF MANUSCRIPT

Cover Sheet	Separate sheet, which does not go out for review. Full title; author names; degrees; professional titles; designation of 1 author as corresponding author with full address, phone number, e-mail address, and fax number.
Abstract	Each article should be summarized in an abstract of not more than 100 words.
Key Words	Please list 5 or 6 keywords that identify manuscript content.
Length	25 pages maximum, including all references, tables, and figures.
Margins	Margins of at least 1 inch on all sides.
Spacing	All parts of the manuscript should be typewritten, double-spaced.

STYLE

Name of Guide	*Publication Manual of the American Psychological Association.*
Subheadings	Not specified.
References	References, citations, and general style of manuscripts should be prepared in accordance with the *APA Publication Manual,* 4th ed. Cite in the text by author and date (Smith, 1983) and include an alphabetical list at the end of the article.
Footnotes	No footnotes preferred. Incorporate into text.
Tables or Figures	Tables and figures (illustrations) should not be embedded in the text, but should be included as separate sheets or files. A short descriptive title should appear above each table with a clear legend

and any footnotes suitably identified below. All units must be included. Figures should be completely labeled, taking into account necessary size reduction. Captions should be typed, double-spaced, on a separate sheet.

REVIEW PROCESS

Type of Review	All review papers in this journal undergo editorial screening and anonymous peer review.
Queries	By e-mail (journal@uic.edu).
Acknowledgment	By e-mail.
Review Time	Approximately 8–12 weeks.
Revisions	See journal.
Acceptance Rate	Not specified.
Return of Manuscript	Only if 9" × 12" self addressed, stamped envelope is enclosed.
Lag Time to Print	Approximately 6–12 months.

CHARGES TO AUTHOR

Author Alterations	Not specified.
Page Charges	Not specified.
Processing	Color illustrations will be considered for publication; however, the author will be required to bear the full cost involved in color art reproduction. Color art can be purchased for online-only reproduction or for print and online reproduction. Color reprints can only be ordered if print and online reproduction costs are paid. Rates for color art reproduction are: Online-Only Reproduction: $225 for the first page of color; $100 per page for the next three pages of color. A maximum charge of $525 applies.
	Print and Online Reproduction: $900 for the first page of color; $450 per page for the next 3 pages of color. A custom quote will be provided for articles with more than 4 pages of color.

REPRINT, SUBSCRIPTION, AND CONTACT INFORMATION

Reprint Policy	Page proofs are sent to the designated author using Taylor & Francis' Central Article Tracking System (CATS). They must be carefully checked and returned within 48 hours of receipt. Reprints of individual articles are available for order at the time authors review page proofs. A discount on reprints is available to authors who order before print publication. Each corresponding author will receive 3 complete issues in which the article publishes and a complimentary PDF. The corresponding author is responsible for distributing the material to co-authors.
Book Reviews	None.
Subscriptions	Institutional print and online subscription – US $1,166.00.
	Institutional online-only subscription – US $1,108.00.
	Individual print and online subscription – US $240.00.
	Individual online-only subscription – US $228.00.
	Subscribe at www.informaworld.com/WJOR or phone toll free 1-800-354-1420, press 4.
Affiliation	Taylor & Francis Group.
E-Mail Address	journal@uic.edu
Website	www.informaworld.com/WJOR

JOURNAL OF PAIN & PALLIATIVE CARE PHARMACOTHERAPY

Current Title	*Journal of Pain & Palliative Care Pharmacotherapy*
Previous Title	*The Hospice Journal*
Editorial Focus	*Journal of Pain & Palliative Care Pharmacotherapy* addresses advances in acute, chronic, and end-of-life symptom management. The journal publishes original research, timely review articles, case reports, commentaries, book and media reviews, and articles on efficacy, safety, cost-effectiveness, availability, delivery systems, ethics, policy, philosophy, and other issues relevant to pharmacotherapy in the management of acute, chronic, and end-of-life pain and related symptoms.
Audience	Clinicians, investigators, and analysts from the disciplines of bioethics, medicine, nursing, pharmaceutical sciences, psychology, social work, and health care policy.
Special Themes	Applied research and evaluation studies.
Where Indexed/ Abstracted	Biology Digest; Current Abstracts; EBSCOhost; Family Database; International Pharmaceutical Abstracts; MEDLINE; PsycINFO; SCOPUS.
Year Established	1993.
Circulation	Not specified.
Frequency	Quarterly.
Months Issued	Not specified.
No. of Articles per Issue	6–10 per issue.

SUBMISSIONS

Postal Mailing Address	Dr. Arthur G. Lipman, Editor, *Journal of Pain & Palliative Care Pharmacotherapy*, 30 S 2000 E Room 258, University of Utah Health Sciences Center, Salt Lake City, UT 84112-5820.
Method for Submission	Manuscripts or letters for publication consideration may be submitted as e-mail attachments sent directly to the editor at arthur.lipman@utah.edu. If e-mail submission of a manuscript is impractical, authors may mail a computer disk or three hard copies of the final manuscript.
Number of Copies	3 if sent by regular mail.
Disk Submission	Author can submit a disk by regular mail if e-mail submission is not possible.
Online or E-mail Submission Allowed or Required	E-mail submission preferred. Online submission system not available.

FORMAT OF MANUSCRIPT

Cover Sheet	The title page should include the name(s), degree(s), and affiliation(s) of all authors as they wish them to appear in the published manuscript.
Abstract	Submit an abstract that summarizes the paper in 150–200 words.
Key Words	Submit a list of key words. Number not specified.
Length	Articles are normally 20–30 pages in length exclusive of references, figures, and tables, and reports are normally 10–20 pages long. Longer manuscripts may be considered by the editor and may be divided into sections for publication in successive journal issues.
Margins	1 inch on all sides.
Spacing	Double-spaced.

STYLE

Name of Guide	The reference format is that used by the *Journal of the American Medical Association*.
Subheadings	Not specified.
References	The number of references normally should be limited to 50. Higher numbers of references for extensive review articles may be included at the editor's discretion.
Footnotes	Footnotes not preferred, incorporate into text.
Tables or Figures	Each table should be numbered, captioned, and computer printed or typewritten on a separate page following the references in the manuscript.

REVIEW PROCESS

Type of Review	Blind peer review.
Queries	Authors are encouraged to read the journal to determine whether their subject matter would be appropriate.
Acknowledgment	Not specified.

Review Time	Publication decisions normally are communicated to the corresponding author within 60 days of receipt of the manuscript.
Revisions	Not specified.
Acceptance Rate	Not specified.
Return of Manuscript	Not specified.
Lag Time to Print	Most manuscripts are published 6–9 months following formal acceptance.

REPRINT, SUBSCRIPTION, AND CONTACT INFORMATION

Reprint Policy	Each corresponding author will receive 1 complimentary copy of the journal issue. The corresponding author can also register with RightsLink, the journal's authorized reprint provider, to receive 10 complimentary reprints. The author will need to create a personal account and register with RightsLink for this free service. Complimentary reprints are not available after publication. An order form for discounted reprints will be sent to the corresponding author of each paper with the galley proofs several weeks prior to the issue publication date.
Book Reviews	Books, monographs, audio and videotapes, software, and other relevant media may be submitted to the editor for review. Formal Book and Media Reviews are published in each issue.
Subscriptions	Available through the website at: http://www.informaworld.com/smpp/title~db=all~content=t792304028~tab=subscribe.
Affiliation	National Hospice Organization (NHO).
E-Mail Address	arthur.lipman@utah.edu
Website	http://www.informaworld.com/smpp/title~content=t792304028~link=cover

JOURNAL OF PEACE RESEARCH

Current Title	*Journal of Peace Research*
Previous Title	N/A.
Editorial Focus	The journal encourages a wide conception of peace, but focuses on the causes of violence and conflict resolution. Without sacrificing the requirements for theoretical rigor and methodological sophistication, articles directed towards ways and means of peace are favored.
Audience	Researchers, faculty, students, libraries, organizations.
Special Themes	Civil War, Democratic Peace, Datasets.
Where Indexed/ Abstracted	A Matter of Fact; Abstracts of Military Bibliography; Academic Abstracts FullTEXT Elite; Academic Index; Academic Search Elite; Academic Search; Premier; America: History and Life; Annotated Bibliography for English Studies; Book Review Index; British Humanities Index; Business Source Corporate; Communication Abstracts; Criminal Justice Abstracts; CSA Worldwide Political Science Abstracts; Current Contents/Social and Behavioral Sciences; EconLit; Economic Literature Index; Expanded Academic Index; Future Survey; Health Source: Nursing/Academic Edition; Historical Abstracts; HRI Reporter; Humanities International Index; IBZ: International Bibliography of Periodical Literature; Index of Economic Articles; Information-Documentation; Inforpaz; International Bibliography of Book Reviews of Scholarly Literature on the Humanities and Social Sciences; International Bibliography of Periodical Literature on the Humanities and Social Sciences; International Bibliography of the Social Sciences; International Political Science Abstracts; Journal of Economic Literature; Lancaster Index to Defense and International Security Literature; Middle East Abstracts & Index; Monthly Bibliography of the UN Library; Newsearch; OCLC Public Affairs Information Service; Peace Research Abstracts; Periodical Abstracts; Political Science Abstracts (Part of CSA Worldwide Political Science Abstracts); Political Science Index; Research Alert; Risk Abstracts; Science Culture; Science Direct Navigator; Social Science Abstracts; Social Science Source; Social Sciences Citation Index; Social Sciences Index; Social SciSearch; Social Services Abstracts; Social Work Abstracts; Sociofile; Sociological Abstracts; Southeast Asia Abstracts & Index; The Alternative Newsletter; Violence & Abuse Abstracts; Vocational Search; World Affairs Online; Worldwide Political Science Abstracts.
Year Established	1964.
Circulation	5,000.
Frequency	Bimonthly.
Months Issued	January, March, May, July, September, and November.
No. of Articles per Issue	6–8.

SUBMISSIONS

Postal Mailing Address	*Journal of Peace Research*, International Peace Research Institute, Olso (PRIO), P.O. Box 9229 Grønland, NO-0134 OSLO, Norway.
Method for Submission	Electronic form via website.
Number of Copies	Not specified.
Disk Submission	No.
Online or E-mail Submission Allowed or Required	Required.

FORMAT OF MANUSCRIPT

Cover Sheet	Yes, can be brief.
Abstract	200–300 words.
Key Words	None.
Length	Maximum 10,000 words for regular articles, 6,000 words for Viewpoint and Special Data Features, 5,000 words for Review Essays.
Margins	1 inch on all sides.
Spacing	Double-spaced or 1.5.

STYLE

Name of Guide	Provided by the editor.
Subheadings	See style guide.

References	See style guide.
Footnotes	Use endnotes only.
Tables or Figures	See style guide.

REVIEW PROCESS

Type of Review	Double-blind peer review, usually 3 reviewers.
Queries	Yes, within reason.
Acknowledgment	Online (e-mail).
Review Time	Approximately 3–4 months.
Revisions	When needed.
Acceptance Rate	Approximately 15%–20%.
Return of Manuscript	No.
Lag Time to Print	Approximately 12 months after acceptance (working to shorten the lag).

REPRINT, SUBSCRIPTION, AND CONTACT INFORMATION

Reprint Policy	Electronic, from publisher.
Book Reviews	Book notes (max. 300 words); Review Essays.
Subscriptions	Sage Pub: http://www.sagepub.com/journalsSubscribe.nav?prodId=Journal200751.
Affiliation	International Peace Research Institute, Oslo (PRIO).
E-Mail Address	jpr@prio.no
Website	http://www.prio.no/jpr

JOURNAL OF PEDIATRIC PSYCHOLOGY

Current Title	*Journal of Pediatric Psychology*
Previous Title	N/A.
Editorial Focus	The main emphasis of the journal is on original research. Analytical reviews of research, brief scientific reports, scholarly case studies, and comments to the editor will also be considered for publication.
Audience	Psychologists, physicians, nurses, social workers.
Special Themes	The journal publishes articles related to theory, research, and professional practice in pediatric psychology. Pediatric psychology is an interdisciplinary field addressing physical, cognitive, social, and emotional functioning and development as they relate to health and illness issues in children, adolescents, and families.
Where Indexed/ Abstracted	Beck Medical Information; Behavioral Medicine Abstracts; Biological Abstracts; Child and Youth Services; Child Development Abstracts and Bibliography; Cumulative Index to Nursing and Allied Health Literature; Current Contents; Exceptional Child Education Resources; Excerpta Medica; Family Resources Database; Health Instrument File; Index Medicus; Mental Health Abstracts; Psychological Abstracts; Referativnyi Zhurnal; Sage Family Studies Abstracts; Science Citation Index; Selected List of Tables of Contents of Psychiatric Periodicals; Social Work Research & Abstracts; Sociological Abstracts; Special Educational Needs Abstracts; The Psychological Reader's Guide; Zeitschrift fur Kinder- und Jugendpsychiatric.
Year Established	1976.
Circulation	2,550.
Frequency	Bimonthly.
Months Issued	February, April, June, August, October, December.
No. of Articles per Issue	10–12.

SUBMISSIONS

Postal Mailing Address	Dennis Drotar, PhD, Editorial Office: 2515 Edgehill Road, Cleveland, OH 44106.
Method for Submission	Electronic submission via website: http://mc.manuscriptcentral.com/jpepsy.
Number of Copies	N/A.
Disk Submission	No.
Online or E-mail Submission Allowed or Required	Required.

FORMAT OF MANUSCRIPT

Cover Sheet	A separate title page listing the name and academic affiliations of all authors, the full mailing address of corresponding author, and personal acknowledgements; authors are to avoid identifying information in the body of the manuscript.
Abstract	A structured abstract of not more than 150 words should be included. The abstract should include the following parts: Objective (brief statement of the purpose of the study); Methods (summary of the participants, designs, measures, procedures); Results (the primary findings of this work); Conclusions (statement of implications of these data).
Key Words	Key words should be included, consistent with APA style.
Length	Original research articles should not exceed 25 pages, in total, including title page, references, figures, tables, etc. Brief scientific reports should not exceed 12 pages, including a maximum of two tables and/or figures. Scholarly reviews should not exceed 30 pages total. Case reports should not exceed 12 pages. Commentaries should not exceed 4 pages.
Margins	1 inch on all sides.
Spacing	Double-spaced.

STYLE

Name of Guide	*Publication Manual of the American Psychological Association.*
Subheadings	See style guide.
References	See style guide.
Footnotes	See style guide.
Tables or Figures	See style guide. Tables should be double-spaced, numbered, and referred to by number in the text. Each table should be placed on a separate sheet of paper and have a brief descriptive title.

Figures or illustrations are to be numbered in 1 consecutive series of Arabic numerals. For the initial submission, figures may be laser prints or photocopies. On acceptance, one set of glossy prints, showing high contrast, must be provided. Each figure should have an accompanying caption, with all captions typed as 1 list on a separate sheet of paper.

REVIEW PROCESS

Type of Review	Double-blind anonymous peer review. 2 reviewers plus the editor read the manuscript.
Queries	To the editorial office: 2515 Edgehill Road, Cleveland, OH 44106 or by e-mail: jpepsy@gmail.com.
Acknowledgment	E-mail.
Review Time	Approximately 2–3 months.
Revisions	To be decided by the editor. Directions will be given at that time.
Acceptance Rate	Approximately 41%.
Return of Manuscript	N/A.
Lag Time to Print	Approximately 3.3 weeks from acceptance to the day published online.

CHARGES TO AUTHOR

Author Alterations	None.
Page Charges	None.
Processing	None; Open Access charge if the author chooses Open Access publication model (information available here: http://www.oxfordjournals.org/our_journals/jpepsy/for_authors/msprep_submission.html.

REPRINT, SUBSCRIPTION, AND CONTACT INFORMATION

Reprint Policy	special.sales@oxfordjournals.org.
Book Reviews	Yes.
Subscriptions	www.jpepsy.oxfordjournals.org/subscriptions
Affiliation	Not specified.
E-Mail Address	jpepsy@oxfordjournals.org
Website	http://jpepsy.oxfordjournals.org/

JOURNAL OF PERSONALITY AND SOCIAL PSYCHOLOGY

Current Title	*Journal of Personality and Social Psychology*
Previous Title	N/A.
Editorial Focus	*Journal of Personality and Social Psychology* publishes original papers in all areas of personality and social psychology. It emphasizes empirical reports but may include specialized theoretical, methodological, and review papers.
Audience	Researchers in the discipline, faculty, libraries.
Special Themes	Not specified.
Where Indexed/ Abstracted	Academic Index; Applied Social Sciences Index & Abstracts; Child Development Abstracts; Communication Abstracts; Criminal Justice Abstracts; Current Contents; Current Index to Journals in Education; Educational Administration Abstracts; Index Medicus; Linguistics & Language Behavior Abstracts; Management Contents; PsycINFO; Sage Family Studies Abstracts; Social Sciences Citation Index; Social Sciences Index; Social Work Research & Abstracts; Studies on Women and Gender Abstracts.
Year Established	1965.
Circulation	Not specified.
Frequency	Monthly.
Months Issued	Monthly.
No. of Articles per Issue	15.

SUBMISSIONS

Postal Mailing Address	http://www.apa.org/journals/psp/description.html.
Method for Submission	Electronic to one of 3 editors.
Number of Copies	Not specified.
Disk Submission	Not specified.
Online or E-mail Submission Allowed or Required	Online portal required at web address above.

FORMAT OF MANUSCRIPT

Cover Sheet	Refer to Instructions to Authors in each issue.
Abstract	All manuscripts must include an abstract containing a maximum of 250 words typed on a separate page.
Key Words	After the abstract, please supply up to 5 keywords or brief phrases.
Length	Not specified.
Margins	See style guide.
Spacing	Double-spaced.

STYLE

Name of Guide	*Publication Manual of the American Psychological Association.*
Subheadings	See style guide.
References	List references in alphabetical order. Each listed reference should be cited in text, and each text citation should be listed in the References section.
Footnotes	See style guide.
Tables or Figures	Graphics files are welcome if supplied as TIFF, EPS, or PowerPoint files. The minimum line weight for line art is 0.5 point for optimal printing.

REVIEW PROCESS

Type of Review	Masked review only if requested by author.
Queries	Not query letters.
Acknowledgment	Editor acknowledges submission by mail.
Review Time	Usually 60–90 days.
Revisions	Most manuscripts are initially rejected; most published manuscripts have gone through 1 or 2 revisions.
Acceptance Rate	Approximately 17%.
Return of Manuscript	Manuscripts are not usually returned.
Lag Time to Print	Approximately 6 months.

CHARGES TO AUTHOR

Author Alterations	Authors are billed for alterations in proofs.
Page Charges	Not specified.
Processing	Not specified.

REPRINT, SUBSCRIPTION, AND CONTACT INFORMATION

Reprint Policy	Authors may purchase reprints of their articles.
Book Reviews	None.
Subscriptions	http://www.apa.org/journals/psp/pricing.html
Affiliation	Published by the American Psychological Association.
E-Mail Address	Not specified.
Website	http://www.apa.org/journals/psp/description.html

JOURNAL OF PHYSICAL AND OCCUPATIONAL THERAPY IN GERIATRICS

Current Title	*Journal of Physical and Occupational Therapy In Geriatrics*
Previous Title	N/A.
Editorial Focus	Current trends in geriatrics. Focus on rehabilitation of the geriatric client to share information, clinical experience, research, and therapeutic practice. Each issue focuses on current practice and emerging issues in the care of the older client, including rehabilitation and long-term care in institutional and community settings, and innovative programming; the entire range of problems experienced by the elderly; and the current skills needed for working with older clients. Contributors consider the current methods of managing older people at home, in assisted living, alone, or with families. Contributors address policy issues that affect the styles of living of older people, and discuss projects relating to research and teaching as they may affect practice in the field of gerontology.
Audience	Not specified.
Special Themes	Manuscripts submitted to *Physical & Occupational Therapy in Geriatrics* (*POTG*) should address topics related to geriatric rehabilitation, long-term care and wellness. All inquiries should be directed to the Editor. Submissions can be made in the form of Original Research, Case Reports, Systemic Reviews, and Theory/Perspective studies related to older adults.
Where Indexed/ Abstracted	Abstracts in Social Gerontology: Current Literature on Aging, National Council on the Aging; Academic Abstracts/CD-ROM; Brown University Geriatric Research Application Digest "Abstracts Section"; CINAHL (Cumulative Index t Nursing & Allied Health Literature); CNPIEC Reference Guide: Chinese National Directory of Foreign Periodicals; Communication Abstracts; Excerpta Medica/Secondary Publishing Division; Family Studies Database (online and CD-ROM); Health Source; Health Source Plus; Human Resources Abstracts (HRA); INTERNET ACCESS (and additional networks) Bulletin Board for Libraries ("BUBL"), coverage of information resources on INTERNET, JANET, and other networks; Occupational Therapy Database (OTDBASE); Occupational Therapy Index; OT BibSys; Psychological Abstracts/ PsycINFO; Public Affairs Information Bulletin (PAIS); Social Work Abstracts; Sport Database/Discus.
Year Established	1980.
Circulation	Not specified.
Frequency	Quarterly.
Months Issued	Not specified.
No. of Articles per Issue	6–10.

SUBMISSIONS

Postal Mailing Address	Not specified.
Method for Submission	Electronically via webiste. Manuscripts should be submitted electronically to *POTG*'s electronic submissions and peer review website, ScholarOne's Manuscript Central; http://mc.manuscript central.com/wpog. Please include a Microsoft Word file (.doc) cover sheet that should include all identifying information. A second Microsoft Word file should include the manuscript (abstract, text, references). Tables or figures should also be uploaded as separate documents. Authors should not include their names, telephone numbers, fax numbers, or e-mail addresses inside the body of the manuscript or on any figures or tables. All identifying information will be kept confidential by the journal office.
Number of Copies	4.
Disk Submission	N/A.
Online or E-mail Submission Allowed or Required	Electronically via website.

FORMAT OF MANUSCRIPT

Cover Sheet	Submit a title page with the manuscript, indicating only the title (this is used for anonymous refereeing). Title page should be uploaded as a separate MS word file. Title Page (uploaded as a separate MS Word file) should include: A title that is concise and reflects the content of the manuscript, The full name(s) of each author; footnote with authors' academic degrees, professional titles, and affiliations; and mailing and e-mail address of corresponding author (i.e. "Address correspondence to:"), Acknowledgement of research support or other credit.

Key Words	Below the abstract provide 3–10 keywords for index purposes.
Length	Maximum 20 typed pages with the above formatting (excluding abstract and references).
Margins	Leave at least 1 inch margin on all 4 sides: set all notes as endnotes.
Spacing	Double-spaced, including endnotes and references. Times New Roman, 12 point. A header and footer on each page.

STYLE

Name of Guide	*Publication Manual of the American Psychological Association.*
Subheadings	Use as needed to guide reader. No more than 4 levels
References	References, citations, and general style of manuscripts for this journal should follow APA style (as outlined in the latest edition of the *Publication Manual of the American Psychological Association*).
Footnotes	None preferred. Incorporate into text.
Tables or Figures	Tables and figures should be uploaded electronically as separate files. Use only those illustrations that clarify and augment the text. Captions must be saved separately, as part of the file containing the complete text of the paper, and numbered correspondingly. Digital files are recommended for highest quality reproduction and should follow these guidelines: 300 dpi or higher and sized to fit on journal page. Specific permission for facial photographs of patients is required. A letter of consent must accompany the photographs of patients in which a possibility of identification exists. It is not sufficient to cover the eyes to mask identity.

REVIEW PROCESS

Type of Review	Peer reviewed. Manuscripts submitted to *POTG* undergo an anonymous review by 2 members of the Editorial Board.
Queries	Authors are encouraged to read the journal to see whether their subject matter would be appropriate.
Acknowledgment	Submissions will be acknowledged via e-mail.
Review Time	Approximately 10–15 weeks.
Revisions	When the recommendation is to revise, authors should resubmit the manuscript within 60 days after the revisions are requested. If the revised manuscript is not received within 60 days, the manuscript file will be closed. An extension of the deadline may be requested. Papers are frequently accepted by the editor contingent upon changes that are mandated by anonymous specialist referees and/or members of the editorial board. If the editor returns your manuscript for revisions, you are responsible for incorporating these revisions.
Acceptance Rate	Not specified.
Return of Manuscript	Not specified.
Lag Time to Print	Approximately 6–12 months.

CHARGES TO AUTHOR

Author Alterations	See website.
Page Charges	Any figure submitted as a color original will appear in color in the journal's online edition free of charge and can be downloaded. Paper copy color reproduction will only be considered on condition that authors contribute to the associated costs. Charges are: 500/US$1030 for the first color page and 250/US$515 for each color page after per article. Color costs will be waived for invited Review Articles.
Processing	Proofs: The designated author for correspondence will receive a copy of the proofs, which should be read carefully for errors. The corrected proof must be returned to the Publisher within 48 hours. Authors will be asked to defray the expense of any major alterations to the proofs that are departures from the original manuscript.

REPRINT, SUBSCRIPTION, AND CONTACT INFORMATION

Reprint Policy	Each corresponding author will receive 1 copy of the issue in which the article appears. Additional copies of the journal can be purchased separately at the author's preferential rate of 15.00/US$25.00 per copy. Reprints of individual articles are available to order at the time authors review page proofs. A discount on reprints is available to authors who order before print publication.
Book Reviews	Address journal editor.
Subscriptions	http://www.informaworld.com/smpp/title~db=all~content=t792304026~tab=subscribe.
Affiliation	Not specified.
E-Mail Address	Not specified.
Website	http://www.informaworld.com/smpp/title~db=all~content=t792304026~tab=summary

JOURNAL OF POETRY THERAPY: THE INTERDISCIPLINARY JOURNAL OF PRACTICE, THEORY, RESEARCH, AND EDUCATION

Current Title	*Journal of Poetry Therapy: The Interdisciplinary Journal of Practice, Theory, Research, and Education.*
Previous Title	N/A.
Editorial Focus	The general focus of this interdisciplinary journal is on promoting growth and healing through language, symbol, and story. Poetry therapy relates to the use of the language arts in therapeutic, educational, and community-building capacities. The purview of *JPT* includes bibliotherapy, narrative therapy, journal therapy, drama therapy, healing and writing, and creative expression. *JPT* welcomes a wide variety of scholarly articles including theoretical, historical, practice, and research (qualitative and quantitative) studies. Additional features include book reviews, dissertation abstracts, and original poetry.
Audience	The intended audience of *JPT* includes those in the allied helping professions and education, as well as those in literary/artistic fields with a concern toward promoting growth and healing through language, symbol, and story.
Special Themes	Individual, family, group, and community practice; social welfare; gender and cultural issues; interpersonal violence; health/mental health and writing; narrative therapy; grief and bereavement; prevention; related expressive arts therapies; trauma; suicide; at-risk populations; literary exemplars; disaster recovery; therapeutic use of metaphors; storytelling; and lyrical expression.
Where Indexed/ Abstracted	Abstracted or Indexed in Articles First (OCLC); Bibliography of Periodicals Literature; CSA Sociological Abstracts; Current Index to Journals in Education (CIJE); Educational Resources Information (ERIC); Google Scholar; International Bibliography of Periodical Literature on the Humanities and Social Sciences (IBZ); International Bibliography of Book Reviews of Scholarly Literature on the Humanities and Social Sciences (IBR); Linguistics and Language Behavior Abstracts (LLBA); LOCATORplus (National Library of Medicine); Modern Language Association (MLA).
Year Established	1987.
Circulation	500.
Frequency	Quarterly.
Months Issued	March, June, September, December.
No. of Articles per Issue	4–5 articles; 3–5 poems.

SUBMISSIONS

Postal Mailing Address	Nicholas Mazza, PhD, Editor, *Journal of Poetry Therapy*, Florida State University, College of Social Work, 2505 University Center-C, 296 Champions Way, Tallahassee, FL 32306-2570 (e-mail: nfmazza@fsu.edu).
Method for Submission	E-mail.
Number of Copies	E-mail attachment only.
Disk Submission	No.
Online or E-mail Submission Allowed or Required	E-mail required.

FORMAT OF MANUSCRIPT

Cover Sheet	Full title, author names, degrees, author affiliation, complete mailing address, phone number, e-mail address, and fax number.
Abstract	Empirical: 100–150 words; practice/theory: 75–100 words.
Key Words	Up to 5 key words.
Length	14–30 pages for full-length manuscript; 4–8 pages for brief reports.
Margins	1 inch on all sides.
Spacing	Double-spaced.

STYLE

Name of Guide	*Publication Manual of the American Psychological Association.*
Subheadings	See style guide.
References	See style guide.
Footnotes	See style guide.
Tables or Figures	Submit camera-ready and include figure legends.

REVIEW PROCESS

Type of Review	Anonymous review by 3 editorial board members.
Queries	Accepted.
Acknowledgment	E-mail acknowledgment sent upon receipt of manuscript.
Review Time	3 months.
Revisions	Major revision: revised manuscript sent out for review. Minor revision: handled between author and editor only.
Acceptance Rate	Approximately 40% articles; 5% poetry.
Return of Manuscript	Returned.
Lag Time to Print	Approximately 3–9 months.

REPRINT, SUBSCRIPTION, AND CONTACT INFORMATION

Reprint Policy	Corresponding authors can receive 50 free reprints, free online access to their article through our website (http://www.informaworld.com/), and a complimentary copy of the issue containing their article. Complimentary reprints are available through Rightslink, and additional reprints can be ordered through Rightslink when proofs are received. If you have any queries, please contact our reprints department at reprints@tandf.co.uk.
Book Reviews	Please send all inquiries regarding book reviews to the Book Review Editor, Charles Rossiter, PhD, at Charles.Rossiter@poetrypoetry.com.
Subscriptions	Routledge (Taylor& Francis Group), 4 Park Square, Milton Park, Abington, Oxon, OX14, 4RN, United Kingdom.
	GBP: Institutional (print & online) $440, Institutional online $418, Personal $61.
	USD: Institutional (print & online) $663, Institutional online $630, Personal $94.
	EUR: Institutional (print & online) $528, Institutional online $502, Personal $74.
Affiliation	Sponsored by the National Association of Poetry Therapy.
E-Mail Address	Editor: nfmazza@fsu.edu
Website	http://www.tandf.co.uk/journals/titles/08893675.asp

JOURNAL OF POLICE CRISIS NEGOTIATIONS

Current Title	*Journal of Police Crisis Negotiations: An International Journal*
Previous Title	*The Journal of Police Negotiations, Crisis Management and Suicidology & prior Journal of Crisis Negotiations.*
Editorial Focus	Police hostage and crisis negotiations, crisis management/intervention and suicide.
Audience	Police negotiators; plus all others interested in these areas specifically related to police and related groups.
Special Themes	Hostage and crisis negotiations, crisis interventions, suicide and related areas that provide practical information as well as theory. Practical input from field negotiators and from academics is welcome.
Where Indexed/ Abstracted	See Website.
Year Established	1996.
Circulation	300.
Frequency	Semi-annually.
Months Issued	Approximately March and November.
No. of Articles per Issue	6–8.

SUBMISSIONS

Postal Mailing Address	Dr. James L. Greenstone, Editor-in-Chief, 222 West Fourth Street, Suite 212, Fort Worth, TX 76102; Editorial Office: 817-882-9415.
Method for Submission	E-mail.
Number of Copies	Microsoft Word Attachment.
Disk Submission	Microsoft Word Attachment.
Online or E-mail Submission Allowed or Required	Yes.

FORMAT OF MANUSCRIPT

Cover Sheet	Title, authors, affiliations, address and phone numbers.
Abstract	500 words.
Key Words	6 key words.
Length	10–15 pages.
Margins	Standard.
Spacing	Double-spaced.

STYLE

Name of Guide	*Publication Manual of the American Psychological Association (APA, latest edition).*
Subheadings	See style guide.
References	See style guide.
Footnotes	See style guide.
Tables or Figures	See style guide.

REVIEW PROCESS

Type of Review	Peer reviewed.
Queries	Welcome.
Acknowledgment	Please provide self addressed, stamped postcard.
Review Time	Approximately 8–10 weeks.
Revisions	Author is responsible in most cases.
Acceptance Rate	Approximately 60%–70%.
Return of Manuscript	Not returned.
Lag Time to Print	Approximately 4–5 months.

CHARGES TO AUTHOR

Author Alterations	Varies.
Page Charges	Varies.
Processing	Not indicated.

REPRINT, SUBSCRIPTION, AND CONTACT INFORMATION

Reprint Policy	See website.
Book Reviews	Send books for review to Editor-in-Chief.
Subscriptions	See website.
Affiliation	Taylor and Francis Group, by Routledge.
E-Mail Address	drjlg1@charter.net
Website	http://www.informaworld.com/smpp/title~content=t792322385~db=all

JOURNAL OF POLICY ANALYSIS AND MANAGEMENT

Current Title	*Journal of Policy Analysis and Management*
Previous Title	N/A.
Editorial Focus	The journal strives for quality, relevance, and originality in its feature articles. The editors give priority to manuscripts that relate their conclusions broadly to a number of substantive fields of public policy or that deal with issues of professional practice in policy analysis and public management. Although an interdisciplinary perspective is usually most appropriate, manuscripts that use the tools of a single discipline are welcome if they have substantial relevance and if they are written for a general rather than disciplinary audience. The editors welcome proposals for articles that review the state of knowledge in particular policy areas. For the "Insights" section, the editors seek manuscripts that present novel policy ideas, challenge common wisdom, report surprising research findings, draw lessons from experience, or illustrate the application of an analytical or managerial method. Wit and verve, and occasionally irreverence, are welcome. For "Curriculum and Case Notes" the editors believe the journal should play a role in improving professional education in policy analysis and public management, and therefore welcome short manuscripts that deal with broad issues of curriculum or specific aspects of pedagogy.
Audience	Academics, government research staff, government practitioners, consultants; all with public policy and management concerns.
Special Themes	Not specified.
Where Indexed/ Abstracted	Not specified.
Year Established	1981.
Circulation	3,500.
Frequency	Quarterly.
Months Issued	December, March, June, September.
No. of Articles per Issue	4–6, plus shorter pieces.

SUBMISSIONS

Postal Mailing Address	N/A.
Method for Submission	Electronic form via website.
Number of Copies	1
Disk Submission	Not accepted.
Online or E-mail Submission Allowed or Required	Online submission required.

FORMAT OF MANUSCRIPT

Cover Sheet	Title and affiliation of authors.
Abstract	125 words.
Key Words	Not specified.
Length	25–40 pages.
Margins	Wide.
Spacing	Double-spaced.

STYLE

Name of Guide	*Chicago Manual of Style.*
Subheadings	Beginning at the left margin, use initial capitalization for major section headings. Subheadings should be paragraphed, underlined, with period at the end. The text should follow without paragraph. Do not use numbers or letters to identify sections.
References	Cite references in the text and footnotes within brackets that contain the author names and the year of publication. Consult the journal's notes on style for more details.
Footnotes	Incorporate footnotes into text when possible. If inclusion proves difficult, that is a strong argument for dropping the point. If, exceptionally, the author decides the idea must be included, then it may be carried in a footnote. Number footnotes consecutively and place them at the end of the manuscript.
Tables or Figures	Rough in first submission; camera-ready for accepted manuscripts. Provide only data relevant to the textual argument. Select headings that communicate the argument being made. Avoid design-

ing tables on dimensions that require printing at right angles to the normal reading position. Number and title all tables.

REVIEW PROCESS

Type of Review	Blind.
Queries	Optional.
Acknowledgment	By card or e-mail.
Review Time	Approximately 5–7 weeks.
Revisions	Not specified.
Acceptance Rate	Approximately 8 %.
Return of Manuscript	Not returned.
Lag Time to Print	Approximately 3 months.

REPRINT, SUBSCRIPTION, AND CONTACT INFORMATION

Reprint Policy	Available at a fee from Wiley-Blackwell Inc.
Book Reviews	Submitted to Bill McGregor, SPEA 225, Indiana University, 1315 East 10th Street, Bloomington, IN 47405.
Subscriptions	Available from Wiley-Blackwell Inc.
Affiliation	Journal of the Association for Policy Analysis and Management.
E-Mail Address	jpam@indiana.edu or e-mail the Editor-in-Chief, Maureen A. Pirog at: Pirog@indiana.edu.
Website	http://www3.interscience.wiley.com/journal/34787/home

JOURNAL OF POLICY PRACTICE

Current Title	*Journal of Policy Practice.*
Previous Title	*Social Policy Journal.*
Editorial Focus	*Journal of Policy Practice* endeavors to publish the highest quality research and scholarship on policy practice, social policy, social policy analysis, the creation and administration of social policy and programs and related topics.
Audience	Academics, practitioners, and students in the social policy and social work areas.
Special Themes	Advocacy, policy practice, and evaluation of social policy; studies of the impact of social policy.
Where Indexed/ Abstracted	ABC Pol Sci; Alternative Press Index; Current Contents: Behavioral, Social and Educational Sciences; Current Index to Journals in Education; Medical Socioeconomic Research Sources; Social Sciences Citations Index; Social Sciences Index.
Year Established	2001 (changed name from *Social Policy Journal* to *Journal of Policy Practice* in 2006).
Circulation	Not specified.
Frequency	Quarterly.
Months Issued	January, April, July, October.
No. of Articles per Issue	4–6.

SUBMISSIONS

Postal Mailing Address	E-mail submission is required: rhoefer@uta.edu.
Method for Submission	E-mail.
Number of Copies	1.
Disk Submission	Not specified.
Online or E-mail Submission Allowed or Required	Required.

FORMAT OF MANUSCRIPT

Cover Sheet	Follow style guide.
Abstract	100 words.
Key Words	3–7 words.
Length	20–27 pages.
Margins	1 inch.
Spacing	Double-spaced.

STYLE

Name of Guide	*Publication Manual of the American Psychological Association* (APA, latest edition).
Subheadings	See style guide.
References	See style guide.
Footnotes	See style guide.
Tables or Figures	See style guide.

REVIEW PROCESS

Type of Review	Anonymous peer review.
Queries	Acceptable, but not necessary.
Acknowledgment	Sent via e-mail.
Review Time	Approximately 2–3 months.
Revisions	Explained in letter requesting revisions.
Acceptance Rate	Approximately 30%.
Return of Manuscript	No.
Lag Time to Print	Approximately 3 months.

REPRINT, SUBSCRIPTION, AND CONTACT INFORMATION

Reprint Policy	Contact Taylor and Francis, http://www.tandf.co.uk/journals/ or Taylor & Francis, Inc., 325 Chestnut Street, Suite 800, Philadelphia, PA 19106.
Book Reviews	Send to editor, Richard Hoefer, rhoefer@uta.edu or book review editor, John McNutt, mcnuttjg@udel.edu

Subscriptions   http://www.informaworld.com/smpp/title~content=t792306913~tab=subscribe~db=all

Affiliation   Social Policy and Policy Practice Group.

E-Mail Address   rhoefer@uta.edu use for inquiries and submissions of articles.

Website   http://www.tandf.co.uk/journals/titles/15588742.asp

JOURNAL OF PRACTICE TEACHING AND LEARNING

Current Title	*Journal of Practice Teaching and Learning*
Previous Title	*Journal of Practice Teaching in Health and Social Work.*
Editorial Focus	Education for social work and related fields in health and care, with special emphasis on workplace education, field instruction, practice teaching, etc.
Audience	Educators in social work and related fields, managers in those fields, academics.
Special Themes	Special issues from time to time.
Where Indexed/ Abstracted	Applied Social Sciences Index; Bibliographie Zeitschriftenliteratur aller Gebieten des Wissens; Social Care Update; Social Work Abstracts; Sociological Abstracts.
Year Established	1998.
Circulation	Not specified.
Frequency	3 times per year.
Months Issued	April, August, December.
No. of Articles per Issue	6–8.

SUBMISSIONS

Postal Mailing Address	C/O Whiting and Birch Ltd, 90 Dartmouth Road, London SE23 3HZ, England.
Method for Submission	E-mail.
Number of Copies	1.
Disk Submission	E-mail is preferred.
Online or E-mail Submission Allowed or Required	Preferred.

FORMAT OF MANUSCRIPT

Cover Sheet	Yes.
Abstract	Less than 200 words.
Key Words	Up to 8 key words.
Length	2,500 to 6,000 words. Longer by prior agreement.
Margins	No requirement.
Spacing	Single- or Double-spaced.

STYLE

Name of Guide	See notes for contributors in journal, or publisher's website for more detail. Refer to *Publication Manual of the American Psychological Association* for points of detail.
Subheadings	3 levels or fewer. Minimize capitalization.
References	Harvard.
Footnotes	Endnotes permitted only if absolutely essential.
Tables or Figures	Tables or figures: See publisher's website (www.whitingbirch.net) for full details. Graphics for figures and charts must be supplied to at least 300 dpi in tiff or .pdf format. Charts and figures must work in monochrome.

REVIEW PROCESS

Type of Review	Double anonymous.
Queries	Editors welcome queries.
Acknowledgment	By e-mail.
Review Time	Approximately 3 months.
Revisions	Material may be accepted subject to minor revisions, rejected, or more substantial revision required, in which case resubmission may be required.
Acceptance Rate	Approximately 40%.
Return of Manuscript	Not relevant, as submissions should be by e-mail.
Lag Time to Print	Target approximately 12 months or less.

CHARGES TO AUTHOR

Author Alterations	US$10 per page for significant and foreseeable alterations.
Page Charges	None.
Processing	None.

REPRINT, SUBSCRIPTION, AND CONTACT INFORMATION

Reprint Policy	2 free copies of journal, and a .pdf file. Offprints can be provided at cost for those who want them.
Book Reviews	Published.
Subscriptions	Whiting & Birch Ltd, 90 Dartmouth Road, London SE23 3HZ, United Kingdom; www.whitingbirch.net. North America rates: US $250.00 for libraries, US $60.00 for individuals.
Affiliation	None.
E-Mail Address	enquiries@whitingbirch.net
Website	www.whitingbirch.net

JOURNAL OF PREVENTION & INTERVENTION IN THE COMMUNITY

Current Title	*Journal of Prevention & Intervention in the Community*
Previous Title	N/A.
Editorial Focus	Research and theoretical articles. Each issue is focused on a current topic.
Audience	Scientists and faculty, students, libraries, human service and social welfare professionals.
Special Themes	Geographic information system, homelessness, sexual assault/violence, depression in women, psychology in the community, Healthy Families America, HIV/AIDS, community action research, etc.
Where Indexed/ Abstracted	Current Contents; ERIC; Social Science Index; Social Work Abstracts; and others.
Year Established	1984.
Circulation	Not specified.
Frequency	4 issues per year.
Months Issued	January, April, June, September.
No. of Articles per Issue	Approximately 6–8 articles.

SUBMISSIONS

Postal Mailing Address	*Journal of Prevention & Intervention in the Community*, DePaul University, Department of Psychology, 2219 North Kenmore Avenue, Chicago, IL 60614.
Method for Submission	Disk.
Number of Copies	2.
Disk Submission	Yes.
Online or E-mail Submission Allowed or Required	No.

FORMAT OF MANUSCRIPT

Cover Sheet	Include author's name and a shortened version of the title suitable for the running head, not exceeding 50 character spaces.
Abstract	Each article should be summarized in an abstract of not more than 100–150 words. Avoid abbreviations, diagrams, and reference to the text in the abstract.
Key Words	None.
Length	Manuscript length should be 8–18 typed pages.
Margins	At least 1 inch on all sides.
Spacing	Double-spaced.

STYLE

Name of Guide	*Publication Manual of the American Psychological Association* (APA).
Subheadings	Use as needed; no more than 3 levels.
References	References, citations, and general style of manuscripts should be prepared in accordance with the *APA Publication Manual*, 4th ed. Cite in the text by author and date.
Footnotes	No footnotes preferred; incorporate into text.
Tables or Figures	Tables and figures (illustrations) should not be embedded in the text, but should be included as separate sheets or files. A short descriptive title should appear above each table with a clear legend and any footnotes suitably identified below. All units must be included. Figures should be completely labeled, taking into account necessary size reduction. Captions should be typed, double-spaced, on a separate sheet.

REVIEW PROCESS

Type of Review	All research articles in this journal have undergone rigorous peer review, based on initial Guest Editor screening and anonymous refereeing by 1 or 2 referees arranged by the Guest Editor.
Queries	Query letters are discouraged.
Acknowledgment	Guest editor is phoned or written concerning status.
Review Time	As soon as possible.
Revisions	In general, the guest editor and the editor-in-chief read revisions.
Acceptance Rate	Because the papers are pulled together by a guest editor, the acceptance rate is high.

Return of Manuscript All accepted manuscripts, artwork, and photographs become the property of the publisher.

Lag Time to Print Approximately 12 or more weeks.

CHARGES TO AUTHOR

Author Alterations Not specified.

Page Charges Color illustrations will be considered for publication; however, the author will be required to bear the full cost involved in color art reproduction. Color art can be purchased for online-only reproduction or for print and online reproduction. Color reprints can only be ordered if print and online reproduction costs are paid. Rates for color art reproduction are: Online-Only Reproduction: $225 for the first page of color; $100 per page for the next 3 pages of color. A maximum charge of $525 applies. Print and Online Reproduction: $900 for the first page of color; $450 per page for the next 3 pages of color. A custom quote will be provided for articles with more than 4 pages of color.

Processing Not specified.

REPRINT, SUBSCRIPTION, AND CONTACT INFORMATION

Reprint Policy Reprints of individual articles are available for order at the time authors review page proofs. A discount on reprints is available to authors who order before print publication. Each corresponding author will receive 3 complete issues in which the article publishes and a complimentary PDF. This file is for personal use only and may not be copied and disseminated in any form without prior written permission from Taylor and Francis Group, LLC.

Book Reviews None.

Subscriptions Taylor & Francis, Attention: Customer Service, 325 Chestnut Street, Suite 800, Philadelphia, PA 19106, or customerservice@taylorandfrancis.com

Affiliation N/A.

E-Mail Address jferrari@depaul.edu

Website www.informaworld.com/wpic

JOURNAL OF PROGRESSIVE HUMAN SERVICES

Current Title	*Journal of Progressive Human Services*
Previous Title	*Catalyst*
Editorial Focus	The only journal of its kind in the United States, the *Journal of Progressive Human Services* covers political, social, personal, and professional problems in human services from a progressive perspective.
Audience	Not specified.
Special Themes	Developing knowledge about theories, social policies, clinical practice, organizing, administration, research, and history that reflects and responds to progressive concerns.
Where Indexed/ Abstracted	Alternative Press Index; Applied Social Sciences Index & Abstracts; CNPIEC References Guide: Chinese Directory of Foreign Periodicals; Family Studies Database (online and CD-ROM); International Bibliography of Periodical Literature; Index to Periodical Articles Related to Law; INTERNET ACCESS (and additional networks) Bulletin Board for Libraries ("BUBL"), coverage of information resources on INTERNET, JANET, and other networks; Left Index; National Library Database on Homelessness; Public Affairs Information Bulletin (PAIS); Referativnyi Zhurnal (Abstracts Journal of the Institute of Scientific Information of the Republic of Russia); Social Planning/Policy & Development Abstracts (SOPODA); Social Work Abstracts; Sociological Abstracts (SA); Sociology of Education Abstracts; Special Educational Needs Abstracts; Urban Affairs Abstracts; Violence & Abuse Abstracts: A Review of Current Literature on Interpersonal Violence (VAA).
Year Established	1990.
Circulation	650+.
Frequency	Twice a year.
Months Issued	Not specified.
No. of Articles per Issue	Approximately 8.

SUBMISSIONS

Postal Mailing Address	Marcia Cohen, University of New England, Westbrook College Campus, School of Social Work, 716 Stevens Avenue, Portland, ME 04103-2670.
Method for Submission	Electronic strongly encouraged; mcohen@une.edu.
Number of Copies	Triplicate; paper or disk.
Disk Submission	If submitting a disk, it should be prepared using MS Word or WordPerfect and should be clearly labeled with the authors' names, file name, and software program. A hardcopy printout that exactly matches the disk must be supplied in triplicate.
Online or E-mail Submission Allowed or Required	Electronic strongly encouraged. Send to: mcohen@une.edu.

FORMAT OF MANUSCRIPT

Cover Sheet	Separate sheet, which does not go out for review. Full title; author names; degrees; professional titles; and designation of 1 author as corresponding author with full address, phone numbers, e-mail address, and fax number and date of submission.
Abstract	100 words.
Key Words	5–6 key words that identify article content.
Length	15–25 pages, including references and abstract. Lengthier manuscripts may be considered, but only at the discretion of the editor. Sometimes, lengthier manuscripts may be considered if they can be divided into sections for publication in successive issues.
Margins	1 inch
Spacing	Double-spaced.

STYLE

Name of Guide	*Publication Manual of the American Psychological Association* (APA).
Subheadings	Use as needed to guide reader through the article. No more than 4 levels.
References	References, citations, and general style of manuscripts should be prepared in accordance with the *APA Publication Manual*, 4th ed.
Footnotes	No footnotes preferred; incorporate into text.
Tables or Figures	Tables and figures (illustrations) should not be embedded in the text, but should be included as separate sheets or files. A short descriptive title should appear above each table with a clear legend

and any footnotes suitably identified below. All units must be included. Figures should be completely labeled, taking into account necessary size reduction. Captions should be typed, double-spaced, on a separate sheet.

REVIEW PROCESS

Type of Review	"Double-blind" anonymous peer review. 3 reviewers plus editor-in-chief read the manuscript in an anonymous review.
Queries	Authors are encouraged to read the journal to determine whether their subject matter would be appropriate.
Acknowledgment	Enclose a regular self-addressed, stamped envelope with submission.
Review Time	Approximately 3–4 months.
Revisions	See journal.
Acceptance Rate	Not specified.
Return of Manuscript	Only if 9" × 12" self-addressed, stamped envelope is enclosed.
Lag Time to Print	Approximately 6–12 months.

CHARGES TO AUTHOR

Author Alterations	Page proofs are sent to the designated author using Taylor & Francis' Central Article Tracking System (CATS). They must be carefully checked and returned within 48 hours of receipt.
Page Charges	Not specified.
Processing	Not specified.

REPRINT, SUBSCRIPTION, AND CONTACT INFORMATION

Reprint Policy	http://www.informaworld.com/smpp/journals_reprints~db=all.
Book Reviews	http://www.informaworld.com/smpp/journals_reprints~db=all.
Subscriptions	See website.
Affiliation	Social Welfare Action Alliance (formerly Bertha Capen Reynolds Society).
E-Mail Address	mcohen@une.edu
Website	http://www.informaworld.com/smpp/title~db=all~content=t792306943

JOURNAL OF PSYCHOSOCIAL ONCOLOGY

Current Title	*Journal of Psychosocial Oncology*
Previous Title	N/A.
Editorial Focus	*Journal of Psychosocial Oncology* is an essential source for up-to-date clinical and research material geared toward health professionals who provide psychosocial services to cancer patients, their families, and their caregivers. The journal—the first interdisciplinary resource of its kind—is in its third decade of examining exploratory and hypothesis testing and presenting program evaluation research on critical areas, including: the stigma of cancer; employment and personal problems facing cancer patients; patient education; family involvement in patient care; children with cancer; the psychosocial needs of cancer patients; hospital and hospice staff; and volunteers
Audience	Professional social work clinicians, administrators, educators, and researchers committed to the enhancement of the psychological services to cancer patients and their families.
Special Themes	Contemporary clinical and research materials as well as exploratory, hypothesis testing, and program evaluation research for health professionals.
Where Indexed/ Abstracted	Academic Search Complete; Academic Search Premier; CINAHL Database; Social Service Abstracts; Current Abstracts; Health & Psychological Instruments; MEDLINE; Orere - Pastoral Abstracts; PILOTS Database; PsycINFO; Social Science Citation Index; Sociological Abstract; Studies on Women & Gender Abstracts; Swets Information Services.
Year Established	1983.
Circulation	Approximately 1,340.
Frequency	Quarterly.
Months Issued	Not specified.
No. of Articles per Issue	6–10.

SUBMISSIONS

Postal Mailing Address	James R. Zabora, ScD, MSW, Editor, *Journal of Psychosocial Oncology,* Dean. National Catholic School of Social Services, The Catholic University of America, 100 Shahan Hall, 620 Michigan Avenue NE, Washington, DC 20064 USA
Method for Submission	Online preferable: zabora@cua.edu OR mailforkrish@gmail.com
Number of Copies	Not specified.
Disk Submission	Not specificd.
Online or E-mail Submission Allowed or Required	Online preferable: zabora@cua.edu OR mailforkrish@gmail.com

FORMAT OF MANUSCRIPT

Cover Sheet	Authors must complete a Copyright Transfer Form. Each manuscript must be accompanied by a statement that it has not been published elsewhere and that it has not been submitted simultaneously for publication elsewhere.
Abstract	100 words.
Key Words	Not specified.
Length	20 pages, including references and abstract. Lengthier manuscripts may be considered, but only at the discretion of the editor. Sometimes, lengthier manuscripts may be considered if they can be divided into sections for publication in successive issues.
Margins	1 inch.
Spacing	Double-spaced.

STYLE

Name of Guide	*Publication Manual of the American Psychological Association* (APA).
Subheadings	Use as needed to guide reader through the article. No more than 4 levels.
References	References, citations, and general style of manuscripts should be prepared in accordance with the APA Publication Manual, 4th ed.
Footnotes	No footnotes preferred; incorporate into text.
Tables or Figures	Tables and figures (illustrations) should not be embedded in the text, but should be included as separate sheets or files. A short descriptive title should appear above each table with a clear legend and any footnotes suitably identified below. All units must be included. Figures should be completely

labeled, taking into account necessary size reduction. Captions should be typed, double-spaced, on a separate sheet.

REVIEW PROCESS

Type of Review	All articles have undergone anonymous double-blind review by at least 2 referees.
Queries	Authors are encouraged to read the journal to determine whether their subject matter would be appropriate.
Acknowledgment	Enclose a regular self-addressed, stamped envelope with submission.
Review Time	Approximately 3–4 months.
Revisions	See journal.
Acceptance Rate	Not specified.
Return of Manuscript	Only if 9" × 12" self-addressed, stamped envelope is enclosed.
Lag Time to Print	Approximately 6–12 months.

CHARGES TO AUTHOR

Author Alterations	Page proofs are sent to the designated author using Taylor & Francis' Central Article Tracking System (CATS). They must be carefully checked and returned within 48 hours of receipt.
Page Charges	Not specified.
Processing	Not specified.

REPRINT, SUBSCRIPTION, AND CONTACT INFORMATION

Reprint Policy	Reprints of individual articles are available for order at the time authors review page proofs. A discount on reprints is available to authors who order before print publication. Each corresponding author will receive 3 complete issues in which the article publishes and a complimentary PDF. This file is for personal use only and may not be copied and disseminated in any form without prior written permission from Taylor and Francis Group, LLC.
Book Reviews	Yes.
Subscriptions	Haworth Inc.: See website
Affiliation	Haworth Inc.: See website
E-Mail Address	zabora@cua.edu OR mailforkrish@gmail.com
Website	http://www.informaworld.com/smpp/title~content=t792306912~db=all

JOURNAL OF POVERTY

Current Title	*Journal of Poverty*
Previous Title	N/A.
Editorial Focus	The journal's broad understanding of poverty—more inclusive than the traditional view—keeps the focus on people's need for education, employment, safe and affordable housing, nutrition, and adequate medical care, and on interventions that range from direct practice to community organization to social policy analysis. The journal's articles will increase your knowledge and awareness of oppressive forces such as racism, sexism, classism, and homophobia that contribute to the maintenance of poverty and inequality.
Audience	Researchers, academics, social workers, and others who work with the poor.
Special Themes	Not specified.
Where Indexed/ Abstracted	Criminal Justice Abstracts; Current Abstracts; EBSCOhost; Education Research Index; Family & Society Studies Worldwide; Family Index; Risk Abstracts (Online); SCOPUS; Social Services Abstracts; Social Work Abstracts; Sociological Abstracts.
Year Established	1997.
Circulation	Not specified.
Frequency	Quarterly.
Months Issued	Not specified.
No. of Articles per Issue	5–6.

SUBMISSIONS

Postal Mailing Address	Editors, *Journal of Poverty*, School of Social Work, Loyola University Chicago, Water Tower Campus, 820 North Michigan Avenue, Chicago, IL 60611.
Method for Submission	Manuscripts should be submitted electronically to the Editors of *Journal of Poverty* at the following e-mail address: mvidal@luc.edu.
Number of Copies	1 copy.
Disk Submission	Not required.
Online or E-mail Submission Allowed or Required	E-mail submission required.

FORMAT OF MANUSCRIPT

Cover Sheet	Not specified.
Abstract	Provide an abstract of approximately 100 words.
Key Words	Below the abstract provide 3–10 keywords for index purposes.
Length	5–30 pages. Longer length articles may be considers at the discretion of the editors.
Margins	1 inch all around.
Spacing	Double-spaced.

STYLE

Name of Guide	*Publication Manual of the American Psychological Association* (APA).
Subheadings	Follow style guide.
References	Follow style guide.
Footnotes	Follow style guide.
Tables or Figures	Tables and figures (illustrations) should not be embedded in the text, but should be included as separate sheets or files. A short descriptive title should appear above each table with a clear legend and any footnotes suitably identified below. All units must be included. Figures should be completely labeled, taking into account necessary size reduction. Captions should be typed, double-spaced, on a separate sheet.

REVIEW PROCESS

Type of Review	All research articles in this journal have undergone rigorous peer review, based on initial editor screening and blind review by 3 anonymous referees.
Queries	Contact editors.
Acknowledgment	Not specified.
Review Time	Not specified.
Revisions	Per editor instruction.

Acceptance Rate	Not specified.
Return of Manuscript	Not specified.
Lag Time to Print	Not specified.

CHARGES TO AUTHOR

Author Alterations	Not specified.
Page Charges	Not specified.
Processing	Not specified.

REPRINT, SUBSCRIPTION, AND CONTACT INFORMATION

Reprint Policy	Reprints of individual articles are available for order at the time authors review page proofs. A discount on reprints is available to authors who order before print publication. Each corresponding author will receive 3 complete issues in which the article publishes and a complimentary PDF. This file is for personal use only and may not be copied and disseminated in any form without prior written permission from Taylor and Francis Group, LLC.
Book Reviews	Contact Editors.
Subscriptions	Available through the website at www.informaworld.com.
Affiliation	Not specified.
E-Mail Address	mvidal@luc.edu
Website	http://www.units.muohio.edu/journalofpoverty/

JOURNAL OF RELIGION AND SPIRITUALITY IN SOCIAL WORK: SOCIAL THOUGHT

Current Title	*Journal of Religion and Spirituality in Social Work: Social Thought*
Previous Title	*Social Thought (Journal of Religion in the Social Services).*
Editorial Focus	In *Journal of Religion and Spirituality in Social Work: Social Thought,* scholars, researchers, and practitioners examine issues of social justice and religion as they relate to the development of policy and delivery of social services. In addition to timely literature reviews, the journal presents up-to-date, in-depth, expert information on sectarian and nonsectarian approaches to spirituality and ethics; justice and peace; philosophically oriented aspects of religion in the social services; conceptual frameworks; the philosophy of social work; and a great deal more.
Audience	Social work practitioners, researchers, academics, and students
Special Themes	Faith-based social service organizations; controversial issues between social work and religion; social work ethics.
Where Indexed/ Abstracted	Not specified.
Year Established	1974
Circulation	625
Frequency	Quarterly.
Months Issued	January, April, July, November.
No. of Articles per Issue	5

SUBMISSIONS

Postal Mailing Address	Frederick L. Ahearn, Editor, JRSSW, Shahan Hall, CUA/NCSSS, Washington, DC 20064.
Method for Submission	E-mail.
Number of Copies	1
Disk Submission	N/A.
Online or E-mail Submission Allowed or Required	Encouraged.

FORMAT OF MANUSCRIPT

Cover Sheet	Yes.
Abstract	Yes.
Key Words	Yes, 5–6 key words.
Length	20–25 pages.
Margins	1 inch.
Spacing	Double-spaced.

STYLE

Name of Guide	*Publication Manual of the American Psychological Association* (APA, latest edition).
Subheadings	See style guide.
References	See style guide.
Footnotes	See style guide.
Tables or Figures	See style guide.

REVIEW PROCESS

Type of Review	All research articles in this journal have undergone rigorous peer review, based on initial editor screening and anonymous refereeing by 2 referees.
Queries	Welcomed.
Acknowledgment	Yes, usually via e-mail.
Review Time	Approximately 3–5 months.
Revisions	Revisions are usually required.
Acceptance Rate	Approximately 10% without revisions; 40% with revisions.
Return of Manuscript	No.
Lag Time to Print	Approximately 12 months.

REPRINT, SUBSCRIPTION, AND CONTACT INFORMATION

Reprint Policy	Authors receive 2 reprints each.
Book Reviews	In each issue.

Subscriptions   GBP: Institutional (print & online) $275, Institutional online $261, Personal $84.
USD: Institutional (print & online) $363, Institutional online $345, Personal 109.
EUR: Institutional (print & online) $358, Institutional online $340, Personal $109.

Affiliation   The Society for Spirituality in Social Work.

E-Mail Address   Ahearn@cua.edu

Website   http://www.tandf.co.uk/journals/titles/15426432.asp

JOURNAL OF PUBLIC CHILD WELFARE

Current Title	*Journal of Public Child Welfare*
Previous Title	*N/A.*
Editorial Focus	*Journal of Public Child Welfare* provides a broad forum for theory-based and applied research in child welfare. Rather than limit itself to primarily private agencies, this essential journal provides the quality research and comprehensive information that child welfare professionals and public agencies need most. The legal mandate of vital public child welfare programs is safety, permanence, and child and family well-being. With this in mind, *Journal of Public Child Welfare* presents quantitative, qualitative, and mixed-methods theory-based or applied research, cogent reviews of the literature, policy analyses, and program evaluation articles about child welfare.
Audience	Social workers, psychologists, counselors, juvenile court judges, attorneys, and other child welfare professionals.
Special Themes	Not specified.
Where Indexed/ Abstracted	CSA Worldwide Political Science Abstracts; Current Abstracts; EBSCOhost; Education Research Abstracts Online; Family Index; Risk Abstracts; SCOPUS; Social Service Abstracts; Sociology of Education Abstracts.
Year Established	2007.
Circulation	Not specified.
Frequency	Quarterly.
Months Issued	Not specified.
No. of Articles per Issue	5–7 per issue.

SUBMISSIONS

Postal Mailing Address	Manuscripts should be submitted through e-mail.
Method for Submission	Authors are strongly encouraged to submit manuscripts electronically. Manuscripts should be prepared using MS Word or WordPerfect. Please e-mail electronic files to Co-editor Alberta J. Ellett at aellett@uga.edu, and indicate that it is a submission for the *Journal of Public Child Welfare* in the subject line.
Number of Copies	1 copy.
Disk Submission	Not specified.
Online or E-mail Submission Allowed or Required	E-mail submission encouraged.

FORMAT OF MANUSCRIPT

Cover Sheet	Not specified.
Abstract	Each article should be summarized in an abstract of not more than 100 words. Avoid abbreviations, diagrams, and reference to the text in the abstract.
Key Words	Not specified.
Length	Not specified.
Margins	1 inch on all sides.
Spacing	Double-spaced.

STYLE

Name of Guide	*Publication Manual of the American Psychological Association* (APA, 5th edition).
Subheadings	See style guide.
References	See style guide.
Footnotes	See style guide.
Tables or Figures	Tables and figures (illustrations) should not be embedded in the text, but should be included as separate sheets or files. A short descriptive title should appear above each table with a clear legend and any footnotes suitably identified below. All units must be included. Figures should be completely labeled, taking into account necessary size reduction. Captions should be typed, double-spaced, on a separate sheet.

REVIEW PROCESS

Type of Review	Double-blind peer and editorial review with feedback to the authors.
Queries	Contact the editor.

Acknowledgment	Not specified.
Review Time	Not specified.
Revisions	Per editor instruction.
Acceptance Rate	Not specified.
Return of Manuscript	Not specified.
Lag Time to Print	Not specified.

CHARGES TO AUTHOR

Author Alterations	Not specified.
Page Charges	Not specified.
Processing	Not specified.

REPRINT, SUBSCRIPTION, AND CONTACT INFORMATION

Reprint Policy	Reprints of individual articles are available for order at the time authors review page proofs. A discount on reprints is available to authors who order before print publication. Each corresponding author will receive 3 complete issues in which the article publishes and a complimentary PDF. This file is for personal use only and may not be copied and disseminated in any form without prior written permission from Taylor and Francis Group, LLC.
Book Reviews	Contact editor.
Subscriptions	Available through the website at www.informaworld.com.
Affiliation	Not specified.
E-Mail Address	aellett@uga.edu
Website	www.informaworld.com

JOURNAL OF SEX AND MARITAL THERAPY

Current Title	*Journal of Sex and Marital Therapy*
Previous Title	N/A.
Editorial Focus	Featured topics in the journal include: sexual dysfunctions, ranging from dysparenia to auto-gynephelia to pedophilia; therapeutic techniques, including psychopharmacology and sexual counseling for a wide range of dysfunctions; clinical considerations, sexual dysfunction and its relationship to aging, unemployment, alcoholism, and more; theoretical issues, such as the ethics of pornography in the AIDS era; and marital relationships, including psychological intimacy and marital stability in women abused as children.
Audience	Sex therapists, marriage and family therapists, psychiatrists, psychologists, allied health and mental health practitioners, counselors, clinical social workers, physicians, nurses, clergy practitioners, and pastoral counselors.
Special Themes	Not specified.
Where Indexed/ Abstracted	EBSCO Academic Search Premier; Elsevier EMBASE/Excerpta Medica; Family Index Database; ISI Current Contents: Social & Behavioral Sciences; ISI Social Science Citation Index; MEDLINE/ Index Medicus; OCLC ArticleFirst; OCLC Electronic Collections Online; PsycFirst; Psychological Abstracts/PsycINFO; Sage Family Studies Abstracts.
Year Established	1976.
Circulation	Not specified.
Frequency	5 times per year.
Months Issued	Not specified.
No. of Articles per Issue	Not specified.

SUBMISSIONS

Postal Mailing Address	R.T. Segraves, MD, MHMC-Psychiatry, 2500 MetroHealth Drive, Cleveland, OH 44109-1998.
Method for submission	See website instructions for authors. Surface mail; however, we strongly encourage you to send the final, revised version of your article electronically, by e-mail, to Dr. R.T. Segraves at rsegraves@metrohealth.org. This will ensure that it can be dealt with quickly and will reduce errors at the typesetting stage. This guide sets out the procedures which will allow us to process your article efficiently.
Number of Copies	See website instructions for authors; 3 copies of each manuscript.
Disk Submission	Authors are strongly encouraged to submit manuscripts on disk. The disk should be prepared using MS Word or WordPerfect and should be clearly labeled with the authors' names, file name, and software program. A hardcopy printout that exactly matches the disk must be supplied.
Online or E-mail Submission Allowed or Required	***Note to Authors: please make sure your contact address information is clearly visible on the outside of all packages you are sending to Editors.***Three copies of each manuscript and return postage should be sent to: R.T. Segraves, MD, MHMC-Psychiatry, 2500 MetroHealth Drive, Cleveland, OH 44109-1998. Authors are strongly encouraged to submit manuscripts on disk. The disk should be prepared using MS Word or WordPerfect and should be clearly labeled with the authors' names, file name, and software program. A hardcopy printout that exactly matches the disk must be supplied. Each manuscript must be accompanied by a statement that it has not been published elsewhere and that it has not been submitted simultaneously for publication elsewhere. Authors are responsible for obtaining permission to reproduce copyrighted material from other sources and are required to sign an agreement for the transfer of copyright to the publisher. All accepted manuscripts, artwork, and photographs become the property of the publisher.

FORMAT OF MANUSCRIPT

Cover Sheet	See website instructions for authors. Include full names of authors, academic and/or other professional affiliations and the complete mailing address of the author to whom proofs and correspondence would be sent on the title pages. Please include phone, fax, and e-mail address, if available.
Abstract	100 words.
Key Words	Not specified.
Length	Not specified.
Margins	1 inch.
Spacing	Double-spaced.

STYLE

Name of Guide	*Publication Manual of the American Psychological Association* (APA, 4th edition).
Subheadings	Not specified.
References	See style guide.
Footnotes	See below.
Tables or Figures	Tables and figures should not be embedded in the text, but should be included as separate sheets or files. A short descriptive title should appear above each table with a clear legend and any footnotes suitably identified below. All units must be included. Figures should be completely labeled, taking into account necessary size reduction. Captions should be typed, double-spaced, on a separate sheet. All original figures should be clearly marked in pencil on the reverse side with the number, author's name, and top edge indicated.
	Illustrations submitted (line drawings, halftones, photos, photomicrographs, etc.) should be clean originals or digital files. Digital files are recommended for highest quality reproduction and should follow these guidelines: 300 dpi or higher; sized to fit on journal page; EPS, TIFF, or PSD format only; submitted as separate files; not embedded in text files. Color illustrations will be considered for publication; however, the author will be required to bear the full cost involved in their printing and publication. The charge for the first figure is $1,200.00. Subsequent figures, totaling no more than 4 text pages, are $500.00 each. Good-quality color prints should be provided in their final size. Figures needing reduction or enlargement will be charged an additional 25 %. The publisher has the right to refuse publication of any artwork deemed unacceptable.

REVIEW PROCESS

Type of Review	All review papers in this journal have undergone editorial screening and peer review.
Queries	Not specified.
Acknowledgment	Not specified.
Review Time	Not specified.
Revisions	Not specified.
Acceptance Rate	Not specified.
Return of Manuscript	Not specified.
Lag Time to Print	Not specified.

CHARGES TO AUTHOR

Author Alterations	All proofs must be corrected and returned to the publisher within 48 hours of receipt. If the manuscript is not returned within the allotted time, the editor will proofread the article and it will be printed per the editor's instruction. Only correction of typographical errors is permitted. The author will be charged for additional alterations to text at the proof stage.
Page Charges	Color illustrations will be considered for publication; however, the author will be required to bear the full cost involved in their printing and publication. The charge for the first figure is $1,200.00. Subsequent figures, totaling no more than 4 text pages, are $500.00 each. Good-quality color prints should be provided in their final size. Figures needing reduction or enlargement will be charged an additional 25 %. The publisher has the right to refuse publication of any artwork deemed unacceptable.
Processing	We strongly encourage you to send the final, revised version of your article electronically, by e-mail, to Dr. R.T. Segraves at rsegraves@metrohealth.org. This will ensure that it can be dealt with quickly and will reduce errors at the typesetting stage. This guide sets out the procedures which will allow us to process your article efficiently.

REPRINT, SUBSCRIPTION, AND CONTACT INFORMATION

Reprint Policy	The corresponding author of each article will receive 1 complete copy of issue in which the article appears. Offprints of an individual article may be ordered from Taylor & Francis by using the offprint order form included with page proofs.
Book Reviews	Yes. Editor: Leonore Tiefer, PhD, New York, NY.
Subscriptions	See website: http://www.informaworld.com/smpp/title~db=all~content=t713723519~tab=subscribe
Affiliation	Taylor and Francis.
E-Mail Address	rsegraves@metrohealth.org
Website	http://www.informaworld.com/smpp/title~content=t713723519~db=all

JOURNAL OF SEXUAL AGGRESSION

Current Title	*Journal of Sexual Aggression*
Previous Title	N/A.
Editorial Focus	*Journal of Sexual Aggression* provides an international and interdisciplinary forum for the dissemination of research findings and the development of theory, policy and practice regarding sexual aggression in all its forms. The Editor welcomes the opportunity to consider papers which examine the nature and impact of sexual aggression, as well as its prevention and treatment. Priority is afforded to articles containing original material that are likely to contribute to the advancement of knowledge in the field. As such, several types of contribution are welcomed: (1) research and conceptual developments, papers reporting the findings of empirical research or the development of theory/ conceptual models. (2) reviews, literature reviews or commentaries focusing upon specific issues of relevance. (3) practice, articles presenting clinical practice or programme descriptions. (4) debate, brief responses to articles which have appeared in previous issues of the Journal.
Audience	As an interdisciplinary and international publication, *Journal of Sexual Aggression* is relevant to a wide range of professional disciplines, such as psychology, psychiatry, social work, probation, and other allied health and social care professions. Emphasising research, theory, and practice, the journal is a forum for a diverse professional community, including researchers, practitioners, managers, and policy makers.
Special Themes	The scope of the journal extends to the expression of sexual aggression across childhood and adulthood, with regard to abusers, victims, and survivors, irrespective of gender, culture, and sexual preference.
Where Indexed/ Abstracted	Community Care; Criminal Justice Abstracts; Educational Research Abstracts online (ERA); Family Studies Database; International Bibliography of the Social Sciences; PsycINFO; PASCAL Database; Studies on Women and Gender Abstracts; Violence and Abuse Abstracts (SAGE).
Year Established	1994.
Circulation	Not specified.
Frequency	3 times per year.
Months Issued	March, July and November.
No. of Articles per Issue	Approximately 7–9 articles.

SUBMISSION

Postal Mailing Address	http://mc.manuscriptcentral.com/tjsa.
Method for Submission	See below: electronically.
Number of Copies	2; one should be a complete text, while in the second all document information identifying the author should be removed from files to allow them to be sent anonymously to referees. When uploading files, authors will then be able to define the nonanonymous version as "File not for review."
Disk Submission	N/A.
Online or E-mail Submission Allowed or Required	Yes. Manuscripts may be submitted in any standard format, including Word, PostScript, and PDF. These files will be automatically converted into a PDF file for the review process. LaTeX files should be converted to PDF prior to submission because Manuscript Central is not able to convert LaTeX files into PDFs directly. This journal does not accept Microsoft Word 2007 documents. Please use Word's "Save As" option to save your document as an older (.doc) file type. See: http://mc.manuscriptcentral.com/tjsa.

FORMAT OF MANUSCRIPT

Cover Sheet	Yes, all the authors of a paper should include their full names, affiliations, postal addresses, telephone and fax numbers and e-mail addresses on the cover page only of the manuscript. One author should be identified as the corresponding author.
Abstract	150 words.
Key Words	6 key words.
Length	A typical article (Research and Conceptual Development) will not exceed 6,000 words; Reviews up to 8,000 words; Practice articles between 2,000 and 4,000 words; Debate articles between 750 and 1,500 words. Papers that greatly exceed this will be critically reviewed with respect to length. Authors should include a word count with their manuscript.
Margins	4-cm minimum margins.
Spacing	Double-spaced throughout.

STYLE

Name of Guide	Please consult the Instructions for Authors on the journal website for points of detail: www.tandf.co.uk/journals/tjsa.
Subheadings	(A) bold initial cap only; (B) bold italic initial cap only; (C) italic initial cap only; (D) italic initial cap only. Text runs on.
References	Please use the *Publication Manual of the American Psychological Association* (APA) for points of detail.
Footnotes	Footnotes are not normally permitted, but endnotes may be used if necessary.
Tables or Figures	Tables should be laid out clearly and supplied on separate pages, with an indication within the text of their approximate location. Vertical lines should be omitted, and horizontal lines limited to those indicating the top and bottom of the table, below column headings and above summed totals. Totals and percentages should be labeled clearly.

REVIEW PROCESS

Type of Review	Double anonymous peer review.
Queries	Please send to adminjsa.hls@coventry.ac.uk.
Acknowledgment	E-mail.
Review Time	Not specified.
Revisions	Material may be accepted subject to minor or major revisions, rejected, or rejected with the option to resubmit.
Acceptance Rate	Not specified.
Return of Manuscript	N/A.
Lag Time to Print	Not specified.

CHARGES TO AUTHOR

Author Alterations	Not specified.
Page Charges	None.
Processing	No fee.

REPRINT, SUBSCRIPTION, AND CONTACT INFORMATION

Reprint Policy	Corresponding authors can receive 50 free reprints, free online access to their article through our website (www.informaworld.com), and a complimentary copy of the issue containing their article. Complimentary reprints are available through Rightslink, and additional reprints can be ordered through Rightslink when proofs are received. If you have any queries, please contact our reprints department at reprints@tandf.co.uk.
Book Reviews	We publish book reviews and accept unsolicited reviews. Books for review should be submitted to the Editorial Office: Book Reviews Editor, *Journal of Sexual Aggression*, c/o Psychology Department, Faculty of Health and Life Sciences JS266, Coventry University, Priory Street, Coventry, CV1 5FB, United Kingdom.
Subscriptions	T&F Customer Services, Sheepen Place, Colchester, Essex, CO3 3LP, United Kingdom; Tel: +44 (0) 207017 5544; Fax: +44 (0) 20 7017 5198 or E-mail: subscriptions@tandf.co.uk.
Affiliation	The National Organization for the Treatment of Abusers (NOTA).
E-Mail Address	adminjsa.hls@coventry.ac.uk
Website	www.tandf.co.uk/journals

JOURNAL OF SOCIAL ISSUES

Current Title	*Journal of Social Issues.*
Previous Title	N/A.
Editorial Focus	*Journal of Social Issues* (*JSI*) is the flagship journal of the Society for the Psychological Study of Social Issues. The goal of *JSI* is to communicate scientific findings and interpretations relevant to pressing social issues in a nontechnical manner, but without the sacrifice of professional standards. Each issue of *JSI* is organized around an integral theme. Issues of the journal are proposed and developed by social researchers, who serve as issue editors under the direction of the *JSI* board. *JSI* does not publish unsolicited manuscripts or book reviews.
Audience	Social scientists and others interested in social issues.
Special Themes	Please note: *JSI* only publishes thematic issues. Each set of papers is coordinated by an issue editor. Individual papers are neither reviewed nor published. Issue editors assemble a proposal for each issue. *JSI* is sponsored by the Society for the Psychological Study of Social Issues (SPSSI). As issue editors develop their proposals, they typically announce the topic of the project in the SPSSI Newsletter. Interested authors can submit items for consideration to the person(s) coordinating the proposal.
Where Indexed/ Abstracted	Over 25 places; see inside cover of the journal.
Year Established	1944
Circulation	Approximately 6,000.
Frequency	Quarterly.
Months Issued	Winter, spring, summer, fall.
No. of Articles per Issue	10–12.

SUBMISSIONS

Postal Mailing Address	See: http://www.spssi.org/index.cfm?fuseaction=page.viewpage&pageid=950.
Method for Submission	E-mail.
Number of Copies	N/A.
Disk Submission	No.
Online or E-mail Submission Allowed or Required	Required.

FORMAT OF MANUSCRIPT

Cover Sheet	Yes.
Abstract	Yes.
Key Words	Per issue editor's instructions.
Length	Per issue editors' instructions.
Margins	1 inch on all sides.
Spacing	Double-spaced.

STYLE

Name of Guide	*Publication Manual of the American Psychological Association* (APA).
Subheadings	See style guide.
References	See style guide.
Footnotes	Discouraged.
Tables or Figures	See style guide.

REVIEW PROCESS

Type of Review	Proposals are reviewed by the *JSI* editorial board and by additional relevant experts.
Queries	Yes.
Acknowledgment	Manuscripts sent to issue editor.
Review Time	Not specified.
Revisions	Not specified.
Acceptance Rate	Not specified.
Return of Manuscript	Not specified.
Lag Time to Print	Approximately 5 months.

REPRINT, SUBSCRIPTION, AND CONTACT INFORMATION

Reprint Policy	Not specified.
Book Reviews	None.
Subscriptions	Included in membership to the Society for the Psychological Study of Social Issues; see http://www.spssi.org/index.cfm?fuseaction=Page.viewPage&pageId=4.
Affiliation	Society for the Psychological Study of Social Issues
E-Mail Address	See website: http://www.spssi.org/index.cfm?fuseaction=page.viewpage&pageid=950
Website	http://www.spssi.org/index.cfm?fuseaction=page.viewpage&pageid=950

JOURNAL OF SOCIAL SERVICE RESEARCH

Current Title	*Journal of Social Service Research*
Previous Title	N/A.
Editorial Focus	Scholarly research papers within the social services arena characterized by sophisticated, appropriate designs and rigorous data analysis. The primary purpose of *JSSR* is to publish funded or non-funded state-of-the-art, evidence-based papers that contribute to enhanced social services in both practice and administrative settings.
Audience	Social service providers, social workers, public health and mental health providers.
Special Themes	Evidence/data based research studies.
Where Indexed/ Abstracted	Academic Search Series; ASSIA: Applied Social Sciences Index and Abstracts; Criminal Justice Abstracts; Family Index Database; Health & Psychological Instruments; PsycINFO; Social Science Citation Index/Journal Citation Report (Impact Factor: .164); Social Service Abstracts.
Year Established	
Circulation	385
Frequency	Quarterly in 2009, 5 issues per year in 2010.
Months Issued	January, March, June, September in 2009.
No. of Articles per Issue	4–6

SUBMISSIONS

Postal Mailing Address	c/o Editor, Sophia F. Dziegielewski, PhD, LISW, University of Cincinnati, 1515 West French Hall, P.O. Box 210108, Cincinnati, OH 45221-0108. Electronic e-mail submissions preferred: Sophia.Dziegielewski@uc.edu and socwork@aol.com.
Method for Submission	E-mail is preferred and electronic submission is requested. Electronic e-mail submissions preferred: Sophia.Dziegielewski@uc.edu and socwork@aol.com.
Number of Copies	Electronic submission requested.
Disk Submission	If electronic, no disk required.
Online or E-mail Submission Allowed or Required	Required.

FORMAT OF MANUSCRIPT

Cover Sheet	Brief statement of the purpose of the scholarly paper and complete contact information for the authors. Submissions currently under review by another journal will not be accepted. When appropriate, author verification that data-based studies involving human subjects have been reviewed and approved by the human subjects institutional review Board at the researcher's institution, hospital or university setting.
Abstract	APA style requested, not more than 100 words. Be sure to include details related to subjects, methods, instruments and procedure, results, and future discussion.
Key Words	Required.
Length	20–25 pages.
Margins	12-point font, standard margins. Please limit footnotes and provide all tables and figures within the document at the end.
Spacing	Double-spaced.

STYLE

Name of Guide	*Publication Manual of the American Psychological Association* (APA).
Subheadings	Not specified.
References	End of document, APA style.
Footnotes	Please limit footnotes and place in body of text when possible.
Tables or Figures	Follow APA style. Place tables and figures at the end of the text with a clear title. At the end of the table or figure provide a brief statement of what the table or figure contributes to the text, outlining the purpose for inclusion. This statement will assist the reviewers in determining the author(s) rationale for inclusion and may be removed prior to publication.

REVIEW PROCESS

Type of Review	All research articles in this journal have undergone rigorous peer review, based on initial editor screening and anonymous refereeing by 2 or 3 referees.

Queries	For comments or questions please contact the editor Sophia.Dzieielewski@uc.edu or socwork@aol.com.
Acknowledgment	Within 1 week of receiving the submission, an e-mail response will be sent that updates the author to whether the article will be sent for peer review, assigning the submission a tracking number.
Review Time	Approximately 6 months.
Revisions	Generally, with acceptance, revisions and clarifications by the reviewers are to be expected.
Acceptance Rate	Approximately 54%.
Return of Manuscript	Decision letters and the anonymous reviewer comments are returned to the author when available.
Lag Time to Print	Your review time plus 12 weeks for T&F production.

CHARGES TO AUTHOR

Author Alterations	No charges.
Page Charges	No charges for standard black and white pages, but if the author wants color the charges are as follows: Color art can be purchased for online-only reproduction or for print and online reproduction. Color reprints can only be ordered if print and online reproduction costs are paid. Rates for color art reproduction are: Online-Only Reproduction: $225 for the first page of color; $100 for the next 3 pages of color. A maximum charge of $525 applies. Print and Online Reproduction: $900 for the first page of color; $450 per page for the next 3 pages of color. A custom quote will be provided for articles with more than 4 pages of color.
Processing	None.

REPRINT, SUBSCRIPTION, AND CONTACT INFORMATION

Reprint Policy	Reprints of individual articles are available for order at the time authors review page proofs. A discount on reprints is available to authors who order before print publication. Each corresponding author will receive 3 complete issues in which the article publishes and a complimentary PDF. This file is for personal use only and may not be copied and disseminated in any form without prior written permission from Taylor and Francis Group, LLC.
Book Reviews	Not specified.
Subscriptions	www.tandf.co.uk/journals/wssr or customer.service@taylorandfrancis.com or 1.800.354.1420, press "4."
Affiliation	N/A.
E-Mail Address	customer.service@taylorandfrancis.com
Website	www.tandf.co.uk/journals/wssr

JOURNAL OF SOCIAL PSYCHOLOGY

Current Title	*Journal of Social Psychology*
Previous Title	N/A.
Editorial Focus	*Journal of Social Psychology* is devoted to experimental, empirical, and field studies of groups, cultural effects, cross-national problems, language, and ethnicity. Cross-cultural and field research are given a higher priority than laboratory research using college students.
Audience	Libraries, faculty.
Special Themes	None.
Where Indexed/ Abstracted	Abstracts for Social Workers; Academic Abstracts; Applied Social Sciences Index and Abstracts; Child Development Abstracts and Bibliography; Current Index to Journals in Education; Current Contents: Social and Behavioral Science; Directory of Title Pages, Indexes, and Contents Pages; Family Resources Database; Health and Psychosocial Instruments; Human Resources Abstracts; Index Medicus; International Political Science Abstracts; Linguistics and Language Behavior Abstracts; Magazine Article Summaries; Mental Health Abstracts; Psychological Abstracts PsycINFO; Research Alert; Social Planning/Policy and Development; Social Science Source; Social Sciences Citation Index; Social Studies/Social Science Education (ERIC); Sociological Abstracts; Sociology of Education Abstracts.
Year Established	1929.
Circulation	1,884.
Frequency	Bimonthly.
Months Issued	February, April, June, August, October, December.
No. of Articles per Issue	Varies; approximately 10.

SUBMISSIONS

Postal Mailing Address	Managing Editor, *Journal of Social Psychology*, 1319 18th Street, NW, Washington, DC 20036-1802.
Method for Submission	Electronic form via website.
Number of Copies	2.
Disk Submission	No.
Online or E-mail Submission Allowed or Required	Yes.

FORMAT OF MANUSCRIPT

Cover Sheet	Authors name, title, and authors' affiliations.
Abstract	120 words; see APA for formatting guidelines.
Key Words	5–7 key words.
Length	5–35 pages.
Margins	1 inch.
Spacing	Double-spaced.

STYLE

Name of Guide	*Publication Manual of the American Psychological Association* (APA, 5th ed.)
Subheadings	Not specified.
References	See style guide.
Footnotes	Discouraged; see submission guidelines.
Tables or Figures	Camera-ready figures; tables set in-house.

REVIEW PROCESS

Type of Review	Blind peer reviewed.
Queries	Accepted.
Acknowledgment	By postcard from publisher.
Review Time	Approximately 2–3 months.
Revisions	2 copies.
Acceptance Rate	Approximately 40%.
Return of Manuscript	Returned if revisions requested.
Lag Time to Print	Approximately 12 months.

REPRINT, SUBSCRIPTION, AND CONTACT INFORMATION

Reprint Policy	Author may purchase reprints through subscription office: heldref@subscriptionoffice.com.
Book Reviews	Contact the Book Review Editor at daviske@mailbox.sc.edu.
Subscriptions	Subscription Department, *Journal of Social Psychology,* 1319 18th Street, NW, Washington, DC 20036-1802. $116 per year.
Affiliation	Helen Dwight Reid Educational Foundation.
E-Mail Address	soc@heldref.org
Website	http://www.heldref.org

JOURNAL OF SOCIOLOGY AND SOCIAL WELFARE

Current Title	*Journal of Sociology and Social Welfare*
Previous Title	N/A.
Editorial Focus	Articles that analyze social welfare institutions, policies, or problems from a social scientific perspective or otherwise attempt to bridge the gap between social science theory and social work practice; also "Research Notes," book reviews, occasional letters and debates.
Audience	Social science and social work faculty and students, libraries, researchers, practitioners.
Special Themes	1–2 annually; calls for papers published in journal and mailed by special editors.
Where Indexed/ Abstracted	Applied Social Sciences Index and Abstracts; Psychological Abstracts; Social Work Abstracts; Sociological Abstracts.
Year Established	1973.
Circulation	600.
Frequency	Quarterly.
Months Issued	March, June, September, December.
No. of Articles per Issue	8–12.

SUBMISSIONS

Postal Mailing Address	*Journal of Sociology and Social Welfare*, School of Social Work, Western Michigan University, Kalamazoo, MI 49008-5034.
Method for Submission	Surface mail and e-mail.
Number of Copies	3.
Disk Submission	Not specified.
Online or E-mail Submission Allowed or Required	rleighn@asu.edu.

FORMAT OF MANUSCRIPT

Cover Sheet	Title, author names, affiliations, mailing address, phone number, e-mail address, any acknowledgments on 1 copy only; title only on other 2 copies.
Abstract	100 words.
Key Words	4–5 key words.
Length	15–18 pages of text; tables and references chosen carefully.
Margins	1 inch on all sides.
Spacing	Double-spaced.

STYLE

Name of Guide	*Publication Manual of the American Psychological Association* (APA).
Subheadings	As needed.
References	Author–date style; see style guide.
Footnotes	If it doesn't fit gracefully into the text, you can probably do without it.
Tables or Figures	See style guide.

REVIEW PROCESS

Type of Review	Anonymous review by 2 editorial board members, sometimes additional reviewers in cases of split decision or when special expertise is required. Editor reads all manuscripts.
Queries	Telephone or e-mail queries welcome, though usually of limited use.
Acknowledgment	Editor will notify author when manuscript goes out for review. This may not happen right away. Feel free to query if anxious.
Review Time	Approximately 120 days. Feel free to ask editor for status report.
Revisions	Editor will advise.
Acceptance Rate	Approximately 25%–30%.
Return of Manuscript	Not returned.
Lag Time to Print	Approximately 9–12 months.

CHARGES TO AUTHOR

Author Alterations	None.
Page Charges	None.
Processing	None.

REPRINT, SUBSCRIPTION, AND CONTACT INFORMATION

Reprint Policy   Consult with Managing Editor.

Book Reviews   Send queries to Book Review Editors: Marguerite Rosenthal, mrosenthal@salemstate.edu; Jennifer Zelnick, jzelmocl@salemstate.edu. Send books to Jennifer Zelnick, Salem State College, School of Social Work, 352 Lafayette Street, Salem, MA 01970.

Subscriptions   *Journal of Sociology and Social Welfare*, School of Social Work, Western Michigan University, Kalamazoo, MI 49008-5034 or visit our web site: www.wmich.edu/hhs/newsletters_journals/jssw/index.htm.

Individuals within U.S. $40, Individuals outside the U.S. $45, Institutions inside the U.S. $80 and Institutions outside the U.S. $90.

Affiliation   Western Michigan University and Arizona State University.

E-Mail Address   Editor, Robert Leighninger: rleighn@asu.edu; Managing Editor, Fritz MacDonald: frederick. macdonald@wmich.edu

Website   www.wmich.edu/hhs/newsletters_journals/jssw/index.htm

JOURNAL OF SOCIAL WORK EDUCATION

Current Title	*Journal of Social Work Education*
Previous Title	N/A.
Editorial Focus	*Journal of Social Work Education* is a refereed professional journal concerned with education in social work and social welfare.
Audience	Social work faculty, field instructors, researchers, administrators, students, librarians.
Special Themes	Technology, interprofessional education, program evaluation.
Where Indexed/ Abstracted	Applied Social Sciences Index & Abstracts; Current Contents; Current Index to Journals in Education; ProQuest; Research into Higher Education; Social Sciences Citation Index; Social Sciences Index; Social Work Abstracts; Sociological Abstracts.
Year Established	1964.
Circulation	3,500.
Frequency	3 times per year.
Months Issued	January 15; May 15; September 15.
No. of Articles per Issue	9–10.

SUBMISSIONS

Postal Mailing Address	Council on Social Work Education, 1699 Duke Street, Suite 300, Alexandria, VA 22314-3421.
Method for Submission	Submissions to *JSWE* are accepted only through our online manuscript submission system. Submissions received via mail, fax, or e-mail will be returned unread.
Number of Copies	http://jswe.msubmit.net/cgi-bin/main.plex
Disk Submission	http://jswe.msubmit.net/cgi-bin/main.plex
Online or E-mail Submission Allowed or Required	http://jswe.msubmit.net/cgi-bin/main.plex

FORMAT OF MANUSCRIPT

Cover Sheet	Manuscript title, name of author(s), title and affiliation of author(s).
Abstract	120 words.
Key Words	None.
Length	15–25 without references, tables, etc.
Margins	Not specified.
Spacing	Double-spaced.

STYLE

Name of Guide	*Publication Manual of the American Psychological Association* (APA).
Subheadings	See style guide.
References	The list of references should contain only those works cited in the manuscript. Any exact source material which is the property of a different author or publisher and is reprinted in a manuscript submitted for an article should be accompanied by a written permission from the original author or publisher.
Footnotes	See style guide.
Tables or Figures	See style guide.

REVIEW PROCESS

Type of Review	To ensure anonymity in the peer-review process, all author identification information (name, position, institutional affiliation, mailing address, e-mail address, telephone number) should appear in the cover letter only and should be excluded from your manuscript.
Queries	Accepted on status of manuscript in review process.
Acknowledgment	Sent for all submissions.
Review Time	Approximately 3 months.
Revisions	Accepted for reject/revise ratings.
Acceptance Rate	Approximately 20%.
Return of Manuscript	Not returned.
Lag Time to Print	Approximately 6–9 months.

REPRINT, SUBSCRIPTION, AND CONTACT INFORMATION

Reprint Policy Authors receive 2 free copies; may order additional copies from Boyd Printing Company, 49 Sheridan Avenue, Albany, NY 12201.

Book Reviews By invitation only.

Subscriptions http://www.cswe.org/CSWE/publications/journal/Purchasing+the+JSWE.htm.

Affiliation Council on Social Work Education.

E-Mail Address jswe@cswe.org.

Website http://www.cswe.org/CSWE/publications/journal/

JOURNAL OF SOCIAL WORK IN DISABILITY & REHABILITATION

Current Title	*Journal of Social Work in Disability & Rehabilitation*
Previous Title	N/A.
Editorial Focus	*Journal of Social Work in Disability & Rehabilitation* presents and explores issues related to disabilities and social policy, practice, research, and theory. Reflecting the broad scope of social work in disability practice, this interdisciplinary journal examines vital aspects of the field from innovative practice methods, legal issues, and literature reviews to program descriptions and cutting-edge practice research. Use it to enhance your knowledge and skills and to broaden your professional understanding of the impact of the individual, family, group, community, and social services delivery system on persons with disabilities and on the rehabilitation process. *Journal of Social Work in Disability & Rehabilitation* is based on the concept that a disability can be understood through a number of perspectives, such as moral, medical, minority and social models. These models have influenced the education of social work students and the strategies used by professionals working with persons with disabilities. The journal provides new insight and understanding for students, educators, administrators, and professionals providing services to the community.
Audience	*JSWDR* is a multidisciplinary peer-reviewed journal for students, educators, administrators, and professionals.
Special Themes	Not specified.
Where Indexed/ Abstracted	AMED Database; CINAHL and CINAHL Plus; EBSCO; MEDLINE; OCLC Article First; PSYCLINE; & Social Services Abstracts.
Year Established	2002
Circulation	Not specified.
Frequency	*Journal of Social Work in Disability & Rehabilitation* (ISSN: 1536-710X) is published quarterly by Taylor & Francis Group, LLC, 325 Chestnut Street, Philadelphia, PA 19106.
Months Issued	February, May, August, November.
No. of Articles per Issue	4

SUBMISSIONS

Postal Mailing Address	Authors are strongly encouraged to submit manuscripts electronically. If submitting a disk or by e-mail, it should be prepared using MS Word and should be clearly labeled with the authors' names, file name, and software program. Manuscripts should be submitted in duplicate to: Francis Yuen, Editor, *Journal of Social Work in Disability & Rehabilitation*, Division of Social Work, California State University, Sacramento, 6000 J Street, Sacramento, CA 95819-6090. E-mail: fyuen@csus.edu.
Method for Submission	Disk and E-mail.
Number of Copies	1
Disk Submission	Yes.
Online or E-mail Submission Allowed or Required	Yes.

FORMAT OF MANUSCRIPT

Cover Sheet	On the cover letter, provide information about the author(s): name, title, organizational affiliation, mailing address, e-mail, and phone number. Each manuscript must be accompanied by a statement that it has not been published elsewhere and that it has not been submitted simultaneously for publication elsewhere.
Abstract	Each article should be summarized in an abstract of not more than 100 words. Avoid abbreviations, diagrams, and reference to the text in the abstract.
Key Words	5–10 keywords.
Length	Normally 20–35 double-spaced typed pages.
Margins	All parts of the manuscript should be typewritten, double-spaced, with margins of at least 1 inch on all sides. Number manuscript pages consecutively throughout the paper.
Spacing	Double-spaced.

STYLE

Name of Guide	*American Psychological Association Publication Manual* (APA, 5th edition).
Subheadings	Authors should also supply a shortened version of the title suitable for the running head, not exceeding 50 character spaces.

References	References, citations, and general style of manuscripts should be prepared in accordance with the *APA Publication Manual*, 5th ed. Cite in the text by author and date (Smith, 1983) and include an alphabetical list at the end of the article.

Examples:

Journal: Tsai, M., & Wagner, N. N. (1978). Therapy groups for women sexually molested as children. *Archives of Sexual Behaviour*, 7(6), 417–427.

Book: Millman, M. (1980). *Such a pretty face*. New York: W. W. Norton.

Contribution to a Book: Hartley, J. T., & Walsh, D. A. (1980). Contemporary issues in adult development of learning. In L. W. Poon (ed.), *Ageing in the 1980s* (pp. 239–252). Washington, DC: American Psychological Association.

Footnotes	Allowable, use sparingly.
Tables or Figures	Tables and figures (illustrations) should not be embedded in the text, but should be included as separate sheets or files. A short descriptive title should appear above each table with a clear legend and any footnotes suitably identified below. All units must be included. Figures should be completely labeled, taking into account necessary size reduction. Captions should be typed, double-spaced, on a separate sheet.

REVIEW PROCESS

Type of Review	All research and review articles in this journal will undergo rigorous peer review, based on initial editor screening and anonymous refereeing by 2 referees.
Queries	All questions should be sent to the journal editor. Page proofs are sent to the designated author using Taylor & Francis' Central Article Tracking System (CATS). They must be carefully checked and returned within 48 hours of receipt.
Acknowledgment	Allowable.
Review Time	Approximately 2 months.
Revisions	Varies.
Acceptance Rate	Approximately 30%.
Return of Manuscript	No.
Lag Time to Print	Approximately 3–6 months.

CHARGES TO AUTHOR

Author Alterations	Color Illustrations. Color illustrations will be considered for publication; however, the author will be required to bear the full cost involved in color art reproduction. Color art can be purchased for online-only reproduction or for print and online reproduction. Color reprints can only be ordered if print and online reproduction costs are paid. Rates for color art reproduction are: Online-Only Reproduction: $225 for the first page of color; $100 per page for the next 3 pages of color. A maximum charge of $525 applies. Print and Online Reproduction: $900 for the first page of color; $450 per page for the next 3 pages of color. A custom quote will be provided for articles with more than 4 pages of color.
Page Charges	No.
Processing	No.

REPRINT, SUBSCRIPTION, AND CONTACT INFORMATION

Reprint Policy	Reprints of individual articles are available for order at the time authors review page proofs. A discount on reprints is available to authors who order before print publication. Each corresponding author will receive 3 complete issues in which the article publishes and a complimentary PDF. This file is for personal use only and may not be copied and disseminated in any form without prior written permission from Taylor & Francis Group, LLC.
Book Reviews	Yes.
Subscriptions	Annual Subscription, Print ISSN: 1536-710X, Online ISSN: 1536-7118. Institutional subscribers: $462, £352, 4457 Personal subscribers: $109, £84, 4109 Institutional and individual subscriptions include access to the online version of the journal. (2009).
Affiliation	No.
E-Mail Address	fyuen@csus.edu
Website	http://www.informaworld.com/smpp/title~db=all~content=g911478764~tab=summary

JOURNAL OF SOCIAL WORK PRACTICE IN THE ADDICTIONS

Current Title	*Journal of Social Work Practice in the Addictions*
Previous Title	N/A.
Editorial Focus	*Journal of Social Work Practice in the Addictions* is designed to help social work practitioners stay abreast of the latest developments in the field of addictions. This journal publishes refereed articles on innovative individual, family, group work, and community practice models for treating and preventing substance abuse and other addictions in diverse populations. The journal focuses on research findings, health care, social policies, and program administration directly affecting social work practice in the addictions.
Audience	Social workers, researchers, others working in the field of addiction.
Special Themes	Not specified.
Where Indexed/ Abstracted	Addictions Abstracts; Criminal Justice Abstracts; Current Abstracts; EBSCOhost; Family Index; Peace Research Abstracts Journal; PsycINFO; SCOPUS; Social Service Abstracts; Social Work Abstracts; Studies on Women and Gender Abstracts.
Year Established	2001.
Circulation	Not specified.
Frequency	Quarterly.
Months Issued	Not specified.
No. of Articles per Issue	7–9.

SUBMISSIONS

Postal Mailing Address	Dr. Straussner, SSSW, NYU, 1 Washington Square N., New York, NY 10003.
Method for Submission	Authors are strongly encouraged to submit manuscripts via e-mail as an attached Word document sent to the Editor, Dr. Lala Ashenberg Straussner, DSW, CAS, at: lala.straussner@nyu.edu. If submitting a disk, it should be prepared using MS Word and should be clearly labeled with the authors' names, file name, and software program and mailed to Dr. Straussner, SSSW, NYU, 1 Washington Sq. N., New York, NY 10003.
Number of Copies	1.
Disk Submission	Submissions may be on disk per above instruction.
Online or E-mail Submission Allowed or Required	E-mail submission encouraged.

FORMAT OF MANUSCRIPT

Cover Sheet	Make sure to include a cover page with a title, not exceeding 50 character spaces (and not more than 15 words).
Abstract	No more than 100 words.
Key Words	Must include 6–8 keywords.
Length	Manuscripts should be limited to 23 pages, excluding references and tables.
Margins	At least 1 inch all around.
Spacing	Double-spaced.

STYLE

Name of Guide	*Publication Manual of the American Psychological Association* (APA, 6th edition).
Subheadings	Follow style guide.
References	Follow style guide.
Footnotes	Follow style guide.
Tables or Figures	Tables and figures (illustrations) should not be embedded in the text, but should be included as separate sheets or files. A short descriptive title should appear above each table with a clear legend and any footnotes suitably identified below. All units must be included. Figures should be completely labeled, taking into account necessary size reduction. Captions should be typed, double-spaced, on a separate sheet.

REVIEW PROCESS

Type of Review	Not specified.
Queries	Contact editor.
Acknowledgment	Not specified.

Review Time	Not specified.
Revisions	Per editor instruction.
Acceptance Rate	Not specified.
Return of Manuscript	Not specified.
Lag Time to Print	Not specified.

CHARGES TO AUTHOR

Author Alterations	Not specified.
Page Charges	Not specified.
Processing	Not specified.

REPRINT, SUBSCRIPTION, AND CONTACT INFORMATION

Reprint Policy	Reprints of individual articles are available for order at the time authors review page proofs. A discount on reprints is available to authors who order before print publication. Each corresponding author will receive 3 complete issues in which the article is published and a complimentary PDF, both to be distributed to coauthors. The PDF is for personal use only and may not be copied and disseminated in any form without prior written permission from Taylor and Francis Group, LLC.
Book Reviews	Submissions should be sent to the Book Review Editor: Audrey Begun: begun.5@osu.edu or College of Social Work, Ohio State University, 1947 College Road, 325D Stillman Hall, Columbus, OH 43210;
Subscriptions	Available online through www.informaworld.com.
Affiliation	Not specified.
E-Mail Address	lala.straussner@nyu.edu
Website	www.informaworld.com

JOURNAL OF SOCIAL WORK VALUES AND ETHICS

Current Title	*Journal of Social Work Values and Ethics*
Previous Title	N/A.
Editorial Focus	*Journal of Social Work Values and Ethics* examines the ethical and values issues that impact and are interwoven with social work practice, research, and theory development. *JSWVE* addresses ethical and value issues that encompass the full range of social problems and issues that social workers encounter. The journal provides the necessary historical perspectives on the development of social work values and ethics, as well as present articles providing value and ethical dilemmas stemming from state-of-the-art developments. Manuscripts submitted to the journal should be relevant to the mission of *JSWVE*. *Journal of Social Work Values and Ethics* focuses on areas such as development of models for analyzing and resolving value and ethical conflicts. Discussion of ethical and value dilemmas related to the development of new technologies; research studies on the influence of values and ethics in social work practice decision-making and in agency program development; examples of good practice that clearly highlight ethical and value considerations; theoretical articles that explain the origin, development, and evolution of social work values and ethics; reviews and analyzes scholarly and practice books, monographs, and articles written on the topic of social work values and ethics.
Audience	Those interested in human service ethics.
Special Themes	Special issues are proposed by the readership and editorial board. Examples include academic honesty, disability, and international research.
Where Indexed/ Abstracted	Academic Search Complete; Directory of Open Access Journals (see: http://www.doaj.org/); Social Service Abstracts; Social Work Abstracts.
Year Established	2004
Circulation	6,000
Frequency	2 editions annually, with additional special editions; total of 2–3 annually.
Months Issued	October, April (3rd issues appear in December or June).
No. of Articles per Issue	3–5.

SUBMISSIONS

Postal Mailing Address	smarson@nc.rr.com (*JSWVE* does not accept hard copies).
Method for Submission	E-mail.
Number of Copies	1 electronic only.
Disk Submission	E-mail attachment.
Online or E-mail Submission Allowed or Required	Required.

FORMAT OF MANUSCRIPT

Cover Sheet	Required.
Abstract	150–250 words.
Key Words	5 keywords.
Length	25 pages maximum.
Margins	1 inch.
Spacing	APA style.

STYLE

Name of Guide	*Publication Manual of the American Psychological Association* (APA).
Subheadings	See style guide.
References	See style guide.
Footnotes	See style guide.
Tables or Figures	See style guide. (Submitted as JPG file, not embedded in manuscript).

REVIEW PROCESS

Type of Review	Blind peer review.
Queries	Queries are accepted and encouraged.
Acknowledgment	Within 5 days, the first author receives an e-mail acknowledging the receipt of the manuscript. If the author does not receive a reply within 5 days, assume that the manuscript never arrived.

Review Time	Approximately 2 weeks to 3 months.
Revisions	2 revisions accepted based on editorial comments.
Acceptance Rate	Approximately .5% as submitted; 25%–30% after revision.
Return of Manuscript	Manuscripts are not returned, as the journal accepts electronic submissions only.
Lag Time to Print	Approximately 3–6 months.

CHARGES TO AUTHOR

Author Alterations	None.
Page Charges	None.
Processing	None.

REPRINT, SUBSCRIPTION, AND CONTACT INFORMATION

Reprint Policy	Not applicable, as the journal is available free online. Permission is required to reprint articles from *JSWVE* in another publication.
Book Reviews	1–4 per issue; journal has a staff of 10 book reviewers, but welcomes submissions.
Subscriptions	Subscriptions are available free of charge online at http://www.socialworker.com/jswve.
Affiliation	Published by White Hat Communications.
E-Mail Address	smarson@nc.rr.com for submissions.
Website	http://www.socialworker.com/jswve/

JOURNAL OF SPECIALISTS IN GROUPWORK

Current Title	*Journal of Specialists in Groupwork*
Previous Title	
Editorial Focus	The journal publishes articles in the following categories: Research, Practice, Training, Reflection, and Commentary.
Audience	The readers include counselors in all settings, psychologists, therapists, researchers, social workers, and university instructors.
Special Themes	All topics related to group work are welcomed.
Where Indexed/ Abstracted	ASSIA: Applied Social Sciences Index & Abstracts; CINAHL: Cumulative Index to Nursing and Allied Health Literature, CSA Risk Abstracts; CSA Social Services Abstracts; CSA Sociological Abstracts; CSA Worldwide Political Science Abstracts; EBSCO SocINDEX; ERIC Database/ CIJE: Current Index to Journals in Education; Family Index Database; Higher Education Abstracts; NISC Family & Society Studies Worldwide Database; OCLC ArticleFirst; OCLC Electronic Collections Online; Psychological Abstracts/PsycINFO; Social Work Abstracts; Windows Live Academic.
Year Established	Published continuously since 1976
Circulation	Base run for each printing is 2,100
Frequency	*JSGW* in published four times per year.
Months Issued	March, June, September, December.
No. of Articles per Issue	Varies (generally 5–6).

SUBMISSIONS

Postal Mailing Address	Not needed. Manuscripts submitted online.
Method for Submission	Manuscripts should be submitted online at: http://mc.manuscriptcentral.com/usgw
Number of Copies	1 online.
Disk Submission	No disks are requested. Documents should be in Microsoft Word 2003. At present, Manuscript Central does not handle documents in Microsoft Word 2007.
Online or E-mail Submission Allowed or Required	Online only.

FORMAT OF MANUSCRIPT

Cover Sheet	Title and running head only. Manuscripts are blind reviewed.
Abstract	Abstracts should be 100 words or less.
Key Words	3–5 keywords are required.
Length	Generally, manuscripts should be less than 35 double-spaced pages including reference list, tables, and figures. Longer manuscripts are considered if space is available.
Margins	1 inch all sides
Spacing	Double-spaced.

STYLE

Name of Guide	*Publication Manual of the American Psychological Association* (5th ed.)
Subheadings	Authors discretion, adhere to APA style.
References	APA style.
Footnotes	Only essential footnotes should be used, placed at the bottom of the page and numbered consecutively using Arabic numerals.
Tables or Figures	

REVIEW PROCESS

Type of Review	Manuscripts are blind peer reviewed.
Queries	Queries are welcome if the information is not included in author guidelines.
Acknowledgment	Receipt of manuscript is acknowledged electronically.
Review Time	Average time to first decision is 66 days.
Revisions	If revisions are invited, instructions for submission via the journal's website are included in the decision letter.
Acceptance Rate	25%–30% of manuscripts are eventually accepted.

Return of Manuscript	N/A
Lag Time to Print	Currently 3–6 months.

CHARGES TO AUTHOR

Author Alterations	No charge for minor editorial corrections to proofs.
Page Charges	There are no page charges.
Processing	There are no processing charges.

REPRINT, SUBSCRIPTION, AND CONTACT INFORMATION

Reprint Policy	Authors receive complementary copies of the journal in which their article appears. Reprints can be purchased as well. Reprint information is available at http://www.informaworld.com/smpp/journals_reprints~db=all.
Book Reviews	No book reviews are published in this journal.
Subscriptions	Subscriptions are a benefit of membership in the Association for Specialists in Group Work. Individual print subscriptions are $94.00 per year. Subscription information is available at http://www.informaworld.com/smpp/title~content=t713658627~tab=subscribe~db=all.
Affiliation	Association for Specialists in Group Work
E-Mail Address	The editor can be contacted at sherib@u.arizona.edu.
Website	http://www.tandf.co.uk/journals/titles/01933922.asp

JOURNAL OF SPIRITUALITY IN MENTAL HEALTH

Current Title	*Journal of Spirituality in Mental Health*
Previous Title	*American Journal of Pastoral Counseling.*
Editorial Focus	Deepen understandings of explicit and implicit spiritualities that inform and guide psychotherapeutic activity. Provide a forum for the articulation of primary spiritual assumptions embedded in a wide range of counseling/psychotherapeutic activities.
Audience	Broadly based.
Special Themes	Spirituality and psychotherapy.
Where Indexed/ Abstracted	Academic Search Complete; CINAHL Databases; Current Abstracts; Family Index Database; H.W. Wilson; Index Copernicus; Index to Jewish Periodicals; MasterFile Premier; Pastoral Abstracts; Social Work Abstracts; SocIndex; Swets Information Services; TOCPremier.
Year Established	1997.
Circulation	400–500.
Frequency	Quarterly.
Months Issued	Not specified.
No. of Articles per Issue	5.

SUBMISSIONS

Postal Mailing Address	Dr. William Schmidt, Loyola University Chicago, 820 N. Michigan Avenue, Chicago, IL 60611.
Method for Submission	E-mail.
Number of Copies	1.
Disk Submission	Not specified.
Online or E-mail Submission Allowed or Required	E-mail required.

FORMAT OF MANUSCRIPT

Cover Sheet	Yes.
Abstract	Yes.
Key Words	Yes.
Length	Any.
Margins	1 inch on all sides.
Spacing	Double-spaced.

STYLE

Name of Guide	*Publication Manual of the American Psychological Association* (APA).
Subheadings	See style guide.
References	See style guide.
Footnotes	See style guide.
Tables or Figures	See style guide. Tables and figures (illustrations) should not be embedded in the text, but should be included as separate sheets or files. A short descriptive title should appear above each table with a clear legend and any footnotes suitably identified below. All units must be included. Figures should be completely labeled, taking into account necessary size reduction. Captions should be typed, double-spaced, on a separate sheet.

REVIEW PROCESS

Type of Review	Double-blind.
Queries	Yes.
Acknowledgment	Yes.
Review Time	Approximately 6–8 weeks.
Revisions	Yes, if required in select cases.
Acceptance Rate	Approximately 40%.
Return of Manuscript	No.
Lag Time to Print	Approximately 6–12 months.

REPRINT, SUBSCRIPTION, AND CONTACT INFORMATION

Reprint Policy	Reprints of individual articles are available for order at the time authors review page proofs. A discount on reprints is available to authors who order before print publication. Each corresponding author will receive 3 complete issues in which the article publishes and a complimentary PDF. The file is for personal use only and may not be copied and disseminated in any form without prior written permission from Taylor and Francis Group, LCC.
Book Reviews	says see attachment but not in attachment – e-mailed editor
Subscriptions	http://www.informaworld.com/smpp/title~db=all~content=t792306967~tab=subscribe.
Affiliation	Taylor and Francis Group.
E-Mail Address	Not specified.
Website	http://www.informaworld.com/smpp/title~content=t792306967

JOURNAL OF STUDIES ON ALCOHOL AND DRUGS

Current Title	*Journal of Studies on Alcohol and Drugs*
Previous Title	*Journal of Studies on Alcohol* and *Quarterly Journal of Studies on Alcohol*
Editorial Focus	*JSAD* publishes peer-reviewed studies on a wide range of topics related to the consumption of alcoholic beverages as well as the use of, abuse of, and dependence on illegal drugs (e.g., marijuana, heroin) and legal drugs other than alcohol (e.g., tobacco, prescription medication).
Audience	Not specified.
Special Themes	The range of materials includes biological, medical, epidemiological, social, psychological, and other aspects of alcohol and other drug use, abuse, and dependence
Where Indexed/ Abstracted	Not specified.
Year Established	1940
Circulation	Not specified.
Frequency	6 per year.
Months Issued	January, March, May, July, September, November.
No. of Articles per Issue	Not specified.

SUBMISSIONS

Postal Mailing Address	The Editor, c/o Patricia Castellano, Editorial Secretary, *Journal of Studies on Alcohol and Drugs*, Center of Alcohol Studies, Rutgers, The State University of New Jersey, 607 Allison Road, Piscataway, NJ 08854-8001, USA.
Method for Submission	http://www.jsad.com/jsad/login/&src=submission; online preferred.
Number of Copies	Alternatively, 2 clean copies, double-spaced in 12-point type on 8.5" × 11 inch paper, accompanied by a diskette or a CD.
Disk Submission	See above.
Online or E-mail Submission Allowed or Required	Online.

FORMAT OF MANUSCRIPT

Cover Sheet	Each manuscript should be accompanied by a cover letter indicating whether the paper is submitted as an original study, a brief report, a rapid communication, or a review or theoretical article. The cover letter should also contain (1) the name, address, e-mail address, and telephone/fax numbers of the corresponding author; (2) a statement that the paper contains original material, not submitted, in press, or published elsewhere in any form; (3) a note describing whether the manuscript is one of several papers derived from the same dataset or whether similar or overlapping data are reported in any other manuscripts and, if so, how the current submission differs from the others (this should also be stated clearly in the introduction to the manuscript); (4) a statement that each author has contributed significantly to the work and agrees to the submission; (5) a note describing any conflict of interest regarding the paper or a statement that no conflict exists; (6) an explanation of the contribution of the present manuscript to the literature; (7) if desired, suggestions for possible reviewers; and finally (8) the signatures of all authors. If revisions are requested, all authors must also sign the cover letter accompanying the revised paper.
Abstract	Abstracts should be 250 or fewer words and must include the following information under these four headings: (1) Objective: the background and purpose of the study; (2) Method: the study design, setting, participants (including manner of sample selection, number and gender of participants), and interventions; (3) Results: details of major findings; and (4) Conclusions: main inferences drawn from results and potential application of findings.
Key Words	Not specified.
Length	Original Studies: The recommended length for these reports is 20 double-spaced typewritten pages, excluding the title page, abstract, and references but including tables and figures. Brief Reports: These papers are limited in length to 8 double-spaced typewritten pages, excluding the references but including tables and figures. Reviews and Theoretical Articles: A limited number of comprehensive reviews and theoretical treatises will be published as space permits. Although there are occasional exceptions, these reports should be limited to 20 double-spaced typewritten pages, excluding the title page, abstract, and references but including tables and figures.

Margins	1 inch.
Spacing	Double-spaced.

STYLE

Name of Guide	See website: http://www.jsad.com/jsad/static/contributors.html.
Subheadings	See website: http://www.jsad.com/jsad/static/contributors.html.
References	Citations in text should include the author's name and year of publication. With more than two authors, the text citation should contain the name of the first author followed by "et al." and the date of the publication. If reference is made to more than 1 publication by the same authors in the same year, suffixes a, b, c, etc. should be added to the year, both in the text citation and in the reference list (e.g., use citations "Smith et al. 1991a" and "Smith et al. 1991b" even if the subsequent authors in the reference are different). The "a," "b," and "c" are determined by the order of the references in the reference list.
Footnotes	Not specified.
Tables or Figures	Each table should be typewritten on a separate page and should be numbered consecutively with Arabic numerals. Each table must have a concise descriptive heading and should be constructed as simply as possible: Preferably use only tabs and text typed directly in the word processing document or Word's table function. Tables must be intelligible without reference to the text. Footnotes to tables should be referred to by italicized lowercase superscript letters (a, b, c etc.) and should appear beneath the table involved, not on a separate page of the manuscript. Do not use any functions or tools that format footnotes, but instead set footnotes in plain type below the table.
	Figure Captions: These should be numbered consecutively in Arabic numerals and should appear on a separate page of the manuscript. Captions should explain the figures in sufficient detail so that repeated reference to the text is unnecessary. Abbreviations in the captions should conform to those in the text.
	Figures: One set of graphs and diagrams must be submitted as original prints, with the figure number and the author's name indicated on the front of each print (at the top of the print, above the material to be reproduced). Copies of all figures must be embedded within the word processing file at the end of the manuscript. Figures will be photo-reproduced and thus must be supplied fully camera ready. Figures preferably should be black and white only, with black and white hatching or design used in the place of gray or color. (If a figure requires grayscale and cannot be altered to contain black and white only, create a file of the figure in .tif format with 300 dpi. If a file requires color, create a high-resolution CMYK .eps file with 300 dpi. Authors will be charged a fee for the use of color.) Symbols, numbers, and letters should be supplied in 11–14-point boldface (2.5–3.5 mm); all borders, rules, and lines should also be printed in boldface. The title of each figure should appear in the caption rather than on the figure itself. Line drawings and graphs should be professionally drawn and lettered; freehand or typewritten lettering is unacceptable.

REVIEW PROCESS

Type of Review	Peer reviewed.
Queries	Not specified.
Acknowledgment	Yes.
Review Time	It is important to us that authors can feel confident that their work will be reviewed quickly. Therefore, each paper receives a quick reading at the time of submission, and approximately 10% of authors hear from us within a week or so of submission. These answers usually indicate that the paper is not quite appropriate for us and that the author(s) might turn elsewhere. In this instance, very little time has passed, and the author has the chance to quickly submit the manuscript elsewhere. The remaining 90% or so of the papers are assigned to an associate editor to be sent out for review, a process that takes approximately 1 week. Reviewers are asked to return the manuscripts within a month to 6 weeks if at all possible, with the final result that most authors hear from the journal in approximately 6–8 weeks, others even sooner.
Revisions	When an article is considered as a possible candidate for publication but the reviewers request changes, the author(s) is urged to return the revised manuscript to the associate editor within a maximum of 3 months. The purpose of this turnaround is so the same manuscript can be sent back to the same reviewers, if necessary. Asking reviewers to look at a paper they saw more than 3 months ago places an extra burden on them, as they are likely to have forgotten their reactions and might have to start over from scratch. However, if an author feels there are reasons why 3 months is not appropriate, an extension beyond that date can be granted on the judgment of

the associate editor. Even in the worst-case scenario, the paper is not simply rejected because it comes back after 3 months. Rather, new reviewers are selected.

Acceptance Rate	Not specified.
Return of Manuscript	Not specified.
Lag Time to Print	Not specified.

CHARGES TO AUTHOR

Author Alterations	Galley proofs will be sent to the corresponding author and should be returned within 72 hours. A reprint order form and price list will accompany galley proofs.
Page Charges	*JSAD* does not assess page charges on its contributors except for the use of color in figures.
Processing	Not specified.

REPRINT, SUBSCRIPTION, AND CONTACT INFORMATION

Reprint Policy	Not specified.
Book Reviews	Not specified.
Subscriptions	See website: http://www.jsad.com/jsad/static/contributors.html.
Affiliation	Center of Alcohol Studies, Rutgers University, Piscataway, NJ.
E-Mail Address	Not specified.
Website	http://www.jsad.com/

JOURNAL OF TEACHING IN SOCIAL WORK

Current Title	*Journal of Teaching in Social Work*
Previous Title	N/A.
Editorial Focus	Articles that focus on the teacher, the teaching process, the learner, and the learning process, as well as new contexts of teaching are considered for publication in the journal.
Audience	Not specified.
Special Themes	Not specified.
Where Indexed/ Abstracted	Applied social Sciences Index & Abstracts; Behavioral Medicine Abstracts; Caredata CD: the social and community care database; CNPIEC Reference Guide: Chinese National Directory of Foreign Periodicals; Contents pages in Education; Family Studies Database (online and CD-ROM); Human Resources Abstracts (HRA); IBZ International Bibliography of Periodical Literature; Index to Periodical Articles Related to Law; International Bulletin of Bibliography on Education; INTERNET ACCESS (and additional networks) bulletin Board for Libraries ("BUBL"), coverage of information resources on INTERNET JANET and other networks; Referativnyi Zhurnal (Abstracts Journal of the Institute of Scientific Information of the Republic of Russia); Social Planning/Policy & Development Abstracts (SOPODA); Social Work Abstracts; Sociological Abstracts (SOPODA); Studies on Women Abstracts.
Year Established	1987.
Circulation	200+.
Frequency	4 times per year.
Months Issued	By Volume/Issue.
No. of Articles per Issue	Approximately 6.

SUBMISSIONS

Postal Mailing Address	Article: Editor, Florence Vigilante, DSW, Hunter College School of Social Work, 129 East 79th Street, New York, NY 10075 Book Review: Book Review Editor, Dr. Charles Guzzetta, Professor, Hunter College School of Social Work, 129 East 79th Street, New York, NY 10075.
Method for Submission	Not specified.
Number of Copies	Triplicate.
Disk Submission	Authors of accepted manuscripts are asked to submit a disk, preferably in Microsoft Word.
Online or E-mail Submission Allowed or Required	Not specified.

FORMAT OF MANUSCRIPT

Cover Sheet	States not being considered elsewhere; Submit a cover page with the manuscript, indicating only the article title (this is used for anonymous refereeing). Include a regular title page as a separate document.
Abstract	100 words.
Key Words	5–6 key words that identify article content.
Length	5–20 pages.
Margins	1 inch.
Spacing	Double-spaced.

STYLE

Name of Guide	*Publication Manual of the American Psychological Association* (APA, current edition).
Subheadings	Use as needed to guide reader through the article. No more than 4 levels.
References	Author-date citation style; see APA style guide.
Footnotes	Not footnotes preferred; incorporate into text.
Tables or Figures	Tables and figures (illustrations) should not be embedded in the text, but should be included as separate sheets or files. A short descriptive title should appear above each table with a clear legend and any footnotes suitably identified below. All units must be included. Figures should be completely labeled, taking into account necessary size reduction. Captions should be typed, double-spaced, on a separate sheet.

REVIEW PROCESS

Type of Review	"Double-blind" anonymous peer review. 3 reviewers plus editor-in-chief read the manuscript in an anonymous review.

Queries	Authors are encouraged to read the journal to determine whether their subject matter would be appropriate.
Acknowledgment	Enclose a regular self-addressed, stamped envelope with submission.
Review Time	Approximately 3–4 months.
Revisions	See journal.
Acceptance Rate	Not specified.
Return of Manuscript	Only if a 9" × 12" self-addressed, stamped envelope is enclosed.
Lag Time to Print	Approximately 6–12 months.

CHARGES TO AUTHOR

Author Alterations	Page proofs are sent to the designated author using Taylor & Francis' Central Article Tracking System (CATS). They must be carefully checked and returned within 48 hours of receipt.
Page Charges	Not specified.
Processing	Not specified.

REPRINT, SUBSCRIPTION, AND CONTACT INFORMATION

Reprint Policy	Reprints of individual articles are available for order at the time authors review page proofs. A discount on reprints is available to authors who order before print publication. Each corresponding author will receive 3 complete issues in which the article publishes and a complimentary PDF. This file is for personal use only and may not be copied and disseminated in any form without prior written permission from Taylor and Francis Group, LLC.
Book Reviews	Yes.
Subscriptions	The Haworth Press, Inc. 10 Alice Street, Binghamton, NY 13904-1580.
Affiliation	Not specified.
E-Mail Address	Not specified.
Website	http://www.informaworld.com/smpp/title~db=all~content=g910217244~tab=summary

JOURNAL OF TECHNOLOGY IN HUMAN SERVICES

Current Title	*Journal of Technology in Human Services*
Previous Title	*Computers in Human Services.*
Editorial Focus	Technology and human services.
Audience	Human service professionals.
Special Themes	Technology.
Where Indexed/ Abstracted	Many places, contact publisher.
Year Established	1985.
Circulation	Contact publisher.
Frequency	Quarterly.
Months Issued	January–March, etc.
No. of Articles per Issue	Depends on article length.

SUBMISSIONS

Postal Mailing Address	N/A: only online submissions via e-mail.
Method for Submission	E-mail.
Number of Copies	N/A.
Disk Submission	N/A.
Online or E-mail Submission Allowed or Required	Only online submissions via e-mail.

FORMAT OF MANUSCRIPT

Cover Sheet	Yes.
Abstract	Yes.
Key Words	Yes, 3–5 key words.
Length	12–18 pages.
Margins	1 inch.
Spacing	Double-spaced.

STYLE

Name of Guide	*Publication Manual of the American Psychological Association* (APA, latest edition).
Subheadings	See style guide.
References	See style guide.
Footnotes	See style guide.
Tables or Figures	See style guide.

REVIEW PROCESS

Type of Review	Anonymous peer review.
Queries	Yes.
Acknowledgment	E-mail.
Review Time	Approximately 6 weeks.
Revisions	Required if suggested.
Acceptance Rate	Approximately 25%.
Return of Manuscript	N/A.
Lag Time to Print	Approximately 6 months.

CHARGES TO AUTHOR

Author Alterations	N/A.
Page Charges	N/A.
Processing	N/A.

REPRINT, SUBSCRIPTION, AND CONTACT INFORMATION

Reprint Policy	3 issues and a PDF.
Book Reviews	Yes.

Subscriptions	Check publisher, Taylor and Francis.
Affiliation	HUSITA.
E-Mail Address	Schoech@uta.edu
Website	http://www2.uta.edu/cussn/jths/

JOURNAL OF TRAUMATIC STRESS

Current Title	*Journal of Traumatic Stress*
Previous Title	N/A.
Editorial Focus	Publication of peer-review original articles on biopsychosocial aspects of psychological trauma. Papers focus on theoretical formulations, research, treatment, prevention education/training, and legal and policy concerns. The journal publishes original articles; brief reports; review papers; commentaries; case reports; and, from time to time, special issues devoted to a single topic. CE credits are available for reading selected articles.
Audience	Professionals who study and treat people exposure to highly stressful and traumatic events.
Special Themes	Traumatic events such as war, disaster, sexual or physical violence or abuse, terrorism, and serious accidents.
Where Indexed/ Abstracted	Cambridge Scientific Abstracts (CSA/CIG); CSA Biological Sciences Database (CSA/CIG); CSA Environmental Sciences & Pollution Management Database (CSA/CIG); Current Abstracts (EBSCO); Current Contents/Social & Behavioral Sciences (Thomson ISI); Index Medicus/ MEDLINE/PubMed (NLM); Journal Citation Reports/Social Science Edition (Thomson ISI); PASCAL Database (INIST/CNRS); PILOTS (CSA/National Center for PTSD); Psychological Abstracts/PsycINFO (APA); Social Sciences Citation Index (Thomson ISI); Social SciSearch (Thomson ISI); Social Services Abstracts (CSA/CIG); SocINDEX (EBSCO); Sociological Abstracts (CSA/CIG); Web of Science (Thomson ISI).
Year Established	1988
Circulation	NA.
Frequency	Bimonthly.
Months Issued	February, April, June, August, October, December.
No. of Articles per Issue	12–15.

SUBMISSIONS

Postal Mailing Address	*Journal of Traumatic Stress*, Paula P. Schnurr, PhD, Editor-in-Chief, National Center for PTSD (116D), VA Medical Center, White River Junction, VT 05009, USA. The preferred address for submitting manuscripts is http://mc.manuscriptcentral.com/jots.
Method for Submission	Electronic via website.
Number of Copies	N/A.
Disk Submission	N/A.
Online or E-mail Submission Allowed or Required	Yes.

FORMAT OF MANUSCRIPT

Cover Sheet	The title page should include the title of the article, author's name (no degrees), author's affiliation, acknowledgments, and suggested running head. The affiliation should comprise the department, institution (usually university or company), city and state (or nation) and should be typed as a footnote to the author's name. The suggested running head should be fewer than 80 characters (including spaces) and should comprise the article title or an abbreviated version thereof. Also include the word count, the complete mailing address, telephone and fax numbers, and e-mail address for the corresponding author during the review process, and, if different, a name and address to appear in the article footnotes for correspondence after publication.
Abstract	120-word abstract in APA style.
Key Words	4–6 to facilitate indexing.
Length	Limits are 6,000 words for Regular Articles, 7,500 words for Special Articles, 2,500 words for Brief Reports, and 1,000 words for Commentaries. Word count should include text, references, tables, and figures, with each page of figures and double-spaced tables counted as 200 words.
Margins	1 inch.
Spacing	Double-spaced.

STYLE

Name of Guide	*Publication Manual of the American Psychological Association* (APA).
Subheadings	See style guide.
References	See style guide.

Footnotes Footnotes are discouraged; when used, they should be formatted according to APA style.

Tables or Figures See style guide.

REVIEW PROCESS

Type of Review The journal uses a policy of unmasked review. Author identities are known to reviewers; reviewer identities are not known to authors or other reviewers. During the submission process, authors may request that specific individuals not be selected as reviewers; the names of preferred reviewers also may be provided. Authors may request blind review by contacting jots@dartmouth.edu prior to submission.

Queries Authors are encouraged to consult the website before submitting a query.

Acknowledgment An e-mail message with an assigned manuscript number for tracking is sent to the author upon receipt of his or her manuscript.

Review Time 2–3 months

Revisions Authors should submit a revised manuscript and a detailed letter describing the revision through the website.

Acceptance Rate Approximately 20%.

Return of Manuscript N/A.

Lag Time to Print Approximately 4–6 months from when a final copy is received.

REPRINT, SUBSCRIPTION, AND CONTACT INFORMATION

Reprint Policy Reprints are available to authors, and order forms with the current price schedule are sent with proofs. Authors may also access PDFs of their articles through Author Services on the journal's website.

Book Reviews None.

Subscriptions Wiley Subscription Services, Inc., a Wiley Company, 111 River St., Hoboken, NJ 07030-5744. Journal Customer Services: For ordering information, claims and any inquiry concerning your journal subscription please go to interscience.wiley.com/support or contact your nearest office: Americas: E-mail: cs-journals@wiley.com; Tel: +1 781 388 8598 or 1 800 835 6770 (Toll free in the USA & Canada). Europe, Middle East, and Africa: E-mail: cs-journals@wiley.com; Tel: +44 (0) 1865 778315 Asia Pacific: E-mail: cs-journals@wiley.com; Tel: +65 6511 8000.

Affiliation *Journal of Traumatic Stress* is published for the International Society for Traumatic Stress Studies, http://www.istss.org.

E-Mail Address jots@dartmouth.edu

Website http://mc.manuscriptcentral.com/jots

JOURNAL OF VISUAL IMPAIRMENT AND BLINDNESS

Current Title	*Journal of Visual Impairment and Blindness*
Previous Title	N/A.
Editorial Focus	*Journal of Visual Impairment & Blindness (JVIB)* is the international, interdisciplinary journal of record on blindness and visual impairment that publishes scholarship and information and serves as a forum for the exchange of ideas, airing of controversies, and discussion of issues
Audience	Practitioners (primarily nonmedical) in the field of blindness and visual impairment (e.g., orientation and mobility instructors, rehabilitation counselors, etc.), teachers, university professor, social scientists, administrators (e.g., principals of public schools, principals of residential schools for the blind, directors of rehabilitation agencies, etc.), consumers, and parents.
Special Themes	This is only a sampling: The Americans with Disabilities Act, specialized services, employment, attitudes toward blindness, orientation and mobility, public policy, literacy, Braille literacy, aging, low vision, early intervention, transition, family issues, deaf-blindness, disability studies.
Where Indexed/ Abstracted	Academic Search; Cumulative Index to Nursing & Allied Health Literature; Current Contents: Social and Behavioral Sciences; Current Index to Journals in Education; Education Index; EMBASE; EP Collection; Exceptional Child Education Resources; Homework Helper; Linguistics and Language Behavior Abstracts; Masterfile, OCLC; Psychological Abstracts/PsycINFO; PsycLIT; Social Sciences Citation Index; Social Work Abstracts; Sociological Abstracts; Telebase; UnCover.
Year Established	1907.
Circulation	3,000.
Frequency	Monthly.
Months Issued	Monthly.
No. of Articles per Issue	Approximately 6.

SUBMISSIONS

Postal Mailing Address	Duane R. Geruschat, PhD, Editor-in-Chief, JVIB, Lions Vision Center, 550 North Broadway, 6th Floor, Baltimore, MD 21205; e-mail: jvibeditor@afb.net.
Method for Submission	Submissions sent through traditional mail should include 1 paper copy and 1 CD copy of the manuscript. *JVIB* uses Microsoft Word as its standard word processor for text, but manuscripts may also be submitted in Rich Text Format or ASCII.
Number of Copies	2. See above.
Disk Submission	Yes. See above.
Online or E-mail Submission Allowed or Required	E-mail preferred; Online submissions should be in the form of e-mail attachments.

FORMAT OF MANUSCRIPT

Cover Sheet	Authors' names, academic degrees, professional affiliations with addresses, title of manuscript; also, phone number, fax number, and e-mail address for contact author (usually lead author).
Abstract	Abstracts are required for full articles only. Abstracts should be limited to 50 words.
Key Words	None.
Length	The maximum length of full manuscripts is 5,000 words. Maximum lengths of Research Reports and Practice Reports are 2,500 words. The word count includes all tables and references, but does not include the cover page. Note that one double-spaced word-processed page equals approximately 250 words.
Margins	1 inch.
Spacing	Double-spaced.

STYLE

Name of Guide	*Publication Manual of the American Psychological Association* (APA, 5th edition).
Subheadings	As needed; up to 3 levels.
References	See style guide.
Footnotes	None, information should be incorporated into text.
Tables or Figures	Figures and tables should **not** be embedded in text files. Each one should be saved as a separate file. Figures should be created in black and white or grayscale only and in a mainstream graphics software package, such as Word, Adobe Illustrator, Free Hand, Adobe Photoshop, or Excel.

Reserve tables and figures to present crucial data directly related to the text of the manuscript and to simplify a discussion that would otherwise be dense with numbers. These elements should in all cases supplement, not duplicate, the text.

REVIEW PROCESS

Type of Review	"Blind," anonymous outside peer review (2–4 reviewers) plus 3 "blind" in-house reviewers (managing editor and 2 consulting editors, research), and the editor-in-chief (who knows identity of authors).
Queries	E-mail encouraged for initial contact; letters and phone calls accepted.
Acknowledgment	Letter with copyright transfer agreement enclosed.
Review Time	Approximately 3 months.
Revisions	Submit original plus 5 copies with a cover letter detailing the changes made and explaining why any changes were not made.
Acceptance Rate	Approximately 15%.
Return of Manuscript	Only if manuscript is rejected. If peer review determination is to revise the manuscript, even if authors never comply, manuscript is not returned.
Lag Time to Print	Approximately 6–12 months.

REPRINT, SUBSCRIPTION, AND CONTACT INFORMATION

Reprint Policy	Reprints of single copies of *JVIB* articles can be ordered for $15.00 from the Information Center, American Foundation for the Blind; phone: 800-AFB-LINE (232-5463) or 212-502-7661; e-mail: <afbinfo@afb.net>. Reprints in multiples of 100 can be ordered from The Sheridan Press; phone: 800-352-2210 or 717-632-3535; fax: 717-633-8929; web site: <www.sheridanreprints.com>.
Book Reviews	An evaluation of a recent book that assesses its value for *JVIB* readers. Unsolicited manuscripts are not considered. Scholarly books should be sent to the Editor-in-Chief for consideration; general interest books about blindness or disability should be sent to AFB Press.
Subscriptions	See website: http://www.afb.org/jvibspecial.asp.
Affiliation	American Foundation for the Blind
E-Mail Address	jvib@afb.net
Website	http://www.afb.org/afbpress/pubjvib.asp?DocID=jvib0306toc

JOURNAL OF WOMEN AND AGING

Current Title	*Journal of Women and Aging*
Previous Title	N/A.
Editorial Focus	Original research preferred.
Audience	Faculty, students, and professionals in the helping professions: social work, medicine, nursing, psychology, gerontology, physical therapy, education, counseling, and other related professions.
Special Themes	Thematic topics are solicited. There is generally one special thematic issue every 2 years. Thematic issues are frequently double issues, containing 10 to 12 articles. Book reviews may or may not appear in special thematic issues.
Where Indexed/ Abstracted	Abstracts in Social Gerontology; Academic Search Series (EBSCOhost); AgeLine; CINAHL Databases; Gender Watch; MEDLINE/PubMed; PsycINFO; Social Science Citation Index (Impact Factor: .333); Sociological Abstracts; Studies on Women & Gender Abstracts.
Year Established	1989.
Circulation	257 total subscribers.
Frequency	Quarterly.
Months Issued	February, May, August, November.
No. of Articles per Issue	5–6.

SUBMISSIONS

Postal Mailing Address	Dr. Dianne Garner, Editor, *Journal of Women & Aging*, 1348 Cottonwood Trail, Sarasota, FL 34232.
Method for Submission	Surface mail, required for initial submission: disk or CD, required for final submission, e-mail, required for final submission, electronic form via Web.
Number of Copies	Electronic submission preferred.
Disk Submission	Yes.
Online or E-mail Submission Allowed or Required	Electronic submission preferred.

FORMAT OF MANUSCRIPT

Cover Sheet	Yes.
Abstract	Yes.
Key Words	Yes.
Length	20-page limit unless content justifies additional pages. No more than 25 pages when exception to 20-page limit is granted.
Margins	Standard margins.
Spacing	Double-spaced.

STYLE

Name of Guide	*Publication Manual of the American Psychological Association* (APA).
Subheadings	Yes.
References	Yes.
Footnotes	As needed.
Tables or Figures	Preferred.

REVIEW PROCESS

Type of Review	Blind peer review.
Queries	Yes.
Acknowledgment	As appropriate.
Review Time	Approximately 3 months.
Revisions	Usually required. Very rarely is a manuscript accepted "as is."
Acceptance Rate	Approximately 40%. Most articles are accepted pending revisions.
Return of Manuscript	Only if SASE provided.
Lag Time to Print	Approximately 3 months after final acceptance.

CHARGES TO AUTHOR

Author Alterations
May be required depending on the outcome of blind reviews.

Page Charges
No charges for pages printed in black and white. Color art can be purchased for online-only reproduction or for print and online reproduction. Color reprints can only be ordered if print and online reproduction costs are paid. Rates for color art reproduction are: Online-Only Reproduction: $225 for the first page of color; $100 per page for the next 3 pages of color. A maximum charge of $525 applies. Print and Online Reproduction: $900 for the first page of color; $450 per page for the next 3 pages of color. A custom quote will be provided for articles with more than 4 pages of color.

Processing
Not specified.

REPRINT, SUBSCRIPTION, AND CONTACT INFORMATION

Reprint Policy
Reprints of individual articles are available for order at the time authors review page proofs. A discount on reprints is available to authors who order before print publication. Each corresponding author will receive 3 complete issues in which the article publishes and a complimentary PDF. This file is for personal use only and may not be copied and disseminated in any form without prior written permission from Taylor and Francis Group, LLC.

Book Reviews
Generally 2 per issue.

Subscriptions
Online-Only Personal Sub: $104; Online-Only Institutional Sub: $497; Print/Online Personal Sub: $109; Print/Online Institutional Sub: $523. The option to pay in other currencies is available.

Affiliation
None.

E-Mail Address
diannegarner@verizon.net

Website
www.taylorandfrancis.com

JOURNAL OF WOMEN, POLITICS AND POLICY

Current Title	*Journal of Women, Politics and Policy*
Previous Title	N/A.
Editorial Focus	*Journal of Women, Politics & Policy* explores women's roles in the political process—as voters, activists, leaders in interest groups and political parties; and office holders in the legislative, executive, and judicial branches of government, including the increasingly relevant international bodies such as the European Union and the World Trade Organization. It examines the impact of public policies on women's lives, examining areas such as tax and budget issues; poverty reduction and income security; education and employment; care giving; and health and human rights, including violence, safety, and reproductive rights. Throughout, the journal places a special emphasis on the intersection of gender, race/ethnicity, class, and other dimensions of women's experiences.
Audience	Not specified.
Special Themes	Not specified.
Where Indexed/ Abstracted	Academic Search Premier (EBSCO); Academic Source Complete (EBSCO); America: History & Life; BEFO; Cambridge Scientific Abstracts; Contemporary Women's Issues; Current Abstracts (EBSCO); Current Legal Sociology; EBSCOhost Electronic Journals Services (EJS); Electronic Collections Online (OCLC); Elsevier Eflow-I; Elsevier SCOPUS; Family & Society Studies Worldwide (NISC); Family Index Database; Family Violence & Sexual Assault Bulletin; Feminist Majority Foundation; Feminist Periodicals; GenderWatch (CSA); Historical Abstracts; International Bibliography of Periodical Literature on the Humanities and Social Sciences (IBZ); Index to Periodical Articles Related to Law; International Political Science Abstracts; ISI Current Contents: Social & Behavioral Sciences; ISI Social Science Citation Index; JournalSeek; Links@Ovid; MasterFILE Elite (EBSCO); NewJour; OCLC ArticleFirst; Ovid Linksolver; Periodicals Index Online (CSA); Research Library; Social Sciences Index; Social Work Abstracts (NASW); Social Work Access Network (SWAN); Sociological Abstracts (CSA); TOC Premier (EBSCO); Women in Politics; Women's Studies International (NISC); Worldwide Political Science Abstracts (CSA).
Year Established	
Circulation	
Frequency	4 times per year.
Months Issued	
No. of Articles per Issue	Approximately 6 per issue.

SUBMISSIONS

Postal Mailing Address	Heidi Hartmann, PhD Co-Editor, Journal of Women, Politics & Policy Institute for Women's Policy Research 1707 L Street NW, Suite 750 Washington D.C. 20036
Method for Submission	Authors are strongly encouraged to submit manuscripts electronically. If submitting a disk, it should be prepared using MS Word or WordPerfect and should be clearly labeled with the authors' names, file name, and software program. Please e-mail electronic files to Co-editor Heidi Hartmann, PhD at jwpp@gwu.edu. Each manuscript must be accompanied by a statement that it has not been published elsewhere and that it has not been submitted simultaneously for publication elsewhere. Authors are responsible for obtaining permission to reproduce copyrighted material from other sources and are required to sign an agreement for the transfer of copyright to the publisher. All accepted manuscripts, artwork, and photographs become the property of the publisher.
Number of Copies	Authors are strongly encouraged to submit manuscripts electronically.
Disk Submission	If submitting a disk, it should be prepared using MS Word or WordPerfect and should be clearly labeled with the authors' names, file name, and software program
Online or E-mail Submission Allowed or Required	Authors are strongly encouraged to submit manuscripts electronically.

FORMAT OF MANUSCRIPT

Cover Sheet	Each manuscript must be accompanied by a statement that it has not been published elsewhere and that it has not been submitted simultaneously for publication elsewhere.

Abstract	Authors should also supply a shortened version of the title suitable for the running head, not exceeding 50 character spaces. Each article should be summarized in an abstract of not more than 100 words. Avoid abbreviations, diagrams, and reference to the text in the abstract.
Key Words	Not specified.
Length	Not specified.
Margins	1 inch.
Spacing	Double-spaced.

STYLE

Name of Guide	*American Political Science Association Guide, 2001.*
Subheadings	See style guide.
References	References, citations, and general style of manuscripts should be prepared in accordance with the *Chicago Manual of Style,* 14th Edition and the American Political Science Association's *Style Manual for Political Science* (2001). Cite in the text by author and date (Smith 1983) and include an alphabetical list at the end of the article.
Footnotes	Illustrations submitted (line drawings, halftones, photos, photomicrographs, etc.) should be clean originals or digital files. Digital files are recommended for highest quality reproduction and should follow these guidelines: 300 dpi or higher; sized to fit on journal page; EPS, TIFF, or PSD format only; and submitted as separate files, not embedded in text files.
Tables or Figures	Tables and figures (illustrations) should not be embedded in the text, but should be included as separate sheets or files. A short descriptive title should appear above each table with a clear legend and any footnotes suitably identified below. All units must be included. Figures should be completely labeled, taking into account necessary size reduction. Captions should be typed, double-spaced, on a separate sheet.

REVIEW PROCESS

Type of Review	All papers in this journal have undergone editorial screening and peer reviews.
Queries	jwpp@gwu.edu
Acknowledgment	Not specified.
Review Time	Not specified.
Revisions	Not specified.
Acceptance Rate	Not specified.
Return of Manuscript	Not specified.
Lag Time to Print	Not specified.

CHARGES TO AUTHOR

Author Alterations	Page proofs are sent to the designated author using Taylor & Francis' Central Article Tracking System (CATS). They must be carefully checked and returned within 48 hours of receipt.
Page Charges	See website for any page charges.
Processing	See website for any page charges. Color illustrations will be considered for publication; however, the author will be required to bear the full cost involved in color art reproduction. Color art can be purchased for online-only reproduction or for print and online reproduction. Color reprints can only be ordered if print and online reproduction costs are paid. Rates for color art reproduction are: Online-Only Reproduction: $225 for the first page of color; $100 for the next 3 pages of color. A maximum charge of $525 applies. Print and Online Reproduction: $900 for the first page of color; $450 for the next 3 pages of color. A custom quote will be provided for articles with more than 4 pages of color. Art not supplied at a minimum of 300 dpi will not be considered for print.

REPRINT, SUBSCRIPTION, AND CONTACT INFORMATION

Reprint Policy	Reprints of individual articles are available for order at the time authors review page proofs. A discount on reprints is available to authors who order before print publication. Each corresponding author will receive 3 complete issues in which the article publishes and a complimentary PDF. This file is for personal use only and may not be copied and disseminated in any form without prior written permission from Taylor and Francis Group, LLC.
Book Reviews	Not specified.
Subscriptions	http://www.informaworld.com/smpp/title~db=all~content=t792306983~tab=subscribe.
Affiliation	See website.
E-Mail Address	jwpp@gwu.edu
Website	http://www.informaworld.com/smpp/title~content=t792306983~db=all

JOURNAL OF WORKPLACE BEHAVIORAL HEALTH

Current Title	*Journal of Workplace Behavioral Health*
Previous Title	*Employee Assistance Quarterly*
Editorial Focus	Publishes articles on: best practices in EAPs, workplace violence, behavior risk management, quality of work life, labor issues, workplace conflict resolution, behavioral health care, older workers, workplace stress and trauma, gender issues, performance-based contracting, work/family, international issues, and much more!
Audience	Employee assistant professionals, workplace human service administrators, counselors, and consultants.
Special Themes	Emerging issues in the employee assistance field, cost management, industrial social work, new modes of outpatient, and employee assistance programs for the postindustrial era.
Where Indexed/ Abstracted	Computer and Information Systems Abstracts Journal; Current Abstracts; EBSCOhost; Environmental Engineering Abstracts Online; Family & Society Studies Worldwide; International Abstracts of Human Resources; PsycINFO; Social Services Abstracts; Social Work Abstracts; Sociological Abstracts.
Year Established	1985.
Circulation	Not specified.
Frequency	Quarterly.
Months Issued	Not specified.
No. of Articles per Issue	6–10 per issue.

SUBMISSIONS

Postal Mailing Address	R. Paul Maiden, PhD, Editor-in-Chief, University of Southern California, 669 W. 34th Street, MRF 210, Los Angeles, CA 90089-0411.
Method for Submission	Manuscripts may be mailed or e-mailed to the editor.
Number of Copies	3.
Disk Submission	Not specified.
Online or E-mail Submission Allowed or Required	Manuscripts may be e-mailed to the editor at: rmaiden@usc.edu. No online submissions.

FORMAT OF MANUSCRIPT

Cover Sheet	Separate sheet that does not go out for review. Full authorship should be listed, as well as an introductory note with authors' academic degrees, professional titles, affiliations, mailing and e-mail addresses, and any desired acknowledgement of research support or other credit.
Abstract	Each article should be summarized in an abstract of not more than 100 words.
Key Words	Provide 3–10 words for indexing purposes.
Length	Up to 25 pages including references and abstract. Brief reports (10 pages or less) are also encouraged.
Margins	1 inch on all sides.
Spacing	Double-spaced.

STYLE

Name of Guide	*Publication Manual of the American Psychological Association* (APA, 5th edition).
Subheadings	See style guide.
References	See style guide.
Footnotes	See style guide.
Tables or Figures	See style guide.

REVIEW PROCESS

Type of Review	Double-blind anonymous peer review.
Queries	Authors are encouraged to read the journal to determine whether their subject matter would be appropriate.
Acknowledgment	Enclose a regular self-addressed, stamped envelope with submission.
Review Time	Not specified.
Revisions	Not specified.
Acceptance Rate	Not specified.

Return of Manuscript	Only if 9" × 12" self-addressed, stamped envelope is enclosed.
Lag Time to Print	Not specified.

CHARGES TO AUTHOR

Author Alterations	Not specified.
Page Charges	Not specified.
Processing	Not specified.

REPRINT, SUBSCRIPTION, AND CONTACT INFORMATION

Reprint Policy	Reprints of individual articles are available for order at the time authors review page proofs. A discount on reprints is available to authors who order before print publication. Each corresponding author will receive 3 complete issues in which the article publishes and a complimentary PDF.
Book Reviews	Not specified.
Subscriptions	Available online through: http://www.informaworld.com.
Affiliation	Employee Assistance Society of North America.
E-Mail Address	rmaiden@usc.edu
Website	http://www.tandf.co.uk/journals/journal.asp?issn=1555-5240&linktype=1

JOURNAL OF YOUTH AND ADOLESCENCE

Current Title	*Journal of Youth and Adolescence*
Previous Title	N/A.
Editorial Focus	The journal publishes papers based on experimental evidence and data, theoretical papers, and comprehensive review articles. The journal especially welcomes empirically rigorous papers that take policy implications seriously.
Audience	Psychologists, psychiatrists, biologists, criminologists, educators, and professionals in many other allied disciplines.
Special Themes	Not specified.
Where Indexed/ Abstracted	Academic Search Alumni Edition; Academic Search Complete; Academic Search Elite; Academic Search Premier; AgeLine; AGRICOLA; Bibliography of Asian Studies; Cengage; CSA Social Services Abstracts; CSA Sociological Abstracts; Current Abstracts; Current Contents/Social & Behavioral Sciences; Dietrich's Index Philosophicus; Educational Management Abstracts; Educational Research Abstracts Online (ERA); EMCare; ERIC System Database; ERIH; Expanded Academic; FRANCIS; Google Scholar; Higher Education Abstracts; IBIDS; International Bibliography of Book Reviews (IBR); Journal Citation Reports/Science Edition; LGBT Life; Multicultural Education Abstracts; N.C.J.R.S. Catalogue; OCLC ArticleFirst Database; OCLC FirstSearch Electronic Collections Online; OmniFile Mega; OmniFile Select; OmniFile V Full Text; PASCAL; PsycINFO; RILM Abstracts of Music Literature; SCOPUS; Social Science Citation Index; Social Science Index; Sociology of Education Abstracts; Special Education Needs Abstracts; Studies on Women & Gender Abstracts; Summon by Serial Solutions; Technical Education & Training Abstracts; TOC Premier; Wilson Social Science Abstracts.
Year Established	1971.
Circulation	3,000.
Frequency	10 times per year.
Months Issued	Not published in June or December.
No. of Articles per Issue	Approximately 12.

SUBMISSIONS

Postal Mailing Address	Contact the Editor if you are unable to submit the manuscript electronically or have questions about the submission process. Roger J.R. Levesque, JD, PhD, 302 Sycamore Hall, Indiana University, Bloomington, IN 47405. e-mail: rlevesqu@indiana.edu.
Method for Submission	Electronically via website. The Editor requires manuscript submission through Editorial Manager, a fully web-enabled online manuscript submission and review system.
Number of Copies	Not specified.
Disk Submission	Not specified.
Online or E-mail Submission Allowed or Required	Preferred; see website.

FORMAT OF MANUSCRIPT

Cover Sheet	The title page should include: the title of the article, author names (no degrees), author affiliation, and suggested running head. The journal considers only original manuscripts, written in English. Conduct all correspondence through e-mail. https://www.editorialmanager.com/joyo/.
Abstract	Provide an abstract of 100–150 words, typed on a separate page. Abstracts of empirical articles must describe the problem under investigation, specify pertinent characteristics of participants, report findings and conclusions, and use the third-person perspective.
Key Words	For review articles, consult the *APA Publication Manual*. Directly below the abstract, provide 3–5 key words that express the manuscript's precise content.
Length	Manuscripts should not exceed 25–30 pages (including text, references, tables and figures); the Editor considers exceptions only if authors provide adequate justifications. Number all your pages. Type all components double-spaced, including
Margins	1 inch on all sides.
Spacing	Double-spaced.

STYLE

Name of Guide	*Publication Manual of the American Psychological Association.*
Subheadings	Effective manuscripts tend to divide sections into subsections. Use at least 2 subheadings if you provide any subheading under a higher level subheading (see APA style guide).
References	All publications cited in the text must be presented in a list of references following the text of the manuscript. References within the text must cite the author's names followed by the date of publication, in chronological order
Footnotes	Avoid using footnotes, unless explicitly requested otherwise
Tables or Figures	See style guide.

REVIEW PROCESS

Type of Review	The Editor and Editorial Board members control manuscript review and selection. Manuscripts are reviewed by the Editor, the Editorial board, and perhaps by invited reviewers with special competence in the area represented by the manuscript. The Editor determines whether the manuscript will be sent for review. The Editor's decision depends on the relative importance, scientific rigor, and appropriateness of submissions to the journal readership. The Editor retains the discretion to integrate solicited reviews with his own opinions and recommendations into a determinative response.
Queries	Not specified.
Acknowledgment	Upon receipt of manuscript. See website.
Review Time	Approximately 6 months.
Revisions	Not specified.
Acceptance Rate	Not specified.
Return of Manuscript	Not specified.
Lag Time to Print	Not specified.

CHARGES TO AUTHOR

Author Alterations	Not specified.
Page Charges	The journal makes no page charges. Authors can purchase reprints; order forms with the current price schedule will accompany page proofs.
Processing	Not specified.

REPRINT, SUBSCRIPTION, AND CONTACT INFORMATION

Reprint Policy	Consult with editor.
Book Reviews	None.
Subscriptions	See website.
Affiliation	American Society of Adolescence Psychiatry.
E-Mail Address	rlevesqu@indiana.edu
Website	http://www.springerlink.com/content/104945/

JOURNAL OF YOUTH STUDIES

Current Title	*Journal of Youth Studies.*
Previous Title	N/A.
Editorial Focus	*Journal of Youth Studies* is an international scholarly journal devoted to a theoretical and empirical understanding of young people's experiences and life contexts. Over the last decade, changing socioeconomic circumstances have had important implications for young people; new opportunities have been created, but the risks of marginalization and exclusion have also become significant. *Journal of Youth Studies* aims to become the key multidisciplinary journal for academics with interests relating to youth and adolescence.
	Journal of Youth Studies is focused young people within a range of contexts, such as education, the labor market, and the family, and highlights key research themes such as the construction of identity, the use of leisure time, involvement in crime, consumption, and political behavior. The journal particularly encourages the submission of articles that highlight interconnections between the different spheres of young people's lives (such the transition from school to work) and articles that offer a critical perspective on social policies that affect young people.
Audience	Journal of Youth Studies brings together social scientists working in a range of disciplines. These include sociology, psychology, education, social policy, political science, economics, anthropology and social geography.
Special Themes	Not specified.
Where Indexed/ Abstracted	Caredata Abstracts; Contents Pages in Education; Educational Management Abstracts; Gezinswetenschappelijke Documentatie; PsycINFO; Social Planning/Policy and Development Abstracts; Social Science Citation Index; Sociological Abstracts; Sociology of Education Abstracts; family and society studies worldwide.
Year Established	1998.
Circulation	In 2008, a total of 18,879 article downloads were recorded.
Frequency	6 issues per year.
Months Issued	February, April, June, August, October and December.
No. of Articles per Issue	Approximately 7.

SUBMISSIONS

Postal Mailing Address	All submissions via Manuscript Central website.
Method for Submission	Electronic form via website.
Number of Copies	N/A.
Disk Submission	N/A.
Online or E-mail Submission Allowed or Required	Required http://mc.manuscriptcentral.com/cjys

FORMAT OF MANUSCRIPT

Cover Sheet	No.
Abstract	Yes.
Key Words	Yes.
Length	5,000–8,000 words.
Margins	See: http://www.tandf.co.uk/journals/authors/style/reference/tf_X.pdf.
Spacing	Not specified.

STYLE

Name of Guide	*See: http://www.tandf.co.uk/journals/authors/style/reference/tf_X.pdf.*
Subheadings	Not specified.
References	Harvard.
Footnotes	Not specified.
Tables or Figures	Not specified.

REVIEW PROCESS

Type of Review	Blind peer review.
Queries	Not specified.
Acknowledgment	Immediate electronically.

Review Time	Approximately 66 days.
Revisions	Not specified.
Acceptance Rate	Approximately 40% after revisions.
Return of Manuscript	N/A.
Lag Time to Print	Approximately 6 months.

CHARGES TO AUTHOR

Author Alterations	Charges only for major alterations at proof stage.
Page Charges	N/A.
Processing	N/A.

REPRINT, SUBSCRIPTION, AND CONTACT INFORMATION

Reprint Policy	Considered on a case by case basis.
Book Reviews	No.
Subscriptions	http://www.tandf.co.uk/journals/subscription.asp#subs
Affiliation	None.
E-Mail Address	editor: a.furlong@educ.gla.ac.uk
Website	http://mc.manuscriptcentral.com/cjys
	http://www.routledge.com/9780415445405
	http://www.mcgraw-hill.co.uk/html/0335223621.html

MARRIAGE & FAMILY REVIEW

Current Title	*Marriage & Family Review*
Previous Title	N/A.
Editorial Focus	*Marriage & Family Review* publishes a mix of open-submission articles as well as thematic issues that bring together the most current research, practice, advances in theory development, and applications of knowledge on a particular topic in the field.
Audience	Counselors, psychologists, health professionals, and social workers.
Special Themes	Leisure time activities, traditional and nontraditional family relationships, societal pressures and impacts on families, and cross-cultural studies on the family.
Where Indexed/ Abstracted	Abstracts in Social Gerontology: Current Literature on Aging, National Council on the Aging; Abstracts of Research in Pastoral Care & Counseling; Academic Abstracts/CD-ROM; AGRICOLA Database; Applied Social Sciences Index & Abstracts; Current Contents: Clinical Medicine/Life Sciences (CC:CM/LS); Family Life Educator "Abstracts Section"; Family Violence & Sexual Assault Bulletin; Guide to Social Science & Religion in Periodical Literature; Index to Periodical Articles Related to Law; Inventory of Marriage and Family Literature; PASCAL Bibliography T205: Sciences de l'Information Documentation; Periodical Abstracts, Research; Periodical Abstracts, Research II; Population Index; Psychological Abstracts/PsycINFO; Sage Family Studies Abstracts (SFSA); Social Planning/Policy and Development Abstracts; Sociological Abstracts (SA); Special Educational Needs Abstracts; Studies on Women and Gender Abstracts; Violence & Abuse Abstracts: A Review of Current Literature on Interpersonal Violence (VAA).
Year Established	1978.
Circulation	400+.
Frequency	2–3 times per year; some combined issues for 4 issues per volume (they report 8 issues per year but a review does not show that for several years).
Months Issued	Not specified.
No. of Articles per Issue	Average 6.

SUBMISSIONS

Postal Mailing Address	Department of Individual and Family Studies, College of Human Resources, University of Delaware, Newark, DE 19716.
Method for Submission	Julie Ehlers (julie.ehlers@taylorandfrancis.com)
Number of Copies	You will be advised if a hard copy of your manuscript is needed.
Disk Submission	Not specified.
Online or E-mail Submission Allowed or Required	The complete manuscript including a cover sheet, tables and figures, references, and appendix should be in a single file as an e-mail attachment, except for tables and figure that are not in a word-processing format. The editor will remove all identifying information, including those hidden under properties. Please make sure that you have removed this information if you are sending a figure or table as a pdf file.

FORMAT OF MANUSCRIPT

Cover Sheet	Separate sheet, which does not go out for review. Full title; author names, degrees, and professional titles; designation of one author as corresponding author with full address, phone numbers, e-mail address, and fax number; date of submission.
Abstract	Not more 125 words.
Key Words	Not specified.
Length	20 pages, including references and abstract. Lengthier manuscripts may be considered, but only at the discretion of the editor. Sometimes, lengthier manuscripts may be considered if they can be divided into sections for publication is successive issues.
Margins	1 inch.
Spacing	Double-spaced for all copy, except title page.

STYLE

Name of Guide	*Publication Manual of the American Psychological Association* (APA).
Subheadings	Use as needed to guide reader through the article. No more than 4 levels.
References	Author–date citation style; see style guide.
Footnotes	No footnotes preferred; incorporate into text.

Tables or Figures	Table or figures that are not in a word-processing format (such as PDF, pp, jpg, and excel) should be sent as separate files.

REVIEW PROCESS

Type of Review	"Double-blind" anonymous peer review. 3 reviewers plus editor-in-chief read the manuscript in an anonymous review.
Queries	Authors are encouraged to read the journal to determine if their subject matter would be appropriate.
Acknowledgment	Enclose a regular self-addressed, stamped envelope with submission.
Review Time	Approximately 3–4 months.
Revisions	See journal.
Acceptance Rate	Not specified.
Return of Manuscript	Only if 9" × 12" self-addressed, stamped envelope is enclosed.
Lag Time to Print	Approximately 6–12 months.

CHARGES TO AUTHOR

Author Alterations	Page proofs are sent to the designated author using Taylor & Francis' Central Article Tracking System. They must be carefully checked and returned within 48 hours of receipt.
Page Charges	Not specified.
Processing	Not specified.

REPRINT, SUBSCRIPTION, AND CONTACT INFORMATION

Reprint Policy	Reprints of individual articles are available for order at the time authors review page proofs. A discount on reprints is available to authors who order before print publication. Each corresponding author will receive 3 complete issues in which the article publishes and a complimentary PDF. This file is for personal use only and may not be copied and disseminated in any form without prior written permission from Taylor and Francis Group, LLC.
Book Reviews	Send request to editor.
Subscriptions	See website.
Affiliation	Not specified.
E-Mail Address	julie.ehlers@taylorandfrancis.com
Website	http://www.informaworld.com/smpp/title~content=t792306931

MERRILL-PALMER QUARTERLY: JOURNAL OF DEVELOPMENTAL PSYCHOLOGY

Current Title	*Merrill-Palmer Quarterly: Journal of Developmental Psychology*
Previous Title	N/A.
Editorial Focus	This internationally acclaimed periodical features empirical and theoretical papers on child development and family–child relationships.
Audience	Researchers, writers, teachers, and practitioners.
Special Themes	
Where Indexed/ Abstracted	Child Development Abstracts and Bibliography; Current Contents/Social and Behavioral Sciences; Current Index to Journals in Education; Linguistics and Language Behavior Abstracts; Psychological Abstracts; PsycSCAN: Developmental Psychology; Sage Family Studies Abstracts; Social Work Research and Abstracts; Sociological Abstracts; Sociology of Education Abstracts (British).
Year Established	1959.
Circulation	Approximately 1,300.
Frequency	Quarterly.
Months Issued	January, April, July, October.
No. of Articles per Issue	Approximately 5.

SUBMISSIONS

Postal Mailing Address	Dr. Gary W. Ladd, Editor, Merrill-Palmer Quarterly Editorial Office, Department of Family and Human Development, P.O. Box 872502, Arizona State University, Tempe, AZ 85287-2502.
Method for Submission	Surface mail or electronically via website.
Number of Copies	5 high-quality copies.
Disk Submission	See below.
Online or E-mail Submission Allowed or Required	Manuscripts can be submitted either electronically or via surface mail. Send electronic submissions (manuscript and cover letter) in the form of MSWord documents to mpq@asu.edu. To submit by surface mail, print 5 high-quality copies of the manuscript (please retain the original) on white paper and send them to the following address: Dr. Gary W. Ladd, Editor, Merrill-Palmer Quarterly Editorial Office, Department of Family and Human Development, P.O. Box 872502, Arizona State University, Tempe, AZ 85287-2502. E-mail: mpq@asu.edu, Phone: (480) 727-7199; Fax: (480) 965-0334.

SUBMISSIONS

Cover Sheet	A separate title page should be attached to each copy of the manuscript. Place all information about the authors (e.g., institutional affiliations, contact information, etc.) on this page only, using the APA 3 paragraph format (i.e., affiliation, acknowledgments, contact information). Blind review requires that information that might identify the authors or their affiliations be removed from all pages of the manuscript except the title page.
Abstract	150 words.
Key Words	Not required.
Length	Do not exceed 30 to 40 pages, all-inclusive (i.e., including references, tables, and figures). Additional page space may, at times, be permitted for critical reviews of literature, theoretical papers, or manuscripts that contain multiple studies.
Margins	1 inch minimum on all sides.
Spacing	Double-space *everything,* including text, tables, and references. Please use 12-point font. Text should be left-justified, and words should not be divided at the end of lines.

STYLE

Name of Guide	*Publication Manual of the American Psychological Association* (APA, 5th edition).
Subheadings	3 levels; see APA style guide.
References	See style guide.
Footnotes	See style guide.
Tables or Figures	See style guide.

REVIEW PROCESS

Type of Review	The Editors of *Merrill-Palmer Quarterly* have changed the journal's peer review policy to that of blind peer review. Thus, only manuscripts that have been prepared for blind peer review can be considered for publication.

Queries	Inquiries about manuscripts should be directed to the Editorial Office via e-mail (mpq@asu.edu) or fax (480-965-0334).
Acknowledgment	Receipt of manuscripts will be acknowledged via e-mail.
Review Time	3 months.
Revisions	Not specified.
Acceptance Rate	Approximately 16%–24%.
Return of Manuscript	Not returned; author should retain copies.
Lag Time to Print	Approximately 6–12 months.

CHARGES TO AUTHOR

Author Alterations	Not specified.
Page Charges	If excessive, publisher may charge author.
Processing	Not specified.

REPRINT, SUBSCRIPTION, AND CONTACT INFORMATION

Reprint Policy	Not specified.
Book Reviews	Not specified.
Subscriptions	See website: http://www.asu.edu/clas/ssfd/mpq/subscribe.htm.
Affiliation	Wayne State University Press.
E-Mail Address	mpq@asu.edu
Website	http://www.asu.edu/clas/ssfd/mpq/submit.htm and http://wsupress.wayne.edu/journals/merrill.htm

THE NEW SOCIAL WORKER: THE MAGAZINE FOR SOCIAL WORK STUDENTS AND RECENT GRADUATES

Current Title	*The New Social Worker: The Magazine for Social Work Students and Recent Graduates*
Previous Title	N/A.
Editorial Focus	Career guidance, news, and educational articles for social work students and new graduates. Each issue includes educational articles on field placement issues and social work ethics. Includes articles on practice specialties, book reviews, social work role models, job search tips, news from the profession and from schools of social work, and resources for social workers.
Audience	Social work students, recent graduates, faculty, practitioners, libraries, career placement centers.
Special Themes	Social work ethics, social work field placement.
Where Indexed/ Abstracted	Social Work Abstracts; Sociological Abstracts.
Year Established	1994
Circulation	6,000
Frequency	Quarterly.
Months Issued	January, April, July, October.
No. of Articles per Issue	Approximately 10.

SUBMISSIONS

Postal Mailing Address	E-mail to lindagrobman@socialworker.com (preferred) or postal mail to Linda Grobman, ACSW, LSW, Editor, *The New Social Worker,* P.O. Box 5390, Harrisburg, PA 17110-0390.
Method for Submission	Surface mail, e-mail.
Number of Copies	1
Disk Submission	If you are not able to send via e-mail attachment, please send manuscript on disk in a Word or PC compatible file.
Online or E-mail Submission Allowed or Required	E-mail submission to lindagrobman@ socialworker.com is preferred.

FORMAT OF MANUSCRIPT

Cover Sheet	Please include a cover sheet with the author's full name, title, degrees, agency or university affiliation, address, phone numbers, e-mail address, and fax number.
Abstract	None.
Key Words	None.
Length	1,500–2,000 words (4–6 double-spaced pages).
Margins	0.5–1 inch on all sides.
Spacing	Double-spaced.

STYLE

Name of Guide	Use *Publication Manual of the American Psychological Association* for formatting citations/ references. Articles are written in conversational feature style or news style. Please see a back issue for examples of our style.
Subheadings	Use as needed.
References	Minimal references preferred. May include "Recommended Readings" at the end of article. If references are included, please use APA format.
Footnotes	No footnotes.
Tables or Figures	Our articles typically do not have tables or figures. If there are tables, figures, or other illustrations, please submit them in separate graphics files (GIF or JPG).

REVIEW PROCESS

Type of Review	All articles are reviewed by the editor.
Queries	Query letters are welcome. However, manuscripts may be submitted without a prior query.
Acknowledgment	Approximately 1 month, when status of manuscript is determined.
Review Time	Approximately 1 month.
Revisions	Revisions may be requested by the editor. Submit 1 copy of revisions to the editor.
Acceptance Rate	Approximately 50%.
Return of Manuscript	Manuscripts are not returned. Author should retain copies.
Lag Time to Print	Approximately 3–12 months.

CHARGES TO AUTHOR

Author Alterations   N/A.

Page Charges   N/A.

Processing   N/A.

REPRINT, SUBSCRIPTION, AND CONTACT INFORMATION

Reprint Policy   Not applicable, as *The New Social Worker* is now an online publication and is freely available. Permission is required for reprinting articles from *The New Social Worker* in another publication.

Book Reviews   By invitation only. Send books for review or your qualifications for reviewing books to the editor.

Subscriptions   Subscriptions: *The New Social Worker* is available in electronic format only, free of charge, from http://www.socialworker.com. Subscribe free at http://www.socialworker.com/home/menu/Subscribe/

Affiliation   *The New Social Worker* is published by White Hat Communications.

E-Mail Address   lindagrobman@socialworker.com

Website   http://www.socialworker.com

NONPROFIT AND VOLUNTARY SECTOR QUARTERLY

Current Title	*Nonprofit and Voluntary Sector Quarterly*
Previous Title	N/A.
Editorial Focus	*Nonprofit and Voluntary Sector Quarterly* (*NVSQ*) provides cutting-edge research, discussion, and analysis of the field and leads its readers to understanding the impact the nonprofit sector has on society.
Audience	*Nonprofit and Voluntary Sector Quarterly* provides a forum for researchers from around the world to publish timely articles from a variety of disciplinary perspectives. *NVSQ* is dedicated to enhancing our knowledge of nonprofit organizations, philanthropy, and voluntarism. This goal can be achieved only through the cumulative efforts of many different disciplines. Among the disciplines represented in *NVSQ* are: anthropology, aarts and humanities, economics, education, health, history, law, management, political science, psychology, public administration, religious studies, social work, sociology, and urban affairs.
Special Themes	*Nonprofit and Voluntary Sector Quarterly* occasionally supplements its broad coverage with special issues featuring in-depth studies of particular topics of interest. *Nonprofit and Voluntary Sector Quarterly* is the journal of the Association for Research on Nonprofit Organizations and Voluntary Action (ARNOVA). Visit the ARNOVA website at www.arnova.org.
Where Indexed/ Abstracted	Applied Social Sciences Index & Abstracts (ASSIA); Biological Sciences Abstracts; Current Contents: Social & Behavioral Sciences; EconLit; Family & Society Studies Worldwide (NISC); FRANCIS Database; Health & Safety Sciences Abstracts; Human Resources Abstracts; IBZ (International Bibliography of Periodical Literature on the Humanities and Social Sciences); International Political Science Abstracts; NISC; Periodical Abstracts – ProQuest; Risk Abstracts; Safety Science & Risk Abstracts; SCOPUS; Social Care Online; Social Sciences Citation Index (Web of Science); Social SciSearch; Social Services Abstracts; Sociological Abstracts; Standard Periodical Directory (SPD).
Year Established	1972.
Circulation	Not specified.
Frequency	Bimonthly.
Months Issued	February, April, June, August, October, December.
No. of Articles per Issue	Not specified.

SUBMISSIONS

Postal Mailing Address	Manuscripts should be submitted to Manuscript Central at http://mc.manuscriptcentral.com/nvsq. Send queries or manuscript submissions to: Julianna Koksarova, Managing Editor, *Nonprofit and Voluntary Sector Quarterly,* 550 W. North Street, Suite 301, Indianapolis, IN, 46202, Phone: (317) 278-8981; Fax: (317) 684-8900 or nvsq@iupui.edu.
Method for Submission	Manuscripts should be submitted to Manuscript Central at http://mc.manuscriptcentral.com/nvsq.
Number of Copies	Not specified.
Disk Submission	Not specified.
Online or E-mail Submission Allowed or Required	Manuscripts should be submitted to Manuscript Central at http://mc.manuscriptcentral.com/nvsq.

FORMAT OF MANUSCRIPT

Cover Sheet	On the title page, include each authors' name, affiliation, address, phone number, fax number, e-mail address, and discipline of specialty and a short (2–3 sentence) biography of each author. In the main document, remove all identifying information.
Abstract	Include an abstract of 150 words or less.
Key Words	For specific instructions on manuscript submission and publication please see the *NVSQ* website at http://www.spea.iupui.edu/nvsq.
Length	Text in the main document should be generally limited to 20 pages maximum.
Margins	For specific instructions on manuscript submission and publication, please see the *NVSQ* website at http://www.spea.iupui.edu/nvsq.
Spacing	Double-space and left-justify everything with a ragged right-hand margin (no full justification).

STYLE

Name of Guide See website. Any questions can be answered by the help section on the site (click "Get Help Now" at the top of any screen), through the 24-hour support line, or can be e-mailed to the editorial office at nvsq@iupui.edu.

Subheadings Any questions can be answered by the help section on the site (click "Get Help Now" at the top of any screen), through the 24-hour support line, or can be e-mailed to the editorial office at nvsq@iupui.edu.

References All in-text citations are included in the reference list; all references have in-text citations. Follow the APA style for your citations and reference list.

Footnotes There are no footnotes. End notes are used for discursive purposes only. They should be grouped on a separate page.

Tables or Figures Insert "markers" indicating placement of tables/figures ([Table 1 Here]). Begin each section on a separate page and in this sequence: abstract, text, appendix (es), notes, references, each table, each figure. Figures are camera-ready; they appear exactly as they should in the journal, except for sizing.

REVIEW PROCESS

Type of Review Any questions can be answered by the help section on the site (click "Get Help Now" at the top of any screen), through the 24-hour support line, or can be e-mailed to the editorial office at nvsq@iupui.edu.

Queries Send queries or manuscript submissions to: Julianna Koksarova, Managing Editor, *Nonprofit and Voluntary Sector Quarterly*, 550 W. North Street, Suite 301, Indianapolis, IN, 46202, Phone: (317) 278-8981; Fax: (317) 684-8900 or nvsq@iupui.edu.

Acknowledgment Not specified.

Review Time Not specified.

Revisions Not specified.

Acceptance Rate Not specified.

Return of Manuscript Not specified.

Lag Time to Print Not specified.

CHARGES TO AUTHOR

Author Alterations Any questions can be answered by the help section on the site (click "Get Help Now" at the top of any screen), through the 24-hour support line, or can be e-mailed to the editorial office at nvsq@iupui.edu.

Page Charges Not specified.

Processing Not specified.

REPRINT, SUBSCRIPTION, AND CONTACT INFORMATION

Reprint Policy Reprints of individual articles are available for order at the time authors review page proofs. A discount on reprints is available to authors who order before print publication. Each corresponding author will receive 3 complete issues in which the article publishes and a complimentary PDF. This file is for personal use only and may not be copied and disseminated in any form without prior written permission from Taylor and Francis Group, LLC.

Book Reviews Send inquiries on book reviews to: Jeffrey L. Brudney, Book Review Editor, Albert A. Levin Chair of Urban Studies and Public Service, Maxine Goodman Levin College of Urban Affairs, Cleveland State University, 2121 Euclid Avenue, Cleveland, OH 44115, Phone: (216) 687-5269; Fax: (216) 687-9342 or nvsqbook@csuohio.edu.

Subscriptions See website: http://www.sagepub.com/journalsProdDesc.nav?prodId=Journal200775.

Affiliation http://intl-nvs.sagepub.com/

E-Mail Address nvsq@iupui.edu.

Website http://nvs.sagepub.com/ or http://intl-nvs.sagepub.com/.

OCCUPATIONAL THERAPY IN HEALTH CARE

Current Title	*Occupational Therapy in Health Care*
Previous Title	N/A.
Editorial Focus	*Occupational Therapy in Health Care* emphasizes practice-related articles and reports, features regular reviews of OT-related books and software, discusses educational strategies, and deals with the theoretical and philosophical issues that provide the foundation for occupational therapy evaluation and treatment approaches
Audience	Occupational therapists and occupational therapy assistants.
Special Themes	Not specified.
Where Indexed/ Abstracted	Abstracts in Social Gerontology: Current Literature on Aging; Academic Abstracts/CD-ROM; Biology Digest; Cambridge Scientific Abstracts; CINAHL (Cumulative Index to Nursing & Allied Health Literature); CNPIEC Reference Guide: Chinese National Directory of Foreign Periodicals; Communication Abstracts; Exceptional Child Education Resources (ECER); Excerpta Medica/Secondary Publishing Division; Health Source; Health Source Plus; Human Resources Abstracts (HRA); INTERNET ACCESS (and additional networks) Bulletin Board for Libraries ("BUBL"), coverage of information resources on INTERNET, JANET, and other networks; Occupational Therapy Database (OTDBASE); Occupational Therapy Index; OT BibSys; Social Work Abstracts; Sport Database/Discus; Violence & Abuse Abstracts: A Review of Current Literature on Interpersonal Violence (VAA).
Year Established	1984.
Circulation	435+.
Frequency	Quarterly.
Months Issued	Not specified.
No. of Articles per Issue	Approximately 6.

SUBMISSIONS

Postal Mailing Address	Anne E. Dickerson, PhD, OTR/L, FAOTA, Professor and Chair, Department of Occupational Therapy, School of Allied Health Sciences, 3305 E East Carolina University, Greenville, NC 27858-4354.
Method for Submission	Electronically via website: http://mc.manuscriptcentral.com/wohc.
Number of Copies	Not specified.
Disk Submission	Not specified.
Online or E-mail Submission Allowed or Required	Electronically via website: http://mc.manuscriptcentral.com/wohc.

FORMAT OF MANUSCRIPT

Cover Sheet	Title page (uploaded as a separate MS Word file) should include: a title that is concise and reflects the content of the manuscript; the full name(s) of each author; footnote with authors' academic degrees, professional titles, and affiliations; mailing and e-mail address of corresponding author (i.e., "Address correspondence to:"); acknowledgement of research support or other credit.
Abstract	100 words.
Key Words	3–6 key words below abstract.
Length	5–20 pages excluding references, etc.
Margins	1 inch.
Spacing	Double-spaced; make endnotes if notes are needed.

STYLE

Name of Guide	*Publication Manual of the American Psychological Association* (APA).
Subheadings	Not specified.
References	Informa Healthcare is participating in reference linking for journal articles. (To obtain information on reference linking initiatives, please consult the CrossRef Web site at www.crossref.org). When citing a journal article, include the article's Digital Object Identifier (DOI), when available, as the last item in the reference. A DOI is a persistent, authoritative, and unique identifier that a publisher assigns to each article. Because of its persistence, DOIs will enable Informa Healthcare and other publishers to link to the article referenced, and the link will not break over time.

Footnotes	No footnotes preferred; incorporate into text.
Tables or Figures	Tables and figures (including legend, notes, and sources) should be no larger than 4 ½ × 6 ½ inches. Type within tables or figures should be no smaller than 8 point. Tables and figures should be uploaded electronically as separate files. Use only those illustrations that clarify and augment the text. Tables and figures must be referred to in the text and numbered in order of their appearance. Each table and figure should have a complete, descriptive title; and each table column an appropriate heading. Each table and/or figure must have a title that explains its purpose without reference to the text. Please format graphs, figures, etc. mindful that these will be reproduced in black and white. The use of differing line types and symbols are more clearly distinguished by readers than subtle differences in color and identical line and symbol types. Please see below for further details on color figures. Captions must be saved separately, as part of the file containing the complete text of the paper, and numbered correspondingly.

REVIEW PROCESS

Type of Review	Manuscripts submitted to *OTHC* undergo an anonymous review by 2 or 3 members of the Editorial Board. Authors receive the reviews by e-mail and will receive a letter from the Editor summarizing the reviews and the status of the manuscript (accepted, revise, not accepted).
Queries	All editorial inquiries should be directed to the Editor.
Acknowledgment	Not specified.
Review Time	Every effort is made to complete the review process in 10–15 weeks.
Revisions	When the recommendation is to revise, authors should resubmit the manuscript within 90 days after the revisions are requested. If the revised manuscript is not received within 90 days, the manuscript file will be closed. An extension of the deadline may be requested.
Acceptance Rate	Not specified.
Return of Manuscript	Not specified.
Lag Time to Print	Approximately 6–12 months.

CHARGES TO AUTHOR

Author Alterations	Not specified.
Page Charges	Not specified.
Processing	Not specified.

REPRINT, SUBSCRIPTION, AND CONTACT INFORMATION

Reprint Policy	The designated author for correspondence will receive an e-mail that instructs them to respond to the proofs of the manuscript. This should be read carefully for errors and be completed within the time frame allocated. Authors will be asked to defray the expense of any major alterations to the proofs that are departures from the original manuscript.
Book Reviews	No.
Subscriptions	Need to register for subscription information.
Affiliation	Informa HealthCare.
E-Mail Address	dickersona@ecu.edu
Website	http://www.informaworld.com/smpp/title~db=jour~content=t792304022

OCCUPATIONAL THERAPY IN MENTAL HEALTH

Current Title	*Occupational Therapy in Mental Health*
Previous Title	N/A.
Editorial Focus	An essential journal for all OTs in mental health fields, Occupational Therapy in Mental Health provides professionals with a forum in which to discuss today's challenges-identifying the philosophical and conceptual foundations of the practice; sharing innovative evaluation and treatment techniques; learning about and assimilating new methodologies developing in related professions; and communicating information about new practice settings and special problem areas particular to psychiatric occupational therapy.
Audience	Occupational therapists in mental health.
Special Themes	Not specified.
Where Indexed/ Abstracted	Abstracts in Social Gerontology: Current Literature on Aging, National Council on the Aging; CINAHL (Cumulative Index to Nursing & Allied Health Literature); CNPIEC Reference Guide: Chinese National Directory of Foreign Periodicals; Developmental Medicine & Child Neurology; Exceptional Child Education Resources (ECER); Excerpta Medica/Secondary Publishing Division; Family Studies Database (online and CD-ROM); INTERNET ACCESS (and additional networks) Bulletin Board for Libraries ("BUBL"), coverage of information resources on INTERNET, JANET, and other networks; Mental Health Abstracts (online through DIALOG); Occupational Therapy Database (OTDBASE); Occupational Therapy Index; OT BibSys; PASCAL International Bibliography T205: Sciences de l'Information Documentation; Psychiatric Rehabilitation Journal; Social Work Abstracts; Sport Database/Discus.
Year Established	1980.
Circulation	Not specified.
Frequency	Quarterly.
Months Issued	Not specified.
No. of Articles per Issue	Approximately 5.

SUBMISSIONS

Postal Mailing Address	Marie-Louise Blount, AM, OT, FAOTA: mlb2@nyu.edu, 35 Young Avenue, Croton-on-Hudson, NY 10520 or Mary V. Donohue, PhD, OT, FAOTA: mvd1@nyu.edu, 38 Lakeview Avenue, Lynbrook, NY 11563.
Method for Submission	Electronically via website preferred but will accept surface mail.
Number of Copies	If submitting a disk, it should be prepared using MS Word and should be clearly labeled with the authors' names, file name, and software program used.
Disk Submission	Authors are strongly encouraged to submit manuscripts electronically. If submitting a disk, it should be prepared using MS Word and should be clearly labeled with the authors' names, file name, and software program used.
Online or E-mail Submission Allowed or Required	Authors are strongly encouraged to submit manuscripts electronically. If submitting a disk, it should be prepared using MS Word and should be clearly labeled with the authors' names, file name, and software program used.

FORMAT OF MANUSCRIPT

Cover Sheet	Separate sheet, which does not go out for review. Full title; author names, degrees, and professional titles; designation of one author as corresponding author with full address, phone numbers, e-mail address, and fax number; and date of submission.
Abstract	100 words. Avoid abbreviations, diagrams, and reference to the text in the abstract.
Key Words	Not specified.
Length	20 pages, including references and abstract. Lengthier manuscripts may be considered, but only at the discretion of the editor. Sometimes, lengthier manuscripts may be considered if they can be divided into sections for publication in successive issues.
Margins	1 inch.
Spacing	Double-spaced.

STYLE

Name of Guide	*Publication Manual of the American Psychological Association* (APA).
Subheadings	Use as needed to guide reader through article; no more than 4 levels.
References	References, citations, and general style of manuscripts should be prepared in accordance with the *APA Publication Manual*, 4th ed.

Footnotes	No footnotes preferred; incorporate into text.
Tables or Figures	Tables and figures (illustrations) should not be embedded in the text, but should be included as separate sheets or files. A short descriptive title should appear above each table with a clear legend and any footnotes suitably identified below. All units must be included. Figures should be completely labeled, taking into account necessary size reduction. Captions should be typed, double-spaced, on a separate sheet.

REVIEW PROCESS

Type of Review	"Double-blind" anonymous peer review. 3 reviewers plus editor-in-chief read the manuscript in an anonymous review.
Queries	Authors are encouraged to read the journal to determine whether their subject matter would be appropriate.
Acknowledgment	Not specified.
Review Time	Approximately 3–4 months.
Revisions	See journal/website.
Acceptance Rate	Not specified.
Return of Manuscript	Not specified.
Lag Time to Print	Approximately 6–12 months.

CHARGES TO AUTHOR

Author Alterations	Page proofs are sent to the designated author using Taylor & Francis' Central Article Tracking System. They must be carefully checked and returned within 48 hours of receipt.
Page Charges	Illustrations submitted (line drawings, halftones, photos, photomicrographs, etc.) should be clean originals or digital files. Digital files are recommended for highest quality reproduction and should follow these guidelines: 300 dpi or higher; sized to fit on journal page; EPS, TIFF, or PSD format only; and submitted as separate files, not embedded in text files. Color illustrations will be considered for publication; however, the author will be required to bear the full cost involved in color art reproduction. Color art can be purchased for online-only reproduction or for print and online reproduction. Color reprints can only be ordered if print and online reproduction costs are paid. Rates for color art reproduction are: Online-Only Reproduction: $225 for the first page of color; $100 per page for the next 3 pages of color. A maximum charge of $525 applies. Print and Online Reproduction: $900 for the first page of color; $450 per page for the next 3 pages of color. A custom quote will be provided for articles with more than 4 pages of color.
Processing	Not specified.

REPRINT, SUBSCRIPTION, AND CONTACT INFORMATION

Reprint Policy	Reprints of individual articles are available for order at the time authors review page proofs. A discount on reprints is available to authors who order before print publication. Each corresponding author will receive 3 complete issues in which the article publishes and a complimentary PDF. This file is for personal use only and may not be copied and disseminated in any form without prior written permission from Taylor and Francis Group, LLC.
Book Reviews	Lisette N. Kautzmann, EdD, OT, FAOTA, Sheboygan, WI: Book Review Editor.
Subscriptions	Need to register for subscription info (true for all informaworld journals).
Affiliation	Not specified.
E-Mail Address	See above.
Website	http://www.informaworld.com/smpp/title~content=t792306940~db=all

OMEGA: JOURNAL OF DEATH AND DYING

Current Title	*Omega: Journal of Death and Dying*
Previous Title	N/A.
Editorial Focus	Research articles are a top priority. The journal also publishes quality case studies, theoretical, and review contribution. Original contributions on nontrivial topics are welcomed. Readers include sophisticated researchers, educators, and practitioners from a variety of fields. Manuscripts should respect the existing knowledge and offer facts, ideas, or experiences that make a difference. The base fact that a manuscript is "about death" does not automatically qualify it for publication in *Omega*. The journal looks for incisive, thoughtful, challenging manuscripts.
Audience	Not specified.
Special Themes	Contact the editor to express interest in a theme.
Where Indexed/ Abstracted	Abstracts for Social Workers; Applied Social Sciences Index & Abstracts; Behavioral Abstracts; Bibliographic Index of Health Education Periodicals; BioScience Information Service of Biological Abstracts; Chicago Psychoanalytic Literature Index; Excerpta Medica; Family Abstracts; Mental Health Digest; PRE-PSYC Database; PREV; Psychological Abstracts; Social Work Abstracts; Sociological Abstracts.
Year Established	1970.
Circulation	Approximately 1,500.
Frequency	8 per year.
Months Issued	Not specified.
No. of Articles per Issue	Approximately 6.

SUBMISSIONS

Postal Mailing Address	Kenneth J. Doka, PhD, Editor, The Center for Palliative Care and Death Education, The College of New Rochelle, New Rochelle, NY 10805.
Method for Submission	Surface mail, disk, e-mail, and electronic form via website.
Number of Copies	3.
Disk Submission	Yes.
Online or E-mail Submission Allowed or Required	Allowed.

FORMAT OF MANUSCRIPT

Cover Sheet	Name, address (include zip code), phone number, fax number.
Abstract	100–150 words.
Key Words	Not specified.
Length	No maximum or minimum, average length 20 pages.
Margins	Wide.
Spacing	Double-spaced.

STYLE

Name of Guide	*Publication Manual of the American Psychological Association.*
Subheadings	Include.
References	See style guide.
Footnotes	Include only for acknowledgement and for special circumstances. Generally, avoid using footnotes.
Tables or Figures	Quality word-processing printout is acceptable. Include each table and figure on a separate page. Avoid abbreviations. Include a legend and heading.

REVIEW PROCESS

Type of Review	Anonymous review by 2 reviewers minimum.
Queries	Not specified.
Acknowledgment	Include self-addressed, stamped envelope or postcard when submitting manuscript.
Review Time	Approximately 6 weeks.
Revisions	Author receives detailed comments from reviewers and editor. Most of the published articles have been revised.
Acceptance Rate	Approximately 15% accepted without revisions; 25%–30% accepted after revisions.

Return of Manuscript	Returned only if requested by author.
Lag Time to Print	Approximately 12 months.

CHARGES TO AUTHOR

Author Alterations	No charge if minor alterations are needed.
Page Charges	Not specified.
Processing	Not specified.

REPRINT, SUBSCRIPTION, AND CONTACT INFORMATION

Reprint Policy	Authors receive 1 free copy of the issue and 20 reprints. Ordering information for additional reprints is sent to author.
Book Reviews	Contact editor. Send a curriculum vita and indicate areas of interest and expertise.
Subscriptions	Baywood Publishing Company, Inc., 26 Austin Avenue, P.O. Box 337, Amityville, NY 11701. Individuals $45; Institutions $145.
Affiliation	Not specified.
E-Mail Address	KnDok@aol.com; other: baywood@baywood.com.
Website	http:// baywood.com

PHYSICAL & OCCUPATIONAL THERAPY IN GERIATRICS

Current Title	*Physical and Occupational Therapy In Geriatrics*
Previous Title	N/A.
Editorial Focus	Current trends in geriatrics. Focus on rehabilitation of the geriatric client to share information, clinical experience, research, and therapeutic practice. Each issue focuses on current practice and emerging issues in the care of the older client, including rehabilitation and long-term care in institutional and community settings, and innovative programming; the entire range of problems experienced by the elderly; and the current skills needed for working with older clients. Contributors consider the current methods of managing older people at home, in assisted living, alone, or with families. Contributors address policy issues that affect the styles of living of older people, and discuss projects relating to research and teaching as they may affect practice in the field of gerontology.
Audience	Not specified.
Special Themes	Manuscripts submitted to *Physical & Occupational Therapy in Geriatrics* (*POTG*) should address topics related to geriatric rehabilitation, long-term care, and wellness. All inquiries should be directed to the Editor. Submissions can be made in the form of Original Research, Case Reports, Systemic Reviews, and Theory/Perspective studies related to older adults.
Where Indexed/ Abstracted	Abstracts in Social Gerontology: Current Literature on Aging, National Council on the Aging; Academic Abstracts/CD-ROM; Brown University Geriatric Research Application Digest "Abstracts Section"; CINAHL (Cumulative Index to Nursing & Allied Health Literature); CNPIEC Reference Guide: Chinese National Directory of Foreign Periodicals; Communication Abstracts; Excerpta Medica/Secondary Publishing Division; Family Studies Database (online and CD-ROM); Health Source; Health Source Plus; Human Resources Abstracts (HRA); INTERNET ACCESS (and additional networks) Bulletin Board for Libraries ("BUBL"), coverage of information resources on INTERNET, JANET, and other networks; Occupational Therapy Database (OTDBASE); Occupational Therapy Index; OT BibSys; Psychological Abstracts/PsycINFO; Public Affairs Information Bulletin (PAIS); Social Work Abstracts; Sport Database/Discus.
Year Established	1980.
Circulation	Not specified.
Frequency	Quarterly.
Months Issued	Not specified.
No. of Articles per Issue	6–10.

SUBMISSIONS

Postal Mailing Address	Not specified.
Method for Submission	Electronically via webiste. Manuscripts should be submitted electronically to *POTG's* electronic submissions and peer review website, ScholarOne's Manuscript Central; http://mc.manuscriptcentral.com/wpog.
Number of Copies	4.
Disk Submission	N/A.
Online or E-mail Submission Allowed or Required	Electronically via website.

FORMAT OF MANUSCRIPT

Cover Sheet	Submit a title page with the manuscript, indicating only the title (this is used for anonymous refereeing). Title page should be uploaded as a separate MS Word file. Title page should include: a title that is concise and reflects the content of the manuscript; the full name(s) of each author; footnote with authors' academic degrees, professional titles, and affiliations; mailing and e-mail address of corresponding author (i.e. "Address correspondence to:"); and acknowledgement of research support or other credit.
Key Words	Below the abstract provide 3–10 keywords for index purposes.
Length	Maximum 20 typed pages with the above formatting (excluding abstract and references).
Margins	Leave at least 1 inch margin on all four sides: set all notes as endnotes.
Spacing	Double-spaced, including endnotes and references. Times New Roman, 12 point. A header and footer on each page.

STYLE

Name of Guide	*Publication Manual of the American Psychological Association.*
Subheadings	Use as needed to guide reader. No more than 4 levels
References	References, citations, and general style of manuscripts for this journal should follow the APA Style (as outlined in the latest edition of the Publication Manual of the American Psychological Association).
Footnotes	None preferred. Incorporate into text.
Tables or Figures	Tables and figures should be uploaded electronically as separate files. Use only those illustrations that clarify and augment the text. Captions must be saved separately, as part of the file containing the complete text of the paper, and numbered correspondingly. Digital files are recommended for highest quality reproduction and should follow these guidelines: 300 dpi or higher and sized to fit on journal page. Specific permission for facial photographs of patients is required. A letter of consent must accompany the photographs of patients in which a possibility of identification exists. It is not sufficient to cover the eyes to mask identity.

REVIEW PROCESS

Type of Review	Peer reviewed. Manuscripts submitted to *POTG* undergo an anonymous review by 2 members of the Editorial Board.
Queries	Authors are encouraged to read the journal to see whether their subject matter would be appropriate.
Acknowledgment	Submissions will be acknowledged via e-mail.
Review Time	Approximately 10–15 weeks.
Revisions	When the recommendation is to revise, authors should resubmit the manuscript within 60 days after the revisions are requested. If the revised manuscript is not received within 60 days, the manuscript file will be closed. An extension of the deadline may be requested. Papers are frequently accepted by the editor contingent upon changes that are mandated by anonymous specialist referees and/or members of the editorial board. If the editor returns your manuscript for revisions, you are responsible for incorporating these revisions.
Acceptance Rate	Not specified.
Return of Manuscript	Not specified.
Lag Time to Print	Approximately 6–12 months.

CHARGES TO AUTHOR

Author Alterations	See website.
Page Charges	Any figure submitted as a color original will appear in color in the journal's online edition free of charge and can be downloaded. Paper copy color reproduction will only be considered on the condition that authors contribute to the associated costs. Charges are: 500/US$1030 for the first color page and 250/US$515 for each color page after per article. Color costs will be waived for invited Review Articles.
Processing	Proofs: The designated author for correspondence will receive a copy of the proofs, which should be read carefully for errors. The corrected proof must be returned to the Publisher within 48 hours. Authors will be asked to defray the expense of any major alterations to the proofs that are departures from the original manuscript.

REPRINT, SUBSCRIPTION, AND CONTACT INFORMATION

Reprint Policy	Each corresponding author will receive 1 copy of the issue in which the article appears. Additional copies of the journal can be purchased separately at the author's preferential rate of 15.00/US$25.00 per copy. Reprints of individual articles are available to order at the time authors review page proofs. A discount on reprints is available to authors who order before print publication.
Book Reviews	Address journal editor.
Subscriptions	http://www.informaworld.com/smpp/title~db=all~content=t792304026~tab=subscribe.
Affiliation	Not specified.
E-Mail Address	Not specified.
Website	http://www.informaworld.com/smpp/title~db=all~content=t792304026~tab=summary

PHYSICAL & OCCUPATIONAL THERAPY IN PEDIATRICS

Current Title	*Physical & Occupational Therapy in Pediatrics*
Previous Title	N/A.
Editorial Focus	Developmental and physical rehabilitation of infants, children, and youth, with an emphasis on implications and applications for therapy practice. Submissions can be made in the form of original research, case reports, systematic reviews, theory/perspective, and special communications.
Audience	Pediatric physical and occupational therapists.
Special Themes	Not indicated.
Where Indexed/ Abstracted	See attached file PDF.
Year Established	1981.
Circulation	Not indicated.
Frequency	Quarterly
Months Issued	February, May, August, November.
No. of Articles per Issue	Approximately 5–6.

SUBMISSIONS

Postal Mailing Address	Dr. Robert Palisano, Drexel University, Physical Therapy & Rehabilitation Sciences, 245 N. 15th Street, MS 502, Philadelphia, PA 19102.
Method for Submission	Electronic form via website.
Number of Copies	Not indicated.
Disk Submission	Not indicated.
Online or E-mail Submission Allowed or Required	Required http://mc.manuscriptcentral.com/wpop.

FORMAT OF MANUSCRIPT

Cover Sheet	Include a title that is concise and reflects the content of the manuscript; the full name(s) of each author; footnote with authors' academic degrees, professional titles, and affiliations; mailing and e-mail address of corresponding author (i.e., "Address correspondence to:"); and acknowledgement of research support or other credit.
Abstract	Required; maximum of 150 words.
Key Words	Required; maximum of 6.
Length	15 double-spaced pages, not including abstract or references.
Margins	1 inch.
Spacing	Double-spaced.

STYLE

Name of Guide	*Publication Manual of the American Psychological Association.*
Subheadings	Use as needed to guide reader through the article. No more than 4 levels.
References	Use style guide.
Footnotes	No footnotes preferred; incorporate into text.
Tables or Figures	Maximum of 6.

REVIEW PROCESS

Type of Review	Anonymous peer review.
Queries	Accepted.
Acknowledgment	By e-mail.
Review Time	Approximately 10–15 weeks.
Revisions	Determined on an individual basis; must be submitted through website.
Acceptance Rate	Not indicated.
Return of Manuscript	Only if 9" × 12" self-addressed, stamped envelope is enclosed.
Lag Time to Print	Approximately 6–12 months.

CHARGES TO AUTHOR

Author Alterations	Yes, if major.
Page Charges	None.
Processing	None.

REPRINT, SUBSCRIPTION, AND CONTACT INFORMATION

Reprint Policy
Each corresponding author will receive 1 copy of the issue in which the article appears. Additional copies of the journal can be purchased separately at the author's preferential rate of $25.00 per copy. Reprints of individual articles are available to order at the time authors review page proofs. A discount on reprints is available to authors who order before print publication.

Book Reviews
Accepted; contact editor at potp@drexel.edu.

Subscriptions
See http://www.informaworld.com/smpp/268718111-13453998/title~db=all~content= t792304027~tab=subscribe.

Affiliation
None.

E-Mail Address
potp@drexel.edu

Website
http://www.informaworld.com/smpp/268718112-8612073/title~content=t792304027

POLICY AND PRACTICE

Current Title	*Policy and Practice*
Previous Title	*Public Welfare (prior to August 1998).*
Editorial Focus	*Policy and Practice* covers all aspects of the human services and related fields.
Audience	Human service professionals; federal, state, and local administrators and managers; federal and state legislators and other elected officials and their policy staffs; judges and attorneys; directors of private and voluntary social service agencies; leaders of business and consumer groups; and administrators, educators, and students in schools of social work.
Special Themes	???
Where Indexed/ Abstracted	Academic Abstracts; Social Sciences Index and Abstracts; Social Work Abstracts; Sociological Abstracts; and on the Internet at http://www.aphsa.org.
Year Established	1943.
Circulation	5,500.
Frequency	Bimonthly.
Months Issued	February, April, June, August, October, December.
No. of Articles per Issue	30–35.

SUBMISSIONS

Postal Mailing Address	Editor, *Policy and Practice,* American Public Human Services Association, 1133 Nineteenth Street NW, Suite 400, Washington, DC 20036.
Method for Submission	E-mail or electronic form via website.
Number of Copies	1.
Disk Submission	We prefer to receive manuscripts electronically, preferably as a Microsoft Word or otherwise PC-compatible file attached to an e-mail.
Online or E-mail Submission Allowed or Required	Yes.

FORMAT OF MANUSCRIPT

Cover Sheet	Should include for all authors: name, title, professional affiliations, address, phone and fax numbers, and e-mail address. Should also include date of submission and designate 1 author as the corresponding author.
Abstract	Prospective authors should submit a descriptive abstract of no more than 300 words.
Key Words	Social services, human services, Medicaid, child welfare, nutrition assistance.
Length	Target length is 800 words unless arranged beforehand with magazine editor.
Margins	.75 inches on all sides.
Spacing	Double-spaced.

STYLE

Name of Guide	*Publication Manual of the American Psychological Association.*
Subheadings	N/A.
References	*Policy and Practice* prefers an informal style with sources fully identified and worked into the text of the article.
Footnotes	N/A.
Tables or Figures	In general, *Policy and Practice* prefers articles that clearly make their point without need of tables or figures. When they are necessary, 2 rules should apply: They should be simple, direct, and easily understood; and the fewer, the better. All tables or graphics submitted with articles should be camera-ready.

REVIEW PROCESS

Type of Review	Manuscripts submitted for publication are reviewed by the magazine editor. There is no blind peer review.
Queries	Queries are discouraged. Interested authors should read current issues of the magazine; refer to our web site for submission information (www.aphsa.org) http://www.aphsa.org/Publications/Doc/PolicyPractice-Author-Guidelines.pdf.
Acknowledgment	None.
Review Time	Approximately 3–6 months.

Revisions	We will ask for revisions if necessary.
Acceptance Rate	We do not track this information. For unsolicited manuscripts, probably less than 15%; for invited manuscripts, more than 80%.
Return of Manuscript	Not returned. Author should retain copies.
Lag Time to Print	Approximately 3–12 months.

REPRINT, SUBSCRIPTION, AND CONTACT INFORMATION

Reprint Policy	Authors receive a complimentary copy of the issue in which the article appears. Reprint information is available on request.
Book Reviews	By invitation only. Send books for review to the editor.
Subscriptions	American Public Human Services Association (APHSA), 1133 Nineteenth Street NW, Suite 400, Washington, DC 20036.
Affiliation	American Public Human Services Association.
E-Mail Address	frank.solomon@aphsa.org
Website	http://www.aphsa.org

PRACTICE: SOCIAL WORK IN ACTION

Current Title	*Practice: Social Work in Action*
Previous Title	*Practice.*
Editorial Focus	*Practice* provides a forum for the publication of research and knowledge from practice and the experiences of people using services, in a peer-reviewed journal. The journal has a strong base in social work practice and seeks to promote a proactive, reflective, and critical perspective. *Practice* promotes the international dimension of social work and fosters an exchange of learning, knowledge, and values. Academics and researchers are encouraged to translate practice-based research into a format relevant to practicing social workers, whatever their role and task. The journal includes contributions from the field. Practitioners and people using services are encouraged to submit material. The Editorial Board is committed to offering constructive support to those in the early phases of their publishing careers.
Audience	Social work academics and practitioners.
Special Themes	Recent special issues have included Social Work Practice in South Africa and Gender and Sexuality in Social Work. The journal usually has 1 special issue a year.
Where Indexed/ Abstracted	ASSIA; CINAHL (Cumulative Index to Nursing and Allied Health Literature); EBSCO; IBSS; PsycINFO; Social Care Online (SCIE); Social Services Abstracts.
Year Established	1989.
Circulation	Not specified.
Frequency	4 Issues per year. Increasing to 5 issues per year in 2010.
Months Issued	March, June, September, December.
No. of Articles per Issue	Approximately 5 per issues.

SUBMISSIONS

Postal Mailing Address	All submission made via online system, Manuscript Central. Please refer to journal's website www.tandf.co.uk/journals/practice.
Method for Submission	Electronic form via Web (Manuscript Central).
Number of Copies	Not specified.
Disk Submission	Not specified.
Online or E-mail Submission Allowed or Required	Electronic form via Web (Manuscript Central).

FORMAT OF MANUSCRIPT

Cover Sheet	Not specified.
Abstract	200 words.
Key Words	3 keywords.
Length	3,000–5,000 words.
Margins	Ample margins.
Spacing	Double-spaced.

STYLE

Name of Guide	*Chicago Manual of Style.*
Subheadings	For a detailed style guide, please refer to the journal's website: www.tandf.co.uk/journals/practice.
References	Not specified.
Footnotes	Not specified.
Tables or Figures	Not specified.

REVIEW PROCESS

Type of Review	Double blind.
Queries	Not specified.
Acknowledgment	Not specified.
Review Time	Not specified.
Revisions	Not specified.
Acceptance Rate	Not specified.
Return of Manuscript	Not specified.
Lag Time to Print	Not specified.

REPRINT, SUBSCRIPTION, AND CONTACT INFORMATION

Reprint Policy	Not specified.
Book Reviews	Yes.
Subscriptions	Not specified.
Affiliation	The journal is owned by the British Association of Social Workers, and the current editorial office is situated at the University of Bournemouth.
E-Mail Address	practicejournal@bournemouth.ac.uk
Website	www.tandf.co.uk/journals/practice

PROFESSIONAL DEVELOPMENT: THE INTERNATIONAL JOURNAL OF CONTINUING SOCIAL WORK EDUCATION

Current Title	*Professional Development: The International Journal of Continuing Social Work Education*
Previous Title	*Journal of Continuing Social Work Education.*
Editorial Focus	Articles on continuing education and its implications for child welfare, organizational effectiveness, social work education, and community relations, among others.
Audience	Social work faculty, practitioners, librarians, continuing education directors, and research institutions.
Special Themes	Child welfare, international social work, border issues, employee engagement.
Where Indexed/ Abstracted	Social Work Abstracts.
Year Established	1981, retitled in 2008.
Circulation	200
Frequency	Semiannually.
Months Issued	Spring-Summer and Fall-Winter.
No. of Articles per Issue	5–7.

SUBMISSIONS

Postal Mailing Address	UT Austin, School of Social Work, 1 University Station, D3500, Austin, TX 78712.
Method for Submission	E-mail, electronic form via website.
Number of Copies	1
Disk Submission	N/A.
Online or E-mail Submission Allowed or Required	Required at www.profdevjournal.org

FORMAT OF MANUSCRIPT

Cover Sheet	Title, authors, affiliations, e-mail address, mailing address, phone number.
Abstract	75 words or less.
Key Words	None.
Length	4–15 pages.
Margins	No policy.
Spacing	No policy.

STYLE

Name of Guide	*Publication Manual of the American Psychological Association.*
Subheadings	No policy.
References	See style guide.
Footnotes	No policy.
Tables or Figures	No policy.

REVIEW PROCESS

Type of Review	Anonymous review by 3 reviewers.
Queries	Contact Managing Editor.
Acknowledgment	E-mail sent on manuscript receipt.
Review Time	Approximately 6–9 months.
Revisions	Revisions requested by reviewers are outlined in e-mail to authors.
Acceptance Rate	Approximately 60%.
Return of Manuscript	Not returned.
Lag Time to Print	Approximately 9–18 months.

CHARGES TO AUTHOR

Author Alterations	None.
Page Charges	None.
Processing	None.

REPRINT, SUBSCRIPTION, AND CONTACT INFORMATION

Reprint Policy	Reprints may be ordered at $15 per copy; contact Managing Editor.
Book Reviews	Send unsolicited reviews to Noel Landuyt, Managing Editor, UT Austin, School of Social Work, 1 University Station D3500, Austin, TX 78712.
Subscriptions	Noel Landuyt, Managing Editor.
Affiliation	Institute for Organizational Excellence, Center for Social Work Research, UT Austin, School of Social Work.
E-Mail Address	nlanduyt@austin.utexas.edu
Website	www.profdevjournal.org

PSYCHIATRIC SERVICES

Current Title	*Psychiatric Services*
Previous Title	*Hospital & Community Psychiatry* (until 1995)
Editorial Focus	Mental health services (empirical research); service delivery and effectiveness, especially services and programs in the public mental health system targeted to persons with serious and persistent mental illness.
Audience	Mental health professionals in all disciplines, including mental health agency administrators, policy makers, and advocates for people living with mental illnesses.
Special Themes	Evidence-based practices for supporting recovery and community integration; preventing homelessness and incarceration of persons with serious mental illnesses.
Where Indexed/ Abstracted	Cumulative Index to Nursing and Allied Health Literature, Current Contents, Excerpta Medica, HealthSTAR, Index Medicus, MEDLINE, Psychological Abstracts/PsycINFO, Social Science Citation Index, and other indexes and databases.
Year Established	1950
Circulation	22,000
Frequency	Monthly.
Months Issued	Each month.
No. of Articles per Issue	15–20.

SUBMISSIONS

Postal Mailing Address	N/A
Method for Submission	Online submissions only at http://mc.manuscriptcentral.com/appi-ps.
Number of Copies	1 through online submission.
Disk Submission	No.
Online or E-mail Submission Allowed or Required	Online required.

FORMAT OF MANUSCRIPT

Cover Sheet	*Psychiatric Services* uses a double-blind review. When submitting your paper online at Manuscript Central, do not include author information on the title page (Main Body file) or on any supporting files for peer review. (Author information entered during the submission process is internally linked to the manuscript and is not required in the manuscript itself.)
Abstract	All manuscripts should include a structured abstract after the title page with the following information, under the headings indicated: Objective: the primary purpose of the article; Methods: data sources, subjects, design, measurements, and data analysis; Results: key findings; and Conclusions: implications, and future directions. For regular articles, the abstract should not exceed 250 words. For brief reports, the limit is 150 words.
Key Words	Not specified.
Length	In general, articles should not exceed 3,000 words excluding abstract, references, and tables, although some exceptions are made by the Editor. Please do not submit articles of more than 3,000 words without first contacting the Editor or Managing Editor at psjournal@psych.org. In your e-mail, please explain why the paper should exceed the word limit. Attach the abstract of the proposed submission or the paper itself.
Margins	Minimum of 1.5 inches on all sides.
Spacing	Double-spaced.

STYLE

Name of Guide	Follow format in recent issues of the journal.
Subheadings	Follow format in recent issues of the journal.
References	Follow *Psychiatric Services* style for reference punctuation.
Footnotes	Follow format in recent issues of the journal.
Tables or Figures	For regular articles, include no more than 5 tables. Include tables only when they present relevant numerical data more clearly than could be done in text; data in short tables often can be incorporated more concisely in text. Authors will be asked to delete extraneous tables. Follow the table formats used in recent issues of the journal.

REVIEW PROCESS

Type of Review	Peer review (double-blind) by 3 or more independent reviewers.
Queries	psjournal@psych.org
Acknowledgment	Receipt of submission automatically acknowledged by online system.
Review Time	3 months.
Revisions	1 month.
Acceptance Rate	29%
Return of Manuscript	Manuscripts not returned.
Lag Time to Print	4–5 months.

REPRINT, SUBSCRIPTION, AND CONTACT INFORMATION

Reprint Policy	Reprints can be purchased (100 minimum).
Book Reviews	Book review editor e-mail: Jeffrey.geller@umassmed.edu.
Subscriptions	See http://psychservices.psychiatryonline.org for pricing.
Affiliation	American Psychiatric Association.
E-Mail Address	psjournal@psych.org
Website	http://psychservices.psychiatryonline.org/

PSYCHOANALYTIC SOCIAL WORK

Current Title	*Psychoanalytic Social Work*
Previous Title	*Journal of Analytic Social Work.*
Editorial Focus	Clinical, theoretical, and research articles and book reviews germane to psychodynamic social work.
Audience	Clinical social workers, psychoanalysts, social work educators, researchers, allied mental health professionals, libraries, social work programs, psychoanalytic institutes.
Special Themes	Submissions broadly germane to psychoanalytic/psychodynamic theory, practice, research.
Where Indexed/ Abstracted	ASSIA; EBSCO; PsycINFO.
Year Established	1993
Circulation	N/A.
Frequency	Semiannually.
Months Issued	Spring/Fall.
No. of Articles per Issue	4–7.

SUBMISSIONS

Postal Mailing Address	Jerrold R. Brandell, PhD, Editor-in-Chief. Send via e-mail attachment in Word only to: jrbrandell@sbcglobal.net.
Method for Submission	E-mail.
Number of Copies	N/A.
Disk Submission	N/A.
Online or E-mail Submission Allowed or Required	Required.

FORMAT OF MANUSCRIPT

Cover Sheet	Yes.
Abstract	Required; not more than 200 words.
Key Words	Required; 3–6 key words.
Length	Optimal length of 25 pages; longer manuscripts will be considered.
Margins	1 inch all around.
Spacing	Double-spaced for all copy with the exception of the title page.

STYLE

Name of Guide	*Publication Manual of the American Psychological Association.*
Subheadings	As needed throughout article.
References	Author-date citation style; see style guide.
Footnotes	Discouraged; material should be incorporated into text whenever feasible.
Tables or Figures	Submit tables as separate files with descriptive title (See *PSW* "Instructions for Authors" on journal web site for additional details); figures should be camera ready.

REVIEW PROCESS

Type of Review	Double-blind anonymous peer review.
Queries	Address to Editor.
Acknowledgment	Electronically and by request only.
Review Time	12–16 weeks.
Revisions	Requirements vary according to situation; may require resubmission and secondary review.
Acceptance Rate	Approximately 35%.
Return of Manuscript	N/A.
Lag Time to Print	Approximately 9–15 months.

CHARGES TO AUTHOR

Author Alterations	See Taylor & Francis Web Site.
Page Charges	See Taylor & Francis Web Site.
Processing	N/A.

REPRINT, SUBSCRIPTION, AND CONTACT INFORMATION

Reprint Policy 3 complete issues and pdf version are complimentary to corresponding author. Reprints of individual articles available for purchase at time page proofs are reviewed.

Book Reviews By invitation of Book Review Editor only.

Subscriptions Institutional: $495 (US); Personal subscribers: $103. Subscription office: US: Taylor & Francis Group, LLC, 325 Chestnut Street, Philadelphia, PA 19106. Phone: (215) 625-8900; Fax: (215) 625-2940.

Affiliation Not indicated.

E-Mail Address www.taylorandfrancis.com

Website http://www.informaworld.com/smpp/title~content=t792306950~db=all

PSYCHOLOGICAL ASSESSMENT

Current Title	*Psychological Assessment.*
Previous Title	N/A.
Editorial Focus	*Psychological Assessment* publishes empirical research on measurement and evaluation relevant to the broad field of clinical psychology. This journal focuses on the diagnosis and evaluation of psychological characteristics or processes and assessment of the effectiveness of interventions. Topics covered include assessment of personality, psychopathological symptoms, cognitive and neuropsychological processes, and interpersonal behavior. Methodological, theoretical, and review articles address clinical assessment processes, and occasional case studies identify unique contributions to clinical assessment.
Audience	Researchers in the discipline, faculty, and libraries.
Special Themes	Typically by invitation only, but editor will receive and review field initiated proposals for special sections or issues related to the editorial focus of the journal.
Where Indexed/ Abstracted	Academic Index; Addiction Abstract; Applied Social Sciences Index & Abstracts; Biological Abstracts; Child Development Abstracts; Current Advances in Ecological & Environmental Sciences; Current Contents; Current Index to Journals in Education; Ergonomics Abstracts; Index Medicus; Management Contents; PsycINFO; Social Sciences Citation Index; Social Sciences Index.
Year Established	1989.
Circulation	2,500.
Frequency	Quarterly.
Months Issued	March, June, September, and December.
No. of Articles per Issue	16.

SUBMISSIONS

Postal Mailing Address	Refer to Instructions to Authors page in each issue, or at www.apa.org/journals/pas/
Method for Submission	Electronic form via website.
Number of Copies	None.
Disk Submission	Disks will be accepted if you are unable to use the journal's submission portal.
Online or E-mail Submission Allowed or Required	Submit all manuscripts via our Web portal, at www.apa.org/journals/pas/.

FORMAT OF MANUSCRIPT

Cover Sheet	Refer to Instructions to Authors page in each issue, or at www.apa.org/journals/pas/.
Abstract	All manuscripts must include an abstract with a maximum of 180 words.
Key Words	After the abstract, supply up to 5 keywords or brief phrases.
Length	In general, manuscripts should be no longer than 35 pages.
Margins	1 inch.
Spacing	Double-spaced.

STYLE

Name of Guide	*Publication Manual of the American Psychological Association.*
Subheadings	See style guide or refer to Instructions to Authors page at www.apa.org/journals/pas/.
References	See style guide or refer to Instructions to Authors page at www.apa.org/journals/pas/.
Footnotes	See style guide or refer to Instructions to Authors page at www.apa.org/journals/pas/.
Tables or Figures	See style guide or refer to Instructions to Authors page at www.apa.org/journals/pas/.

REVIEW PROCESS

Type of Review	Masked peer reviewed.
Queries	No query letters.
Acknowledgment	Editorial office acknowledges receipt of manuscript by e-mail.
Review Time	Approximately 60–90 days.
Revisions	Editor will notify author if revision is desired (most manuscripts are initially rejected; most published manuscripts have gone through 1 or 2 revisions).
Acceptance Rate	Approximately 15%–20%.

Return of Manuscript	Not applicable, as hard copies of manuscripts are not submitted.
Lag Time to Print	Approximately 7 months.

CHARGES TO AUTHOR

Author Alterations	If exceeds 15% of original.
Page Charges	None, except for color figures.
Processing	None.

REPRINT, SUBSCRIPTION, AND CONTACT INFORMATION

Reprint Policy	Authors may purchase reprints of their articles (order form accompanies proofs).
Book Reviews	None.
Subscriptions	Subscriptions Department, American Psychological Association, 750 First Street NE, Washington, DC 20002-4242 or online at www.apa.org/journals/subscriptions.html. Yearly APA member rates are $55 domestic, $75 international surface, and $86 international airmail. Rates for APA student affiliates are $45 domestic, $65 international surface, and $77 international airmail. Nonmember individual rates are $149 domestic, $174 international surface, and $184 international airmail. Institutional rates are $390 domestic, $432 international surface, and $445 international airmail.
Affiliation	Published by the American Psychological Association.
E-Mail Address	psychassessjournal@gmail.com
Website	www.apa.org/journals/pas/

PSYCHOLOGY AND AGING

Current Title	*Psychology and Aging*
Previous Title	N/A.
Editorial Focus	Although the emphasis is on original research investigations, occasional theoretical analyses of research issues, practical clinical problems, or policy may appear, as well as critical reviews of a content area in adult development and aging. Clinical case studies that have theoretical significance are also appropriate. Brief reports are acceptable with the author's agreement not to submit a full report to another journal.
Audience	Researchers in the disciplines, faculty, and libraries.
Special Themes	Not specified.
Where Indexed/ Abstracted	Applied Social Science Index & Abstracts; Biological Abstracts; Current Contents; EMBASE/ Excerpta Medica; PsycINFO; Social Sciences Citation Index; Social Sciences Index; Social Work Research & Abstract.
Year Established	1986.
Circulation	3,400+.
Frequency	Quarterly.
Months Issued	March, June, September, December.
No. of Articles per Issue	Approximately 6.

SUBMISSIONS

Postal Mailing Address	Fredda Blanchard-Fields, PhD, School of Psychology, Georgia Institute of Technology, Atlanta, GA 30332-0170.
Method for Submission	http://www.jbo.com/jbo3/submissions/dsp_jbo.cfm?journal_code=pag2
Number of Copies	Keep a copy for your records.
Disk Submission	Not specified.
Online or E-mail Submission Allowed or Required	Submission portal only.

FORMAT OF MANUSCRIPT

Cover Sheet	See website instructions for authors.
Abstract	All manuscripts must include an abstract containing a maximum of 250 words typed on a separate page. After the abstract, please supply up to 5 keywords or brief phrases.
Key Words	Up to 5 key words after abstract.
Length	Maximum of 8,000 words/27 pages not including references or tables, etc.
Margins	1 inch.
Spacing	Double-spaced.

STYLE

Name of Guide	*Publication Manual of the American Psychological Association.*
Subheadings	See style guide.
References	See style guide.
Footnotes	See style guide.
Tables or Figures	See style guide. List references in alphabetical order. Each listed reference should be cited in text, and each text citation should be listed in the references section.

REVIEW PROCESS

Type of Review	Masked reviews are optional, and authors who wish masked reviews must specifically request them at submission. Authors requesting masked review should make every effort to see that the manuscript itself contains no clues to their identities. Authors' names, affiliations, and contact information should be included only in the cover letter.
Queries	No query letters.
Acknowledgment	Not specified.
Review Time	Approximately 2–3 months.
Revisions	Editor will notify author if revision is desired (most manuscripts are initially rejected: most published manuscripts have gone through 1 or 2 revisions).
Acceptance Rate	Approximately 34%.

Return of Manuscript	Not usually returned.
Lag Time to Print	Approximately 10 months.

CHARGES TO AUTHOR

Author Alterations	Not specified.
Page Charges	Original color figures can be printed in color at the editor's and publisher's discretion provided the author agrees to pay: $255 for 1 figure, $425 for 2 figures, $575 for 3 figures, $675 for 4 figures, $55 for each additional figure.
Processing	Not specified.

REPRINT, SUBSCRIPTION, AND CONTACT INFORMATION

Reprint Policy	Not specified.
Book Reviews	None
Subscriptions	http://memforms.apa.org/apa/cli/subs/onepub.cfm?publcode=pag.
Affiliation	American Psychological Association.
E-Mail Address	See website.
Website	http://www.apa.org/journals/pag/description.html

PSYCHOTHERAPY THEORY, RESEARCH, PRACTICE AND TRAINING

Current Title	*Psychotherapy Theory, Research, Practice and Training*
Previous Title	N/A.
Editorial Focus	We strive to foster interactions among training, practice, theory, and research because all are essential to psychotherapy
Audience	This journal is an invaluable resource for practicing clinical and counseling psychologists, social workers, and mental health professionals.
`Special Themes	Not specified.
Where Indexed/ Abstracted	Biological Abstracts; Current Contents; PsycINFO; Social Sciences Citation Index.
Year Established	Not specified.
Circulation	Not specified.
Frequency	Quarterly.
Months Issued	March, June, September, December.
No. of Articles per Issue	Approximately 6.

SUBMISSIONS

Postal Mailing Address	Charles J. Gelso, Editor, Department of Psychology, Biology-Psychology Building, University of Maryland, College Park, MD 20742-4411.
Method for Submission	Electronic via portal; also 1 copy to address above http://www.jbo.com/jbo3/submissions/dsp_jbo.cfm?journal_code=pst.
Number of Copies	See above.
Disk Submission	No.
Online or E-mail Submission Allowed or Required	Online portal.

FORMAT OF MANUSCRIPT

Cover Sheet	Not specified.
Abstract	All manuscripts must include an abstract containing a maximum of 250 words typed on a separate page.
Key Words	After the abstract, please supply up to 5 keywords or brief phrases.
Length	Not specified.
Margins	1 inch.
Spacing	Double-spaced.

STYLE

Name of Guide	*Publication Manual of the American Psychological Association.*
Subheadings	See style guide.
References	See style guide. List references in alphabetical order. Each listed reference should be cited in text, and each text citation should be listed in the References section.
Footnotes	See style guide.
Tables or Figures	Graphics files are welcome if supplied as TIFF, EPS, or PowerPoint files. The minimum line weight for line art is 0.5 point for optimal printing. When possible, please place symbol legends below the figure instead of to the side.

REVIEW PROCESS

Type of Review	Masked at author's request.
Queries	Not specified.
Acknowledgment	Not specified.
Review Time	Not specified.
Revisions	Not specified.
Acceptance Rate	Not specified.
Return of Manuscript	Not specified.
Lag Time to Print	Not specified.

CHARGES TO AUTHOR

Author Alterations   Authors of accepted papers must obtain and provide to the editor on final acceptance all necessary permissions to reproduce in print and electronic form any copyrighted work, including, for example, test materials (or portions thereof) and photographs of people.

Page Charges   Original color figures can be printed in color at the editor's and publisher's discretion provided the author agrees to pay: $255 for 1 figure, $425 for 2 figures, $575 for 3 figures, $675 for 4 figures, $55 for each additional figure.

Processing   Not specified.

REPRINT, SUBSCRIPTION, AND CONTACT INFORMATION

Reprint Policy   Not specified.

Book Reviews   No.

Subscriptions   http://memforms.apa.org/apa/cli/subs/onepub.cfm?publcode=pag.

Affiliation   American Psychological Association/Division of Psychotherapy Division 29.

E-Mail Address   gelso@psyc.umd.edu

Website   http://www.apa.org/journals/pst/

QUALITATIVE SOCIAL WORK: RESEARCH AND PRACTICE

Current Title	*Qualitative Social Work: Research and Practice*
Previous Title	N/A.
Editorial Focus	*Qualitative Social Work: Research and Practice* provides a forum for those interested in qualitative research and evaluation and in qualitative approaches to practice. The journal facilitates interactive dialogue and integration between those interested in qualitative research and methodology and those involved in the world of practice. It reflects the fact that these worlds are increasingly international and interdisciplinary in nature. The journal is a forum for rigorous dialogue that promotes qualitatively informed professional practice and inquiry.
	In addition to articles on qualitative research, evaluation and practice, the journal promotes exchange and conversation on the role of critical perspectives within social work, the nature of reflective inquiry and practice, emerging applications of critical realism in social work, and the potential of social constructionist and narrative approaches to research and practice. The basic assumptions of all forms of research and of practice are being challenged. We invite journal contributors to engage that challenge and to do so in the primary contexts of social work and the evaluation of practice. Practitioners and those articulating international and interdisciplinary perspectives are particularly encouraged to submit articles and commentary.
Audience	Social work practitioners, social work educators, social work Masters & Doctoral students.
Special Themes	Generally one special themed issue per year.
Where Indexed/ Abstracted	Academic Search Premier; Caredata Abstracts – Online; CD-ROM – International Bibliography of Book Reviews of Scholarly Literature on the Humanities and Social Sciences; CD-ROM International Bibliography of Periodical Literature on the Humanities and Social Sciences; CINAHL: Cumulative Index to Nursing and Allied Health Literature; Criminal Justice Abstracts; Family Index; IBZ: International Bibliography of Periodical Literature; International Bibliography of Book Reviews of Scholarly Literature on the Humanities and Social Sciences; International Bibliography of Book Reviews of Scholarly Literature on the Humanities and Social; International Bibliography of Periodical Literature on the Humanities and Social Sciences; Journal of Social Work Practice; PsycINFO; Social Services Abstracts; Social Work Abstracts; SocINFO.
Year Established	2002
Circulation	1,900
Frequency	Quarterly.
Months Issued	March, June, September, and December.
No. of Articles per Issue	6

SUBMISSIONS

Postal Mailing Address	Samantha McDermott, Journal Administrator, Department of Social Policy and Social Work, Seebohm Rowntree Building, University of York, Heslington, York, YO10 5DD, United Kingdom.
Method for Submission	Electronic form via website. Website for submissions: Manuscript Central - http://mc.manuscriptcentral.com/qsw
Number of Copies	1.
Disk Submission	No.
Online or E-mail Submission Allowed or Required	Online required

FORMAT OF MANUSCRIPT

Cover Sheet	Yes.
Abstract	Yes; approximately 150 words.
Key Words	Yes; 4–5 key words.
Length	7,000 Words for main articles; 2,750–4,000 words for New Voices; 1,000–1,500 words for Response and Commentary; 2,750–4,000 words for Practice and Teaching of Qualitative Social Work; 1,200–2,500 words for Technical Applications.
Margins	Normal.
Spacing	Double-spaced.

STYLE

Name of Guide The Harvard referencing system is the basic style used by the journal, but we allow discretion, for example in terms of USA or UK English, and prefer first names to be given in full. The style description is specified on the back cover of current issues of *QSW*.

Subheadings Specified on back cover of current issues of *QSW*.

References Specified on back cover of current issues of *QSW*.

Footnotes Specified on back cover of current issues of *QSW*.

Tables or Figures Specified on back cover of current issues of *QSW*.

REVIEW PROCESS

Type of Review Blind review by 2 reviewers from different countries.

Queries Samantha McDermott, Journal Administrator, Department of Social Policy and Social Work, Seebohm Rowntree Building, University of York, Heslington, York, YO10 5DD, United Kingdom. E-mail sm557@york.ac.uk or Ian Shaw, Editor, Department of Social Policy and Social Work, University of York, e-mail: ifs2@york.ac.uk or Roy Ruckdeschel, Editor, School of Social Work, Saint Louis University, St. Louis, MO 63103, USA, e-mail: ruckdesc@slu.edu or Robyn Munford, Associate Editor, Professor of Social Work, Massey University, Palmerston North, New Zealand, e-mail: R.Munford@massey.ac.nz.

Acknowledgment Received via e-mail.

Review Time Approximately 3–6 months.

Revisions Authors who are asked to undertake minor revisions of their submission should do so within 6 weeks of receiving the feedback. Those who are asked to undertake major revisions will be asked to do so within 4 months.

Acceptance Rate Approximately 42%.

Return of Manuscript No.

Lag Time to Print Approximately 9–12 months, but will lessen when the journal initiates OnlineFirst in the near future. This will permit *QSW* to post articles on the Sage Website as soon as they are accepted. This will constitute a form of pending advance access and will mean advance access within 6 months.

CHARGES TO AUTHOR

Author Alterations No charge.

Page Charges No charge.

Processing No charge.

REPRINT, SUBSCRIPTION, AND CONTACT INFORMATION

Reprint Policy No charge.

Book Reviews There is a Reviews Editor: Karen Staller, University of Michigan, e-mail: kstaller@umich.edu.

Subscriptions Institutional subscription, Combined (print & e-access): $679; Institutional subscription, e-access: $611; Institutional subscription, print only: $665; Individual subscription, print only: $83.

Affiliation Sage Publications, Sage Publications Ltd, 1 Oliver's Yard, 55 City Road, London EC1Y 1SP, UK.

E-Mail Address Contact: Louise Skelding <Louise.Skelding@sagepub.co.uk>.

Website http://qsw.sagepub.com/

REFLECTIONS: NARRATIVES OF PROFESSIONAL HELPING

Current Title	*Reflections: Narratives of Professional Helping*
Previous Title	N/A.
Editorial Focus	Narrative inquiry of professional practice. Personal accounts that describe and explain the process of helping others and shaping social change over time; portray practice across diverse populations; demonstrate the concept of failure as well as success; have a literary presence; and offer new practice perspectives.
Audience	Professional helpers such as ethicists, policy makers, community organizers, psychotherapists, case and group workers, family and child practitioners, health and mental health care providers, as well as educators, researchers, students, and administrators in the helping and academic professions.
Special Themes	Narratives about practice: diversity and the range and variety of strategies and systems within the helping professions; justice and ethics. Narratives about the helping process, research, and teaching. Interviews and oral histories.
Where Indexed/ Abstracted	Psychological Abstracts; Social Work Abstracts.
Year Established	1995
Circulation	500
Frequency	Quarterly.
Months Issued	Winter, Spring, Summer, Fall.
No. of Articles per Issue	8–12.

SUBMISSIONS

Postal Mailing Address	*Reflections* – CSULB Department of Social Work, 1250 Bellflower Blvd., Long Beach, CA 90840.
Method for Submission	Surface mail.
Number of Copies	3
Disk Submission	Only upon acceptance.
Online or E-mail Submission Allowed or Required	Surfaced mail preferred.

FORMAT OF MANUSCRIPT

Cover Sheet	Separate sheet that does not go out for review. Put all identifying information on cover sheet only. Be sure to include e-mail and surface mail addresses, phone number, and date submitted.
Abstract	3–5 sentences written in the same language as the narrative.
Key Words	Up to 5 words or phrases (2–3 words maximum) describing the article.
Length	Depends on the temporal sequence of the narrative.
Margins	1 inch on all sides.
Spacing	Double-spaced.

STYLE

Name of Guide	*Publication Manual of the American Psychological Association.*
Subheadings	Use as needed to guide the reader through the article.
References	See style guide.
Footnotes	Footnotes are discouraged. Incorporate content into text.
Tables or Figures	Usually unnecessary.

REVIEW PROCESS

Type of Review	Double-blind, anonymous peer review. 2 reviewers, plus editor.
Queries	Jillian Jimenez, Editor: jjimene7@csulb.edu.
Acknowledgment	Contract for review.
Review Time	Approximately 2–3 months.
Revisions	Supply 3 copies with separate cover sheet replying to reviewers' comments.
Acceptance Rate	Approximately 12%.
Return of Manuscript	Not returned.
Lag Time to Print	Approximately 6–12 months.

CHARGES TO AUTHOR

Author Alterations	Not specified.
Page Charges	Not specified.
Processing	Not specified.

REPRINT, SUBSCRIPTION, AND CONTACT INFORMATION

Reprint Policy	Authors receive 2 complimentary copies of the journal in which their article appears.
Book Reviews	Send query e-mail to Jillian Jimenez, Editor.
Subscriptions	Yearly rate - $40.00 for individuals, $55.00 libraries and institutions. *Reflections* – CSULB Department of Social Work, 1250 Bellflower Blvd., Long Beach, CA 90840. Single copies - $10.00. Outside of US add $15.00.
Affiliation	University Press, California State University Long Beach, Department of Social Work.
E-Mail Address	jjimene7@csulb.edu
Website	http://www.csulb.edu/colleges/chhs/departments/social-work/reflections/

RESEARCH AND PRACTICE IN SOCIAL SCIENCES

Current Title	*Research and Practice in Social Sciences*
Previous Title	N/A.
Editorial Focus	The journal's objective is to give researchers a channel to express their research and practice and involve large number of participants. We provide a venue for such scholars and scholarly works that allow the "subaltern" and "subjugated knowledge(s)" to speak. We sincerely believe that all knowledge is public knowledge, and that everyone should not only have access to knowledge, but also be able to contribute to it.
Audience	Researchers and academics.
Special Themes	Not specified.
Where Indexed/ Abstracted	Not specified.
Year Established	2005.
Circulation	Not specified.
Frequency	Semiannually.
Months Issued	February and August.
No. of Articles per Issue	4–6.

SUBMISSIONS

Postal Mailing Address	Not applicable; submissions should be made by e-mail.
Method for Submission	If you are interested in submitting a paper, please send a copy of your paper via e-mail to researchandpractice@gmail.com along with your name, position, and institutional or organizational affiliation.
Number of Copies	Not specified.
Disk Submission	Not specified.
Online or E-mail Submission Allowed or Required	Not specified.

FORMAT OF MANUSCRIPT

Cover Sheet	The title should be clear and informative and not too long.
Abstract	Include an abstract of less than 150 words.
Key Words	Not specified.
Length	Full-length articles should be between 5,000 and 6,000 words, and small articles or research notes between 2,000 and 2,500 words.
Margins	Standard margins.
Spacing	1.5 inch line spacing with an extra space between paragraphs.

STYLE

Name of Guide	See "Guidelines for Authors" on the website at: http://www.researchandpractice.com/guidelines.php.
Subheadings	See style guide.
References	See style guide.
Footnotes	Convert all footnotes to endnotes so that they appear at the end of the text and before references.
Tables or Figures	Tables and illustrations to be submitted on separate sheets with their location clearly marked in the text.

REVIEW PROCESS

Type of Review	Peer review.
Queries	For further clarification, send an e-mail to researchandpractice@gmail.com and type "inquiry" in the subject field.
Acknowledgment	Not specified.
Review Time	Not specified.
Revisions	Our editorial team will assist authors as needed to improve their texts. The essence of this editorial relationship will be one of utmost respect and cooperation.
Acceptance Rate	Not specified.

Return of Manuscript	Not specified.
Lag Time to Print	Not specified.

CHARGES TO AUTHOR

Author Alterations	Not specified.
Page Charges	Not specified.
Processing	Not specified.

REPRINT, SUBSCRIPTION, AND CONTACT INFORMATION

Reprint Policy	Online journal.
Book Reviews	Reviews of a set of books or films on a particular theme as well data set, theorist, or activist; between 1,000 and 1,500 words.
Subscriptions	Open access journal available through the website.
Affiliation	Not specified.
E-Mail Address	researchandpractice@gmail.com
Website	http://www.researchandpractice.com/index.php

RESEARCH ON SOCIAL WORK PRACTICE

Current Title	*Research on Social Work Practice*
Previous Title	N/A.
Editorial Focus	Empirical research on the outcomes of social work practice; validity studies of measures useful in social work research and practice; systematic reviews and meta-analyses. Only submit articles of the highest quality to this journal, please.
Audience	All social workers and other human service professionals interested in the research base undergirding evidence-based practice.
Special Themes	Occasional special issues appear with various foci.
Where Indexed/ Abstracted	All major indexing and citation services. The journal's 2008 impact factor was .957.
Year Established	1991
Circulation	5,800+
Frequency	6 times a year.
Months Issued	January, March, May, July, September, November.
No. of Articles per Issue	Approximately 10.

SUBMISSIONS

Postal Mailing Address	None. Integrate this content into the text, except for an author's footnote indicating acknowledgements and corresponding information on the title page.
Method for Submission	Electronic form via website.
Number of Copies	Zero. Only electronic submissions are accepted.
Disk Submission	None accepted.
Online or E-mail Submission Allowed or Required	Online submission is required.

FORMAT OF MANUSCRIPT

Cover Sheet	*Publication Manual of the American Psychological Association.*
Abstract	See style guide.
Key Words	5–6 key words.
Length	No page limits on submissions.
Margins	See style guide.
Spacing	See style guide.

STYLE

Name of Guide	*Publication Manual of the American Psychological Association.*
Subheadings	See style guide.
References	See style guide.
Footnotes	None. Integrate this content into the text, except for an author's footnote indicating acknowledgements and corresponding information on the title page.
Tables or Figures	See style guide.

REVIEW PROCESS

Type of Review	Blind.
Queries	These are welcome, and may be directed to the editor at Bthyer@fsu.edu
Acknowledgment	Yes, automatically upon submission.
Review Time	Approximately 2 months or less.
Revisions	Approximately 2 months or less.
Acceptance Rate	Approximately 2 months or less.
Return of Manuscript	N/A.
Lag Time to Print	Approximately less than 12 months.

CHARGES TO AUTHOR

Author Alterations	Minimal charges for minimal changes. Usually no charges are incurred.
Page Charges	Absolutely none.
Processing	Absolutely none.

REPRINT, SUBSCRIPTION, AND CONTACT INFORMATION

Reprint Policy	Authors receive copies of the issue in which their article appears, and they may order reprints via the publisher. They are also provided a PDF of their article.
Book Reviews	These are frequently published and solicited.
Subscriptions	Available via www.sswr.org or http://rsw.sagepub.com/.
Affiliation	Sponsored by the Society for Social Work and Research.
E-Mail Address	Bthyer@fsu.edu
Website	http://rsw.sagepub.com/

RESIDENTIAL TREATMENT FOR CHILDREN AND YOUTH

Current Title	*Residential Treatment for Children and Youth*
Previous Title	N/A.
Editorial Focus	*Residential Treatment for Children and Youth* provides research and case studies to help you plan and assess specialized programs for treatment of substance abuse, dual diagnosis, severe emotional disturbance, and sexual offenders, as well as for children who have suffered maltreatment and abuse.
Audience	Not specified.
Special Themes	Not specified.
Where Indexed/ Abstracted	Child Welfare Information Gateway.
Year Established	1986.
Circulation	750+.
Frequency	Quarterly.
Months Issued	Issues by volume.
No. of Articles per Issue	Approximately 5.

SUBMISSIONS

Postal Mailing Address	John S. Lyons, PhD, Endowed Chair of Child & Youth Mental Health, University of Ottawa, School of Psychology, Children's Hospital of Eastern Ontario, Ottawa, Ontario, Canada.
Method for Submission	Manuscripts should be submitted in triplicate and via e-mail.
Number of Copies	Manuscripts should be submitted in triplicate and via e-mail.
Disk Submission	Authors may submit manuscripts electronically. If submitting a disk, it should be prepared using MS Word or WordPerfect and should be clearly labeled with the authors' names, file name, and software program.
Online or E-mail Submission Allowed or Required	Manuscripts should be submitted in triplicate and via e-mail.

FORMAT OF MANUSCRIPT

Cover Sheet	Not specified.
Abstract	100 words.
Key Words	Below abstract, 3–10 keywords.
Length	Number manuscript pages consecutively throughout the paper with the page number of total (e.g., pg 2 of 7).
Margins	1 inch.
Spacing	Double-spaced.

STYLE

Name of Guide	*Publication Manual of the American Psychological Association.*
Subheadings	As necessary.
References	References, citations, and general style of manuscripts should be prepared in accordance with the *APA Publication Manual.* Cite in the text by author and date (Smith, 1983) and include an alphabetical list at the end of the article.
Footnotes	Footnotes are discouraged.
Tables or Figures	Tables and figures (illustrations) should not be embedded in the text, but should be included as separate sheets or files. A short descriptive title should appear above each table with a clear legend and any footnotes suitably identified below. All units must be included. Figures should be completely labeled, taking into account necessary size reduction. Captions should be typed, double-spaced, on a separate sheet.

REVIEW PROCESS

Type of Review	Peer reviewed.
Queries	jsl329@northwestern.edu or jlyons@uottawa.ca.
Acknowledgment	Yes.
Review Time	Approximately 2 months.
Revisions	As required by editor.

Acceptance Rate	Approximately 85%.
Return of Manuscript	Not returned.
Lag Time to Print	Approximately 9 months.

CHARGES TO AUTHOR

Author Alterations	Page proofs are sent to the designated author using Taylor & Francis' Central Article Tracking System (CATS). They must be carefully checked and returned within 48 hours of receipt.
Page Charges	Color illustrations will be considered for publication; however, the author will be required to bear the full cost involved in color art reproduction. Color art can be purchased for online-only reproduction or for print and online reproduction. Color reprints can only be ordered if print and online reproduction costs are paid. Rates for color art reproduction are: Online-Only Reproduction: $225 for the first page of color; $100 per page for the next 3 pages of color. A maximum charge of $525 applies. Print and Online Reproduction: $900 for the first page of color; $450 per page for the next 3 pages of color. A custom quote will be provided for articles with more than 4 pages of color.
Processing	Not specified.

REPRINT, SUBSCRIPTION, AND CONTACT INFORMATION

Reprint Policy	Reprints of individual articles are available for order at the time authors review page proofs. A discount on reprints is available to authors who order before print publication. Each corresponding author will receive 3 complete issues in which the article publishes and a complimentary PDF. This file is for personal use only and may not be copied and disseminated in any form without prior written permission from Taylor and Francis Group, LLC.
Book Reviews	Yes; edited by Richard A. Epstein.
Subscriptions	See website: http://www.informaworld.com/smpp/title~db=all~content=t792306958~tab=subscribe.
Affiliation	American Association of Children's Residential Centers
E-Mail Address	jsl329@northwestern.edu or jlyons@uottawa.ca
Website	http://www.informaworld.com/smpp/title~content=t792306958~db=all

SCI PSYCHOSOCIAL PROCESS

Current Title	*SCI Psychosocial Process*
Previous Title	N/A.
Editorial Focus	Psychologists and social workers treating people with spinal cord injury.
Audience	Psychologists and social workers.
Special Themes	Psychosocial issues specific to persons with a spinal cord injury.
Where Indexed/ Abstracted	CINAHL; Social Work Abstracts.
Year Established	1987.
Circulation	1,000.
Frequency	Twice a year.
Months Issued	January, June.
No. of Articles per Issue	6–10.

SUBMISSIONS

Postal Mailing Address	E. Jason, Mask, ACSW, Editor, *SCI Psychosocial Process,* Social Work Submission Service (122), Hines VA Hospital, Hines, IL 60141.
Method for Submission	Surface mail, disk, e-mail.
Number of Copies	3 if sent by surface mail.
Disk Submission	One of the 3 methods of submission.
Online or E-mail Submission Allowed or Required	Yes.

FORMAT OF MANUSCRIPT

Cover Sheet	Name, affiliations, and job description.
Abstract	Yes.
Key Words	None.
Length	1,000–5,000 words.
Margins	1.5 inches on all sides.
Spacing	Double-spaced.

STYLE

Name of Guide	*Publication Manual of the American Psychological Association.*
Subheadings	Yes.
References	Yes.
Footnotes	None.
Tables or Figures	Yes.

REVIEW PROCESS

Type of Review	Refereed.
Queries	Yes.
Acknowledgment	Yes.
Review Time	Approximately 3–4 weeks.
Revisions	Yes.
Acceptance Rate	Not specified.
Return of Manuscript	Not returned.
Lag Time to Print	Varies by schedule, but can be very short.

REPRINT, SUBSCRIPTION, AND CONTACT INFORMATION

Reprint Policy	Yes, at author's expense (no markup).
Book Reviews	Yes.
Subscriptions	Free to association members and interested, qualified parties.
Affiliation	American Association of Spinal Cord Injury Psychologists and Social Workers.
E-Mail Address	jason.mask@va.gov
Website	www.aascipsw.org

SCHOOL SOCIAL WORK JOURNAL

Current Title	*School Social Work Journal*
Previous Title	N/A.
Editorial Focus	The focus of the journal is on articles that will assist school social work practitioners in carrying out practice in schools. Original research, integrative and comprehensive reviews, conceptual and practical positions, effective assessment and intervention methodologies, and model service delivery programs are welcome. Implications for school social work practice must be evident.
Audience	School social work practitioners and school social work educators and scholars.
Special Themes	Violence prevention; school-related federal, state and local policies; grief and loss; response to intervention; innovative school-based interventions; child welfare and schools; the role of the school social worker. Topics have included: influences on urban parent involvement, junior high school predictors of high school dropout, facilitating young children's peer relationships, drug traffic intervention through school and community centers, abuse in adolescent dating relationships, boys and media violence, The impact of violence on school achievement and behavior, challenges and service needs of urban children, and the development of a tool for school social work collaboration.
Where Indexed/ Abstracted	British Library Inside, Cambridge Scientific Abstracts, Child Welfare Information Gateway (selected/appropriate articles), Criminal Justice Abstracts (selected/appropriate articles), JournalSeek, Mediafinder, SocINDEX (EBSCO), Ulrich's Periodicals Directory, Zetoc.
Year Established	1972
Circulation	2,200
Frequency	Twice a year
Months Issued	April and September
No. of Articles per Issue	6–7

SUBMISSIONS

Postal Mailing Address	Carol Rippey Massat, Jane Addams College of Social Work, University of Illinois at Chicago, 1040 W. Harrison, M/C 309, Chicago, IL 60607.
Method for Submission	Electronic form via Web.
Number of Copies	1
Disk Submission	Submit via the Web.
Online or E-mail Submission Allowed or Required	Online submission required. Submit by registering with the journal as an author at journals.uic.edu/ SSWJ/information/authors. After registering with the journal as an author, follow the directions to submit online.

FORMAT OF MANUSCRIPT

Cover Sheet	A cover sheet should include the title of the submission and full contact information for all authors, including address, affiliation, phone, e-mail addresses, and fax numbers.
Abstract	A brief abstract (no more than 120 words) should describe the article. On the abstract page, key words should be listed below the abstract.
Key Words	Include key words on the abstract page, for indexing purposes.
Length	15–20 pages.
Margins	1–1.5 inch margins.
Spacing	Double-spaced.

STYLE

Name of Guide	*Publication Manual of the American Psychological Association.*
Subheadings	See style guide.
References	See style guide.
Footnotes	See style guide.
Tables or Figures	See style guide.

REVIEW PROCESS

Type of Review	Blind, peer review by 4 reviewers.
Queries	Submit queries to the editor, Carol Rippey Massat, at cmassat@uic.edu.
Acknowledgment	Manuscript submission will be acknowledged upon receipt.
Review Time	Approximately 9 weeks.

Revisions	If a revise and resubmit decision is made, or a manuscript is accepted with revisions, we ask for revisions to be submitted within 60 days.
Acceptance Rate	Approximately 40%.
Return of Manuscript	Reviewer comments will be sent to the author.
Lag Time to Print	Approximately 6 months to 1 year.

CHARGES TO AUTHOR

Author Alterations	N/A.
Page Charges	N/A.
Processing	N/A.

REPRINT, SUBSCRIPTION, AND CONTACT INFORMATION

Reprint Policy	*School Social Work Journal* is sponsored by the Illinois Association of School Social Workers and is published by Lyceum Books at: Lyceum@LyceumBooks.com, phone (773) 643-1902; fax (773) 643-1903. Reprints can be ordered through Lyceum. Copies of an article may be made for personal or internal use, or for the personal or internal use of specific clients. This consent is given on the condition, however, that the copier pay the stated per-copy fee through the Copyright Clearance Center Inc., 222 Rosewood Drive, Danvers, MA 01923 for copying beyond that permitted by Sections 107 or 108 of the U.S. Copyright Law. This consent does not extend to other kinds of copying, such as copying for general distribution, for advertising or promotional purposes, for creating new collective works, or for resale. Request for special permission or bulk orders should be addressed to *School Social Work Journal,* 341 N. Charlotte Street, Lombard, Illinois 60148.
Book Reviews	Book reviews are solicited by the Book Review Editor, Erin Gleason Leyba, at: erin_leyba@yahoo.com.
Subscriptions	*School Social Work Journal,* 341 N. Charlotte Street, Lombard, Illinois 60148.
Affiliation	Illinois Association of School Social Workers.
E-Mail Address	The editor, Carol Rippey Massat, is available at: cmassat@uic.edu. The managing editor is available at: kopels@illinois.edu. The book review editor, Erin Gleason Leyba, can be reached at: erin_leyba@yahoo.com. Lyceum Books can be reached at: Lyceum@LyceumBooks.com. Illinois Association of School Social Workers can be reached at: iasswck@aol.com.
Website	http://www.iassw.org

SEXUAL ABUSE: A JOURNAL OF RESEARCH AND TREATMENT

Current Title	*Sexual Abuse: A Journal of Research and Treatment*
Previous Title:	
Editorial Focus	*Sexual Abuse: A Journal of Research and Treatment,* the official journal of the Association for the Treatment of Sexual Abusers, provides a forum for the latest original research and scholarly reviews on both clinical and theoretical aspects of sexual abuse. Unlike other publications that present a mix of articles on sexual abuse and human sexuality in general, *Sexual Abuse* is the only one to focus exclusively on this field, thoroughly investigating its etiology, consequences, prevention, treatment, and management strategies.
Audience	Those working in both clinical and academic environments, including psychologists, psychiatrists, social workers, and therapists/counselors, as well as corrections officers and allied professionals in children's services.
Special Themes	Not specified.
Where Indexed/ Abstracted	Criminal Justice Abstracts; Current Abstracts; EBSCOhost; Family Index; MEDLINE; PsycINFO; SCOPUS; Social Services Abstracts; Sociological Abstracts; Swets Information Services.
Year Established	1988
Circulation	Not specified.
Frequency	Quarterly.
Months Issued	March, June, September, December.
No. of Articles per Issue	Approximately 6.

SUBMISSIONS

Postal Mailing Address	N/A
Method for Submission	Articles should be submitted electronically at http://mc.manuscriptcentral.com/sajrt.
Number of Copies	1 copy online.
Disk Submission	Not required.
Online or E-mail Submission Allowed or Required	Online submission required.

FORMAT OF MANUSCRIPT

Cover Sheet	Upon initial submission, the title page should include only the title of the article. An additional title page should be uploaded as a *separate* submission item and should include the title of the article, author's name (no degrees), and author's affiliation. Academic affiliations of all authors should be included.
Abstract	An abstract is to be provided, preferably no more than 250 words.
Key Words	A list of 4–5 key words is to be provided directly below the abstract. Key words should express the precise content of the manuscript, as they are used for indexing purposes.
Length:	
Margins	No less than 1 inch on all sides.
Spacing	Double-spaced.

STYLE

Name of Guide	*Publication Manual of the American Psychological Association.*
Subheadings	Follow style guide.
References	Follow style guide.
Footnotes	Footnotes should be avoided. When their use is absolutely necessary, footnotes should be numbered consecutively using Arabic numerals and should be typed at the bottom of the page to which they refer. Place a line above the footnote, so that it is set off from the text. Use the appropriate superscript numeral for citation in the text.
Tables or Figures	Tables should be numbered (with Roman numerals) and referred to by number in the text. Each table should be typed on a separate page. Center the title above the table, and type explanatory footnotes (indicated by superscript lowercase letters) below the table.

REVIEW PROCESS

Type of Review	Masked peer review.
Queries	Inquiries regarding journal policy, manuscript preparation, and other such general topics should be sent to Managing Editor: Maia Christopher at maia@atsa.com.
Acknowledgment	Through the online system.
Review Time	Not specified.
Revisions	Per editor instruction.
Acceptance Rate	Not specified.
Return of Manuscript	Manuscripts are not returned.
Lag Time to Print	Not specified.

REPRINT, SUBSCRIPTION, AND CONTACT INFORMATION

Reprint Policy	Reprints are available to authors, and order forms with the current price schedule are sent with proofs.
Book Reviews	Contact editor.
Subscriptions	Through the website at: http://sax.sagepub.com/subscriptions/.
Affiliation	Association for the Treatment of Sexual Abuse.
E-Mail Address	maia@atsa.com
Website	http://www.atsa.com/index.html

SMALL GROUP RESEARCH: AN INTERNATIONAL JOURNAL OF THEORY, INVESTIGATION AND APPLICATION

Current Title	*Small Group Research: An International Journal of Theory, Investigation and Application*
Previous Title	*Small Group Behavior.*
Editorial Focus	The only interdisciplinary, international journal focused on research and practice of small group behavior. *Small Group Research* offers research and comprehensive theory relating to all types of groups, such as: intact work groups, family groups, mixed-profession groups, self-help groups, groups in educational settings, social work groups, teams, experimental and laboratory groups, therapy and treatment groups, conflict management, social perception, team productivity, team building, group decision making, mediation, group cohesiveness, status generalization, group development, network analysis.
Audience	Researchers, practitioners, students.
Special Themes	*Small Group Research* occasionally supplements its broad coverage with in-depth studies of critical topics. These special issues are guest-edited by experts in the field, providing a balanced analysis of the subject at hand.
Where Indexed/ Abstracted	Academic Search–EBSCO; Applied Social Sciences Index & Abstracts (ASSIA); Business Source–EBSCO; ComAbstracts; ComIndex; Corporate ResourceNET–EBSCO; Current Citations Express; Current Contents: Social & Behavioral Sciences; EServer.org. FRANCIS Database; Human Resources Abstracts; MasterFILE–EBSCO; NISC; Pascal; Personnel Management Abstracts; Psychological Abstracts/PsycINFO; PsycLIT; Research into Higher Education Abstracts; SCOPUS; Social Sciences Citation Index (Web of Science); Social SciSearch; Social Services Abstracts; Social Work Abstracts; Sociological Abstracts; Standard Periodical Directory (SPD); TOPICsearch–EBSCO.
Year Established	1960
Circulation	Approximately 3,000 worldwide.
Frequency	6 times per year.
Months Issued	February, April, June, August, October, December.
No. of Articles per Issue	5–6.

SUBMISSIONS

Postal Mailing Address	Electronic submission only.
Method for Submission	Electronic form via Web: http://www.sagepub.com/journalsProdDesc.nav?prodId=Journal200891.
Number of Copies	See submission instructions at: http://www.sagepub.com/journalsProdDesc.nav?prodId=Journal200891.
Disk Submission	See submission instructions at: http://www.sagepub.com/journalsProdDesc.nav?prodId=Journal200891.
Online or E-mail Submission Allowed or Required	Electronic submission only.

FORMAT OF MANUSCRIPT

Cover Sheet	See submission instructions at: http://www.sagepub.com/journalsProdDesc.nav?prodId=Journal200891.
Abstract	See submission instructions at website above.
Key Words	See submission instructions at website above.
Length	See submission instructions at website above.
Margins	See submission instructions at website above.
Spacing	See submission instructions at website above.

STYLE

Name of Guide	*Publication Manual of the American Psychological Association.*
Subheadings	See style guide (required).
References	See style guide (required).
Footnotes	See style guide (required).
Tables or Figures	See style guide (required).

REVIEW PROCESS

Type of Review	Anonymous peer review.
Queries	Queries accepted.
Acknowledgment	Automatic through online submission and review process.
Review Time	Approximately 4 months.
Revisions	Depends on review decision.
Acceptance Rate	Approximately 25%.
Return of Manuscript	No.
Lag Time to Print	Approximately 6 months once decision is made.

REPRINT, SUBSCRIPTION, AND CONTACT INFORMATION

Reprint Policy	Please see website.
Book Reviews	Yes.
Subscriptions	Please see website.
Affiliation	Sage Publications.
E-Mail Address	ambrower@wisc.edu, jkeyton@ncsu.edu
Website	http://www.sagepub.com/journalsProdDesc.nav?prodId=Journal200891

SMITH COLLEGE STUDIES IN SOCIAL WORK

Current Title	*Smith College Studies in Social Work*
Previous Title	N/A.
Editorial Focus	This refereed journal addresses issues of mental health, therapeutic process, trauma and recovery, psychopathology, racial and cultural diversity, culturally responsive clinical practice, intersubjectivity, the influence of postmodern theory on clinical practice, community-based practice, and clinical services for specific populations of psychologically and socially vulnerable clients.
Audience	Clinical social work theories, practitioners, researchers, and educators, as well as researchers and practitioners from other mental health disciplines.
Special Themes	The application of theory to practice; children and families; traumatized clients; in-depth treatment approaches; community-based interventions; treatment with individuals, couples, families, and groups; and case reports focusing on process issues. Special issues recently published include: "AIDS and Clinical Practice" and "The Human and Corporate Faces of Managed Behavioral Health Care." Manuscripts are solicited through advertising flyers at conferences, mailing lists, conference presentations, and recommendations from members of the editorial board.
Where Indexed/ Abstracted	Social Work Abstracts.
Year Established	1930.
Circulation	1,270.
Frequency	4 times per year.
Months Issued	Issues vary within volume.
No. of Articles per Issue	Approximately 6.

SUBMISSIONS

Postal Mailing Address	Kathryn Basham, PhD, LICSW, Associate Professor, Smith College School for Social Work, Lilly Hall, Northampton, MA 01063.
Method for Submission	Authors are strongly encouraged to submit manuscripts electronically. kbasham@e-mail.smith.edu.
Number of Copies	3.
Disk Submission	If submitting a disk, it should be prepared using MS Word or WordPerfect and should be clearly labeled with the authors' names, file name, and software program.
Online or E-mail Submission Allowed or Required	Not specified.

FORMAT OF MANUSCRIPT

Cover Sheet	Each manuscript must be accompanied by a statement that it has not been published elsewhere and that it has not been submitted simultaneously for publication elsewhere.
Abstract	100 words.
Key Words	Up to 8 key words or key phrases. (2–3-word maximum) describing central theme of manuscript.
Length	15–25 pages.
Margins	1 inch.
Spacing	Double-spaced.

STYLE

Name of Guide	*Publication Manual of the American Psychological Association.*
Subheadings	See style guide.
References	References, citations, and general style of manuscripts should be prepared in accordance with the *APA Publication Manual.* Cite in the text by author and date (Smith, 1983) and include an alphabetical list at the end of the article.
Footnotes	See style guide.
Tables or Figures	Tables and figures (illustrations) should not be embedded in the text, but should be included as separate sheets or files. A short descriptive title should appear above each table with a clear legend and any footnotes suitably identified below. All units must be included. Figures should be completely labeled, taking into account necessary size reduction. Captions should be typed, double-spaced, on a separate sheet.

REVIEW PROCESS

Type of Review	Peer reviewed.
Queries	Address to editor.
Acknowledgment	Letter sent upon receipt of manuscript.
Review Time	3–4 months.
Revisions	Authors are encouraged to resubmit revised manuscripts. If revisions are major, manuscript is reviewed again by the original reviewers whenever possible. If minor, revisions are handled by the editor. Editor's revisions are sent to the authors for approval.
Acceptance Rate	Approximately 20%.
Return of Manuscript	Not returned. Authors should keep a copy.
Lag Time to Print	Approximately 3–6 months.

CHARGES TO AUTHOR

Author Alterations	Page proofs are sent to the designated author using Taylor & Francis' Central Article Tracking System. They must be carefully checked and returned within 48 hours of receipt.
Page Charges	Not specified.
Processing	Not specified.

REPRINT, SUBSCRIPTION, AND CONTACT INFORMATION

Reprint Policy	Reprints of individual articles are available for order at the time authors review page proofs. A discount on reprints is available to authors who order before print publication. Each corresponding author will receive 3 complete issues in which the article publishes and a complimentary PDF. This file is for personal use only and may not be copied and disseminated in any form without prior written permission from Taylor and Francis Group, LLC
Book Reviews	Book Review Editor: Faye Mishna, PhD, Associate Professor, Margaret & Wallace McCain Chair in Child and Family, University of Toronto School of Social Work, Toronto, Ontario, Canada
Subscriptions	Need to register for subscription info (true for all Informaworld journals)
Affiliation	Smith College School for Social Work
E-Mail Address	kbasham@e-mail.smith.edu
Website	http://www.informaworld.com/smpp/title~db=all~content=t792306960

SOCIAL DEVELOPMENT ISSUES

Current Title	*Social Development Issues.*
Previous Title	N/A.
Editorial Focus	*SDI* is an international refereed journal that serves as a forum for achieving links between multiple disciplines, nations, and cultures. Our purpose is to promote the consideration of issues that affect social justices as well as the development and well-being of individuals and their communities. *SDI* is committed to the advancement of social, cultural, political, and economic theory, policy, and practice within a global context.
Audience	Social workers, academics, and policymakers.
Special Themes	Developmental perspectives and research on international social justices might include—but are not limited to—the following topics: lifespan, gender, and racial issues; the impact of policies, practices, and service delivery systems on urban and rural communities; comparative health/mental health; poverty; income maintenance; and movements such as global feminism, human rights, and peace.
Where Indexed/ Abstracted	Applied Social Sciences Index & Abstracts; Family Index; International Bibliography of the Social Sciences; PAIS International in Print (Annual) (Public Affairs Information Service); Social Work Abstracts; Sociological Abstracts.
Year Established	1978
Circulation	600
Frequency	3 times per year.
Months Issued	March, August, and December.
No. of Articles per Issue	6–8.

SUBMISSIONS

Postal Mailing Address	Joe C. B. Leung, Editor, *Social Development Issues,* Department of Social Work and Social Administration, University of Hong Kong, Pokfulam Road, Hong Kong, China. All submission queries should be directed to: sdi@socwork.hku.hk.
Method for Submission	E-mail.
Number of Copies	1
Disk Submission	Not required.
Online or E-mail Submission Allowed or Required	Yes.

FORMAT OF MANUSCRIPT

Cover Sheet	Separate sheet, which does not go out for review. Full title; author names, degrees, and professional titles; designation of 1 author as corresponding author with full address, phone number, e-mail address, and fax number; date of submission.
Abstract	60 words or less.
Key Words	Required.
Length	Under 5,000 words including tables and references.
Margins	1 inch on all sides.
Spacing	Double-spaced for all copy, except title page.

STYLE

Name of Guide	*Publication Manual of the American Psychological Association.*
Subheadings	Use as needed to guide reader through the article. No more than 2 levels.
References	Author–date citation style; see style guide.
Footnotes	No footnotes preferred; incorporate into text.
Tables or Figures	Place each table or figure on a separate unnumbered page at the end of the manuscript.

REVIEW PROCESS

Type of Review	2 reviewers read the manuscript in an anonymous review.
Queries	Authors are encouraged to read the journal to determine whether their subject matter would be appropriate.
Acknowledgment	Authors receive e-mail message on receipt of manuscript.
Review Time	Approximately 3–4 months.

Revisions	Submit revised manuscript through e-mail.
Acceptance Rate	Approximately 55%.
Return of Manuscript	Not returned; author should retain copies.
Lag Time to Print	Approximately 9–12 months.

REPRINT, SUBSCRIPTION, AND CONTACT INFORMATION

Reprint Policy	No reprints.
Book Reviews	Send books for review to the editor.
Subscriptions	To subscribe to the journal and join the Consortium, complete the form below and give it to a journal representative, or mail it to Lyceum Books, Inc., Subscription Office, 341 N. Charlotte Street, Lombard, IL 60148-0237 USA.
Affiliation	*SDI* is the official journal of The International Consortium for Social Development (ICSD). ICSD is an organization of practitioners, scholars and students in the human services. The organization seeks to develop conceptual frameworks and effective intervention strategies geared to influencing local, national, and international systems. It is committed to creating peaceful solutions to the problems of survival at the local, national, and global levels.
E-Mail Address	lyceumsubscribe@comcast.net
Website	http://sdi.sw.hku.hk

SOCIAL SERVICE REVIEW

Current Title	*Social Service Review*
Previous Title	N/A.
Editorial Focus	Founded in 1927, *Social Service Review* is devoted to the publication of thought-provoking, original research on social welfare policy, organization, and practice. Articles in the *Review* analyze issues from the points of view of various disciplines, theories, and methodological traditions; view critical problems in context; and carefully consider long-range solutions. The *Review* features balanced, scholarly contributions from social work and social welfare scholars, as well as from members of the various allied disciplines engaged in research on human behavior, social systems, history, public policy, and social services. The journal welcomes contributions on a wide range of topics, such as child welfare, poverty, homelessness, community intervention, race and ethnicity, clinical practice, and mental health. The *Review* also features discerning essays and substantive, critical book reviews.
Audience	The journal is read by scholars, policy makers, policy analysts, practitioners, and students.
Special Themes	Not specified.
Where Indexed/ Abstracted	ABC-CLIO; Academic Search Alumni Edition; Academic Search Complete; Academic Search Elite; Academic Search Premier; Applied Social Sciences Index & Abstracts; AgeLine; America: History and Life; Book Review Index; Business Source Alumni Edition; Business Source Complete; Business Source Corporate; Business Source Premier; Business Source Select; Criminal Justice Abstracts; CS Worldwide Political Science Abstracts; Current Abstracts; Current Contents; Econlit; Educational Research Abstracts Online; Executive Daily Brief; International Bibliography of the Social Sciences; Multicultural Education Abstracts; PAIS International in Print; Periodicals Index Online; PsycINFO; Social Sciences Citation Index; Social Sciences Index; Social Services Abstracts; Social Work Abstracts; Sociological Abstracts; SocINDEX; Special Educational Needs Abstracts; Studies on Women and Gender Abstracts.
Year Established	1927
Circulation	Approximately 1,900.
Frequency	Quarterly.
Months Issued	March, June, September, December.
No. of Articles per Issue	5–7.

SUBMISSIONS

Postal Mailing Address	ssr@uchicago.edu; Editor, Social Service Review, 969 East 60th Street, Chicago, IL 60637.
Method for Submission	Surface mail, disk, and e-mail.
Number of Copies	5 if printed copies are submitted.
Disk Submission	Not required but accepted.
Online or E-mail Submission Allowed or Required	E-mail submissions encouraged; submissions may be formatted in Microsoft Word or Corel WordPerfect. For additional instructions, please see http://www.journals.uchicago.edu/page/ssr/instruct.html.

FORMAT OF MANUSCRIPT

Cover Sheet	Title, authors' names, authors' affiliations, acknowledgment note.
Abstract	Fewer than 150 words.
Key Words	Requested upon acceptance.
Length	The *Review* does not impose page limits, but editorial efforts to conserve space are directly related to manuscript length and to the conciseness of the argument presented.
Margins	1 inch.
Spacing	Double-spaced.

STYLE

Name of Guide	*Chicago Manual of Style (15th ed.);* the *Review* considers submissions in any style but requires accepted articles to meet the journal's style.
Subheadings	Use as needed.
References	Author–date citation and reference list; the journal considers submissions in any style and will assist authors in reformatting references if the submission is accepted.
Footnotes	Notes should be used sparingly and only for substantive comments. The journal uses endnotes but submissions may employ footnotes or endnotes.

Tables or Figures	Use judiciously. Tables and figures should present information as clearly and concisely as possible. They may be submitted in Microsoft Word, Corel WordPerfect, or Microsoft Excel.

REVIEW PROCESS

Type of Review	Double-blind peer reviewed.
Queries	Accepted.
Acknowledgment	Via e-mail.
Review Time	Approximately 2–6 months (average is 2.5).
Revisions	Accepted only upon request of the editor.
Acceptance Rate	Not specified.
Return of Manuscript	No.
Lag Time to Print	Approximately 6 months.

CHARGES TO AUTHOR

Author Alterations	No charge for minor changes made to proofs.
Page Charges	No charge.
Processing	No charge.

REPRINT, SUBSCRIPTION, AND CONTACT INFORMATION

Reprint Policy	Lead author receives 10 free copies or 1-year subscription. Reprints are available for a fee.
Book Reviews	By invitation only. Send books for review to Editor, *Social Service Review,* 969 E. 60th Street, Chicago, IL 60637.
Subscriptions	*Social Service Review,* University of Chicago Press, Journals Division, P.O. Box 37005, Chicago, IL 60637. E-mail: subscriptions@press.uchicago.edu. Phone: (773) 753-3347 or toll-free in U.S. and Canada (877) 705-1878.
	For current subscription rates, see http://www.journals.uchicago.edu/page/subs.html.
Affiliation	University of Chicago, School of Social Service Administration; University of Chicago Press.
E-Mail Address	SSR@uchicago.edu
Website	http://www.journals.uchicago.edu/toc/ssr/current

SOCIAL WORK

Current Title	*Social Work*
Previous Title	N/A.
Editorial Focus	New insights into established social work practices, evaluation of new techniques and research, examination of current social problems, critical analyses of problems in the profession.
Audience	Social work practitioners, researchers, faculty, students, libraries, organizations, others in the human services and social welfare.
Special Themes	Multiculturalism, research, public policy, partnership/collaboration, social justice and human rights, ethics.
Where Indexed/ Abstracted	Abstracts in Anthropology; Abstracts in Social Gerontology; Academic Abstracts; Age Line; Applied Social Sciences Index and Abstracts; Caredata; Cumulative Index to Nursing and Allied Health Literature; Current Contents: Social & Behavioral Sciences; ERIC/Counseling and Student Services Clearinghouse; Exceptional Child Resources; Psychological Abstracts/PsycINFO; PsychLIT; Public Affairs Information Service; Quality Review Bulletin; Sage Family Studies Abstracts; Social Planning/Policy & Development Abstracts; Social Science Index/Social Science Abstracts; Social Work Abstracts; Sociological Abstracts.
Year Established	1956
Circulation	163,000
Frequency	Bimonthly.
Months Issued	January, March, May, July, September, November.
No. of Articles per Issue	10–14.

SUBMISSIONS

Postal Mailing Address	Editor, *Social Work,* NASW Press, 750 First Street NE, Suite 700, Washington, DC 20002-4241.
Method for Submission	Postal mail.
Number of Copies	5
Disk Submission	Authors of accepted manuscripts are asked to submit a disk, preferably in Microsoft Word
Online or E-mail Submission Allowed or Required	Forthcoming.

FORMAT OF MANUSCRIPT

Cover Sheet	Separate sheet, which does not go out for review. Full title; author names, degrees, and professional titles; designation of 1 author as corresponding author with full address, phone numbers, e-mail address, and fax number; date of submission.
Abstract	150-word informative abstracts.
Key Words	Up to 5 words or key phrases (2–3-word maximum) describing the article.
Length	14–16 pages including references and tables; manuscripts exceeding 25 pages will be returned.
Margins	1 inch on all sides.
Spacing	Double-spaced for all copy, except title page.

STYLE

Name of Guide	*Writing for the NASWPress: Information for Authors* (free) and *Professional Writing for the Human Services* (for purchase from the NASW Press). Contact NASW Press.
Subheadings	Use as needed to guide readers through the article. No more than 3 levels.
References	Author–date citation style; see style guides.
Footnotes	No footnotes preferred; incorporate into text.
Tables or Figures	Type tables double-spaced. Submit camera-ready art (300 dpi or better) for all figures. Place each table or figure on a separate, numbered page at the end of the manuscript.

REVIEW PROCESS

Type of Review	"Double-blind" anonymous peer review. 3 reviewers, plus the editor-in-chief, all read the manuscript in an anonymous review.
Queries	Query letters are discouraged; authors are encouraged to read the journal and *Writing for the NASW Press* to determine whether their subject matter would be appropriate.
Acknowledgment	The NASW Press sends a postcard on receipt of manuscript.
Review Time	3–4 months.

Revisions	Submit 5 copies with a separate cover sheet (not identifying the author) describing the changes made in the manuscript and replying to the reviewers' comments. In general, the original reviewers and editor-in-chief read revisions.
Acceptance Rate	Approximately 15%.
Return of Manuscript	Not returned, author should retain copies.
Lag Time to Print	Approximately 6 months to 1 year.

CHARGES TO AUTHOR

Author Alterations	No.
Page Charges	No.
Processing	No.

REPRINT, SUBSCRIPTION, AND CONTACT INFORMATION

Reprint Policy	All authors receive 5 complimentary copies of the issue in which the article appears. Authors receive reprint order forms to purchase additional reprinted copies.
Book Reviews	By invitation only. Send books for review to: Book Review Editor, *Social Work*, NASW Press, 750 First Street NE, Suite 700, Washington, D.C. 20002-4241.
Subscriptions	*Social Work*, P.O. Box 431, Annapolis JCT, MD 20701. 1996-97 1-year prices: NASW members, free with membership; individual members, $71; libraries/institutions, $98.
Affiliation	The NASW Press is a division of the National Association of Social Workers.
E-Mail Address	press@naswdc.org
Website	press@naswdc.org

SOCIAL WORK AND CHRISTIANITY: AN INTERNATIONAL JOURNAL

Current Title	*Social Work and Christianity: An International Journal*
Previous Title	N/A.
Editorial Focus	Articles dealing with the issues of the integration of Christian faith and professional practice and other professional concerns that have relevance to Christianity.
Audience	Christians in social work and others who want to understand and interact with a Christian perspective on social work: practitioners, administrators, researchers, educators, students, and libraries.
Special Themes	Values and ethics, approaching issues of diversity with competence and integrity, religion and spirituality in social work practice, practice issues, and research on related topics.
Where Indexed/ Abstracted	Christian Periodical Index; EBSCO; Guide to Social Science and Religion in Periodical Literature; ProQuest; PsycINFO; Social Services Abstracts; Social Work Abstracts; Sociological Abstracts.
Year Established	1974
Circulation	Approximately 1850.
Frequency	Quarterly.
Months Issued	Spring (April); summer (June); fall (September); winter (December).
No. of Articles per Issue	3–5.

SUBMISSIONS

Postal Mailing Address	NACSW, P.O. Box 121, Botsford, CT 06404.
Method for Submission	E-mail.
Number of Copies	1
Disk Submission	No.
Online or E-mail Submission Allowed or Required	Required; E-mail to: david@sherwoodstreet.com.

FORMAT OF MANUSCRIPT

Cover Sheet	Authors name and address, article title, and abstract.
Abstract	150 words or less.
Key Words	Not specified.
Length	10–20 pages.
Margins	Not specified.
Spacing	Double-spaced.

STYLE

Name of Guide	*Publication Manual of the American Psychological Association.*
Subheadings	Not specified.
References	See style guide.
Footnotes	Not specified.
Tables or Figures	Not specified.

REVIEW PROCESS

Type of Review	Anonymous, with 3 reviewers.
Queries	Yes.
Acknowledgment	By mail.
Review Time	Approximately 3–6 months.
Revisions	Major revisions undertaken by the author, editorial revisions by the editor, with extensive editorial revisions reviewed and approved by the author.
Acceptance Rate	Approximately 60%.
Return of Manuscript	Not returned.
Lag Time to Print	Approximately 4–6 months.

REPRINT, SUBSCRIPTION, AND CONTACT INFORMATION

Reprint Policy	Permission to reprint may be requested for academic and personal use for a small fee.
Book Reviews	Send to Book Review Editor Terry Wolfer, University of South Carolina, School of Social Work, Columbia, SC 29208

Subscriptions   Subscriptions are available to libraries and organizations for $107 per year (or $116 in US dollars for Canadian subscriptions, or $124 in US dollars for overseas subscriptions).

Affiliation   North American Association of Christians in Social Work.

E-Mail Address   info@nacsw.org

Website   www.nacsw.org

SOCIAL WORK AND SOCIAL SCIENCES REVIEW

Current Title	*Social Work and Social Sciences Review*
Previous Title	N/A.
Editorial Focus	Links between social work and other social sciences, research, methodology.
Audience	Social workers, health and education personnel, and academics.
Special Themes	Special issues from time to time.
Where Indexed/ Abstracted	APA abstracts; Applied Social Sciences Index; Bibliographie Zeitschriftenliteratur aller Gebieten des Wissens; Social Care Update; Social Work Abstracts; Sociological Abstracts.
Year Established	1990
Circulation	Not specified.
Frequency	3 per year.
Months Issued	April, August, December.
No. of Articles per Issue	6–8.

SUBMISSIONS

Postal Mailing Address	C/O Whiting and Birch Ltd, 90 Dartmouth Road, London SE23 3HZ, England.
Method for Submission	E-mail.
Number of Copies	1.
Disk Submission	E-mail is preferred.
Online or E-mail Submission Allowed or Required	Preferred.

FORMAT OF MANUSCRIPT

Cover Sheet	Yes.
Abstract	Less than 200 words.
Key Words	Up to 8 key words.
Length	2,500 to 6,000 words. Longer by prior agreement.
Margins	No requirement.
Spacing	Single- or Double-spaced.

STYLE

Name of Guide	See notes for contributors in journal, or publisher's website for more detail. Refer to *Publication Manual of the American Psychological Association* for points of details.
Subheadings	3 levels or less. Minimize capitalization.
References	Harvard.
Footnotes	Endnotes permitted only if absolutely essential.
Tables or Figures	See publisher's website (www.whitingbirch.net) for full details. Graphics for figures and charts must be supplied to at least 300 dpi in tiff or .pdf format. Charts and figures must work in monochrome.

REVIEW PROCESS

Type of Review	Double anonymous.
Queries	Editors welcome queries.
Acknowledgment	E-mail.
Review Time	Approximately 3 months.
Revisions	Material may be accepted subject to minor revisions, rejected, or more substantial revision required, in which case resubmission may be required.
Acceptance Rate	Approximately 30%.
Return of Manuscript	Not relevant, as submissions should be by e-mail.
Lag Time to Print	Approximately (target) 12 months or less.

CHARGES TO AUTHOR

Author Alterations	US$10 per page for significant and foreseeable alterations.
Page Charges	None.
Processing	None.

REPRINT, SUBSCRIPTION, AND CONTACT INFORMATION

Reprint Policy	2 free copies of journal, and a .pdf file. Offprints can be provided at cost for those who want them.
Book Reviews	Published.
Subscriptions	Whiting & Birch Ltd, 90 Dartmouth Road, London SE23 3HZ, United Kingdom; www.whitingbirch.net. North America rates: US $250.00 for libraries, US $60.00 for individuals.
Affiliation	None.
E-Mail Address	enquiries@whitingbirch.net
Website	www.whitingbirch.net

SOCIAL WORK & SOCIETY

Current Title	*Social Work & Society – Online Journal for Social Work & Social Policy*
Previous Title	N/A.
Editorial Focus	Social work, social policy, social theory in social work, policy studies in social work, critical social work.
Audience	Researchers, educator, students, and leading professional figures.
Special Themes	Internationalization of social work and social policy research, social work and post-welfare states, policy studies in social work.
Where Indexed/ Abstracted	BASE (http://www.base-search.net); Deutsche Nationalbibliothek; DigiBib (www.digibib.net); DOAJ (http://www.doaj.org/); Google Scholar: (http://scholar.google.de).
Year Established	2003.
Circulation	Open access journal, no subscription required.
Frequency	Twice a year.
Months Issued	July and December.
No. of Articles per Issue	Approximately 10–15.

SUBMISSIONS

Postal Mailing Address	Coordinating Office, *SW&S-Journal,* Duisburg-Essen University, Center for Social Work & Social Policy, Universitätsstrasse 12, 45141 Essen, Germany.
Method for Submission	Electronic form via website.
Number of Copies	One.
Disk Submission	None.
Online or E-mail Submission Allowed or Required	office@socwork.net.

FORMAT OF MANUSCRIPT

Cover Sheet	Not required; please add your name, academic title, institution, and e-mail address, and if available, a link (URL) to your homepage or website.
	General information on *SW&S-Journal:* Format of manuscript differs by section: see "Information for Authors": http://www.socwork.net/informationsauthors.
Abstract	Submissions of papers need to include a summary of the paper of 100–200 words.
Key Words	In case of non-English papers include a summary of 400–500 words.
Length	5 key words.
Margins	Articles (5,000–8,000 words), Research Articles (1,000–3,000 words), Research Reports (400–1,000 words), Essays (1,000–3,000 words), Historical Portraits (3,000–5,000 words), Book Reviews (1,000–3,000 words).
Spacing	No default.
	Double-spaced.

STYLE

Name of Guide	Rich Text Format (.rtf). All manuscripts should be in A4-format throughout. Pages should be numbered serially.
Subheadings	If possible, please do not use more than 2 levels of subheadings in order to divide the text and structure the paper for the convenience of the reader.
References	All references should be placed at the end of the submission (no citation in footnotes). Examples include the following:
	Fabricant, M. B. and Fisher, R. (2002) *Settlement Houses under Siege: The Struggle to Sustain Community Organizations in New York.* New York, Columbia UP
	Beresford, P. and Wilson, A. (1998) Social Exclusion and Social Work: Challenging the Contradictions of Exclusive Debate, in: Barry, M. and Hallett, C. (eds.) *Social Exclusion and Social Work.* Lyme Regis, Russell House, 85-96
	Hasenfeld, Y. (2000) Organizational Forms as Moral Practices: The Case of Welfare Departments, in: *Social Service Review,* 3, 329-351
Footnotes	Authors are asked not to use foot notes extensively, and not to use endnotes.
Tables or Figures	Tables and figures should be provided in .rtf, word- and .gif, .jpg, or tiff format.

REVIEW PROCESS

Type of Review	Double-blind peer review.
Queries	E-mail only.
Acknowledgment	E-mail only.
Review Time	Maximum of 4–6 months.
Revisions	In case of comments by reviewers.
Acceptance Rate	Approximately 40%.
Return of Manuscript	E-mail only.
Lag Time to Print	Maximum of 12 months.

CHARGES TO AUTHOR

Author Alterations	No.
Page Charges	No.
Processing	No.

REPRINT, SUBSCRIPTION, AND CONTACT INFORMATION

Reprint Policy	Open access; articles submitted for publication must not be under consideration for publication elsewhere. Permission to reproduce copyright material must have been obtained by the author.
Book Reviews	Book reviews (1,000–3,000 words). Social work and social policy related publications will be discussed in the Book Review Section. *SW&S Journal* is pleased to receive book reviews on current published books.
Subscriptions	Open access.
Affiliation	Not affiliated with any professional institution.
E-Mail Address	office@socwork.net (Coordinating Office)
Website	http://www.socwork.net

SOCIAL WORK EDUCATION: THE INTERNATIONAL JOURNAL

Current Title	*Social Work Education: The International Journal*
Previous Title	N/A.
Editorial Focus	*Social Work Education* publishes articles of a critical and reflective nature concerned with the theory and practice of social care and social work education at all levels. It presents a forum for international debate on important issues and provides an opportunity for the expression of new ideas and proposals on the structure and content of social care and social work education, training and development. In this way, the journal makes a vital contribution to the development of educational theory and practice in relation to social work and social care, promoting a set of standards in relation to the written presentation of ideas and experience that reflects the needs and requirements of both practice and education. It is most important that all contributions demonstrate and promote antidiscriminatory and antioppressive approaches to training and practice.
Audience	Not specified.
Special Themes	Not specified.
Where Indexed/ Abstracted	ASSIA; British Education Index; Contents Pages in Education; Criminal Justice Abstracts; Education Research Index; FRANCIS; IBSS; Social Care Online (SCIE); PsycINFO; Research into Higher Education Abstracts; SCOPUS; Social Services Abstracts; Sociological Abstracts.
Year Established	Not specified.
Circulation	Not specified.
Frequency	8 issues per year.
Months Issued	Not specified.
No. of Articles per Issue	Not specified.

SUBMISSIONS

Postal Mailing Address	All submissions should be made online at *Social Work Education's* Manuscript Central site. New users should first create an account. Once a user is logged onto the site, submissions should be made via the Author Centre. Authors should prepare and upload 2 versions of their manuscript. One should be a complete text, while in the second all document information identifying the author should be removed from files to allow them to be sent anonymously to assessors. When uploading files, authors will then be able to define the nonanonymous version as "File not for review". If you have difficulties submitting your manuscript, please contact the editorial office at: SocialWorkEducation@ed.ac.uk.
Method for Submission	Electronically via website at *Social Work Education's* Manuscript Central site. New users should first create an account. Once a user is logged onto the site, submissions should be made via the Author Centre.
Number of Copies	Authors should prepare and upload 2 versions of their manuscript. One should be a complete text, while in the second all document information identifying the author should be removed from files to allow them to be sent anonymously to assessors. When uploading files authors will then be able to define the non-anonymous version as "File not for review".
Disk Submission	No.
Online or E-mail Submission Allowed or Required	Electronically via website at Social Work Education's Manuscript Central site.

FORMAT OF MANUSCRIPT

Cover Sheet	The first sheet should include the title of the paper; name(s) of author(s); and for each author, academic and/or professional qualifications as commonly used by the author, main appointment, and address.
Abstract	The second page should repeat the title, and contain an abstract of not more than 200 words, together with 5–10 key words.
Key Words	Not specified.
Length	6,000 words.
Margins	2.5 cm.
Spacing	Double-spaced.

STYLE

Name of Guide	*Harvard System.*
Subheadings	Not specified.

References | References should follow the Harvard system, that is, they should be indicated in the text by giving the authors' names, with the year of publication in parentheses, for example, Smith (1984); or if there are more than 2 authors, Smith et al. (1984). If several papers from the same author(s) and from the same year are cited, (a), (b), (c), etc. should be put after the year of publication. The references should be listed in full alphabetically at the end of the paper on a separate page in the following standard form

Footnotes | Not specified.

Tables or Figures | Tables should be typed on separate pages and should be given Arabic numbers (e.g., Table 3). Their approximate position in the text should be indicated. Units should appear in parentheses in the column heading but not in the body of the table. Words or numerals should be repeated on successive lines; "ditto" or "do" should not be used.

REVIEW PROCESS

Type of Review | All submissions will be subject to anonymous peer review, normally by 2 assessors. At the discretion of the editor, the comments made by referees will be sent to contributors. Contributors are responsible for obtaining permission for any extensive quotations and for ensuring the accuracy and fairness of their contributions.

Queries | SocialWorkEducation@ed.ac.uk.

Acknowledgment | Not specified.

Review Time | Not specified.

Revisions | Not specified.

Acceptance Rate | Not specified.

Return of Manuscript | Not specified.

Lag Time to Print | Not specified.

CHARGES TO AUTHOR

Author Alterations | Proofs are supplied for checking and making essential typographical corrections, not for general revision or alteration. Proofs must be returned within 72 hours of receipt.

Page Charges | Not specified.

Processing | Not specified.

REPRINT, SUBSCRIPTION, AND CONTACT INFORMATION

Reprint Policy | Free article access: Corresponding authors can receive 50 free reprints, free online access to their article through our website (www.informaworld.com), and a complimentary copy of the issue containing their article. Complimentary reprints are available through Rightslink, and additional reprints can be ordered through Rightslink when proofs are received. If you have any queries, please contact our reprints department at reprints@tandf.co.uk.

Book Reviews | Books or any other learning materials suitable for review in the journal, such as CD-ROMs, videos, and other multimedia products should be sent to: Kate Morris, Institute of Applied Social Studies, University of Birmingham, Edgbaston, Birmingham B15 2TT, United Kingdom.

Subscriptions | http://mc.manuscriptcentral.com/cswe.

Affiliation | Not specified.

E-Mail Address | SocialWorkEducation@ed.ac.uk

Website | http://www.informaworld.com/smpp/title~content=t713447070~db=all

SOCIAL WORK FORUM

Current Title	*Social Work Forum*
Previous Title	*Jewish Social Work Forum.*
Editorial Focus	All aspects of social work.
Audience	General social work audience.
Special Themes	N/A
Where Indexed/ Abstracted	Social Work Abstracts; Sociological Abstracts; and others.
Year Established	1962
Circulation	6,000+.
Frequency	1 pcr year.
Months Issued	Fall.
No. of Articles per Issue	5–8.

SUBMISSIONS

Postal Mailing Address	2495 Amsterdam Avenue, Suite 818, New York City, NY 10033.
Method for Submission	Not indicated.
Number of Copies	3
Disk Submission	Yes.
Online or E-mail Submission Allowed or Required	Yes.

FORMAT OF MANUSCRIPTS

Cover Sheet	Title, author, address, e-mail, phone.
Abstract	Yes, 50 words.
Key Words	4–6.
Length	14–30 pages.
Margins	1 inch.
Spacing	Double-spaced.

STYLE

Name of Guide	*Publication Manual of the American Psychological Association.*
Subheadings	Not indicated.
References	See style guide.
Footnotes	No.
Tables or Figures	Provide camera-ready.

REVIEW PROCESS

Type of Review	Peer reviewed.
Queries	Yes.
Acknowledgment	Yes.
Review Time	Approximately 3 months.
Revisions	Author is notified of necessary revisions.
Acceptance Rate	Approximately 50%.
Return of Manuscript	No.
Lag Time to Print	Approximately 6–9 months.

REPRINT, SUBSCRIPTION, AND CONTACT INFORMATION

Reprint Policy	None.
Book Reviews	Yes.
Subscriptions	Daniel Pollack, Co-editor & Managing Editor, WSSW, 2495 Amsterdam Avenue, Suite 818, New York, NY 10033.
Affiliation	Wurzweiler School of Social Work, Yeshiva University.
E-Mail Address	dpollack@yu.edu
Website	http://74.125.95.132/search?q=cache:L0lPjqb34dEJ:www.yu.edu/wurzweiler/page.aspx%3Fid% 3D954+social+work+forum+yeshiva+university

SOCIAL WORK IN HEALTH CARE

Current Title	*Social Work in Health Care*
Previous Title	N/A.
Editorial Focus	Devoted to social work theory, practice, and administration in a wide variety of health care settings, this journal gives you the tools to improve your practice while keeping you up-to-date with the latest crucial information
Audience	Practitioners, supervisors, administrators, researchers, and educators
Special Themes	Health care social work practice, managed care, behavioral health, special populations, chronic illness, community health, health status, public health research.
Where Indexed/ Abstracted	Abstracts in Social Gerontology; Academic Abstracts; Applied Social Sciences Index & Abstracts; Behavioral Medicine Abstracts; Caredata CD: The Social and Community Care Database; CINAHL (Cumulative Index to Nursing & Allied Health Literature); CNPIEC Reference Guide: Chinese National Directory of Foreign Periodicals; Communication Abstracts; Current Contents; Excerpta Medica/Secondary Publishing Division; Family Studies Database; Health Source Pulse; Hospital Literature Index; Human Resources Abstracts (HRA); IBZ International Bibliography of Periodical Literature; Index Medicus; Index to Periodical Articles Related to Law; Institute for Scientific Information; INTERNET ACCESS (and additional networks) Bulletin Board for Libraries ("BUBL"); Psychological Abstracts/PsycINFO; Referativnyi Zhurnal (Abstracts journal of the Institute of Scientific Information of the Republic of Russia); Social Sciences Citation Index; Social Work Abstracts; Sociological Abstracts (SA); SOMED (Social Medicine) Database; Special Educational Needs Abstracts; Studies on Women and Gender Abstracts; Violence & Abuse Abstracts: A Review of Current Literature on Interpersonal Violence (VAA).
Year Established	1975.
Circulation	1,000+.
Frequency	8 per year.
Months Issued	February, May, October, December.
No. of Articles per Issue	5–6 per issue.

SUBMISSIONS

Postal Mailing Address	Gary Rosenberg, PhD, Edith J. Baerwald Professor of Community Medicine (Social Work), The Mount Sinai School of Medicine, One Gustave L. Levy Place, Box 1246, New York, NY 10029 USA.
Method for Submission	Manuscripts should be submitted in triplicate, along with an electronic copy of the manuscript on disk or as an e-mail attachment (formatted in Microsoft Word).
Number of Copies	3 plus e-mail or 3 plus disk.
Disk Submission	See above.
Online or E-mail Submission Allowed or Required	E-mail or mail or disk with 3 copies; Gary.Rosenberg@mountsinai.org.

FORMAT OF MANUSCRIPT

Cover Sheet	Each manuscript should be accompanied by a title page including complete author name(s), affiliations, mailing address, phone, fax, and e-mail information (for multiple author papers, provide complete information for each author and indicate the corresponding author).
Abstract	On separate sheet, up to 100 words.
Key Words	3–10 keywords below abstract.
Length	20 pages.
Margins	1 inch.
Spacing	Double-spaced.

STYLE

Name of Guide	*Publication Manual of the American Psychological Association.*
Subheadings	Use as needed to guide reader through the article.
References	References should be double-spaced, placed in alphabetical order, and listed on separate pages following the text. They should refer only to material cited in the manuscript and should follow the current American Psychological Association style. In text, reference citations should include author and year of publication. Identify subsequent citations in the text in the same way as the

first, not using ibid, op. cit., or loc. cit. If 5 authors or fewer, give names of all authors. For 6 authors or more, use "et al." In the reference list, cite all authors.

Footnotes	The use of footnotes within the text is discouraged. Words should be underlined only when it is intended that they be typeset in italics.
Tables or Figures	Tables and figures should not be embedded in the text but should be included on separate sheets or files. A short descriptive title should appear above each table with a clear legend and any footnotes suitably identified below. All units must be included. Figures should be completely labeled, taking into account necessary size reduction. Figure legends should be typed, double-spaced, on a separate sheet.

REVIEW PROCESS

Type of Review	Submitted manuscripts will undergo blind peer review. Authors should avoid placing any form of identification either on the body of the manuscript or on the required abstract. Manuscripts that do not conform to these requirements will be returned to the authors for correction and will delay the review process.
Queries	Query letters are welcome.
Acknowledgment	A letter of acknowledgement is sent on receipt, with a manuscript number assigned.
Review Time	3–4 months.
Revisions	Submit 4 copies with a manuscript number. Mark revisions either by using a word processing program that highlights the revisions or by marking revisions in red pencil.
Acceptance Rate	Approximately 30%.
Return of Manuscript	Generally, only rejected manuscripts are returned.
Lag Time to Print	Approximately 6–12 months.

CHARGES TO AUTHOR

Author Alterations	Page proofs are sent to the designated author using Taylor & Francis' Central Article Tracking System. They should be carefully checked and returned within 48 hours.
Page Charges	Not specified.
Processing	Not specified.

REPRINT, SUBSCRIPTION, AND CONTACT INFORMATION

Reprint Policy	Reprints of individual articles are available for order at the time authors review page proofs. A discount on reprints is available to authors who order before print publication. Each corresponding author will receive 3 complete issues in which the article publishes and a complimentary PDF. This file is for personal use only and may not be copied and disseminated in any form without prior written permission from Taylor and Francis Group, LLC.
Book Reviews	Yes.
Subscriptions	Not specified.
Affiliation	Not specified.
E-Mail Address	Gary.Rosenberg@mountsinai.org
Website	http://www.informaworld.com/smpp/title~db=all~content=t792306964

SOCIAL WORK IN MENTAL HEALTH

Current Title	*Social Work in Mental Health*
Previous Title	N/A.
Editorial Focus	Mental health issues, mental health research in social work, domestic violence and/or abuse.
Audience	Social workers, psychotherapists.
Special Themes	Yes.
Where Indexed/ Abstracted	Not specified.
Year Established	1999.
Circulation	Not specified.
Frequency	6 issues per year.
Months Issued	Quarterly
No. of Articles per Issue	5–6 articles 140 maximum page count.

SUBMISSIONS

Postal Mailing Address	Gary Rosenberg PhD/Andrew Weissman, PhD, Co-Editors, Mount Sinai School of Medicine, One Gustave L. Levy Place, Box 1246, New York, NY 10029.
Method for Submission	Surface mail, disk, or e-mail.
Number of Copies	4.
Disk Submission	Yes.
Online or E-mail Submission Allowed or Required	Yes.

FORMAT OF MANUSCRIPT

Cover Sheet	Yes.
Abstract	Yes.
Key Words	Yes.
Length	20 pages.
Margins	Not specified.
Spacing	Double-spaced.

STYLE

Name of Guide	*Publication Manual of the American Psychological Association.*
Subheadings	Not specified.
References	See style guide.
Footnotes	The use of footnotes within the text is discouraged.
Tables or Figures	Tables and figures should not be embedded in the text but should be included on separate sheets or files. A short descriptive title should appear above each table with a clear legend and any foot-notes suitably identified below. All units must be included. Figures should be completely labeled, taking into account necessary size reduction. Figure legends should be typed, double-spaced, on a separate sheet. Illustrations submitted (line drawings, halftones, photos, etc.) should be clean originals or digital files. Digital files are recommended for highest quality reproduction and should follow these guidelines: 300 dpi or higher; sized to fit on journal page; EPS, TIFF, or PSD format only; submitted as separate files, not embedded in text files.

REVIEW PROCESS

Type of Review	Peer review.
Queries	Not specified.
Acknowledgment	Upon receipt.
Review Time	Approximately 3–4 months.
Revisions	Approximately 6–8 weeks.
Acceptance Rate	Not specified.
Return of Manuscript	Not specified.
Lag Time to Print	Not specified.

CHARGES TO AUTHOR

Author Alterations   Not specified.

Page Charges   Color illustrations will be considered for publication; however, the author will be required to bear the full cost involved in color art reproduction. Color art can be purchased for online-only reproduction or for print and online reproduction. Color reprints can only be ordered if print + online reproduction costs are paid. Rates for color art reproduction are: Online-Only Reproduction: $225 for the first page with color; $100 per page for the next 3 pages of color. A maximum charge of $525 applies. Print and Online Reproduction: $900 for the first page of color; $450 per page for the next three pages of color. A custom quote will be provided for articles with more than four pages of color.

Processing   Not specified.

REPRINT, SUBSCRIPTION, AND CONTACT INFORMATION

Reprint Policy   Reprints of individual articles are available for order at the time authors review page proofs. A discount on reprints is available to authors who order before print publication. Each corresponding author will receive 3 complete issues in which the article publishes and a complimentary PDF. This file is for personal use only and may not be copied and disseminated in any form without prior written permission from Taylor and Francis Group, LLC.

Book Reviews   Not specified.

Subscriptions   Total volume 6 issues $518 print and on-line subscription. Institutional online-only subscription $492.

Affiliation   Taylor and Francis.

E-Mail Address   customerservice@taylorfrancis.com

Website   Visit Informaworld Librarians Area at: www.informaworld.com/librarians.

SOCIAL WORK IN PUBLIC HEALTH

Current Title	*Social Work in Public Health*
Previous Title	*Journal of Health & Social Policy*
Editorial Focus	Promoting a forum for those interested in debating and discussing policy formulation, as well as for those desirous of analyzing and investigating responses to policies already enacted. The editors and editorial board vigorously pursue the development of a body of knowledge on the differential effects of health and social policy issues on various populations and will encourage manuscripts from minority authors.
Audience	Practitioners, researchers, faculty, students, libraries, organizations involved in public health such as nursing, health education, allied health, social work, urban affairs, pharmacy, psychology, sociology, mental health, and medicine who want to address public and social policy issues.
Special Themes	Current issues.
Where Indexed/ Abstracted	Abstracts in Anthropology; Abstracts in Social Gerontology; Academic Search Alumni Edition (EBSCO); Academic Search Complete (EBSCO); Academic Search Premier (EBSCO); CAB International; Current Abstracts (EBSCO); Gerolit: German Centre of Gerontology; HaPI: Health and Psychosocial Instruments (Ovid); HECLNET - Health Care Literature Information Network; IBZ: Internationale Bibliographie der Zeitschriftenliteratur (Germany); International Political Science Abstracts (Ovid); Master File Premier (EBSCO); SOCIndex (EBSCO); TOC Premier (EBSCO); VINITI: All Russian Scientific and Technical Information.
Year Established	1989.
Circulation	173.
Frequency	4.
Months Issued	January, April, July, October.
No. of Articles per Issue	6.

SUBMISSIONS

Postal Mailing Address	Marvin D. Feit, PhD, Professor, Social Work, Norfolk State University, Ethelyn R. Strong School of Social Work, 700 Park Avenue, Norfolk, VA 23504.
Method for Submission	Surface mail, disk, E-mail.
Number of Copies	3.
Disk Submission	If submitting a disk, it should be prepared using MS Work or WordPerfect and should be clearly labeled with the authors' names, file name, and software program.
Online or E-mail Submission Allowed or Required	Recommended.

FORMAT OF MANUSCRIPT

Cover Sheet	Staple a cover page to each manuscript indicating only the manuscript title on 2 of the hard copies. Also enclose a separate cover sheet that includes full title; author names, degrees, and professional titles; and designation of 1 author as corresponding author with full address, phone numbers, e-mail address, fax number, and date of submission.
Abstract	Each article should be summarized in an abstract of not more than 100 words. Avoid abbreviations, diagrams, and reference to the text in the abstract.
Key Words	3–5 key words.
Length	15–20 pages, including references and tables.
Margins	Minimum of 1 inch on all sides. Number manuscript pages consecutively throughout the paper. Authors should also supply a shortened version of the title suitable for the running head, not exceeding 50 character spaces.
Spacing	Double-spaced.

STYLE

Name of Guide	*Publication Manual of the American Psychological Association.*
Subheadings	See style guide.
References	See style guide.
Footnotes	No footnotes preferred; incorporate into text.

Tables or Figures	Tables and figures (illustrations) should not be embedded in the text, but should be included as separate sheets or files. A short descriptive title should appear above each table with a clear legend and any footnotes suitably identified below. All units must be included. Figures should be completely labeled, taking into account necessary size reduction. Captions should be typed, double-spaced, on a separate sheet.

REVIEW PROCESS

Type of Review	Blind.
Queries	Electronic submission also suggested.
Acknowledgment	A letter is sent upon receipt of manuscript.
Review Time	Approximately 3 months.
Revisions	To be expected.
Acceptance Rate	We work extensively with author to assist in publication, which could take a long time.
Return of Manuscript	Not returned, author should retain copies.
Lag Time to Print	Your review process plus 12 weeks of Taylor and Francis production

CHARGES TO AUTHOR

Author Alterations	Not specified.
Page Charges	Color illustrations will be considered for publication; however, the author will be required to bear the full cost involved in color art reproduction. Color art can be purchased for online-only reproduction or for print and online reproduction. Color reprints can only be ordered if print and online reproduction costs are paid. Rates for color art reproduction are: Online-Only Reproduction: $225 for the first page of color; $100 per page for the next 3 pages of color. A maximum charge of $525 applies. Print and Online Reproduction: $900 for the first page of color; $450 per page for the next 3 pages of color. A custom quote will be provided for articles with more than 4 pages of color. Art not supplied at a minimum of 300 dpi will not considered for print.
Processing	No.

REPRINT, SUBSCRIPTION, AND CONTACT INFORMATION

Reprint Policy	Reprints of individual articles are available for order at the time authors review page proofs. A discount on reprints is available to authors who order before print publication. Each corresponding author will receive 3 complete issues in which the article publishes and a complimentary PDF. This file is for personal use only and may not be copied and disseminated in any form without prior written permission from Taylor and Francis Group, LLC.
Book Reviews	Send book for review to Book Review Editor: Michael Holosko, School of Social Work, University of Windsor, Windsor, Ontario N9B 3P4, Canada.
Subscriptions	www.tandf.co.uk/journals/webs or customer.service@taylorandfrancis.com or 1.800.0354.1420, press "4."
Affiliation	Not specified.
E-Mail Address	Not specified.
Website	www.tandf.co.uk/journals/webs

SOCIAL WORK RESEARCH

Current Title	*Social Work Research*
Previous Title	*Social Work Research and Abstracts* (changed in 1994 when the two journals were separated).
Editorial Focus	Research on issues of concern to social workers and other professionals in human services. Analytical reviews of research, theoretical articles, practice-based research, evaluation studies, and other research studies that contribute to knowledge about social issues and social problems.
Audience	Researchers, faculty, students, researchers and writers in allied disciplines, libraries, schools, and other organizations.
Special Themes	Welfare reform, HIV/AIDS, racial and ethnic diversity, research methodologies.
Where Indexed/ Abstracted	Abstracts in Anthropology; Abstracts in Social Gerontology; Academic Abstracts; AgeLine; Applied Social Sciences Index & Abstracts; Caredata; Cumulative Index to Nursing & Allied Health Literature (CINAHL); Current Contents: Social & Behavioral Sciences; ERIC/Cass; Exceptional Child Education Resources; Psychological Abstracts/PsycINFO/PsycLIT; Public Affairs Information Service Bulletin (PAIS); Sage Family Studies Abstracts; Social Planning/ Policy & Development Abstracts (SOPODA); Social Sciences Index/Social Sciences Abstracts; Social Work Abstracts; Sociological Abstracts (SA).
Year Established	1977
Circulation	3,500
Frequency	Quarterly.
Months Issued	March, June, September, December.
No. of Articles per Issue	Approximately 5.

SUBMISSIONS

Postal Mailing Address	*Social Work Research,* NASW Press, 750 First Street, NE, Suite 700, Washington, DC 20002-4241.
Method for Submission	Not indicated.
Number of Copies	5
Disk Submission	Authors of accepted manuscripts are asked to submit a disk, preferably in Microsoft Word.
Online or E-mail Submission Allowed or Required	Not indicated.

FORMAT OF MANUSCRIPT

Cover Sheet	Separate sheet, which does not go out for review. Full title; author names, degrees, and professional titles; designation of 1 author as corresponding author with full address, phone number, e-mail address and fax number; date of submission.
Abstract	150-word informative abstract.
Key Words	Up to 5 key words or key phrases (2–3-word maximum) describing the article.
Length	Maximum of 20 pages including references and tables.
Margins	1 inch on all sides.
Spacing	Double-spaced on all copy except title page.

STYLE

Name of Guide	*Writing for the NASW Press: Information for Authors* (free) and *Professional Writing for the Human Services* (for purchase from the NASW Press). Contact the NASW Press.
Subheadings	Use as needed to guide the reader through the article. No more than 3 levels.
References	Author–date citation style; see style guidelines.
Footnotes	No footnotes preferred; incorporate into text.
Tables or Figures	Type tables Double-spaced. Submit camera-ready art (300 dpi printer or better) for all figures. Place each table or figure on a separate, numbered page at the end of the manuscript.

REVIEW PROCESS

Type of Review	"Double-blind" anonymous peer review. 3 reviewers plus the editor-in-chief read the manuscript in an anonymous review.
Queries	Query letters are discouraged; authors are encouraged to read the journal and *Writing for the NASW Press* to determine whether their subject matter would be appropriate.
Acknowledgment	The NASW Press sends a letter upon receipt of manuscript.
Review Time	Approximately 3–4 months.

Revisions	Submit 5 copies with a separate cover sheet (not identifying the author) describing the changes made in the manuscript and replying to reviewers' comments. In general, the original reviewers and the editor-in-chief read revisions.
Acceptance Rate	Approximately 20%.
Return of Manuscript	Not returned, authors should retain copies.
Lag Time to Print	Approximately 6–12 months.

CHARGES TO AUTHOR

Author Alterations	Not indicated.
Page Charges	Not indicated.
Processing	Not indicated.

REPRINT, SUBSCRIPTION, AND CONTACT INFORMATION

Reprint Policy	All authors receive 5 complimentary copies of the issue in which the article appears. Authors receive reprint order forms to purchase additional reprinted copies.
Book Reviews	Generally none.
Subscriptions	*Social Work Research*, P.O. Box 431, Annapolis Junction, MD 20701.
Affiliation	The NASW Press is a division of the National Association of Social Workers.
E-Mail Address	press@naswdc.org
Website	www.naswpress.org

SOCIAL WORK WITH GROUPS

Current Title	*Social Work With Groups*
Previous Title	N/A.
Editorial Focus	A journal of community and clinical practice; practice, theory, research, book reviews, video reviews.
Audience	Faculty, students, practitioners, university libraries in social work, and related human services disciplines.
Special Themes	Group work with oppressed populations and in diverse settings.
Where Indexed/ Abstracted	Applied Social Sciences Index & Abstracts; Caredata CD: The Social and Community Care Data-base; CNPIEC Reference Guide; Chinese National Directory of Foreign Periodicals; Current Contents; Expanded Academic Index; Guide to Social Science & Religion in Periodical Literature; Index to Periodical Articles Related to Law; Institute for Scientific Information; International Bulletin of Bibliography on Education; INTERNET ACCESS (and additional networks); Bulletin Board for Libraries ("BUBL"), coverage of information resources on INTERNET, JANET, and other networks; Inventory of Marriage and Family Literature (online and CD-ROM); Psychological Abstracts/PsycINFO; Social Planning/Policy and Development Abstracts (SOPODA); Social Work Abstract; Sociological Abstracts (SA); Special Educational Needs Abstracts; Studies on Women and Gender Abstracts; Violence & Abuse Abstracts: A Review of Current Literature on Interpersonal Violence (VAA).
Year Established	1978
Circulation	1,000
Frequency	Quarterly.
Months Issued	Spring, summer, fall, and winter.
No. of Articles per Issue	Approximately 6 per issue plus editorial commentary and video and book reviews.

SUBMISSIONS

Postal Mailing Address	Andrew Malekoff, Editor-in-Chief, *Social Work with Groups,* c/o North Shore Child and Family Guidance Center, 480 Old Westbury Road, Roslyn Heights, New York, 11577.
Method for Submission	Surface mail and e-mail.
Number of Copies	1 with surface mail and 1 with e-mail.
Disk Submission	No.
Online or E-mail Submission Allowed or Required	Yes.

FORMAT OF MANUSCRIPT

Cover Sheet	Yes.
Abstract	Yes.
Key Words	Yes.
Length	15–20 pages, double-spaced, inclusive of references, tables, charts.
Margins	1 inch on all sides.
Spacing	Double-spaced.

STYLE

Name of Guide	*Publication Manual of the American Psychological Association; Writing for the NASW Press.*
Subheadings	Use as needed.
References	Author–date citation style, see style guides.
Footnotes	Incorporate into text.
Tables or Figures	Must be camera-ready.

REVIEW PROCESS

Type of Review	Juried.
Queries	Interested authors may write for information: Andrew Malekott, Editor, North Shore Child and Family Guidance Center, 480 Old Westbury Road, Roslyn Heights, NY 11577.
Acknowledgment	Letter sent on receipt of manuscript.
Review Time	Approximately 3–6 weeks.
Revisions	Varies.

Acceptance Rate	Approximately 40%.
Return of Manuscript	No.
Lag Time to Print	Approximately 6–12 months.

REPRINT, SUBSCRIPTION, AND CONTACT INFORMATION

Reprint Policy	Contact publisher.
Book Reviews	By invitation only; send books for review to Andrew Malekoff, Editor, *Social Work with Groups*, North Shore Child and Family Guidance Center, 480 Old Westbury Road, Roslyn Heights, NY 11577.
Subscriptions	Taylor & Francis Group, LLC, 325 Chestnut Street, Philadelphia, PA 19107
Affiliation	Publisher.
E-Mail Address	See website.
Website	www.taylorandfrancis.com

SOCIETY

Current Title	*Society*
Previous Title:	
Editorial Focus	New ideas and research findings from all the social sciences.
Audience	Social scientists, journalists, public officials, and others with a proven interest in social, economic, political, and ethical issues.
Special Themes	Social welfare, politics and elections, ethics of life and death, philanthropy, religion and social conflict, professional ethics, international relations, culture and ideas.
Where Indexed/ Abstracted	Ageline; Book Review Index; CSA Political Science and Government; CSA Sustainable Science Abstracts; Current Abstracts; EBSCOhost; Education Research Index; Family Index; International Political Science Abstracts; Peace Research Abstracts Journal; ProQuest Central; Public Administration Abstracts; Race Relations Abstracts; SCOPUS; Social Services Abstracts; Social Work Abstracts; Sociological Abstracts.
Year Established	1963
Circulation	5,000 and online.
Frequency	Bimonthly.
Months Issued	January, March, May, July, September, and November.
No. of Articles per Issue	Approximately 16.

SUBMISSIONS

Postal Mailing Address	J.B. Imber, Dept. of Sociology, Wellesley College, Wellesley, MA 02481
Method for Submission	All manuscripts must be submitted in electronic form, preferably in Microsoft Word.
Number of Copies	1 electronically.
Disk Submission	No.
Online or E-mail Submission Allowed or Required	E-mail required at society@wellesley.edu.

FORMAT OF MANUSCRIPT

Cover Sheet	Not specified.
Abstract	Yes.
Key Words	Yes.
Length	4,000 words.
Margins	At least 1 inch all around.
Spacing	Double-spaced.

STYLE

Name of Guide	All articles should follow the format of *Society*.
Subheadings	Follow format of journal.
References	Follow format of journal.
Footnotes	No footnotes.
Tables or Figures	OK.

REVIEW PROCESS

Type of Review	Not specified.
Queries	Send queries to society@wellesley.edu.
Acknowledgment	Not specified.
Review Time	Not specified.
Revisions	Not specified.
Acceptance Rate	Not specified.
Return of Manuscript	N/A
Lag Time to Print	Not specified.

REPRINT, SUBSCRIPTION, AND CONTACT INFORMATION

Reprint Policy	By permission.
Book Reviews	Yes.

Subscriptions	Contact publisher: journals-ny@springer.com.
Affiliation	None.
E-Mail Address	society@wellesley.edu
Website	http://www.springer.com/social+sciences/sociology/journal/12115

STUDIES IN SOCIAL JUSTICE

Current Title	*Studies in Social Justice*
Previous Title	N/A.
Editorial Focus	*Studies in Social Justice* publishes articles on issues dealing with the social, cultural, economic, political, and philosophical problems associated with the struggle for social justice. This interdisciplinary journal aims to publish work that links theory to social change and the analysis of substantive issues. The journal welcomes heterodox contributions that are critical of established paradigms of inquiry.
Audience	This interdisciplinary journal aims to publish work that links theory to social change and the analysis of substantive issues. The journal welcomes heterodox contributions that are critical of established paradigms of inquiry. The journal focuses on debates that move beyond conventional notions of social justice, and views social justice as a critical concept that is integral in the analysis of policy formation, rights, participation, social movements, and transformations. Social justice is analyzed in the context of processes involving nationalism, social and public policy, globalization, diasporas, culture, gender, ethnicity, sexuality, welfare, poverty, war, and other social phenomena. The journal endeavours to cover questions and debates ranging from governance to democracy, sustainable environments, and human rights, and to introduce new work on pressing issues of social justice throughout the world.
Special Themes	Gender and Violence in Guatemala, Security, Exclusion, Risks and Rights.
Where Indexed/ Abstracted	Not specified.
Year Established	2007.
Circulation	Open access.
Frequency	Semiannually.
Months Issued	Not specified.
No. of Articles per Issue	Approximately 5–7.

SUBMISSIONS

Postal Mailing Address	Not specified.
Method for Submission	Electronic form via website.
Number of Copies	Not specified.
Disk Submission	Not specified.
Online or E-mail Submission Allowed or Required	http://ojs.uwindsor.ca/ojs/leddy/index.php/SSJ/user/register

FORMAT OF MANUSCRIPT

Cover Sheet	N/A.
Abstract	150–200 words.
Key Words	Not specified.
Length	6,000–8,000 words.
Margins	Not specified.
Spacing	Single-spaced.

STYLE

Name of Guide	*Publication Manual of the American Psychological Association.*
Subheadings	Not specified.
References	See style guide.
Footnotes	Footnotes should be avoided; however, if they cannot be avoided, they should be indicated in the text by symbols.
Tables or Figures	All illustrations, figures, and tables are placed within the text at the appropriate points, rather than at the end.

REVIEW PROCESS

Type of Review	The Editors will make an initial judgment on the acceptability of articles. If articles pass this stage they will move into the double-blind review process. Any identifying references to the author(s) should have been removed prior to submission.

Queries	The initial mode of contact should be via our online submission process.
Acknowledgment	E-mail.
Review Time	Approximately 2 months.
Revisions	Submitted through OJS system.
Acceptance Rate	Not specified.
Return of Manuscript	Not specified.
Lag Time to Print	Not specified.

CHARGES TO AUTHOR

Author Alterations	None.
Page Charges	None.
Processing	None.

REPRINT, SUBSCRIPTION, AND CONTACT INFORMATION

Reprint Policy	Not specified.
Book Reviews	Open submissions, indexed, no peer review.
Subscriptions	Open access journal, no subscription required.
Affiliation	University of Windsor.
E-Mail Address	socjust@uwindsor.ca, basok@uwindsor.ca
Website	http://ojs.uwindsor.ca/ojs/leddy/index.php/SSJ/index
	http://www.uwindsor.ca/ socialjustice/

SUBSTANCE ABUSE

Current Title	*Substance Abuse*
Previous Title	N/A.
Editorial Focus	Empirical research papers and reviews in the field of addiction and substance abuse. The journal is primarily a forum for original empirical research but also includes reviews, editorials, letters to the editor, and book reviews.
Audience	Medical educators, clinical researchers, and other health professionals in the field of alcohol and drug abuse.
Special Themes	Clinical and preclinical research, education, health service delivery, and policy in the field of substance abuse.
Where Indexed/ Abstracted	Not indicated.
Year Established	1979
Circulation	Not indicated.
Frequency	Quarterly.
Months Issued	Not indicated.
No. of Articles per Issue	4–5.

SUBMISSIONS

Postal Mailing Address	Marc Galanter, MD, Center for Alcohol and Addiction Studies, Box G-BH, Brown University, Providence, RI 02906.
Method for Submission	Not indicated.
Number of Copies	4
Disk Submission	Not required.
Online or E-mail Submission Allowed or Required	Not indicated.

FORMAT OF MANUSCRIPT

Cover Sheet	Title of the article, author's name (with degree), affiliation, suggested running head.
Abstract	Yes, no more than 150 words.
Key Words	4–5 key words.
Length	No more than 30 pages
Margins	Not indicated.
Spacing	Double-spaced.

STYLE

Name of Guide	Not indicated.
Subheadings	Not indicated.
References	Type double-spaced, numerically in order of text appearance at the end of the paper (after text and before tables and figure caption list).
Footnotes	Should be avoided; if absolutely necessary, should be numbered consecutively with Arabic numerals on the page to which they refer. A line should be placed above the footnote to set it off from the text.
Tables or Figures	Camera-ready copy should be submitted for all tables and figures.

REVIEW PROCESS

Type of Review	All papers are peer reviewed; they are not anonymous.
Queries	Not indicated.
Acknowledgment	By postcard.
Review Time	Approximately 3–4 months.
Revisions	Authors must submit 4 copies of any revisions that are undertaken. Revised manuscripts may be sent out for further review or reviewed by the editor, depending on the extent of the revisions.
Acceptance Rate	Approximately 50%.
Return of Manuscript	Not returned.
Lag Time to Print	Approximately 6–9 months.

CHARGES TO AUTHOR

Author Alterations	Not indicated.
Page Charges	Not indicated.
Processing	Not indicated.

REPRINT, SUBSCRIPTION, AND CONTACT INFORMATION

Reprint Policy	Reprints are made available to the author, and the schedule of charge is distributed by the publisher.
Book Reviews	All books and book reviews may be submitted to the same office. Unsolicited reviews are accepted; however, final decisions on publication are made by the book review editor.
Subscriptions	Routledge (Taylor & Francis Group), 325 Chestnut Street, Philadelphia, PA 19106
Affiliation	Association for Medical Education and Research in Substance Abuse (AMERSA).
E-Mail Address	kcw@brown.edu
Website	Not indicated.

SUICIDE AND LIFE-THREATENING BEHAVIOR

Current Title	*Suicide and Life-Threatening Behavior*
Previous Title	N/A.
Editorial Focus	*Suicide and Life-Threatening Behavior* is devoted to emergent theoretical, clinical, and public health approaches related to violent, self-destructive, and life-threatening behaviors. It is multi-disciplinary and concerned with a broad range of related topics including, but not limited to, suicide, suicide prevention, death, accidents, biology of suicide, epidemiology, crisis intervention, postvention with survivors, nomenclature, standards of care, clinical training and interventions, violence, euthanasia, and assisted suicide
Audience	Practitioners, researchers, support groups, survivors, faculty, students, libraries, organizations, crisis-line workers.
Special Themes	Suicide, suicide prevention, death, accidents, subintentional destruction, violence, standards of care, nomenclature, survivors, methodology, euthanasia, physician-assisted suicide, bereavement.
Where Indexed/ Abstracted	Academic Index; Bell & Howell Information and Learning; Biological Abstracts; Current Contents: Social and Behavioral Sciences; Current Index to Journals in Education; Excerpta Medica/EMBASE; Family Studies Database; Index Medicus/MEDLINE; PsycINFO; Research Alert; Social Sciences Citation Index; Social SciSearch; Sociological Abstracts.
Year Established	1970.
Circulation	2,000.
Frequency	Quarterly.
Months Issued	Winter, spring, summer, and fall.
No. of Articles per Issue	5–6.

SUBMISSIONS

Postal Mailing Address	Thomas E. Joiner, PhD, Florida State University, Department of Psychology, P.O. Box 1270, Tallahassee, FL 32306-1270.
Method for Submission	http://sltb.msubmit.net.
Number of Copies	Quadruplicate.
Disk Submission	Not specified.
Online or E-mail Submission Allowed or Required	joiner@psy.fsu.edu

FORMAT OF MANUSCRIPT

Cover Sheet	With your submission, include a cover letter designating 1 author as correspondent for the review process, and provide a complete address, including phone and fax. In this letter please attest that neither the manuscript nor any other substantially similar paper has been published, except as described in the letter. The corresponding author should also attest that in the case of several authors, each one has studied the manuscript in the form submitted, agreed to be cited as a coauthor, and has accepted the order of authorship. Also indicate agreement by the authors that if the paper is accepted its copyright shall become the property of the publisher.
Abstract	100 words on a separate sheet.
Key Words	Up to 5 key words or key phrases (2–3-word minimum) describing the article.
Length	20 pages, but ordinarily shorter.
Margins	1 inch.
Spacing	Double-spaced.

STYLE

Name of Guide	*Publication Manual of the American Psychological Association.*
Subheadings	Use as needed to guide the reader through the article. No more than 3 levels.
References	Reference lists should be prepared according to the style illustrated in the journal. This approach minimizes punctuation in the specific references, but utilizes the author and date in the text of the articles, to provide maximum information quickly to the reader.
Footnotes	No footnotes preferred; incorporate into text.
Tables or Figures	Tables should be cited in order in the text using Arabic numerals. Each table should be displayed on a separate page, and each must have a title.

REVIEW PROCESS

Type of Review   Manuscripts are generally sent to outside reviewers, and you will be informed of the editorial decision as soon as possible. Ordinarily a decision will be reached in approximately 3 months after submission is acknowledged. A request for revising the manuscript along the lines suggested by the Editor and reviewers does not constitute a decision to publish. All revised manuscripts will be re-evaluated, and the Editors reserve the right to reject a paper at any point during the revision.

Queries   joiner@psy.fsu.edu

Acknowledgment   Editor acknowledges manuscripts upon receipt.

Review Time   Approximately 2–3 months.

Revisions   Each manuscript receives 3 anonymous reviews. Revised manuscript re-read by at least 1 previous reviewer and 1 new reviewer. Decision time for revisions is 1–2 months.

Acceptance Rate   Approximately 30%–35%.

Return of Manuscript   Not returned; author should retain copies.

Lag Time to Print   Approximately 9–12 months.

CHARGES TO AUTHOR

Author Alterations   Charged to authors receiving galley proofs.

Page Charges   N/A.

Processing   N/A.

REPRINT, SUBSCRIPTION, AND CONTACT INFORMATION

Reprint Policy   Reprint order forms will be sent along with the page proofs for your paper.

Book Reviews   Yes.

Subscriptions   Not specified.

Affiliation   American Association of Suicidology.

E-Mail Address   joiner@psy.fsu.edu

Website   http://www.guilford.com/cgi-bin/cartscript.cgi?page=periodicals/jnsl.htm&cart_id=

THE JOURNAL OF CHILD PSYCHOLOGY AND PSYCHIATRY (JCPP)

Current Title	*The Journal of Child Psychology and Psychiatry (JCPP)*
Previous Title	*Journal of Child Psychology and Psychiatry & Allied Disciplines.*
Editorial Focus	*The Journal of Child Psychology and Psychiatry (JCPP)* is internationally recognized to be the leading journal covering both child and adolescent psychology and psychiatry. *JCPP* publishes the highest quality clinically relevant research in psychology, psychiatry, and related disciplines. With a large and expanding global readership, its coverage includes studies on epidemiology, diagnosis, psychotherapeutic and psychopharmacological treatments, behavior, cognition, neuroscience, neurobiology, and genetic aspects of childhood disorders. Articles published include experimental, longitudinal, and intervention studies, especially those that advance our understanding of developmental psychopathology and that inform both theory and clinical practice. An important function of the journal is to bring together empirical research, clinical studies, and reviews of high quality that arise from different points of view, different theoretical perspectives, and different disciplines.
	Coverage: Empirical Papers, Research Reviews, Practitioner Reviews, Annual Research Reviews, Book Reviews. In each volume, 1 issue is devoted to the Annual Research Review. This identifies current and future trends and enables readers to keep up to date with research both in and outside their main area of specialization. *The Journal of Child Psychology and Psychiatry* is one of the journals published by Blackwell on behalf of the Association for Child and Adolescent Mental Health (ACAMH, formerly the Association for Child Psychology and Psychiatry.) Members receive both *JCPP* and *Child and Adolescent Mental Health* as part of their membership benefits. Information on joining ACAMH can be found by visiting the Society website using the link at the top of this page.
Audience	See above.
Special Themes	See above.
Where Indexed/ Abstracted	AMED (Allied and Complimentary Medicine Database); ASSIA (Applied Social Sciences Index & Abstracts); AgeLine, Biological Abstracts; BIOSIS Previews; British Nursing Index; Cumulative Index to Nursing and Allied Health Literature (CINAHL); Current Contents; Education Index; Education Resources Information Center (ERIC); Environmental Sciences and Pollution Management; Exceptional Child Education Resources (Online Edition); Excerpta Medica; Abstract Journals; Family Index; Health and Safety Science Abstracts (Online Edition); Indian Psychological Abstracts and Reviews; Linguistics and Language Behavior Abstracts; MEDLINE; PASCAL; Periodicals Contents Index; Personal Alert; Psychological Abstracts; PsycINFO; PsycSCAN: Developmental Psychology; SCOPUS; Social Sciences Citation Index; Social Sciences Index; Social Services Abstracts; Sociological Abstracts.
Year Established	1959.
Circulation	Over 6,000 institutions with access to current content.
Frequency	12 issues a year (once a month).
Months Issued	Every month.
No. of Articles per Issue	Approximately 12.

SUBMISSIONS

Postal Mailing Address	N/A.
Method for Submission	Electronic form via website.
Number of Copies	N/A.
Disk Submission	None.
Online or E-mail Submission Allowed or Required	Online submission required via http://mc.manuscriptcentral.com/jcpp-camh.

FORMAT OF MANUSCRIPT

Cover Sheet	Title, authors' names and affiliations, address of corresponding author.
Abstract	Maximum of 300 words.
Key Words	Yes, 4–6 key words.
Length	6,000 words including title page, abstracts, references, tables, and figures.
Margins	1 inch on all sides.
Spacing	Double-spaced.

STYLE

Name of Guide	*Publication Manual of the American Psychological Association.* See Notes for Contributors.
Subheadings	Not specified.
References	Not specified.
Footnotes	Not specified.
Tables or Figures	Should be clearly drawn on separate page, with legends for figures and headings for tables on separate sheets and clearly labeled.

REVIEW PROCESS

Type of Review	Anonymous peer review by at least 2 referees. Processing editor reads manuscript. "Blind" review available if requested by author.
Queries	Authors should read the Notes for Contributors carefully to determine if their subject matter is appropriate, but if still in doubt, editors will advise.
Acknowledgment	By e-mail to corresponding author.
Review Time	Approximately 4–5 months.
Revisions	Revisions are not always re-reviewed by referees; this depends on the nature and extent of revisions requested. Revisions are always read by the Editors.
Acceptance Rate	Approximately 20%–25%.
Return of Manuscript	N/A.
Lag Time to Print	Approximately 6–10 months.

CHARGES TO AUTHOR

Author Alterations	No charges unless alterations are extensive.
Page Charges	N/A.
Processing	N/A.

REPRINT, SUBSCRIPTION, AND CONTACT INFORMATION

Reprint Policy	First author receives 50 free reprints automatically, and an order form is sent with proofs on which extra reprints (at author's expense) can be ordered.
Book Reviews	By invitation only. Published in all issues excepted No. 1 (Annual Research Review). Books for review should be sent to: The Book Review Editors (Professor Lionel Hersov), *The Journal of Child Psychology & Psychiatry*, ACPP, St. Saviour's House, 39-41 Union Street, London SE1 1SD, England.
Subscriptions	Journal Customer Service: John Wiley & Sons Inc, 350 Main Street, Malden, MA 02148, USA. Direct Customers: Tel: 781-388-8598 or toll free 800-835-6770. E-mail: cs-journals@wiley.com
Affiliation	*The Journal of Child Psychology and Psychiatry* is published on behalf of the Association for Child and Adolescent Mental Health.
E-Mail Address	ingrid.king@acamh.org.uk
Website	www.blackwellpublishing.com/JCPP

TRAUMATOLOGY

Current Title	*Traumatology*
Previous Title	N/A.
Editorial Focus	*Traumatology: An International Journal* is a primary reference for professionals all over the world who study and treat people exposed to highly stressful and traumatic events, such as terrorist bombings, war disasters, fires, accidents, criminal and familial abuse, hostage-taking, hospitalization, major illness, abandonment, and sudden unemployment.
Audience	Psychologists, medical or nursing professionals, aid workers, social workers, or other disaster/trauma professionals.
Special Themes:	Not specified.
Where Indexed/ Abstracted	PILOTS; PsycINFO.
Year Established	1995.
Circulation	Not specified.
Frequency	Quarterly.
Months Issued	March, June, September, December.
No. of Articles per Issue	9–14.

SUBMISSIONS

Postal Mailing Address	No submissions are accepted by mail.
Method for Submission	All submissions should be sent to http://mc.manuscriptcentral.com/tmt. No submissions are accepted by mail or fax.
Number of Copies	1 copy sent through online system.
Disk Submission	Not required.
Online or E-mail Submission Allowed or Required	Online submission required.

FORMAT OF MANUSCRIPT

Cover Sheet	The title should be brief and meaningful. The authors' first and last names and affiliations should follow the title. The corresponding author should list his or her institutional affiliation, current address, contact information including telephone and fax number, and if the manuscript was orally presented at a meeting, the name of the organization, place, and date it was read. Each additional author should supply an e-mail or phone number.
Abstract	An abstract of approximately 125 words should be provided on a separate sheet of paper. This abstract should be factual and should present the reason for the study, the main findings, and the principal conclusions.
Key Words	The abstract should be followed by 6–8 key words relating to the article.
Length	Not specified.
Margins	1 inch.
Spacing	Double-spaced.

STYLE

Name of Guide	*Publication Manual of the American Psychological Association.*
Subheadings	Follow style guide.
References	Follow style guide.
Footnotes	Follow style guide.
Tables or Figures	Follow style guide.

REVIEW PROCESS

Type of Review	Peer review.
Queries	Contact editor.
Acknowledgment	Online system provides acknowledgment.
Review Time	Not specified.
Revisions	Per editor instruction.
Acceptance Rate	Not specified.
Return of Manuscript	Not specified.
Lag Time to Print	Not specified.

CHARGES TO AUTHOR

Author Alterations   Not specified.

Page Charges   Not specified.

Processing   Not specified.

REPRINT, SUBSCRIPTION, AND CONTACT INFORMATION

Reprint Policy   If you are interested in small quantities of your article, you may purchase individual copies of the back issue that contains the article through our Customer Services: subscriptions@sagepub.co.uk or call +44 (0) 20 7324 8701 for availability.

Book Reviews   Reviews of various media are by invitation only.

Subscriptions   Online, full text available through website at: http://tmt.sagepub.com.

Affiliation   Green Cross Academy of Traumatology

E-Mail Address   Not specified.

Website   http://www.greencross.org

VIOLENCE AGAINST WOMEN

Current Title	*Violence Against Women*
Previous Title	N/A.
Editorial Focus	Publication of research and information on all aspects of the problem of violence against women.
Audience	Researchers, practitioners, clinicians, policy makers.
Special Themes	Domestic violence, sexual assault, incest, sexual harassment, female infanticide, female circumcision, and female sexual slavery.
Where Indexed/ Abstracted	Abstracts in Gerontology; Academic Search (EBSCO); Applied Social Sciences Index & Abstracts (ASSIA); Biological Sciences Abstracts; CINAHL; Corporate ResourceNET (EBSCO); Criminal Justice Abstracts; Current Citations Express; Current Contents: Social & Behavioral Sciences; Family & Society Studies Worldwide (NISC); Family Studies Index (EBSCO); Family Violence & Sexual Assault Bulletin; Feminist Periodicals; Health & Safety Science Abstracts; Health Source Plus; Index to Periodical Articles Related to Law; MAS FullTEXT; MasterFILE (EBSCO); MEDLINE; NCJRS Abstracts Database; NISC; Pollution Abstracts; Prevention Evaluation Research Registry for Youth (PERRY); Psychological Abstracts/PsycINFO; PsycLIT; Risk Abstracts; Safety & Science Risk Abstracts; SCOPUS; Sexual Diversity Studies; Social Sciences Citation Index (Web of Science); Social Science Search; Social Services Abstracts; Sociological Abstracts; Standard Periodical Directory; Studies on Women and Gender Abstracts; TOPICsearch (EBSCO); Urban Studies Abstracts; Violence & Abuse Abstracts; Wilson OmniFile V; Wilson Social Science Index/Abstracts.
Year Established	1994
Circulation	5,000
Frequency	Monthly.
Months Issued	January, February, March, April, May, June, July, August, September, October, November, December.
No. of Articles per Issue	Approximately 6.

SUBMISSIONS

Postal Mailing Address	Claire M. Renzetti, Editor, *Violence Against Women,* Dept. of Sociology, Anthropology, & Social Work, University of Dayton, 300 College Park, Dayton, OH 45469.
Method for Submission	Electronic submission via website.
Number of Copies	1
Disk Submission	No.
Online or E-mail Submission Allowed or Required	Required: http://mc.manuscriptcentral.com/vaw.

FORMAT OF MANUSCRIPT

Cover Sheet	Title; names, affiliations, and full contact information for all authors; authors' note (if any acknowledgments); key words.
Abstract	100 words.
Key Words	3–5 words.
Length	35, inclusive of notes, references, tables, etc.
Margins	Not specified.
Spacing	Double-spaced.

STYLE

Name of Guide	*Publication Manual of the American Psychological Association.*
Subheadings	Not specified.
References	Separate pages.
Footnotes	Separate pages.
Tables or Figures	Separate pages.

REVIEW PROCESS

Type of Review	Anonymous peer review (2).
Queries	By e-mail to the editor: Claire.Renzetti@notes.udayton.edu.
Acknowledgment	By e-mail from the editorial assistant.

Review Time	Approximately 8–12 weeks.
Revisions	If requested by reviewers and/or editor; no deadline.
Acceptance Rate	Approximately 12%.
Return of Manuscript	No.
Lag Time to Print	Approximately 12–18 months after acceptance of production-ready manuscript.

CHARGES TO AUTHOR

Author Alterations	Not specified.
Page Charges	Not specified.
Processing	Not specified.

REPRINT, SUBSCRIPTION, AND CONTACT INFORMATION

Reprint Policy	May be purchased.
Book Reviews	Send queries to the editor via e-mail: Claire.Renzetti@notes.udayton.edu.
Subscriptions	Sage Publications: http://vaw.sagepub.com; Institutional (print & e-access): $1,045; Institutional (e-access only): $941; Institutional (print only): $1,024); Individual (print only): $267.
Affiliation	None.
E-Mail Address	Claire.Renzetti@notes.udayton.edu
Website	http://vaw.sagepub.com

WOMEN AND HEALTH

Current Title	*Women and Health*
Previous Title	N/A.
Editorial Focus	Original papers and critical reviews concerning health and illness and physical and psychological well-being of women, as well as the environmental, lifestyle, and sociocultural factors that are associated with health and disease, which have implications for prevention, early detection and treatment, limitation of disability, and rehabilitation.
Audience	Researchers, policy planners, and all providers of health care for women.
Special Themes	Not specified.
Where Indexed/ Abstracted	PubMed; MEDLINE; more than 40 national/international services.
Year Established	1975
Circulation	1,000
Frequency	8 issues per year.
Months Issued	Not specified.
No. of Articles per Issue	6 per issue.

SUBMISSIONS

Postal Mailing Address	Ellen B. Gold, PhD, Professor and Chair end Editor, *Women and Health,* Department of Public Health Sciences, UC Davis School of Medicine, Davis, CA 95616. Phone: (530) 752-2446, fax: (530) 752-3239, e-mail: ebgold@ucdavis.edu.
Method for Submission	E-mail.
Number of Copies	Not specified.
Disk Submission	Accepted.
Online or E-mail Submission Allowed or Required	Yes, e-mail.

FORMAT OF MANUSCRIPT

Cover Sheet	Yes 2, 1 with author identifiers, and 1 anonymous.
Abstract	Yes, 200 words.
Key Words	Yes.
Length	23 pages, including abstract, text, and references.
Margins	1 inch.
Spacing	Double-spaced.

STYLE

Name of Guide	*Publication Manual of the American Psychological Association.*
Subheadings	See style guide.
References	See style guide.
Footnotes	See style guide.
Tables or Figures	Tables will be reset; figures should be camera-ready; both should be able to stand alone with adequate titles and footnotes and explanation of abbreviations and acronyms.

REVIEW PROCESS

Type of Review	Anonymous peer review.
Queries	Yes.
Acknowledgment	Yes.
Review Time	Approximately 3 months.
Revisions	Must be tracked and e-mailed as attachment with cover letter indicating a point-by-point response to each criticism and the response.
Acceptance Rate	Approximately 30%.
Return of Manuscript	No.
Lag Time to Print	Approximately 8–9 months from submission; 3–4 months from acceptance.

CHARGES TO AUTHOR

Author Alterations	Only if many significant changes are made.
Page Charges	None.
Processing	None.

REPRINT, SUBSCRIPTION, AND CONTACT INFORMATION

Reprint Policy   Reprints of individual articles are available for order at the time authors review page proofs. A discount on reprints is available to authors who order before print publication. Each corresponding author will receive 3 complete issues in which the article publishes and a complimentary PDF. This file is for personal use only and may not be copied and disseminated in any form without prior written permission from Taylor and Francis Group, LLC.

Book Reviews   Occasionally published, but must be solicited.

Subscriptions   http://www.informaworld.com/smpp/title~content=t792306982~tab=subscribe~db=all.

Affiliation   Not specified.

E-Mail Address   womenandhealth@ucdavis.edu.

Website   http://www.tandf.co.uk/journals/journal.asp?issn=0363-0242&linktype=44

WOMEN AND THERAPY

Current Title	*Women and Therapy*
Previous Title	N/A.
Editorial Focus	Psychotherapy
Audience	Therapists working with women clients.
Special Themes	Aging, social class, lesbians, women with disabilities, women across cultures. Journal devotes 3 issues per year to thematic issues that are invited by the editor; check with the editors for upcoming themes.
Where Indexed/ Abstracted	Abstracts of Research in Pastoral Care and Counseling; Academic Abstracts/CD-ROM; Academic Index (online); Alternative Press Index; CNPIEC Reference Guide; Chinese National Directory of Foreign Periodicals; Current Contents: Clinical Medicine/Life Sciences (CC:CM/LS); Digest of Neurology and Psychiatry; Expanded Academic Index; Family Violence and Sexual Assault Bulletin; Feminist Periodicals: A Current Listing of Contents; Health Source; Health Source Plus; Higher Education Abstracts; Index to Periodical Articles Related to Law; INTERNET ACCESS (and additional networks) Bulletin Board for Libraries ("BUBL"), coverage of information resources on INTERNET, JANET, and other networks; Inventory of Marriage and Family Literature (online and CD-ROM); Mental Health Abstracts (online through DIALOG); PASCAL International Bibliography T205: Sciences de l'information Documentation; Periodical Abstracts, Research I; Periodical Abstracts, Research II; PILOTS Database; Psychological Abstracts/PsycINFO; Sage Family Studies Abstracts (SFSA); Social Work Abstracts; Studies on Women and Gender Abstracts; Violence and Abuse Abstracts (VAA); Women Studies Abstracts; Women's Studies Index.
Year Established	1982.
Circulation	2000.
Frequency	4 per year.
Months Issued	Not specified.
No. of Articles per Issue	Approximately 8.

SUBMISSIONS

Postal Mailing Address	Electronic submissions only.
Method for Submission	E-mail.
Number of Copies	1
Disk Submission	N/A.
Online or E-mail Submission Allowed or Required	Yes.

FORMAT OF MANUSCRIPT

Cover Sheet	APA format.
Abstract	Yes.
Key Words	None.
Length	Up to 15 pages.
Margins	1 inch on all sides.
Spacing	Double-spaced.

STYLE

Name of Guide	*Publication Manual of the American Psychological Association.*
Subheadings	See style guide.
References	See style guide.
Footnotes	None.
Tables or Figures	See style guide; must be camera-ready.

REVIEW PROCESS

Type of Review	Blind peer review.
Queries	Editor.
Acknowledgment	By letter.
Review Time	Approximately 3 months.

Revisions	Approximately 3 months.
Acceptance Rate	Approximately 30%.
Return of Manuscript	Yes.
Lag Time to Print	Approximately 6–12 months.

CHARGES TO AUTHOR

Author Alterations	Alterations are discouraged.
Page Charges	None.
Processing	Not specified.

REPRINT, SUBSCRIPTION, AND CONTACT INFORMATION

Reprint Policy	Authors receive 10 free reprints and 1 free copy of the journal issue.
Book Reviews	No.
Subscriptions	See website.
Affiliation	Not specified.
E-Mail Address	(Rothblum) e_rothbl@dewey.uvm.edu; (Hill) rsxg34a@prodigy.com.
Website	Taylor and Francis Publishers.